To Carole.

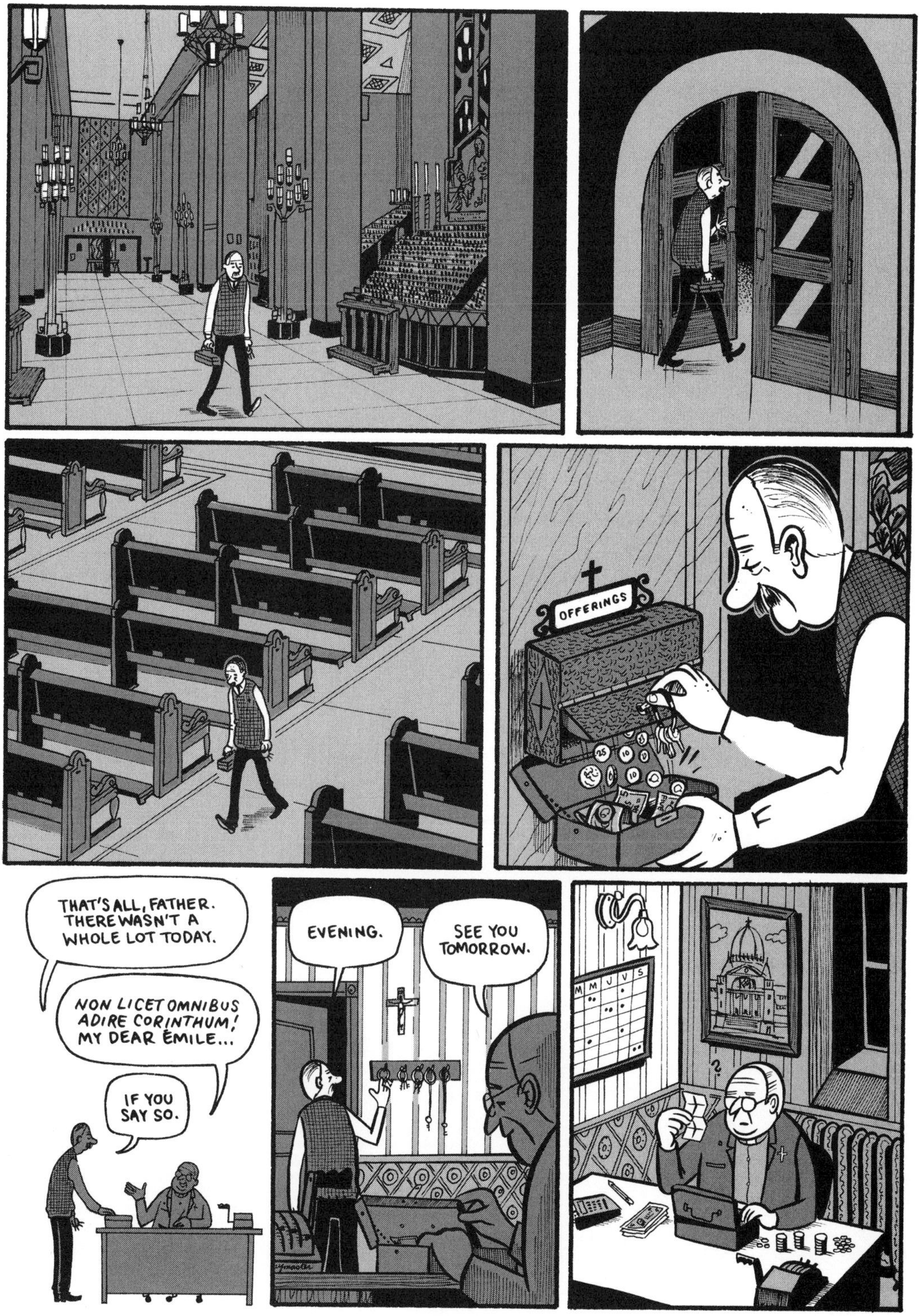
OFFERINGS
THAT'S ALL, FATHER. THERE WASN'T A WHOLE LOT TODAY.
NON LICET OMNIBUS ADIRE CORINTHUM! MY DEAR ÉMILE...
IF YOU SAY SO.
EVENING.
SEE YOU TOMORROW.
M M J V S

Paul goes fishing

Translated by Helge Dascher.
Hand-lettering by Dirk Rehm.

Drawn & Quarterly
Post Office Box 48056
Montreal, Quebec
Canada H2V 4S8
www.drawnandquarterly.com

First edition: February 2008.
Printed in Canada.

10 9 8 7 6 5 4 3 2 1

Library and Archives Canada Cataloguing in Publication
Rabagliati, Michel
    Paul Goes Fishing / Michel Rabagliati; translated by Helge Dascher.
Translation of: Paul à la pêche, published in 2007 by Les Éditions de la Pastèque.
ISBN 978-1-897299-28-9
    I. Dascher, Helge, 1965- II. Title.
PN6734.P3859R3213 2008   741.5'971   C2007-904720-3

Drawn & Quarterly acknowledges the financial contribution of the Government of Canada through the Book Publishing Industry Development Program (BPIDP) and the Canada Council for the Arts for our publishing activities and for support of this edition.

Distributed in the USA by:
Farrar, Straus and Giroux
19 Union Square West
New York, NY 10003
Orders: 888.330.8477

Distributed in Canada by:
Raincoast Books
9050 Shaughnessy Street
Vancouver, BC V6P 6E5
Orders: 800.663.5714

Printed by Imprimerie Transcontinental in Louiseville, Quebec, February 2008.

Michel Rabagliati

translated by Helge Dascher

Paul goes fishing

Drawn & Quarterly

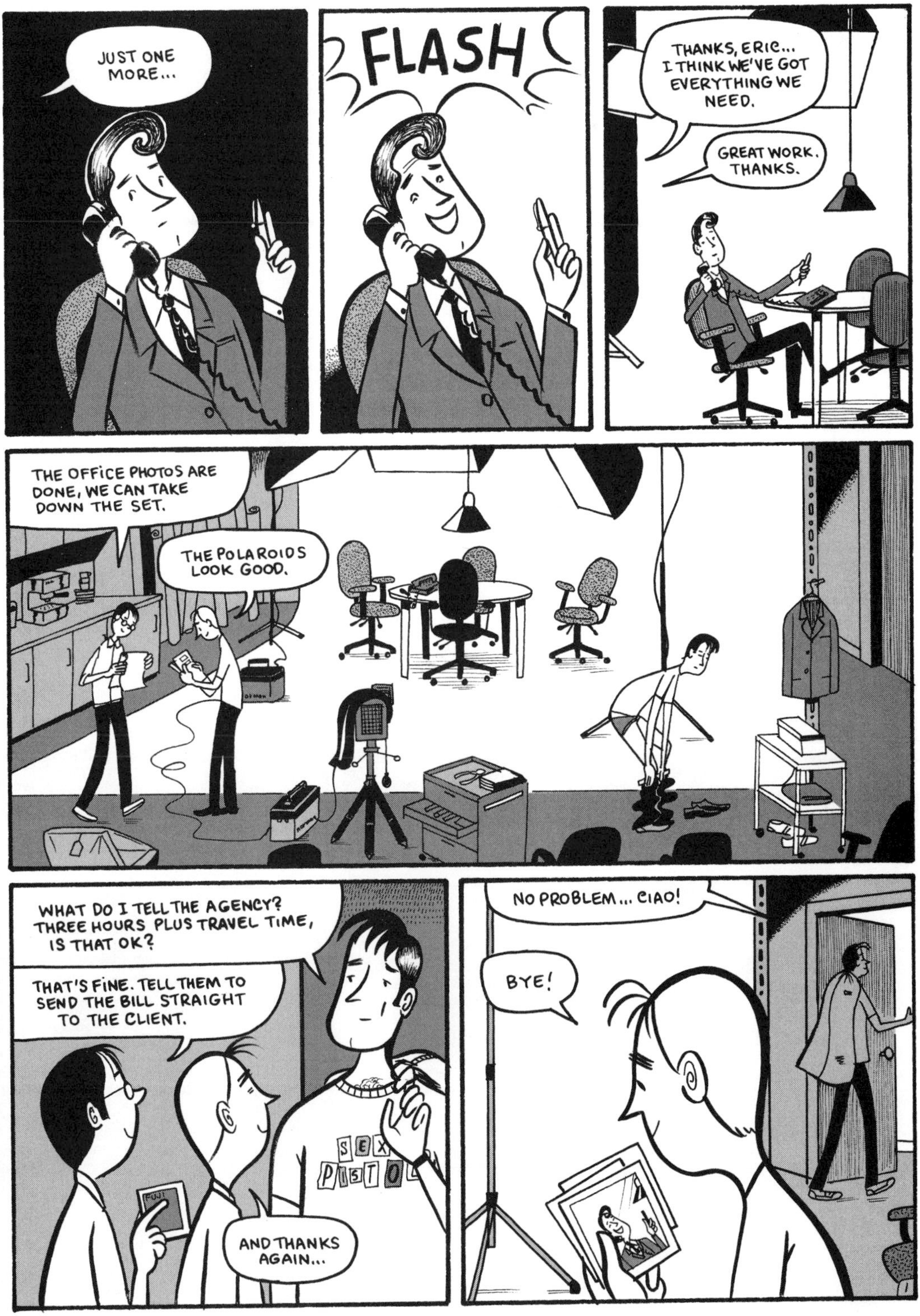
JUST ONE MORE...
FLASH
THANKS, ERIC... I THINK WE'VE GOT EVERYTHING WE NEED.
GREAT WORK. THANKS.
THE OFFICE PHOTOS ARE DONE, WE CAN TAKE DOWN THE SET.
THE POLAROIDS LOOK GOOD.
WHAT DO I TELL THE AGENCY? THREE HOURS PLUS TRAVEL TIME, IS THAT OK?
THAT'S FINE. TELL THEM TO SEND THE BILL STRAIGHT TO THE CLIENT.
SEX PISTOL
AND THANKS AGAIN...
NO PROBLEM... CIAO!
BYE!

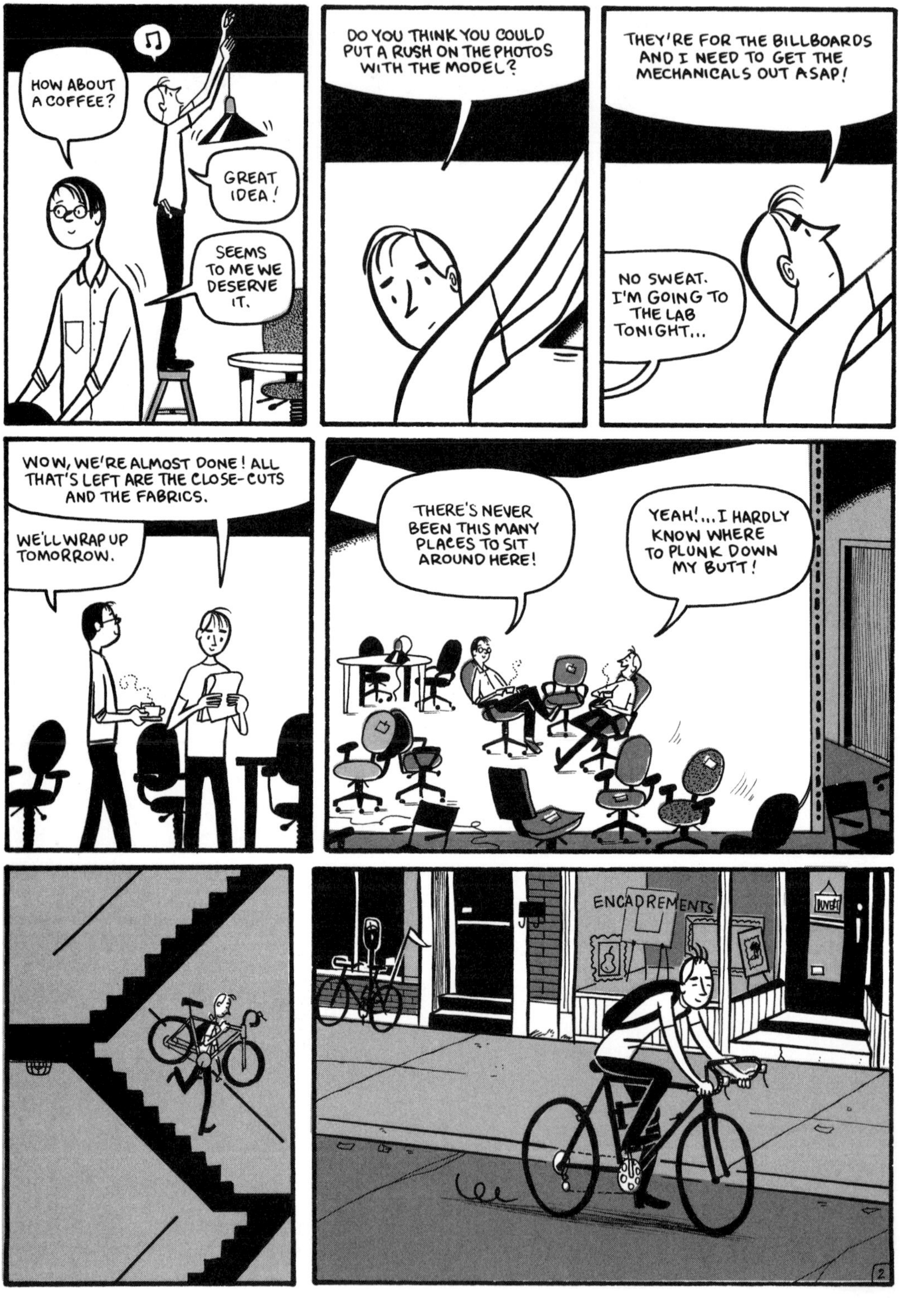

HOW ABOUT A COFFEE?
GREAT IDEA!
SEEMS TO ME WE DESERVE IT.
DO YOU THINK YOU COULD PUT A RUSH ON THE PHOTOS WITH THE MODEL?
THEY'RE FOR THE BILLBOARDS AND I NEED TO GET THE MECHANICALS OUT ASAP!
NO SWEAT. I'M GOING TO THE LAB TONIGHT...
WOW, WE'RE ALMOST DONE! ALL THAT'S LEFT ARE THE CLOSE-CUTS AND THE FABRICS.
WE'LL WRAP UP TOMORROW.
THERE'S NEVER BEEN THIS MANY PLACES TO SIT AROUND HERE!
YEAH!... I HARDLY KNOW WHERE TO PLUNK DOWN MY BUTT!
ENCADREMENTS
OUVERT

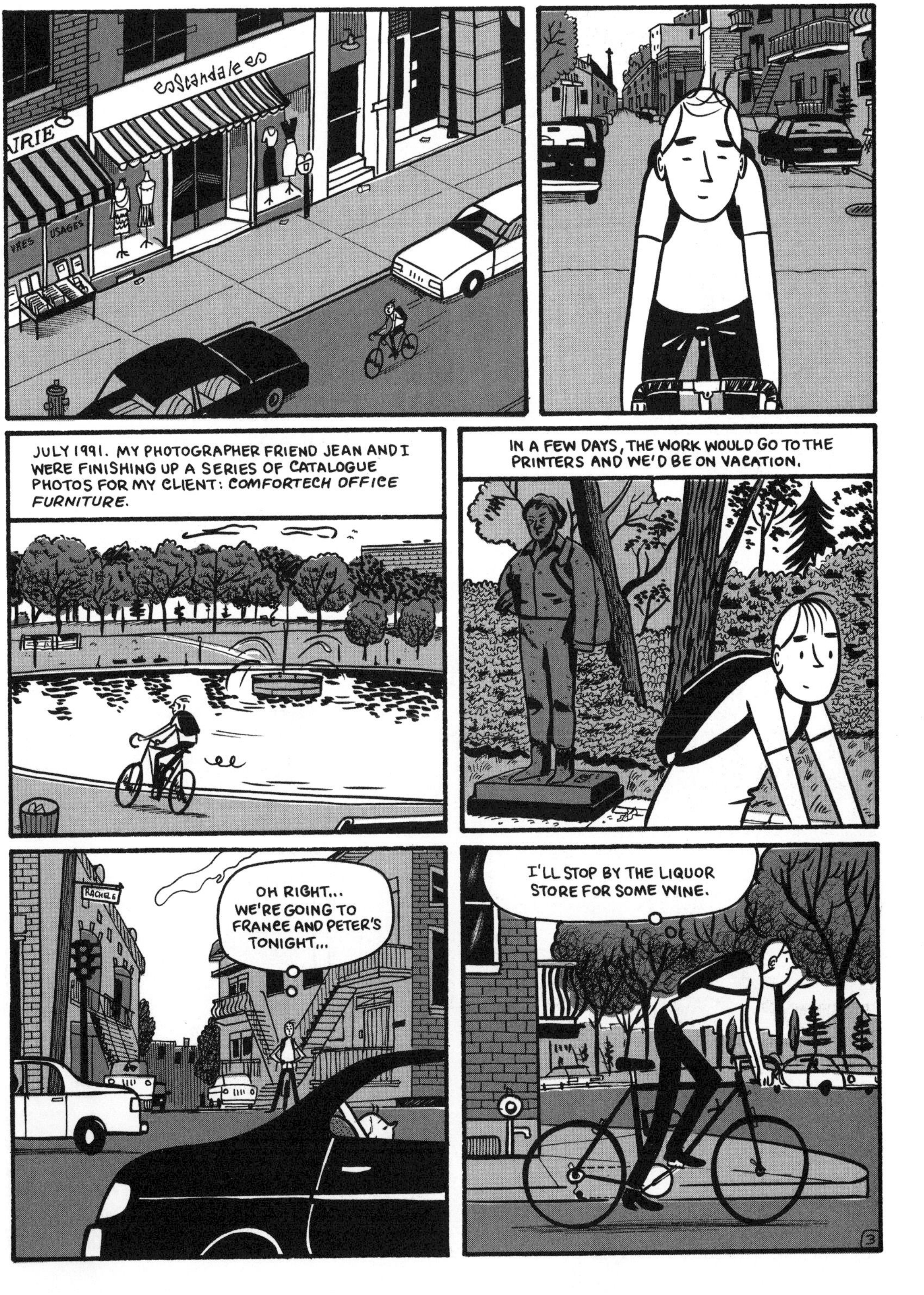
JULY 1991. MY PHOTOGRAPHER FRIEND JEAN AND I WERE FINISHING UP A SERIES OF CATALOGUE PHOTOS FOR MY CLIENT: COMFORTECH OFFICE FURNITURE.
IN A FEW DAYS, THE WORK WOULD GO TO THE PRINTERS AND WE'D BE ON VACATION.
OH RIGHT... WE'RE GOING TO FRANCE AND PETER'S TONIGHT...
I'LL STOP BY THE LIQUOR STORE FOR SOME WINE.

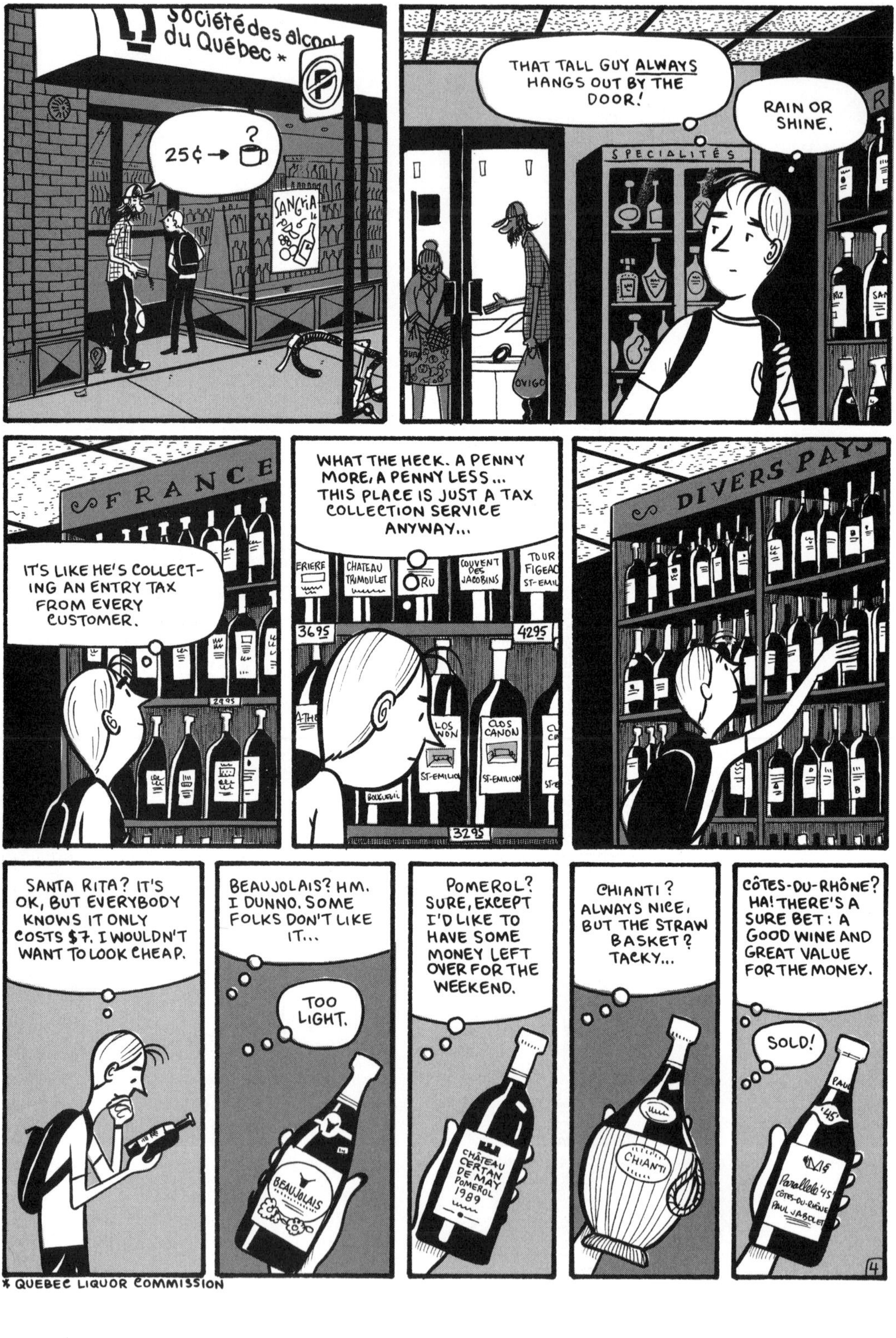
Société des alcools du Québec *
25¢ → ?
SANGRIA
THAT TALL GUY ALWAYS HANGS OUT BY THE DOOR!
RAIN OR SHINE.
SPECIALITÉS
FRANCE
IT'S LIKE HE'S COLLECTING AN ENTRY TAX FROM EVERY CUSTOMER.
WHAT THE HECK. A PENNY MORE, A PENNY LESS... THIS PLACE IS JUST A TAX COLLECTION SERVICE ANYWAY...
CHATEAU TRIMOULET
COUVENT DES JACOBINS
TOUR FIGEAC ST-EMIL
CLOS CANON ST-EMILION
DIVERS PAYS
SANTA RITA? IT'S OK, BUT EVERYBODY KNOWS IT ONLY COSTS $7. I WOULDN'T WANT TO LOOK CHEAP.
BEAUJOLAIS? HM. I DUNNO. SOME FOLKS DON'T LIKE IT...
TOO LIGHT.
BEAUJOLAIS
POMEROL? SURE, EXCEPT I'D LIKE TO HAVE SOME MONEY LEFT OVER FOR THE WEEKEND.
CHÂTEAU CERTAN DE MAY POMEROL 1989
CHIANTI? ALWAYS NICE, BUT THE STRAW BASKET? TACKY...
CHIANTI
CÔTES-DU-RHÔNE? HA! THERE'S A SURE BET: A GOOD WINE AND GREAT VALUE FOR THE MONEY.
SOLD!
Parallèle '45 CÔTES-DU-RHÔNE PAUL JABOULET

* QUEBEC LIQUOR COMMISSION

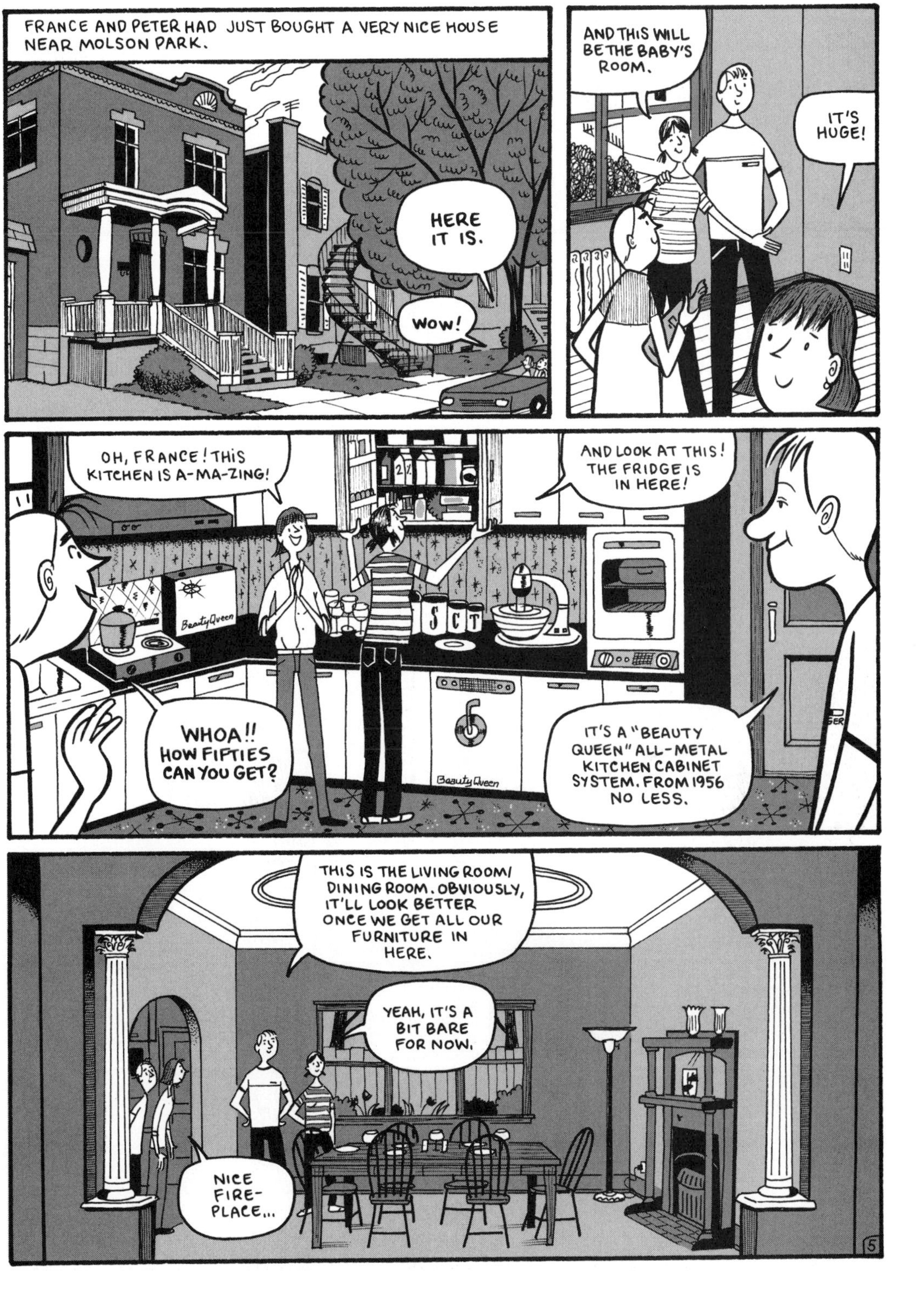

FRANCE AND PETER HAD JUST BOUGHT A VERY NICE HOUSE NEAR MOLSON PARK.
HERE IT IS.
WOW!
AND THIS WILL BE THE BABY'S ROOM.
IT'S HUGE!
OH, FRANCE! THIS KITCHEN IS A-MA-ZING!
AND LOOK AT THIS! THE FRIDGE IS IN HERE!
BeautyQueen
WHOA!! HOW FIFTIES CAN YOU GET?
IT'S A "BEAUTY QUEEN" ALL-METAL KITCHEN CABINET SYSTEM. FROM 1956 NO LESS.
THIS IS THE LIVING ROOM/ DINING ROOM. OBVIOUSLY, IT'LL LOOK BETTER ONCE WE GET ALL OUR FURNITURE IN HERE.
YEAH, IT'S A BIT BARE FOR NOW.
NICE FIRE-PLACE...

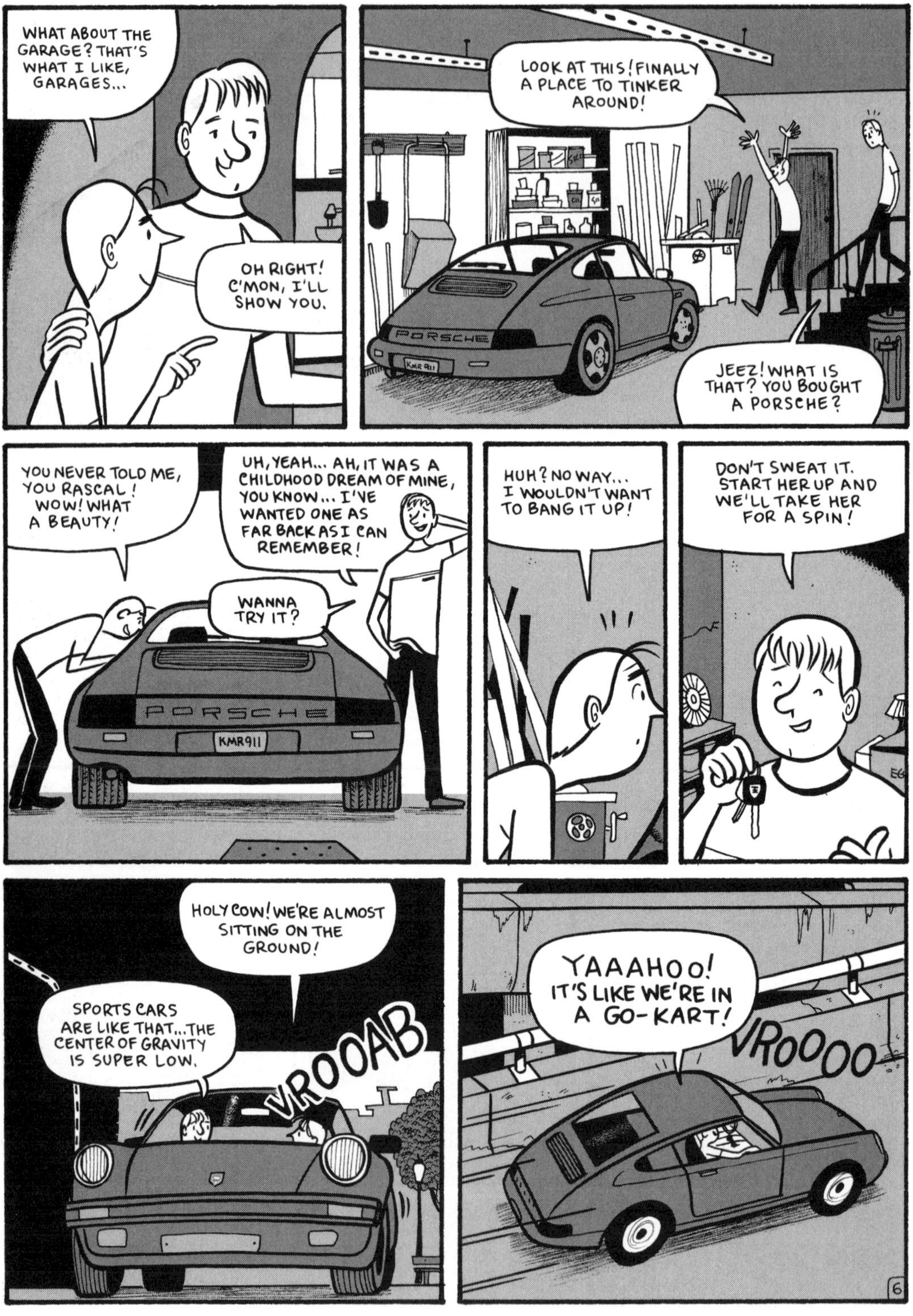
WHAT ABOUT THE GARAGE? THAT'S WHAT I LIKE, GARAGES...
OH RIGHT! C'MON, I'LL SHOW YOU.
LOOK AT THIS! FINALLY A PLACE TO TINKER AROUND!
PORSCHE
KMR 911
JEEZ! WHAT IS THAT? YOU BOUGHT A PORSCHE?
YOU NEVER TOLD ME, YOU RASCAL! WOW! WHAT A BEAUTY!
UH, YEAH... AH, IT WAS A CHILDHOOD DREAM OF MINE, YOU KNOW... I'VE WANTED ONE AS FAR BACK AS I CAN REMEMBER!
WANNA TRY IT?
PORSCHE
KMR911
HUH? NO WAY... I WOULDN'T WANT TO BANG IT UP!
DON'T SWEAT IT. START HER UP AND WE'LL TAKE HER FOR A SPIN!
HOLY COW! WE'RE ALMOST SITTING ON THE GROUND!
SPORTS CARS ARE LIKE THAT... THE CENTER OF GRAVITY IS SUPER LOW.
VROOAB
YAAAHOO! IT'S LIKE WE'RE IN A GO-KART!
VROOOO
6

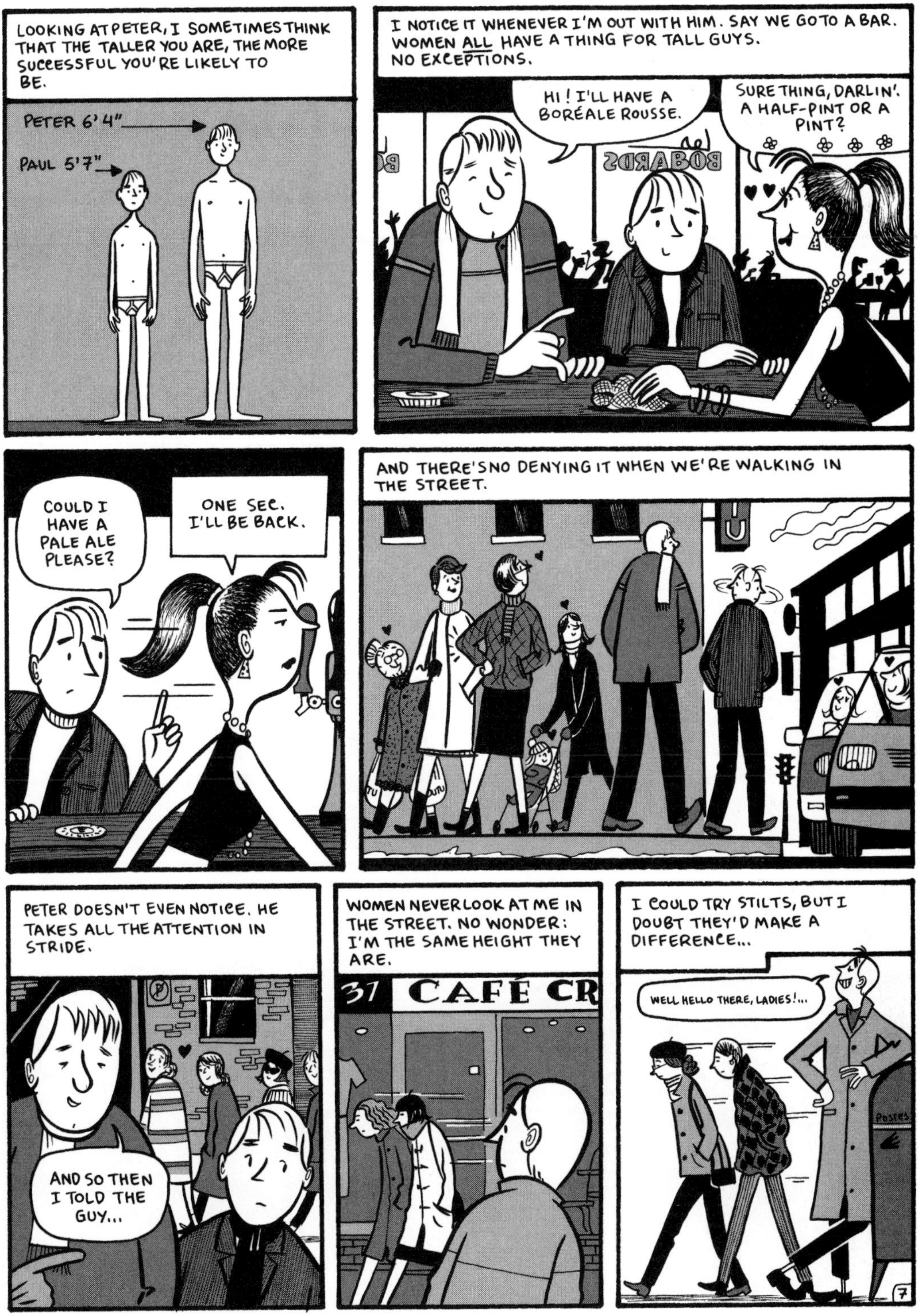
LOOKING AT PETER, I SOMETIMES THINK THAT THE TALLER YOU ARE, THE MORE SUCCESSFUL YOU'RE LIKELY TO BE.
PETER 6' 4"
PAUL 5'7"
I NOTICE IT WHENEVER I'M OUT WITH HIM. SAY WE GO TO A BAR. WOMEN ALL HAVE A THING FOR TALL GUYS. NO EXCEPTIONS.
HI! I'LL HAVE A BORÉALE ROUSSE.
SURE THING, DARLIN'. A HALF-PINT OR A PINT?
COULD I HAVE A PALE ALE PLEASE?
ONE SEC. I'LL BE BACK.
AND THERE'S NO DENYING IT WHEN WE'RE WALKING IN THE STREET.
PETER DOESN'T EVEN NOTICE. HE TAKES ALL THE ATTENTION IN STRIDE.
AND SO THEN I TOLD THE GUY...
WOMEN NEVER LOOK AT ME IN THE STREET. NO WONDER: I'M THE SAME HEIGHT THEY ARE.
31 CAFÉ CR
I COULD TRY STILTS, BUT I DOUBT THEY'D MAKE A DIFFERENCE...
WELL HELLO THERE, LADIES!...
POSTES

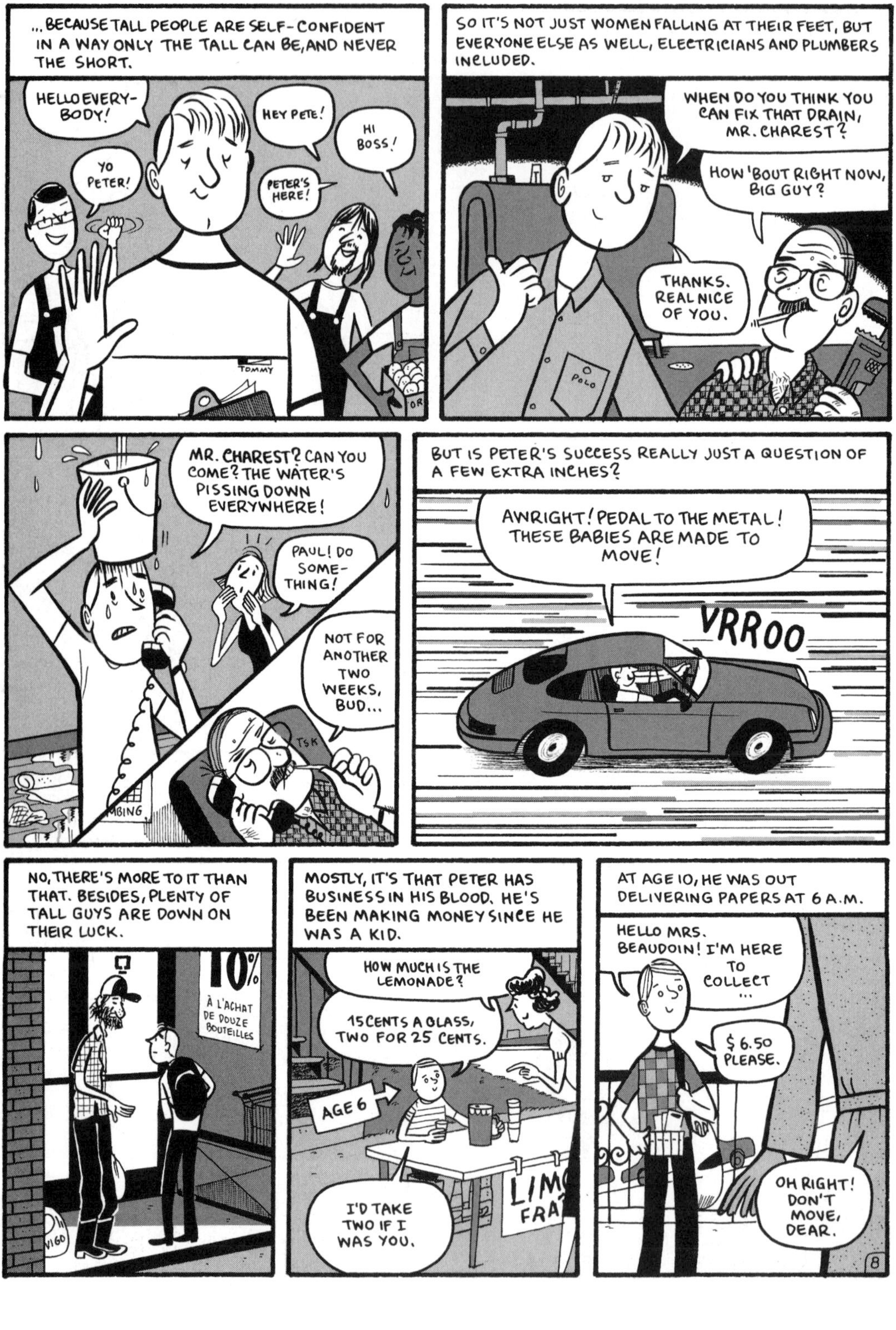

...BECAUSE TALL PEOPLE ARE SELF-CONFIDENT IN A WAY ONLY THE TALL CAN BE, AND NEVER THE SHORT.
HELLO EVERYBODY!
YO PETER!
HEY PETE!
HI BOSS!
PETER'S HERE!
TOMMY
SO IT'S NOT JUST WOMEN FALLING AT THEIR FEET, BUT EVERYONE ELSE AS WELL, ELECTRICIANS AND PLUMBERS INCLUDED.
WHEN DO YOU THINK YOU CAN FIX THAT DRAIN, MR. CHAREST?
HOW 'BOUT RIGHT NOW, BIG GUY?
THANKS. REAL NICE OF YOU.
POLO
MR. CHAREST? CAN YOU COME? THE WATER'S PISSING DOWN EVERYWHERE!
PAUL! DO SOMETHING!
NOT FOR ANOTHER TWO WEEKS, BUD...
TSK
MBING
BUT IS PETER'S SUCCESS REALLY JUST A QUESTION OF A FEW EXTRA INCHES?
AWRIGHT! PEDAL TO THE METAL! THESE BABIES ARE MADE TO MOVE!
VRROO
NO, THERE'S MORE TO IT THAN THAT. BESIDES, PLENTY OF TALL GUYS ARE DOWN ON THEIR LUCK.
10%
À L'ACHAT DE DOUZE BOUTEILLES
VIGO
MOSTLY, IT'S THAT PETER HAS BUSINESS IN HIS BLOOD. HE'S BEEN MAKING MONEY SINCE HE WAS A KID.
HOW MUCH IS THE LEMONADE?
15 CENTS A GLASS, TWO FOR 25 CENTS.
AGE 6
I'D TAKE TWO IF I WAS YOU.
AT AGE 10, HE WAS OUT DELIVERING PAPERS AT 6 A.M.
HELLO MRS. BEAUDOIN! I'M HERE TO COLLECT ...
$ 6.50 PLEASE.
OH RIGHT! DON'T MOVE, DEAR.

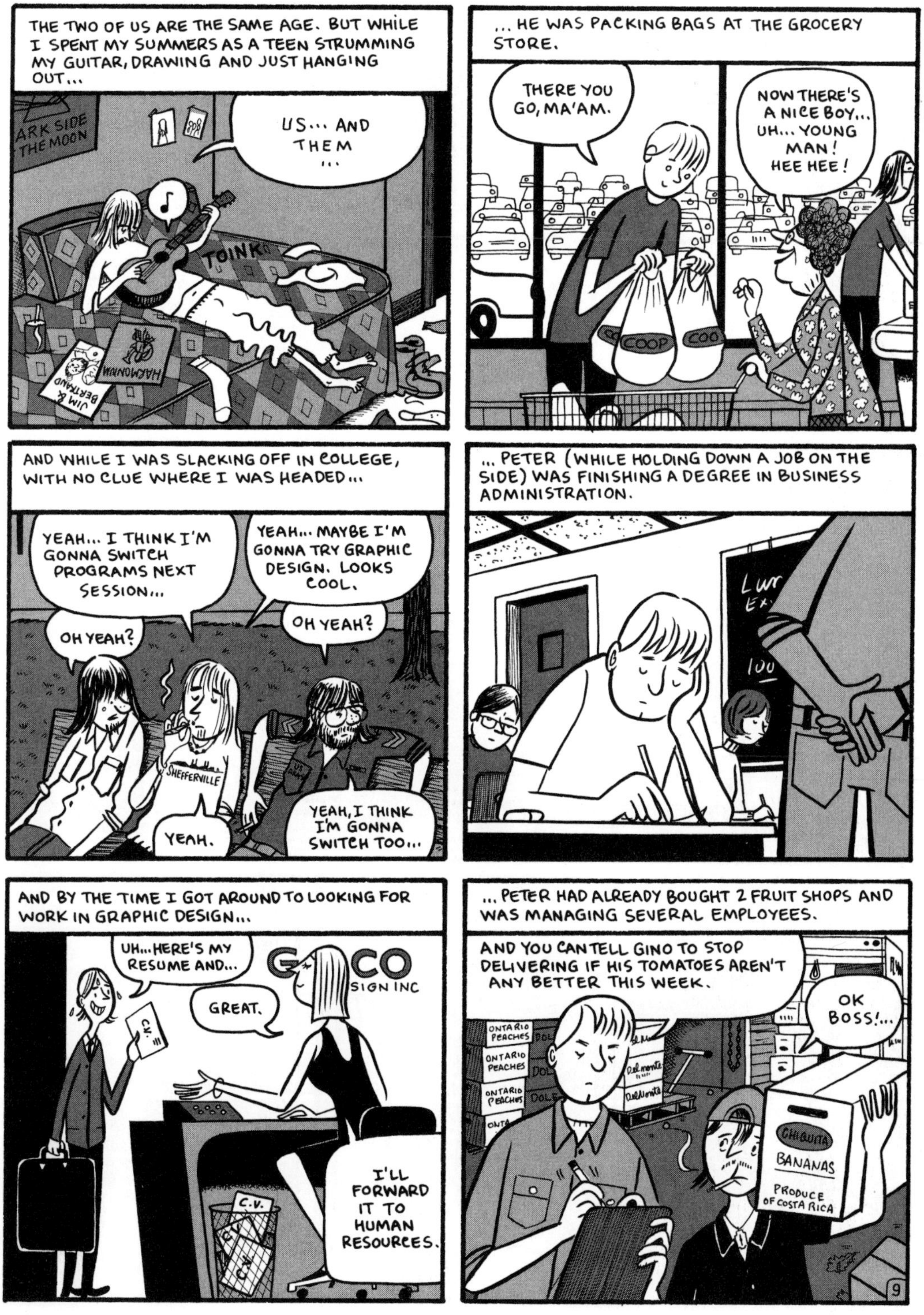
THE TWO OF US ARE THE SAME AGE. BUT WHILE I SPENT MY SUMMERS AS A TEEN STRUMMING MY GUITAR, DRAWING AND JUST HANGING OUT...
ARK SIDE THE MOON
US... AND THEM ...
TOINK
HARMONIUM
JIM & BERTRAND
... HE WAS PACKING BAGS AT THE GROCERY STORE.
THERE YOU GO, MA'AM.
NOW THERE'S A NICE BOY... UH... YOUNG MAN! HEE HEE!
COOP
AND WHILE I WAS SLACKING OFF IN COLLEGE, WITH NO CLUE WHERE I WAS HEADED...
YEAH... I THINK I'M GONNA SWITCH PROGRAMS NEXT SESSION...
YEAH... MAYBE I'M GONNA TRY GRAPHIC DESIGN. LOOKS COOL.
OH YEAH?
OH YEAH?
SHEFFERVILLE
YEAH.
YEAH, I THINK I'M GONNA SWITCH TOO...
... PETER (WHILE HOLDING DOWN A JOB ON THE SIDE) WAS FINISHING A DEGREE IN BUSINESS ADMINISTRATION.
AND BY THE TIME I GOT AROUND TO LOOKING FOR WORK IN GRAPHIC DESIGN...
UH... HERE'S MY RESUME AND...
SIGN INC
GREAT.
C.V.
I'LL FORWARD IT TO HUMAN RESOURCES.
... PETER HAD ALREADY BOUGHT 2 FRUIT SHOPS AND WAS MANAGING SEVERAL EMPLOYEES.
AND YOU CAN TELL GINO TO STOP DELIVERING IF HIS TOMATOES AREN'T ANY BETTER THIS WEEK.
OK BOSS!...
ONTARIO PEACHES
ONTARIO PEACHES
ONTARIO PEACHES
CHIQUITA
BANANAS
PRODUCE OF COSTA RICA

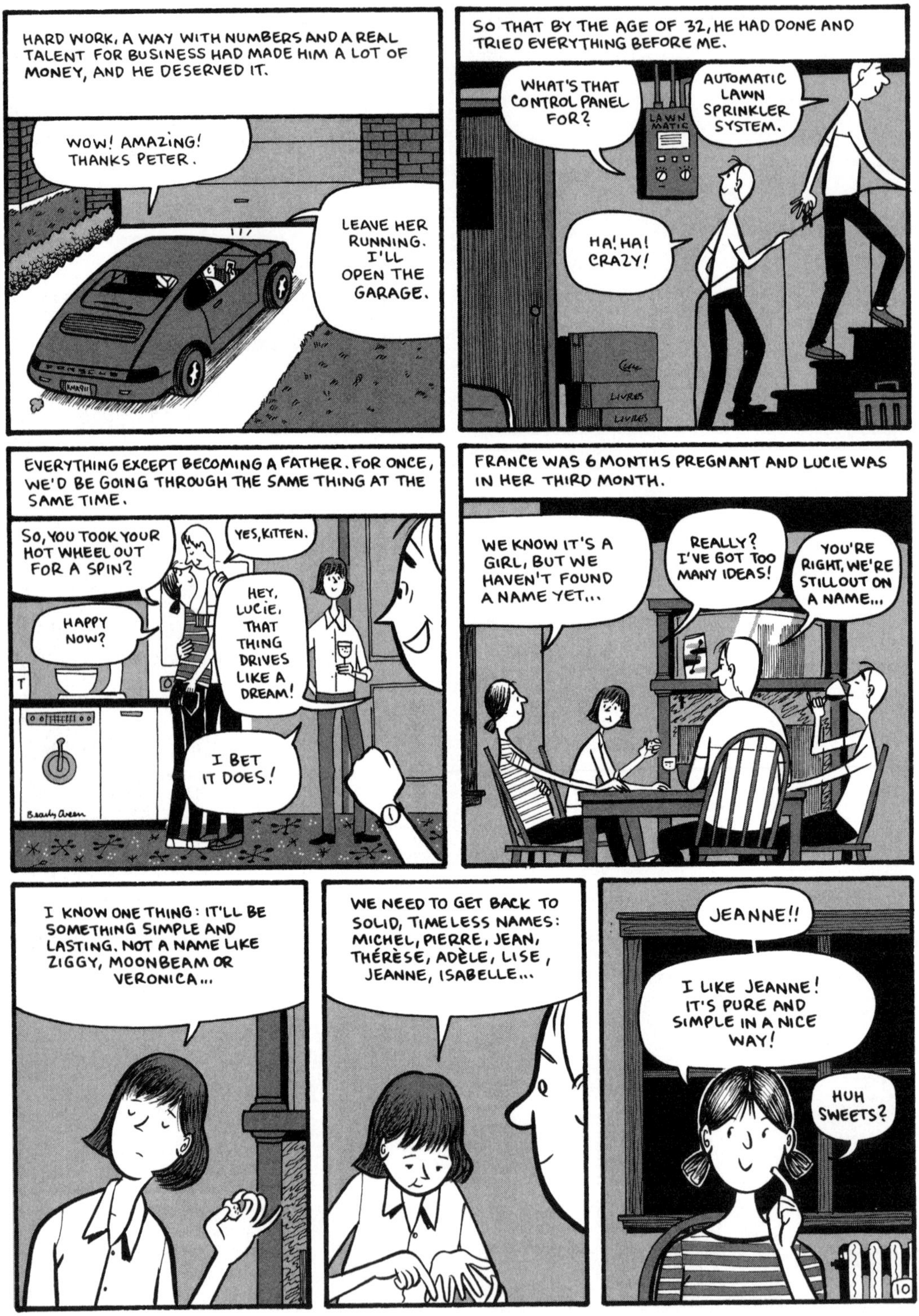
HARD WORK, A WAY WITH NUMBERS AND A REAL TALENT FOR BUSINESS HAD MADE HIM A LOT OF MONEY, AND HE DESERVED IT.
WOW! AMAZING! THANKS PETER.
LEAVE HER RUNNING. I'LL OPEN THE GARAGE.
SO THAT BY THE AGE OF 32, HE HAD DONE AND TRIED EVERYTHING BEFORE ME.
WHAT'S THAT CONTROL PANEL FOR?
AUTOMATIC LAWN SPRINKLER SYSTEM.
LAWN MATIC
HA! HA! CRAZY!
LIVRES
LIVRES
EVERYTHING EXCEPT BECOMING A FATHER. FOR ONCE, WE'D BE GOING THROUGH THE SAME THING AT THE SAME TIME.
SO, YOU TOOK YOUR HOT WHEEL OUT FOR A SPIN?
YES, KITTEN.
HAPPY NOW?
HEY, LUCIE, THAT THING DRIVES LIKE A DREAM!
I BET IT DOES!
FRANCE WAS 6 MONTHS PREGNANT AND LUCIE WAS IN HER THIRD MONTH.
WE KNOW IT'S A GIRL, BUT WE HAVEN'T FOUND A NAME YET...
REALLY? I'VE GOT TOO MANY IDEAS!
YOU'RE RIGHT, WE'RE STILL OUT ON A NAME...
I KNOW ONE THING: IT'LL BE SOMETHING SIMPLE AND LASTING. NOT A NAME LIKE ZIGGY, MOONBEAM OR VERONICA...
WE NEED TO GET BACK TO SOLID, TIMELESS NAMES: MICHEL, PIERRE, JEAN, THÉRÈSE, ADÈLE, LISE, JEANNE, ISABELLE...
JEANNE!!
I LIKE JEANNE! IT'S PURE AND SIMPLE IN A NICE WAY!
HUH SWEETS?

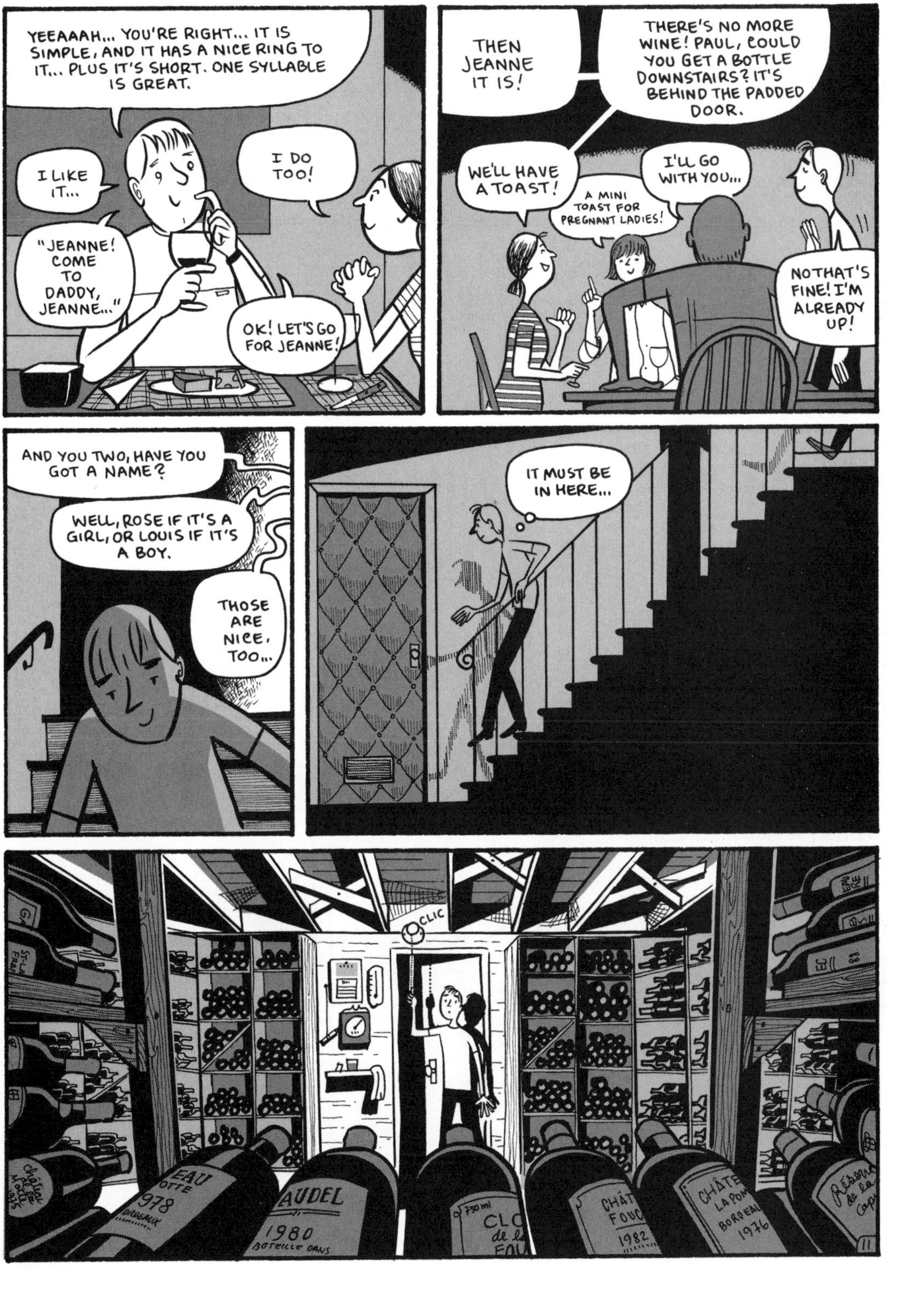

YEEAAAH... YOU'RE RIGHT... IT IS SIMPLE, AND IT HAS A NICE RING TO IT... PLUS IT'S SHORT. ONE SYLLABLE IS GREAT.
I LIKE IT...
I DO TOO!
"JEANNE! COME TO DADDY, JEANNE..."
OK! LET'S GO FOR JEANNE!
THEN JEANNE IT IS!
THERE'S NO MORE WINE! PAUL, COULD YOU GET A BOTTLE DOWNSTAIRS? IT'S BEHIND THE PADDED DOOR.
WE'LL HAVE A TOAST!
A MINI TOAST FOR PREGNANT LADIES!
I'LL GO WITH YOU...
NO THAT'S FINE! I'M ALREADY UP!
AND YOU TWO, HAVE YOU GOT A NAME?
WELL, ROSE IF IT'S A GIRL, OR LOUIS IF IT'S A BOY.
THOSE ARE NICE, TOO...
IT MUST BE IN HERE...
CLIC

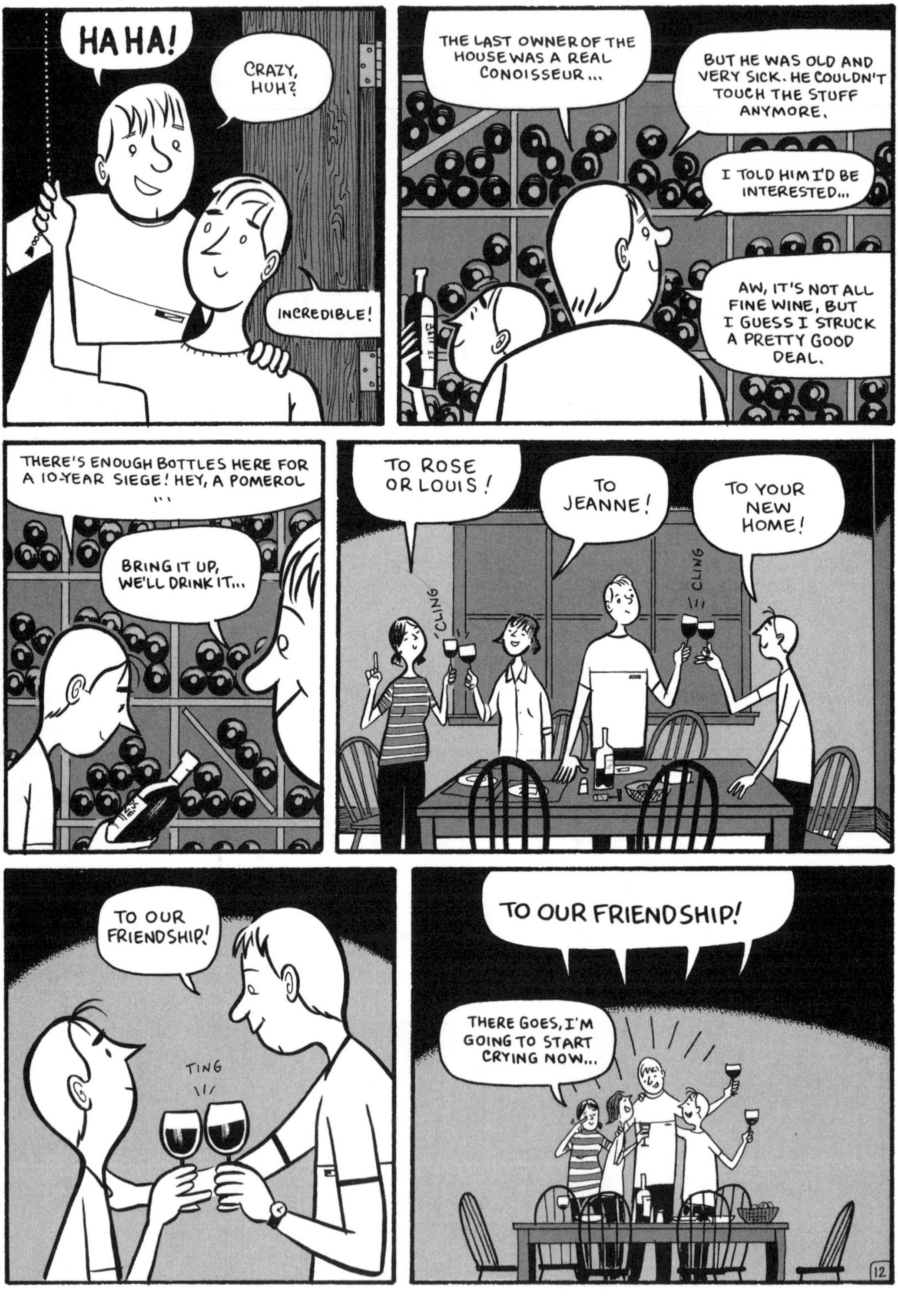
HA HA!
CRAZY, HUH?
INCREDIBLE!
THE LAST OWNER OF THE HOUSE WAS A REAL CONOISSEUR...
BUT HE WAS OLD AND VERY SICK. HE COULDN'T TOUCH THE STUFF ANYMORE.
I TOLD HIM I'D BE INTERESTED...
AW, IT'S NOT ALL FINE WINE, BUT I GUESS I STRUCK A PRETTY GOOD DEAL.
THERE'S ENOUGH BOTTLES HERE FOR A 10-YEAR SIEGE! HEY, A POMEROL ...
BRING IT UP, WE'LL DRINK IT...
TO ROSE OR LOUIS!
TO JEANNE!
TO YOUR NEW HOME!
CLING
CLING
TO OUR FRIENDSHIP!
TING
TO OUR FRIENDSHIP!
THERE GOES, I'M GOING TO START CRYING NOW...

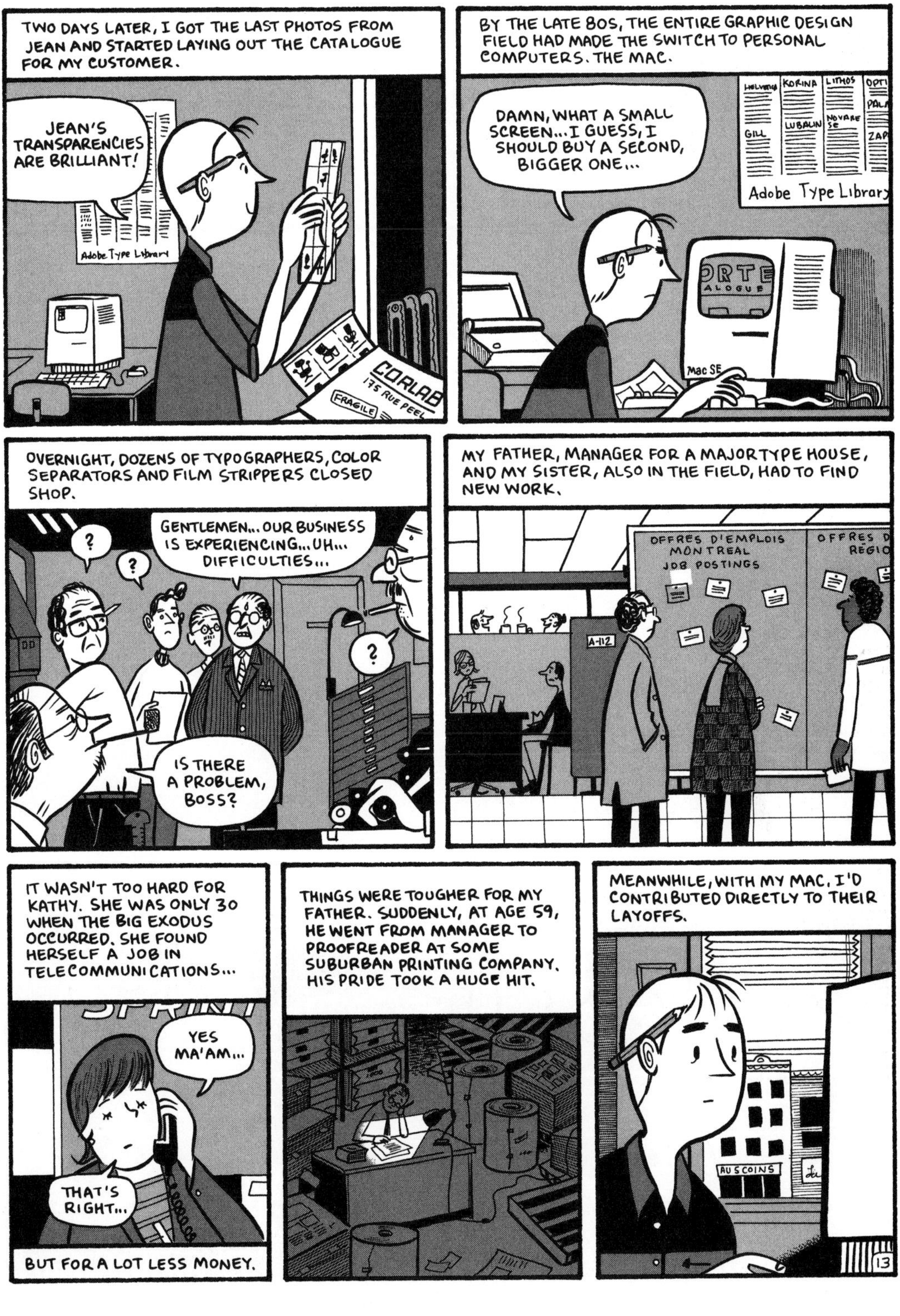
TWO DAYS LATER, I GOT THE LAST PHOTOS FROM JEAN AND STARTED LAYING OUT THE CATALOGUE FOR MY CUSTOMER.
JEAN'S TRANSPARENCIES ARE BRILLIANT!
Adobe Type Library
CORLAB
175 RUE PEEL
FRAGILE
BY THE LATE 80S, THE ENTIRE GRAPHIC DESIGN FIELD HAD MADE THE SWITCH TO PERSONAL COMPUTERS. THE MAC.
DAMN, WHAT A SMALL SCREEN... I GUESS, I SHOULD BUY A SECOND, BIGGER ONE...
HELVETICA
KORINA
LITHOS
GILL
LUBALIN
NOVARESE
Adobe Type Library
Mac SE
OVERNIGHT, DOZENS OF TYPOGRAPHERS, COLOR SEPARATORS AND FILM STRIPPERS CLOSED SHOP.
?
?
GENTLEMEN... OUR BUSINESS IS EXPERIENCING... UH... DIFFICULTIES...
?
IS THERE A PROBLEM, BOSS?
MY FATHER, MANAGER FOR A MAJOR TYPE HOUSE, AND MY SISTER, ALSO IN THE FIELD, HAD TO FIND NEW WORK.
OFFRES D'EMPLOIS MONTREAL JOB POSTINGS
A-112
IT WASN'T TOO HARD FOR KATHY. SHE WAS ONLY 30 WHEN THE BIG EXODUS OCCURRED. SHE FOUND HERSELF A JOB IN TELECOMMUNICATIONS...
YES MA'AM...
THAT'S RIGHT...
BUT FOR A LOT LESS MONEY.
THINGS WERE TOUGHER FOR MY FATHER. SUDDENLY, AT AGE 59, HE WENT FROM MANAGER TO PROOFREADER AT SOME SUBURBAN PRINTING COMPANY. HIS PRIDE TOOK A HUGE HIT.
MEANWHILE, WITH MY MAC, I'D CONTRIBUTED DIRECTLY TO THEIR LAYOFFS.
AUX COINS

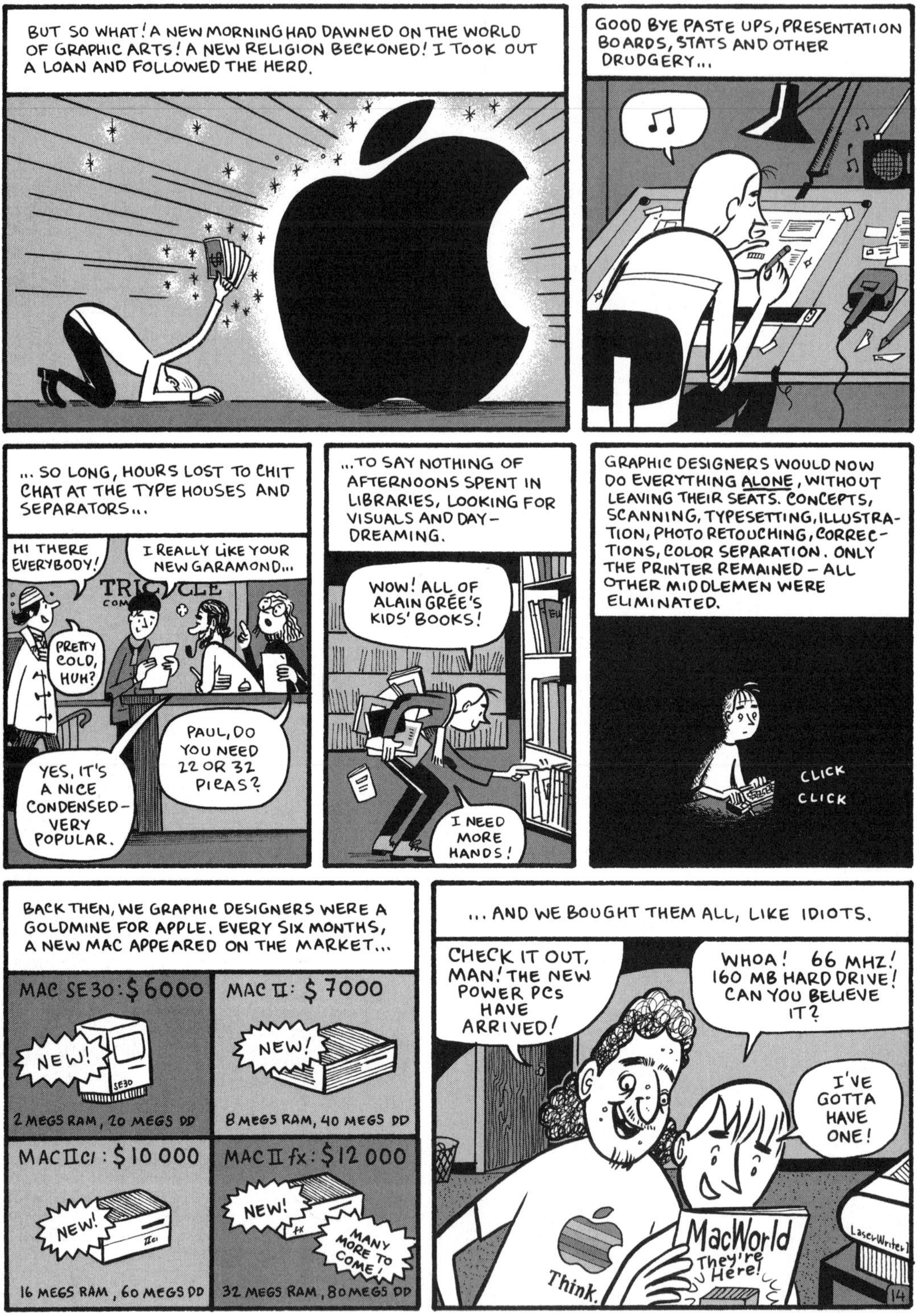

BUT SO WHAT! A NEW MORNING HAD DAWNED ON THE WORLD OF GRAPHIC ARTS! A NEW RELIGION BECKONED! I TOOK OUT A LOAN AND FOLLOWED THE HERD.
GOOD BYE PASTE UPS, PRESENTATION BOARDS, STATS AND OTHER DRUDGERY...
... SO LONG, HOURS LOST TO CHIT CHAT AT THE TYPE HOUSES AND SEPARATORS...
HI THERE EVERYBODY!
I REALLY LIKE YOUR NEW GARAMOND...
PRETTY COLD, HUH?
YES, IT'S A NICE CONDENSED - VERY POPULAR.
PAUL, DO YOU NEED 22 OR 32 PICAS?
...TO SAY NOTHING OF AFTERNOONS SPENT IN LIBRARIES, LOOKING FOR VISUALS AND DAY-DREAMING.
WOW! ALL OF ALAIN GRÉE'S KIDS' BOOKS!
I NEED MORE HANDS!
GRAPHIC DESIGNERS WOULD NOW DO EVERYTHING ALONE, WITHOUT LEAVING THEIR SEATS. CONCEPTS, SCANNING, TYPESETTING, ILLUSTRATION, PHOTO RETOUCHING, CORRECTIONS, COLOR SEPARATION. ONLY THE PRINTER REMAINED – ALL OTHER MIDDLEMEN WERE ELIMINATED.
CLICK
CLICK
BACK THEN, WE GRAPHIC DESIGNERS WERE A GOLDMINE FOR APPLE. EVERY SIX MONTHS, A NEW MAC APPEARED ON THE MARKET...
MAC SE30: $6000
NEW!
SE30
2 MEGS RAM, 20 MEGS DD
MAC II: $7000
NEW!
8 MEGS RAM, 40 MEGS DD
MAC IIci: $10 000
NEW!
IIci
16 MEGS RAM, 60 MEGS DD
MAC II fx: $12 000
NEW!
fx
MANY MORE TO COME!
32 MEGS RAM, 80 MEGS DD
... AND WE BOUGHT THEM ALL, LIKE IDIOTS.
CHECK IT OUT, MAN! THE NEW POWER PCs HAVE ARRIVED!
WHOA! 66 MHZ! 160 MB HARD DRIVE! CAN YOU BELIEVE IT?
I'VE GOTTA HAVE ONE!
Think.
MacWorld
They're Here!
LaserWriter

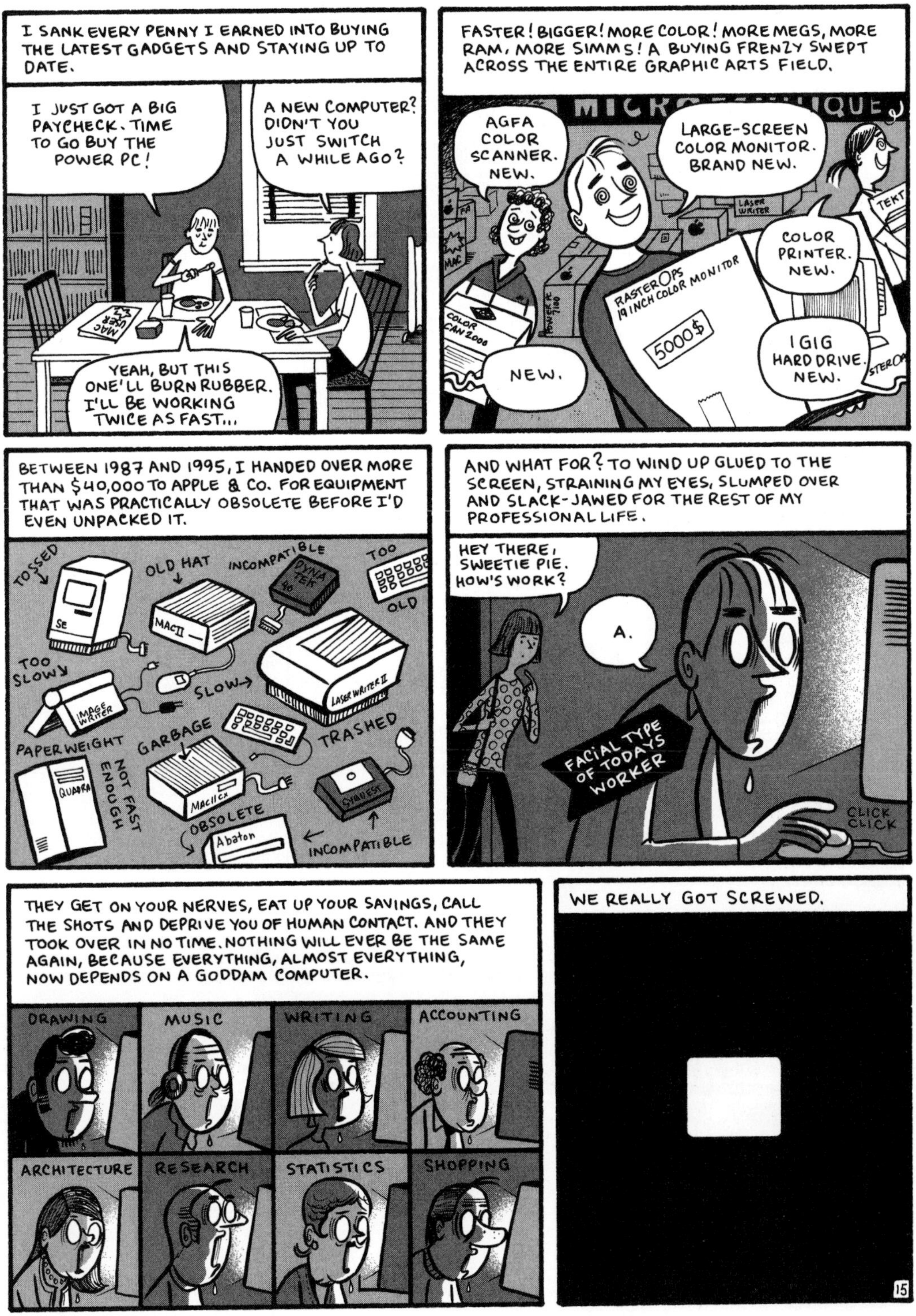
I SANK EVERY PENNY I EARNED INTO BUYING THE LATEST GADGETS AND STAYING UP TO DATE.
I JUST GOT A BIG PAYCHECK. TIME TO GO BUY THE POWER PC!
A NEW COMPUTER? DIDN'T YOU JUST SWITCH A WHILE AGO?
YEAH, BUT THIS ONE'LL BURN RUBBER. I'LL BE WORKING TWICE AS FAST...
MAC USER
FASTER! BIGGER! MORE COLOR! MORE MEGS, MORE RAM, MORE SIMMS! A BUYING FRENZY SWEPT ACROSS THE ENTIRE GRAPHIC ARTS FIELD.
AGFA COLOR SCANNER. NEW.
LARGE-SCREEN COLOR MONITOR. BRAND NEW.
COLOR PRINTER. NEW.
1 GIG HARD DRIVE. NEW.
NEW.
RASTEROPS 19 INCH COLOR MONITOR
5000$
COLOR SCAN 2000
LASER WRITER
BETWEEN 1987 AND 1995, I HANDED OVER MORE THAN $40,000 TO APPLE & CO. FOR EQUIPMENT THAT WAS PRACTICALLY OBSOLETE BEFORE I'D EVEN UNPACKED IT.
TOSSED
SE
OLD HAT
MAC II
INCOMPATIBLE
DYNA TEK 40
TOO OLD
TOO SLOWY
IMAGE WRITER
SLOW
LASER WRITER II
PAPERWEIGHT
QUADRA
NOT FAST ENOUGH
GARBAGE
MAC II CX
TRASHED
SYQUEST
OBSOLETE
Abaton
INCOMPATIBLE
AND WHAT FOR? TO WIND UP GLUED TO THE SCREEN, STRAINING MY EYES, SLUMPED OVER AND SLACK-JAWED FOR THE REST OF MY PROFESSIONAL LIFE.
HEY THERE, SWEETIE PIE. HOW'S WORK?
A.
FACIAL TYPE OF TODAYS WORKER
CLICK CLICK
THEY GET ON YOUR NERVES, EAT UP YOUR SAVINGS, CALL THE SHOTS AND DEPRIVE YOU OF HUMAN CONTACT. AND THEY TOOK OVER IN NO TIME. NOTHING WILL EVER BE THE SAME AGAIN, BECAUSE EVERYTHING, ALMOST EVERYTHING, NOW DEPENDS ON A GODDAM COMPUTER.
DRAWING
MUSIC
WRITING
ACCOUNTING
ARCHITECTURE
RESEARCH
STATISTICS
SHOPPING
WE REALLY GOT SCREWED.

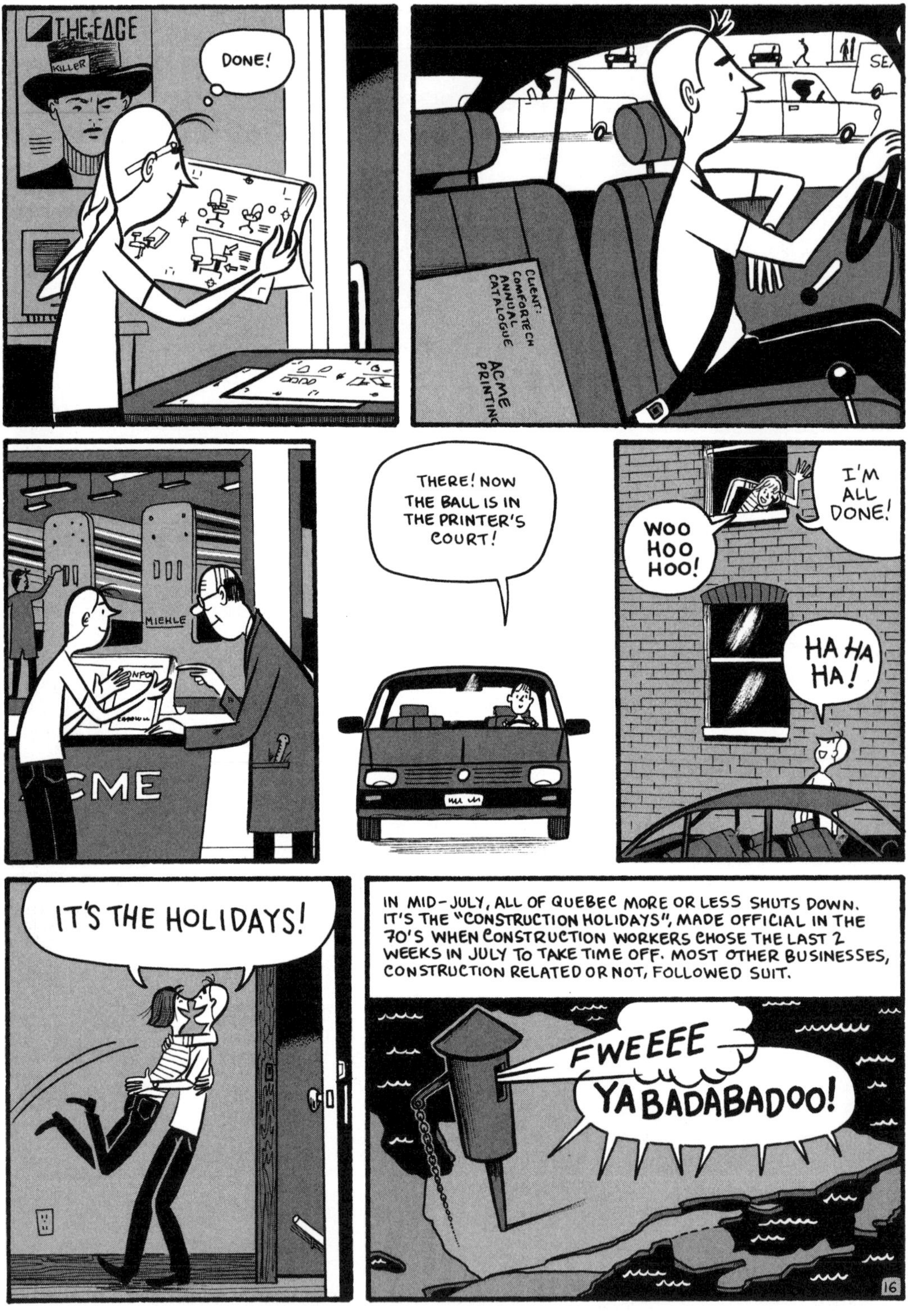
THE FACE
KILLER
DONE!
CLIENT: COMFORTECH ANNUAL CATALOGUE
ACME PRINTING
MIEHLE
ACME
THERE! NOW THE BALL IS IN THE PRINTER'S COURT!
WOO HOO HOO!
I'M ALL DONE!
HA HA HA!
IT'S THE HOLIDAYS!
IN MID-JULY, ALL OF QUEBEC MORE OR LESS SHUTS DOWN. IT'S THE "CONSTRUCTION HOLIDAYS", MADE OFFICIAL IN THE 70'S WHEN CONSTRUCTION WORKERS CHOSE THE LAST 2 WEEKS IN JULY TO TAKE TIME OFF. MOST OTHER BUSINESSES, CONSTRUCTION RELATED OR NOT, FOLLOWED SUIT.
FWEEEE
YABADABADOO!

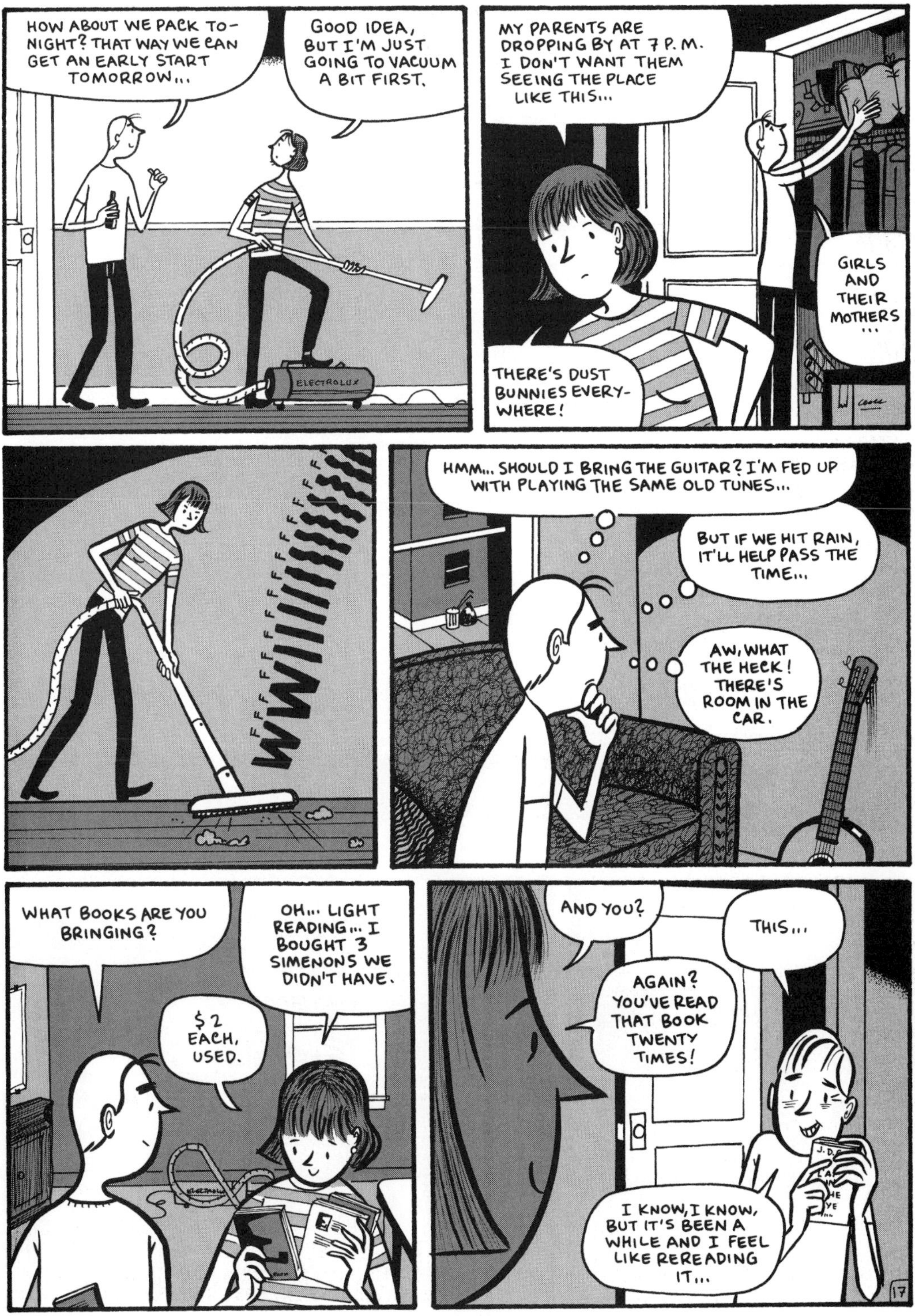
HOW ABOUT WE PACK TO-NIGHT? THAT WAY WE CAN GET AN EARLY START TOMORROW...
GOOD IDEA, BUT I'M JUST GOING TO VACUUM A BIT FIRST.
ELECTROLUX
MY PARENTS ARE DROPPING BY AT 7 P.M. I DON'T WANT THEM SEEING THE PLACE LIKE THIS...
THERE'S DUST BUNNIES EVERY-WHERE!
GIRLS AND THEIR MOTHERS...
WWWIIIIIIIIFFFFFFFFFFF
HMM... SHOULD I BRING THE GUITAR? I'M FED UP WITH PLAYING THE SAME OLD TUNES...
BUT IF WE HIT RAIN, IT'LL HELP PASS THE TIME...
AW, WHAT THE HECK! THERE'S ROOM IN THE CAR.
WHAT BOOKS ARE YOU BRINGING?
OH... LIGHT READING... I BOUGHT 3 SIMENONS WE DIDN'T HAVE.
$2 EACH, USED.
AND YOU?
THIS...
AGAIN? YOU'VE READ THAT BOOK TWENTY TIMES!
I KNOW, I KNOW, BUT IT'S BEEN A WHILE AND I FEEL LIKE REREADING IT...

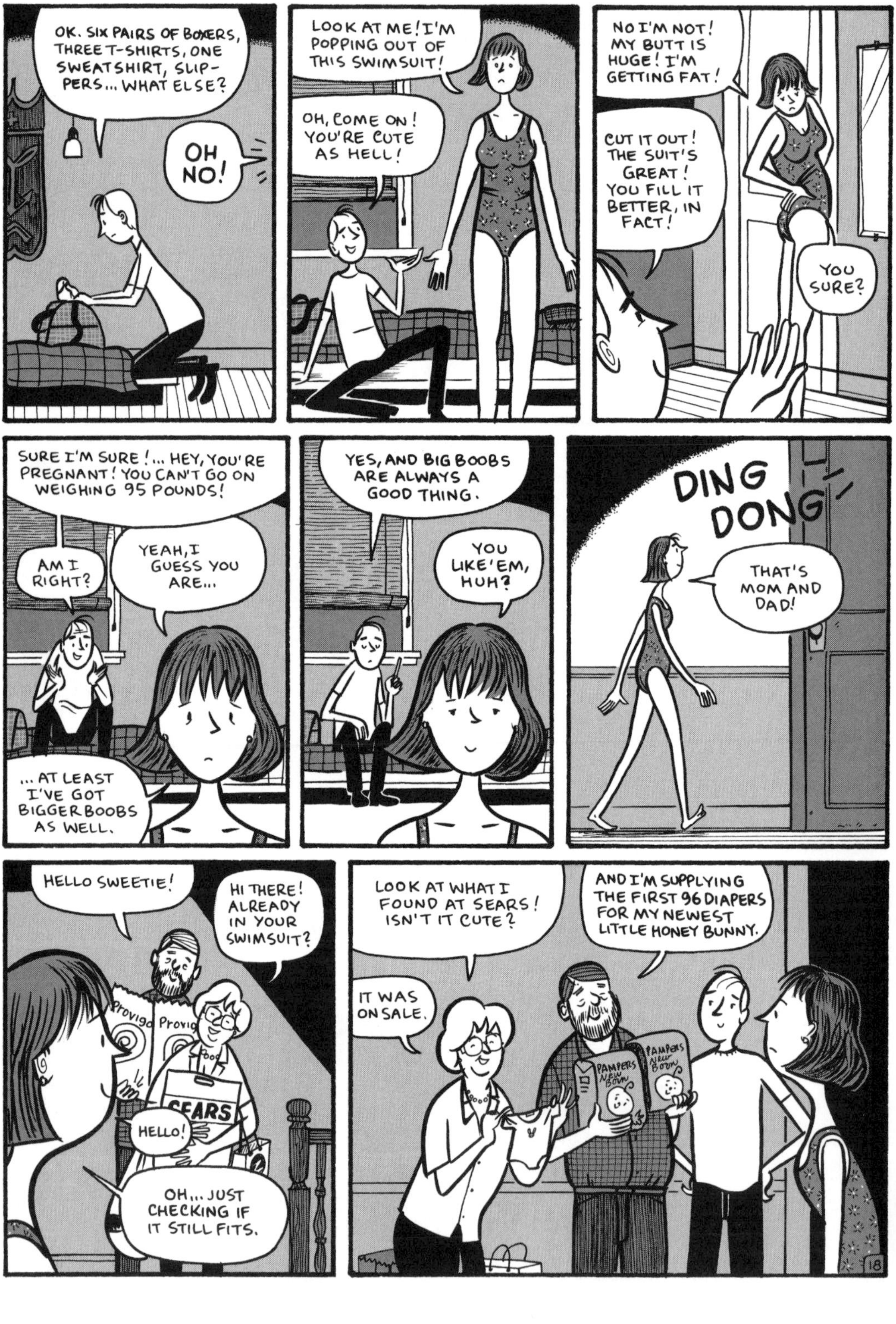
OK. SIX PAIRS OF BOXERS, THREE T-SHIRTS, ONE SWEATSHIRT, SLIPPERS... WHAT ELSE?
OH NO!
LOOK AT ME! I'M POPPING OUT OF THIS SWIMSUIT!
OH, COME ON! YOU'RE CUTE AS HELL!
NO I'M NOT! MY BUTT IS HUGE! I'M GETTING FAT!
CUT IT OUT! THE SUIT'S GREAT! YOU FILL IT BETTER, IN FACT!
YOU SURE?
SURE I'M SURE!... HEY, YOU'RE PREGNANT! YOU CAN'T GO ON WEIGHING 95 POUNDS!
AM I RIGHT?
YEAH, I GUESS YOU ARE...
... AT LEAST I'VE GOT BIGGER BOOBS AS WELL.
YES, AND BIG BOOBS ARE ALWAYS A GOOD THING.
YOU LIKE 'EM, HUH?
DING DONG
THAT'S MOM AND DAD!
HELLO SWEETIE!
HI THERE! ALREADY IN YOUR SWIMSUIT?
Provigo Provigo
SEARS
HELLO!
OH... JUST CHECKING IF IT STILL FITS.
LOOK AT WHAT I FOUND AT SEARS! ISN'T IT CUTE?
AND I'M SUPPLYING THE FIRST 96 DIAPERS FOR MY NEWEST LITTLE HONEY BUNNY.
IT WAS ON SALE.
PAMPERS NEW BORN
PAMPERS NEW BORN

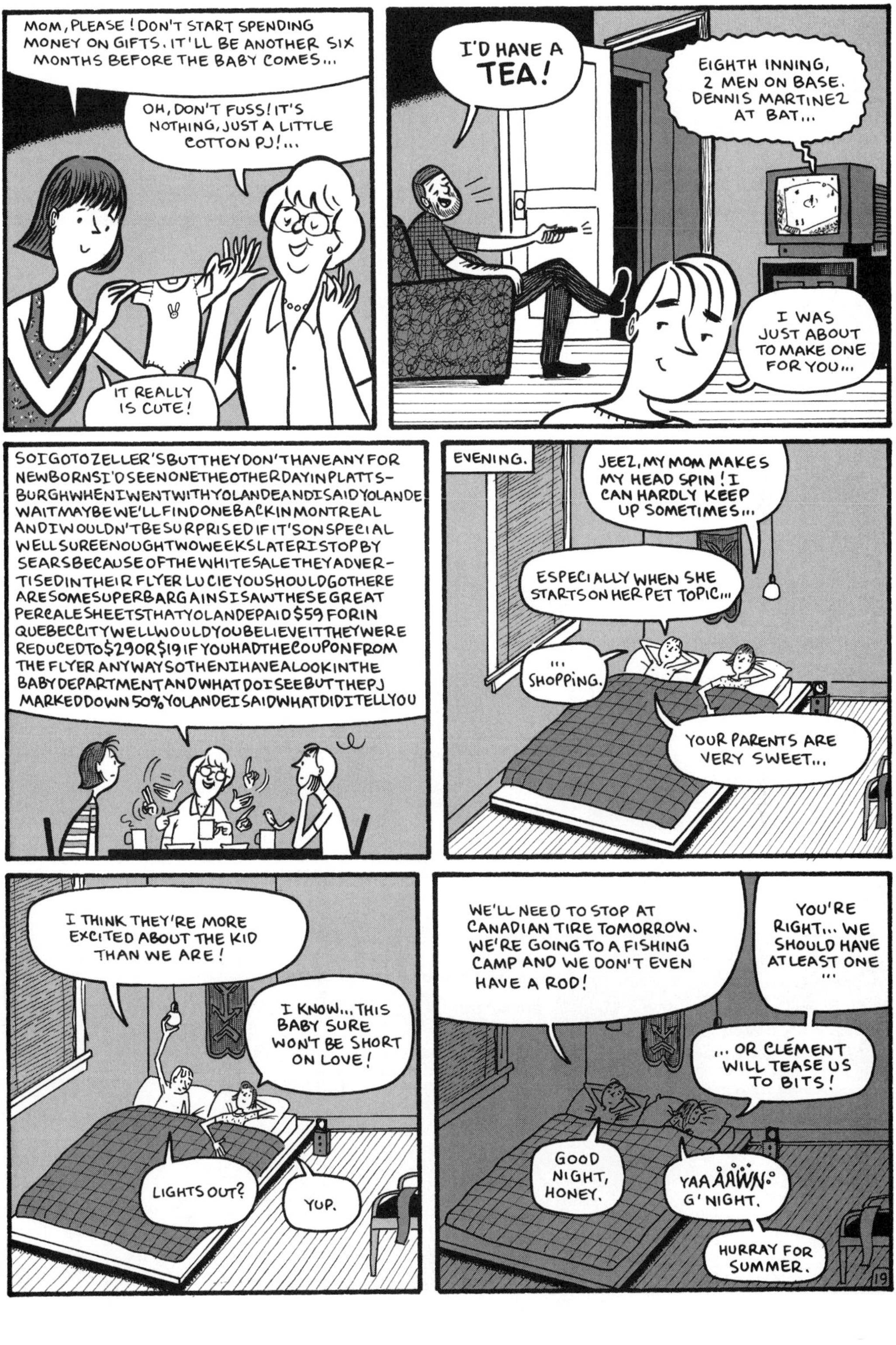
MOM, PLEASE! DON'T START SPENDING MONEY ON GIFTS. IT'LL BE ANOTHER SIX MONTHS BEFORE THE BABY COMES...
OH, DON'T FUSS! IT'S NOTHING, JUST A LITTLE COTTON PJ!...
IT REALLY IS CUTE!
I'D HAVE A TEA!
EIGHTH INNING, 2 MEN ON BASE. DENNIS MARTINEZ AT BAT...
I WAS JUST ABOUT TO MAKE ONE FOR YOU...
SOIGOTOZELLER'SBUTTHEYDON'THAVEANYFOR NEWBORNSI'DSEENONETHEOTHERDAYINPLATTS-BURGHWHENIWENTWITHYOLANDEANDISAIDYOLANDE WAITMAYBEWE'LLFINDONEBACKINMONTREAL ANDIWOULDN'TBESURPRISEDIFIT'SONSPECIAL WELLSUREENOUGHTWOWEEKSLATERISTOPBY SEARSBECAUSEOFTHEWHITESALETHEYADVER-TISEDINTHEIRFLYER LUCIEYOUSHOULDGOTHERE ARESOMESUPERBARGAINSISAWTHESEGREAT PERCALESHEETSTHATYOLANDEPAID$59FORIN QUEBECCITYWELLWOULDYOUBELIEVEITTHEYWERE REDUCEDTO$29OR$19IFYOUHADTHECOUPONFROM THEFLYER ANYWAYSOTHENIHAVEALOOKINTHE BABYDEPARTMENTANDWHATDOISEEBUTTHEPJ MARKEDDOWN50%YOLANDEISAIDWHATDIDITELLYOU
EVENING.
JEEZ, MY MOM MAKES MY HEAD SPIN! I CAN HARDLY KEEP UP SOMETIMES...
ESPECIALLY WHEN SHE STARTS ON HER PET TOPIC...
... SHOPPING.
YOUR PARENTS ARE VERY SWEET...
I THINK THEY'RE MORE EXCITED ABOUT THE KID THAN WE ARE!
I KNOW... THIS BABY SURE WON'T BE SHORT ON LOVE!
LIGHTS OUT?
YUP.
WE'LL NEED TO STOP AT CANADIAN TIRE TOMORROW. WE'RE GOING TO A FISHING CAMP AND WE DON'T EVEN HAVE A ROD!
YOU'RE RIGHT... WE SHOULD HAVE AT LEAST ONE ...
... OR CLÉMENT WILL TEASE US TO BITS!
GOOD NIGHT, HONEY.
YAAAAWN.
G'NIGHT.
HURRAY FOR SUMMER.

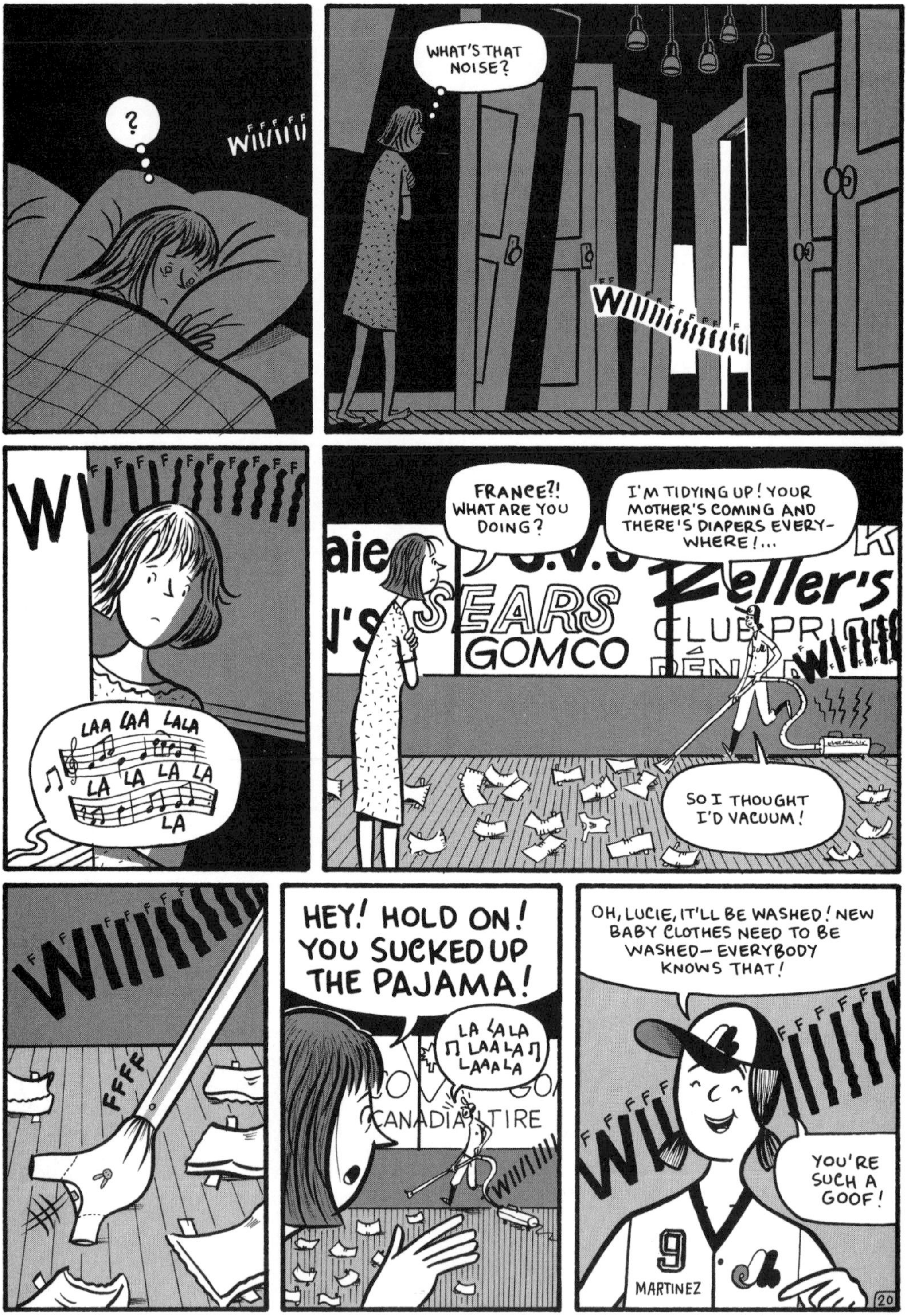
?
WIIIIII FFFF
WHAT'S THAT NOISE?
WIIIIIIIIIIII FFFFFFF
WIIIIIIIIII FFFFFFFFFFF
LAA LAA LALA LA LA LA LA LA
FRANCE?! WHAT ARE YOU DOING?
I'M TIDYING UP! YOUR MOTHER'S COMING AND THERE'S DIAPERS EVERY-WHERE!...
SEARS
GOMCO
Zeller's
CLUB PRI
SO I THOUGHT I'D VACUUM!
WIIIIIIIII FFFFFFF
FFFF
HEY! HOLD ON! YOU SUCKED UP THE PAJAMA!
LA LALA LAA LA LAAA LA
CANADIA TIRE
OH, LUCIE, IT'LL BE WASHED! NEW BABY CLOTHES NEED TO BE WASHED— EVERYBODY KNOWS THAT!
YOU'RE SUCH A GOOF!
9
MARTINEZ

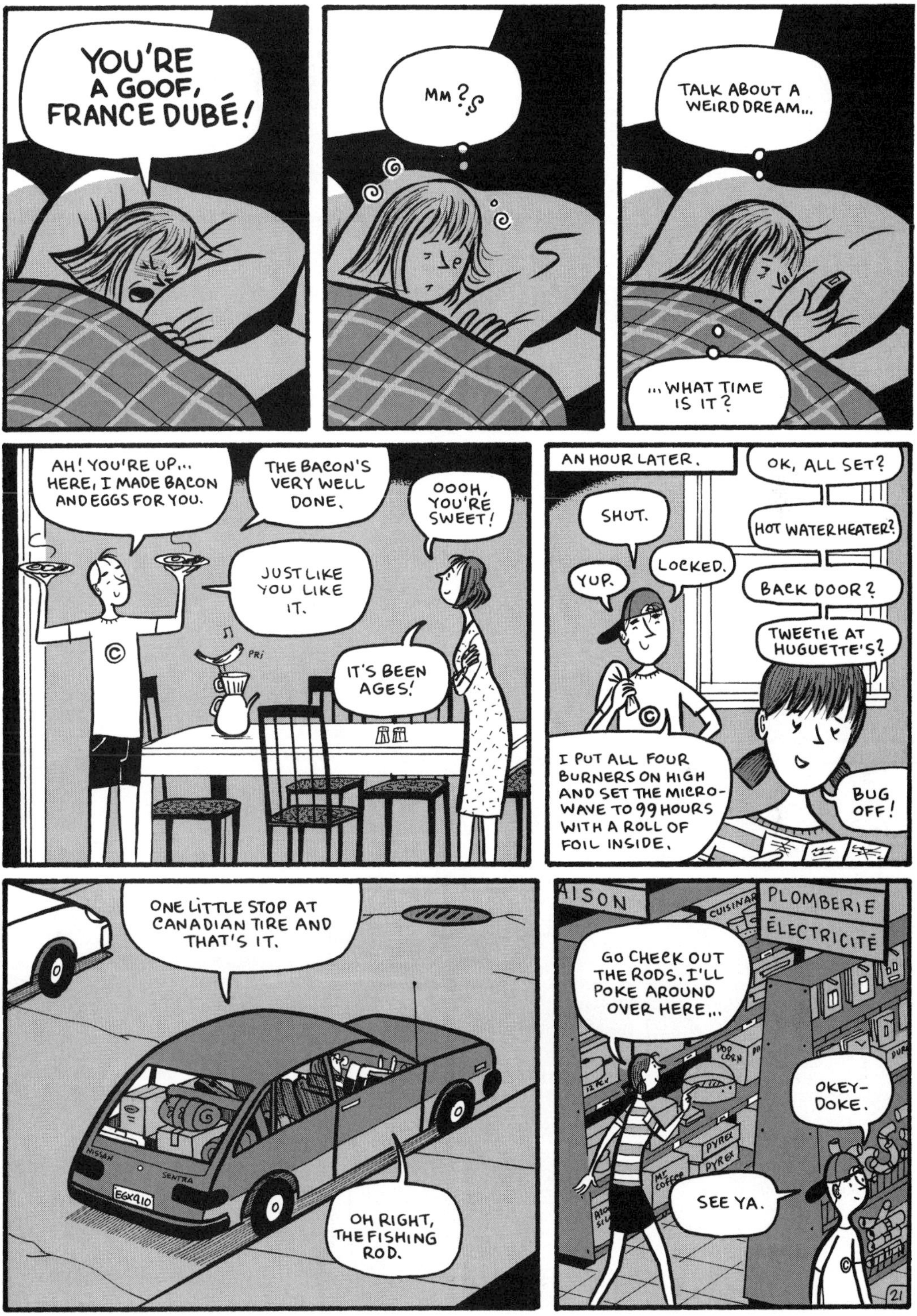
YOU'RE A GOOF, FRANCE DUBÉ!
MM ?S
TALK ABOUT A WEIRD DREAM...
... WHAT TIME IS IT?
AH! YOU'RE UP... HERE, I MADE BACON AND EGGS FOR YOU.
THE BACON'S VERY WELL DONE.
JUST LIKE YOU LIKE IT.
OOOH, YOU'RE SWEET!
IT'S BEEN AGES!
PRI
AN HOUR LATER.
OK, ALL SET?
SHUT.
HOT WATER HEATER?
LOCKED.
YUP.
BACK DOOR?
TWEETIE AT HUGUETTE'S?
I PUT ALL FOUR BURNERS ON HIGH AND SET THE MICRO-WAVE TO 99 HOURS WITH A ROLL OF FOIL INSIDE.
BUG OFF!
ONE LITTLE STOP AT CANADIAN TIRE AND THAT'S IT.
NISSAN
SENTRA
EGK910
OH RIGHT, THE FISHING ROD.
AISON
PLOMBERIE
ÉLECTRICITÉ
GO CHECK OUT THE RODS. I'LL POKE AROUND OVER HERE...
OKEY-DOKE.
PYREX
SEE YA.

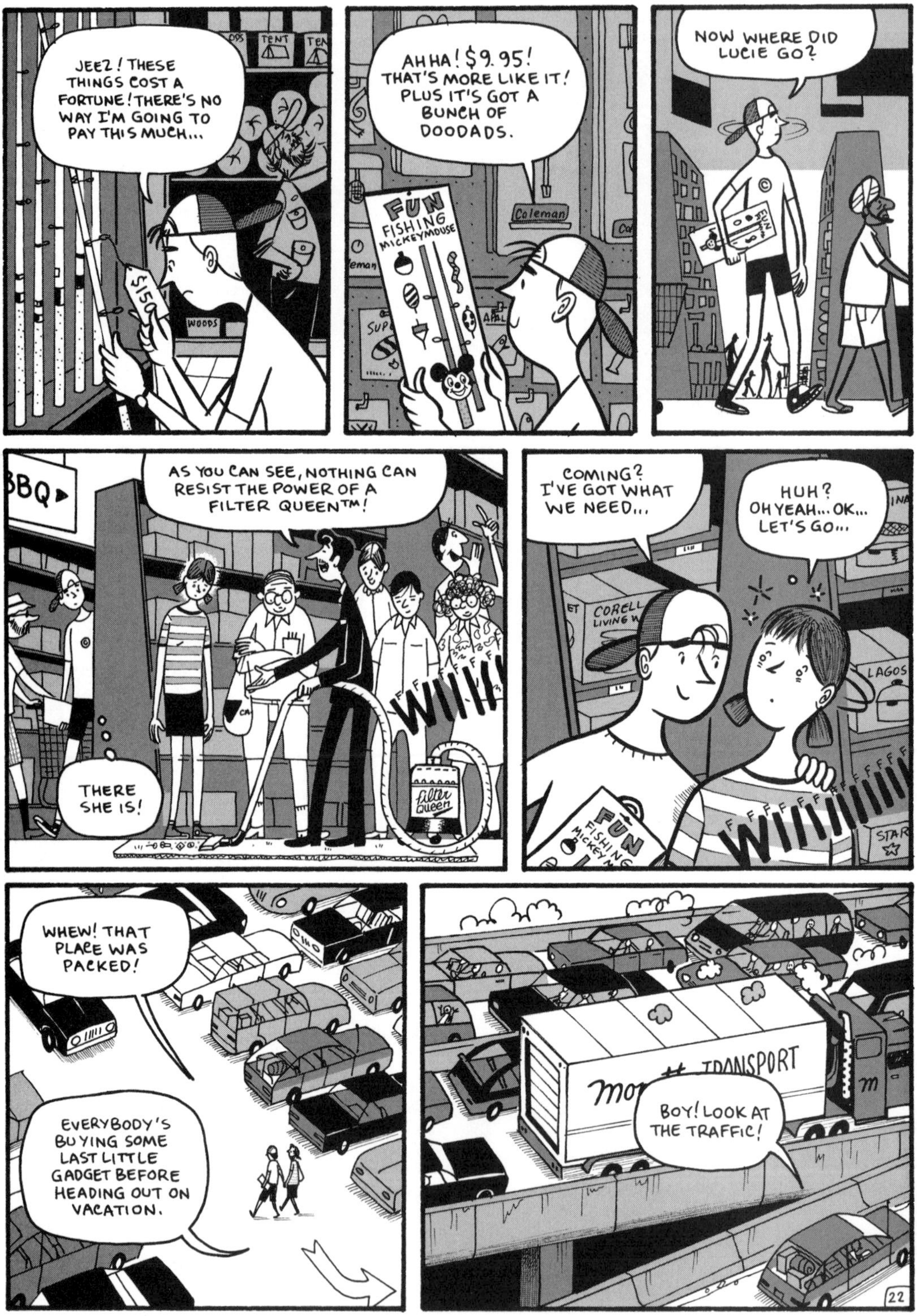

JEEZ! THESE THINGS COST A FORTUNE! THERE'S NO WAY I'M GOING TO PAY THIS MUCH...
$150
AH HA! $9.95! THAT'S MORE LIKE IT! PLUS IT'S GOT A BUNCH OF DOODADS.
FUN FISHING MICKEYMOUSE
Coleman
NOW WHERE DID LUCIE GO?
BBQ
AS YOU CAN SEE, NOTHING CAN RESIST THE POWER OF A FILTER QUEEN™!
THERE SHE IS!
FFFWIIII
COMING? I'VE GOT WHAT WE NEED...
HUH? OH YEAH... OK... LET'S GO...
FFFFFFFWIIIIIIII
WHEW! THAT PLACE WAS PACKED!
EVERYBODY'S BUYING SOME LAST LITTLE GADGET BEFORE HEADING OUT ON VACATION.
TRANSPORT
BOY! LOOK AT THE TRAFFIC!

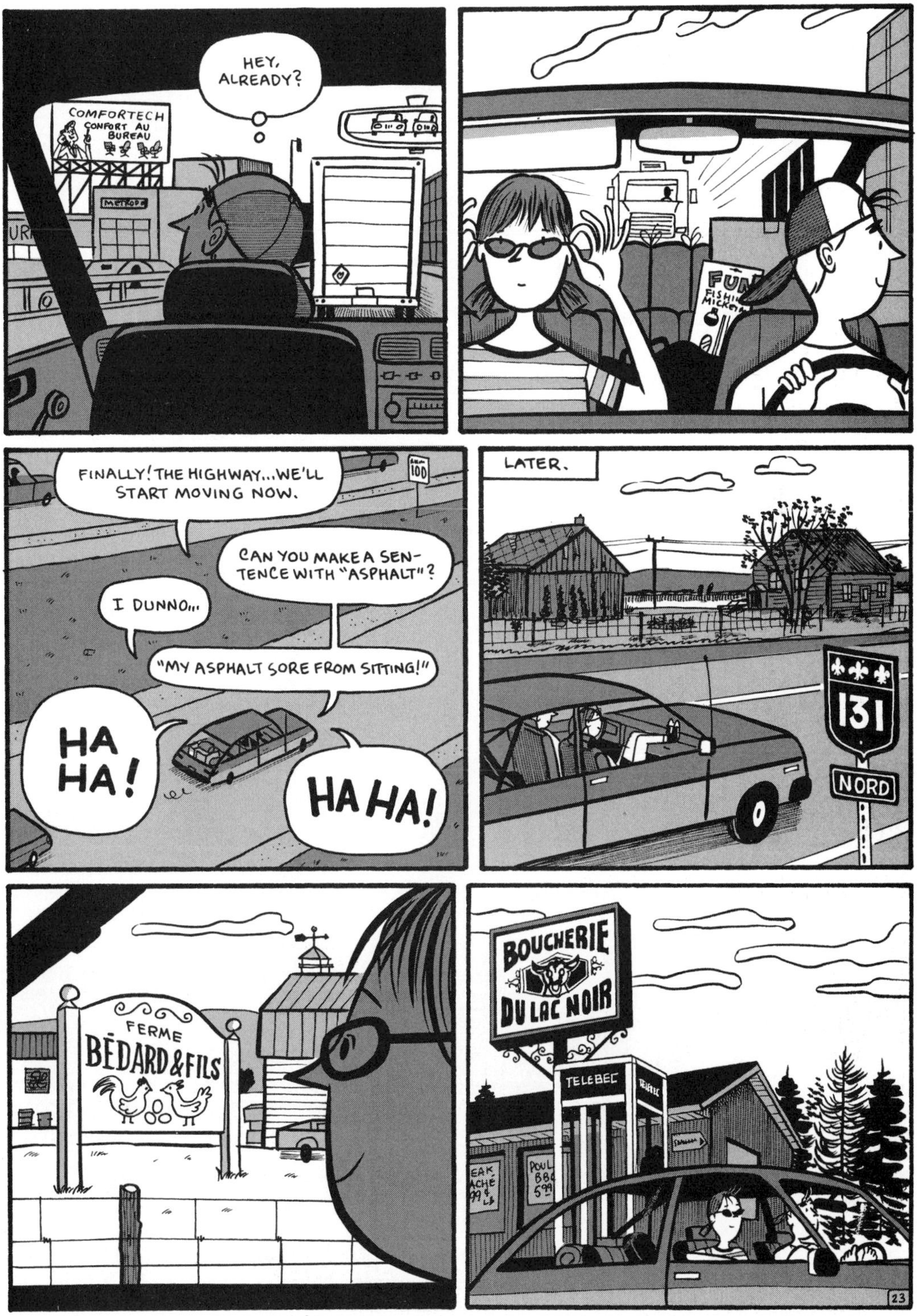
COMFORTECH
CONFORT AU BUREAU
HEY, ALREADY?
FINALLY! THE HIGHWAY... WE'LL START MOVING NOW.
100
CAN YOU MAKE A SENTENCE WITH "ASPHALT"?
I DUNNO...
"MY ASPHALT SORE FROM SITTING!"
HA HA!
HA HA!
LATER.
131
NORD
FERME
BÉDARD & FILS
BOUCHERIE
DU LAC NOIR
TELEBEC

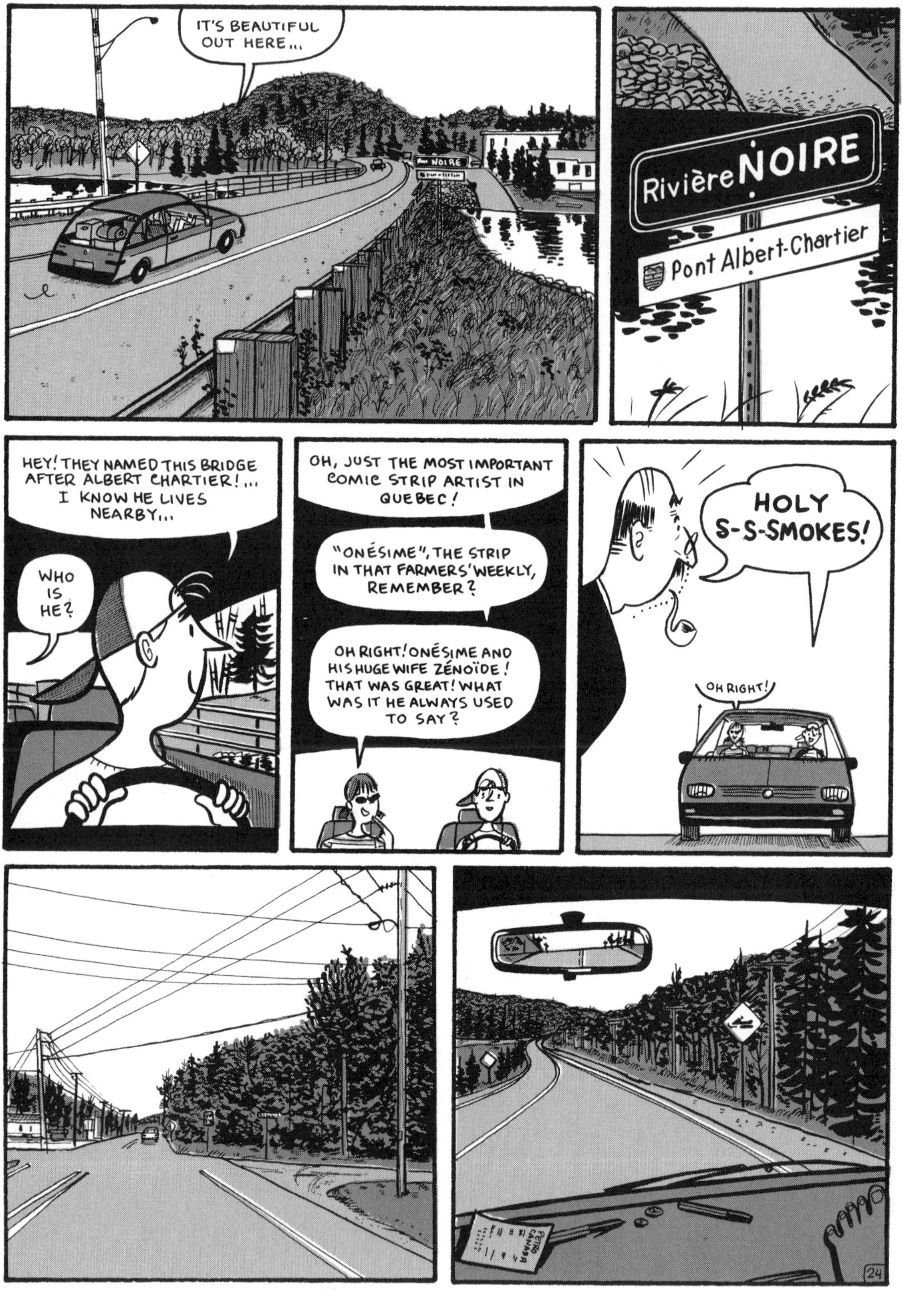
IT'S BEAUTIFUL OUT HERE...
NOIRE
Rivière NOIRE
Pont Albert-Chartier
HEY! THEY NAMED THIS BRIDGE AFTER ALBERT CHARTIER!... I KNOW HE LIVES NEARBY...
WHO IS HE?
OH, JUST THE MOST IMPORTANT COMIC STRIP ARTIST IN QUEBEC!
"ONÉSIME", THE STRIP IN THAT FARMERS' WEEKLY, REMEMBER?
OH RIGHT! ONÉSIME AND HIS HUGE WIFE ZÉNOÏDE! THAT WAS GREAT! WHAT WAS IT HE ALWAYS USED TO SAY?
HOLY S-S-SMOKES!
OH RIGHT!
PETRO CANADA
24

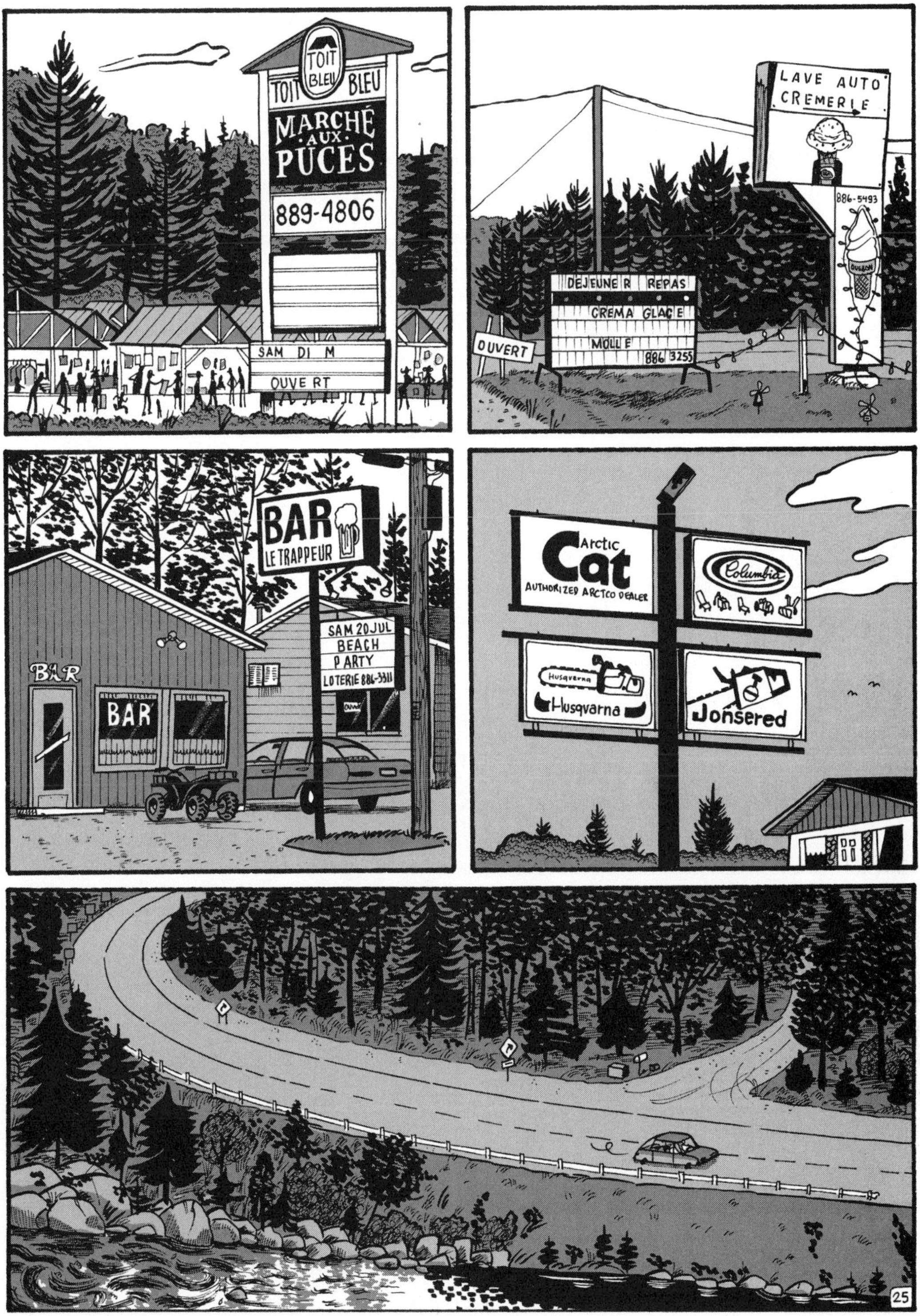
TOIT BLEU
TOIT BLEU TOIT BLEU
MARCHÉ AUX PUCES
889-4806
SAM DI M
OUVE RT
LAVE AUTO
CREMERIE
886-5493
DEJEUNE R REPAS
CREMA GLACE
MOLL E
886 3255
OUVERT
BAR
LE TRAPPEUR
SAM 20 JUL
BEACH
P ARTY
LOTERIE 886-3311
BAR
BAR
Arctic Cat
AUTHORIZED ARCTCO DEALER
Columbia
Husqvarna
Husqvarna
Jonsered

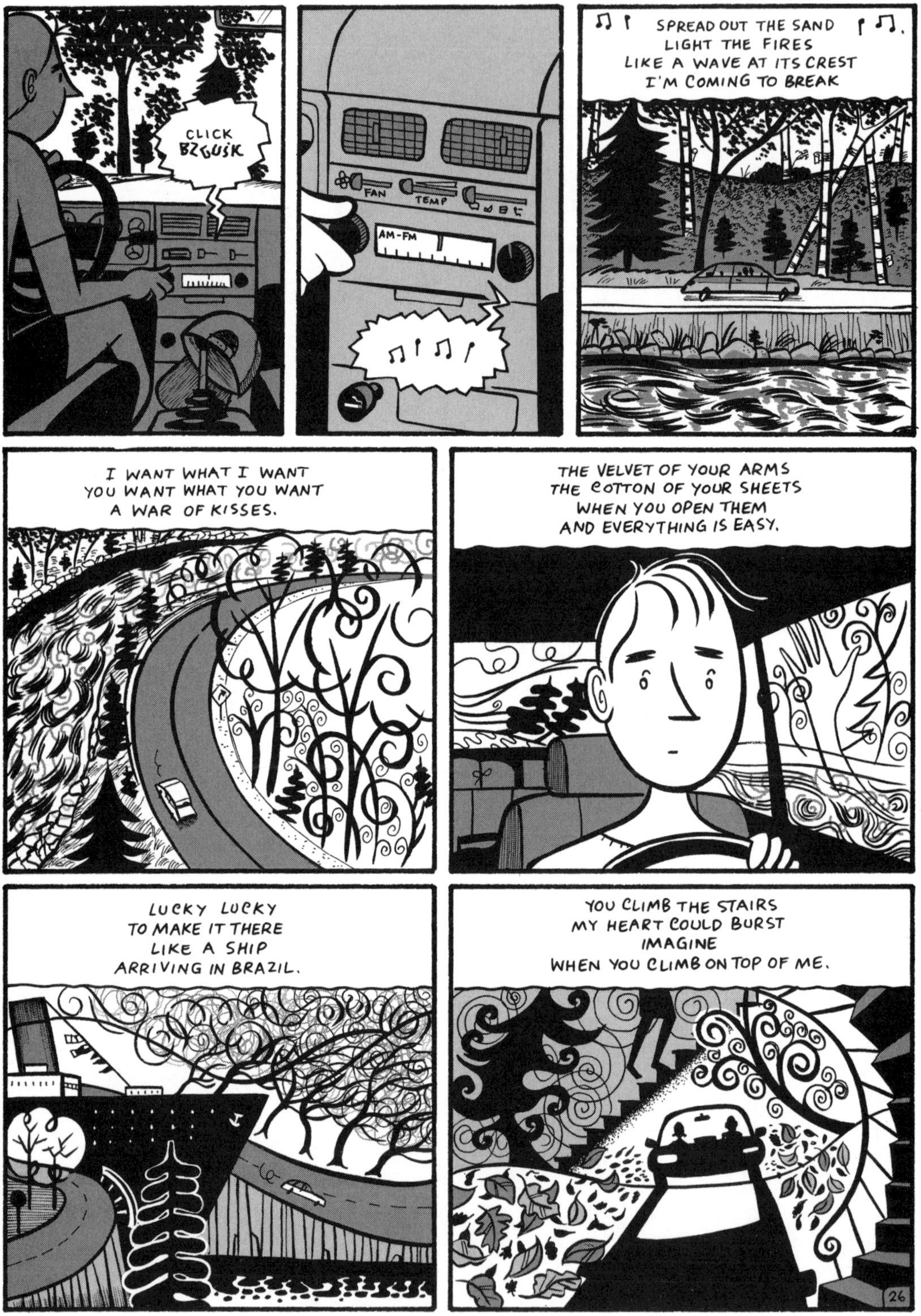
CLICK
BZGUSK
AM-FM
FAN
TEMP
SPREAD OUT THE SAND
LIGHT THE FIRES
LIKE A WAVE AT ITS CREST
I'M COMING TO BREAK
I WANT WHAT I WANT
YOU WANT WHAT YOU WANT
A WAR OF KISSES.
THE VELVET OF YOUR ARMS
THE COTTON OF YOUR SHEETS
WHEN YOU OPEN THEM
AND EVERYTHING IS EASY.
LUCKY LUCKY
TO MAKE IT THERE
LIKE A SHIP
ARRIVING IN BRAZIL.
YOU CLIMB THE STAIRS
MY HEART COULD BURST
IMAGINE
WHEN YOU CLIMB ON TOP OF ME.

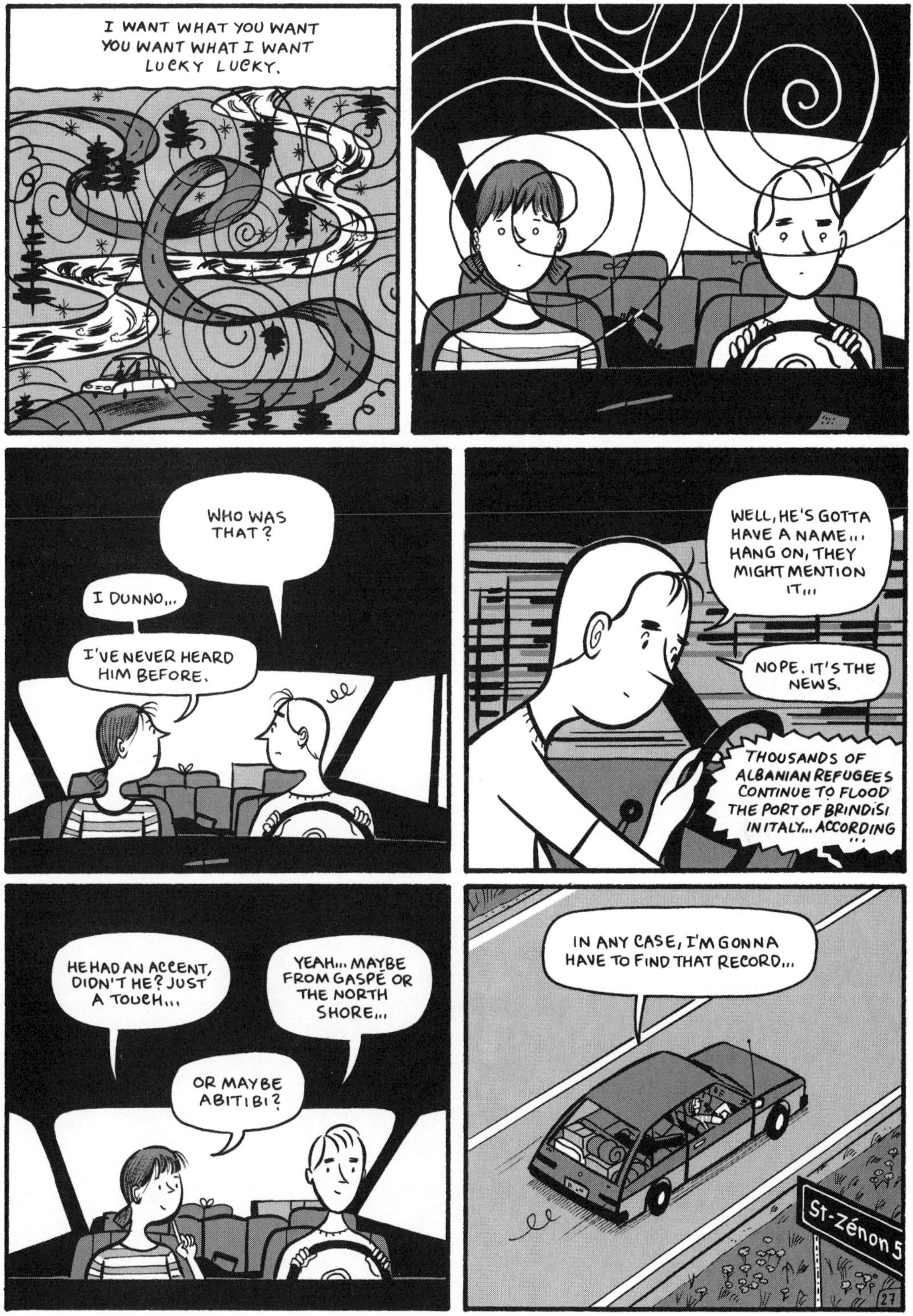
I WANT WHAT YOU WANT
YOU WANT WHAT I WANT
LUCKY LUCKY.
WHO WAS THAT?
I DUNNO...
I'VE NEVER HEARD HIM BEFORE.
WELL, HE'S GOTTA HAVE A NAME... HANG ON, THEY MIGHT MENTION IT...
NOPE. IT'S THE NEWS.
THOUSANDS OF ALBANIAN REFUGEES CONTINUE TO FLOOD THE PORT OF BRINDISI IN ITALY... ACCORDING ...
HE HAD AN ACCENT, DIDN'T HE? JUST A TOUCH...
YEAH... MAYBE FROM GASPÉ OR THE NORTH SHORE...
OR MAYBE ABITIBI?
IN ANY CASE, I'M GONNA HAVE TO FIND THAT RECORD...
St-Zénon 5

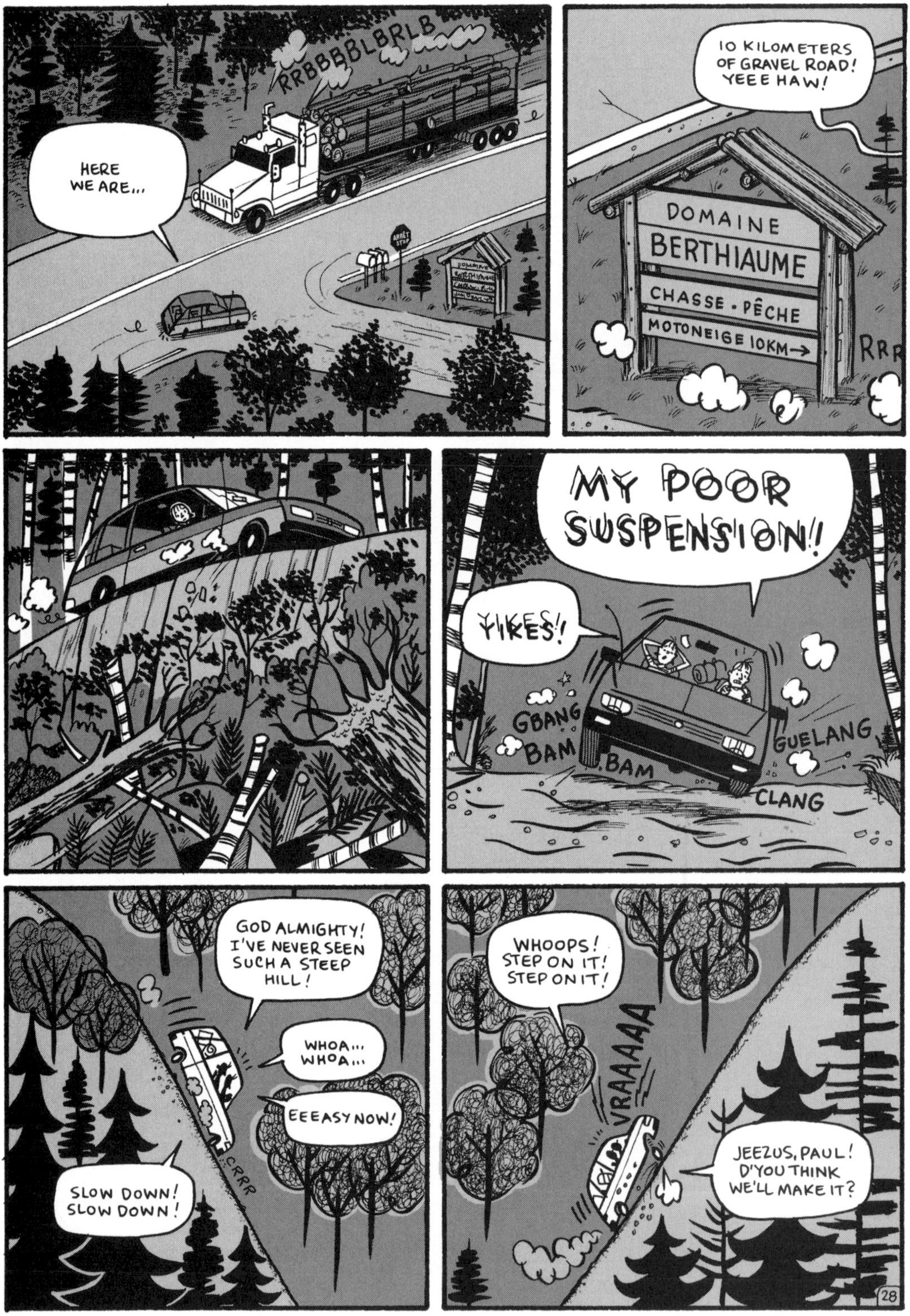
RRBBBBLBRLB
HERE WE ARE...
ARRÊT STOP
10 KILOMETERS OF GRAVEL ROAD! YEEE HAW!
DOMAINE BERTHIAUME
CHASSE - PÊCHE
MOTONEIGE 10KM→
RRR
MY POOR SUSPENSION!!
YIKES!!
GBANG
BAM
BAM
GUELANG
CLANG
GOD ALMIGHTY! I'VE NEVER SEEN SUCH A STEEP HILL!
WHOA... WHOA...
EEEASY NOW!
SLOW DOWN! SLOW DOWN!
CRRR
WHOOPS! STEP ON IT! STEP ON IT!
VRAAAAA
JEEZUS, PAUL! D'YOU THINK WE'LL MAKE IT?

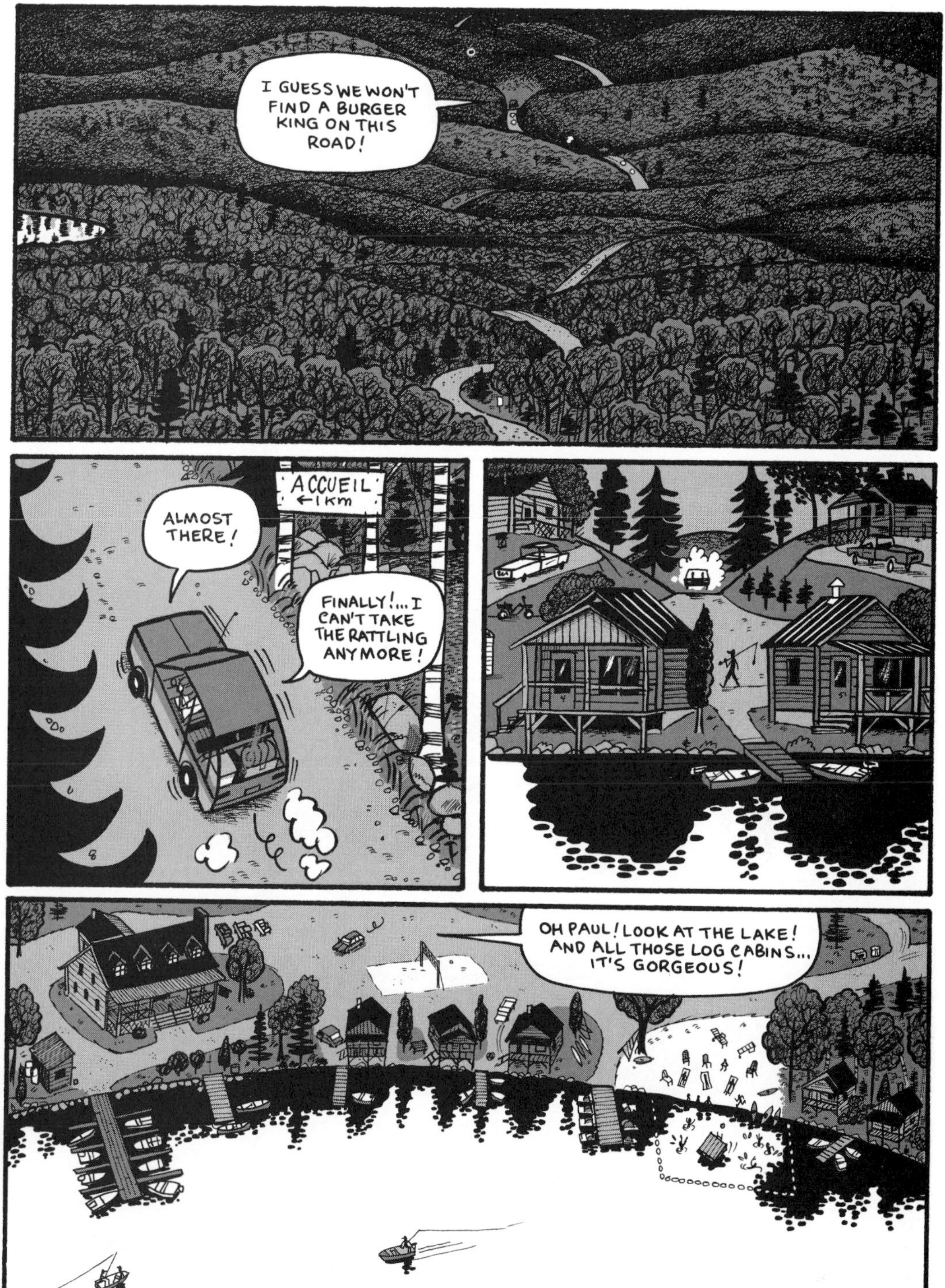
I GUESS WE WON'T FIND A BURGER KING ON THIS ROAD!
ACCUEIL ←1km
ALMOST THERE!
FINALLY!... I CAN'T TAKE THE RATTLING ANYMORE!
OH PAUL! LOOK AT THE LAKE! AND ALL THOSE LOG CABINS... IT'S GORGEOUS!

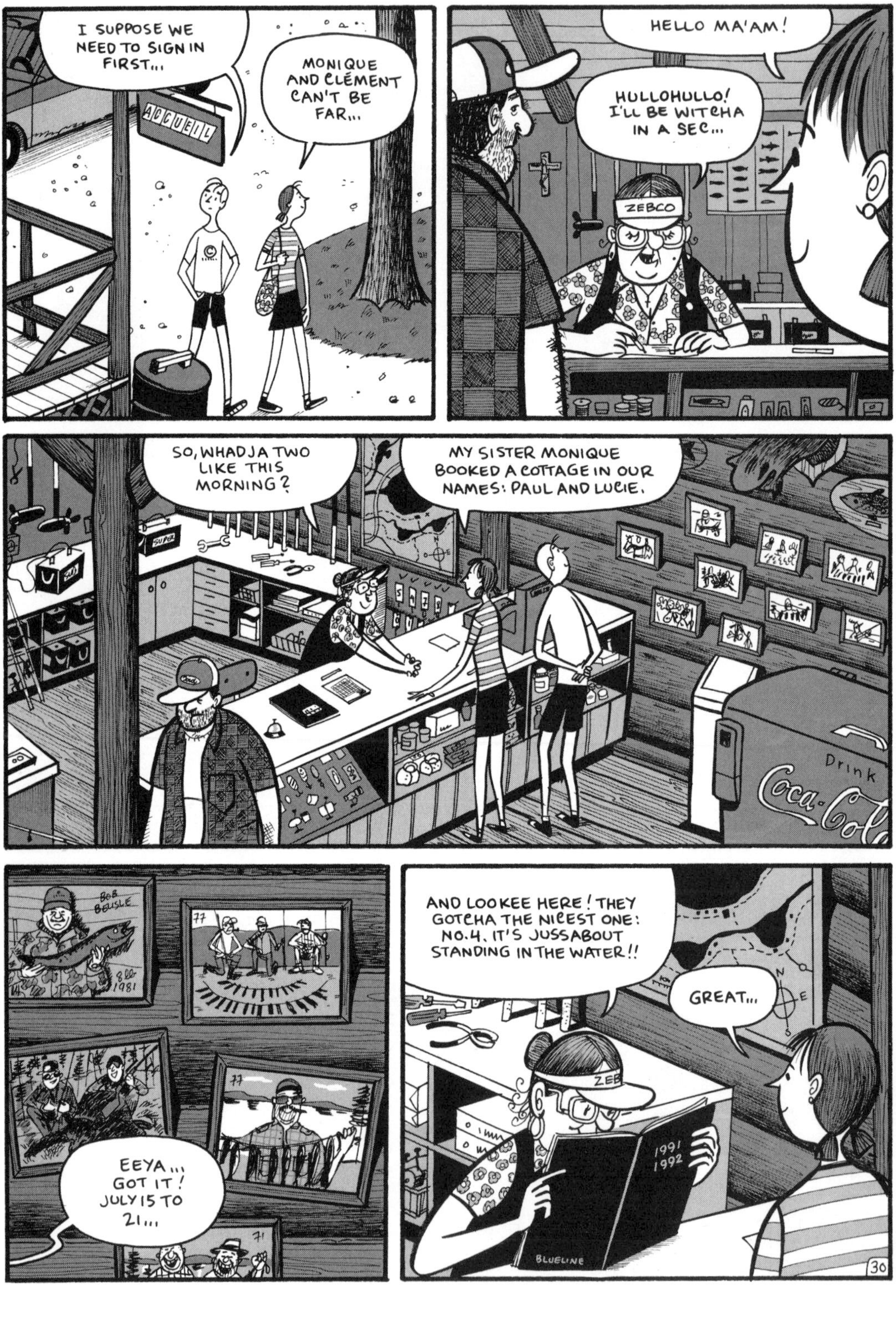
I SUPPOSE WE NEED TO SIGN IN FIRST...
ACCUEIL
MONIQUE AND CLÉMENT CAN'T BE FAR...
HELLO MA'AM!
HULLOHULLO! I'LL BE WITCHA IN A SEC...
ZEBCO
SO, WHADJA TWO LIKE THIS MORNING?
MY SISTER MONIQUE BOOKED A COTTAGE IN OUR NAMES: PAUL AND LUCIE.
Drink Coca-Cola
BOB BELISLE
EEYA... GOT IT! JULY 15 TO 21...
AND LOOKEE HERE! THEY GOTCHA THE NICEST ONE: NO. 4. IT'S JUSSABOUT STANDING IN THE WATER!!
GREAT...
1991 1992
BLUELINE

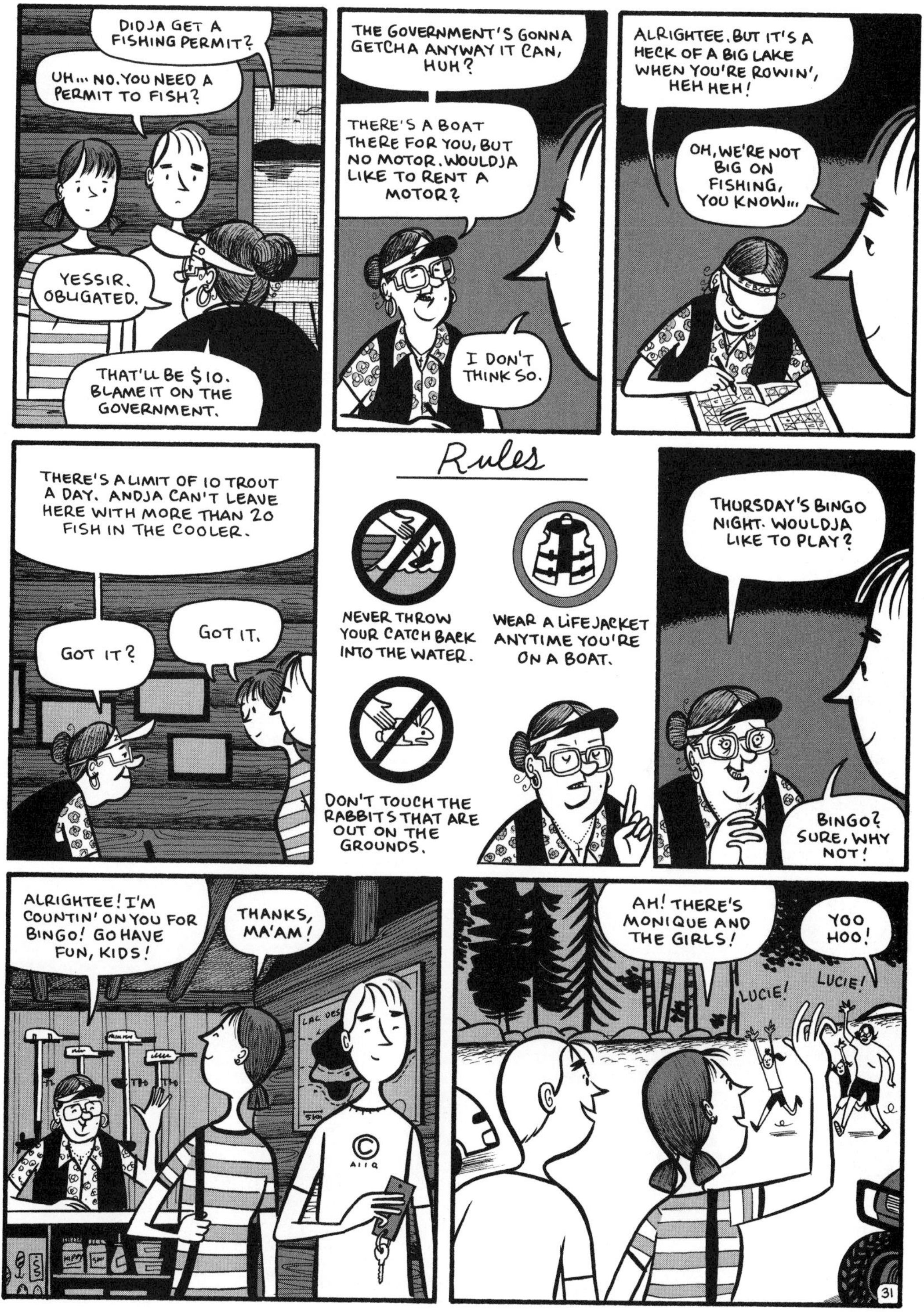
DIDJA GET A FISHING PERMIT?
UH... NO. YOU NEED A PERMIT TO FISH?
YESSIR. OBLIGATED.
THAT'LL BE $10. BLAME IT ON THE GOVERNMENT.
THE GOVERNMENT'S GONNA GETCHA ANYWAY IT CAN, HUH?
THERE'S A BOAT THERE FOR YOU, BUT NO MOTOR. WOULDJA LIKE TO RENT A MOTOR?
I DON'T THINK SO.
ALRIGHTEE. BUT IT'S A HECK OF A BIG LAKE WHEN YOU'RE ROWIN', HEH HEH!
OH, WE'RE NOT BIG ON FISHING, YOU KNOW...
ZEBCO
THERE'S A LIMIT OF 10 TROUT A DAY. ANDJA CAN'T LEAVE HERE WITH MORE THAN 20 FISH IN THE COOLER.
GOT IT?
GOT IT.
Rules
NEVER THROW YOUR CATCH BACK INTO THE WATER.
WEAR A LIFEJACKET ANYTIME YOU'RE ON A BOAT.
DON'T TOUCH THE RABBITS THAT ARE OUT ON THE GROUNDS.
THURSDAY'S BINGO NIGHT. WOULDJA LIKE TO PLAY?
BINGO? SURE, WHY NOT!
ALRIGHTEE! I'M COUNTIN' ON YOU FOR BINGO! GO HAVE FUN, KIDS!
THANKS, MA'AM!
AH! THERE'S MONIQUE AND THE GIRLS!
YOO HOO!
LUCIE!
LUCIE!

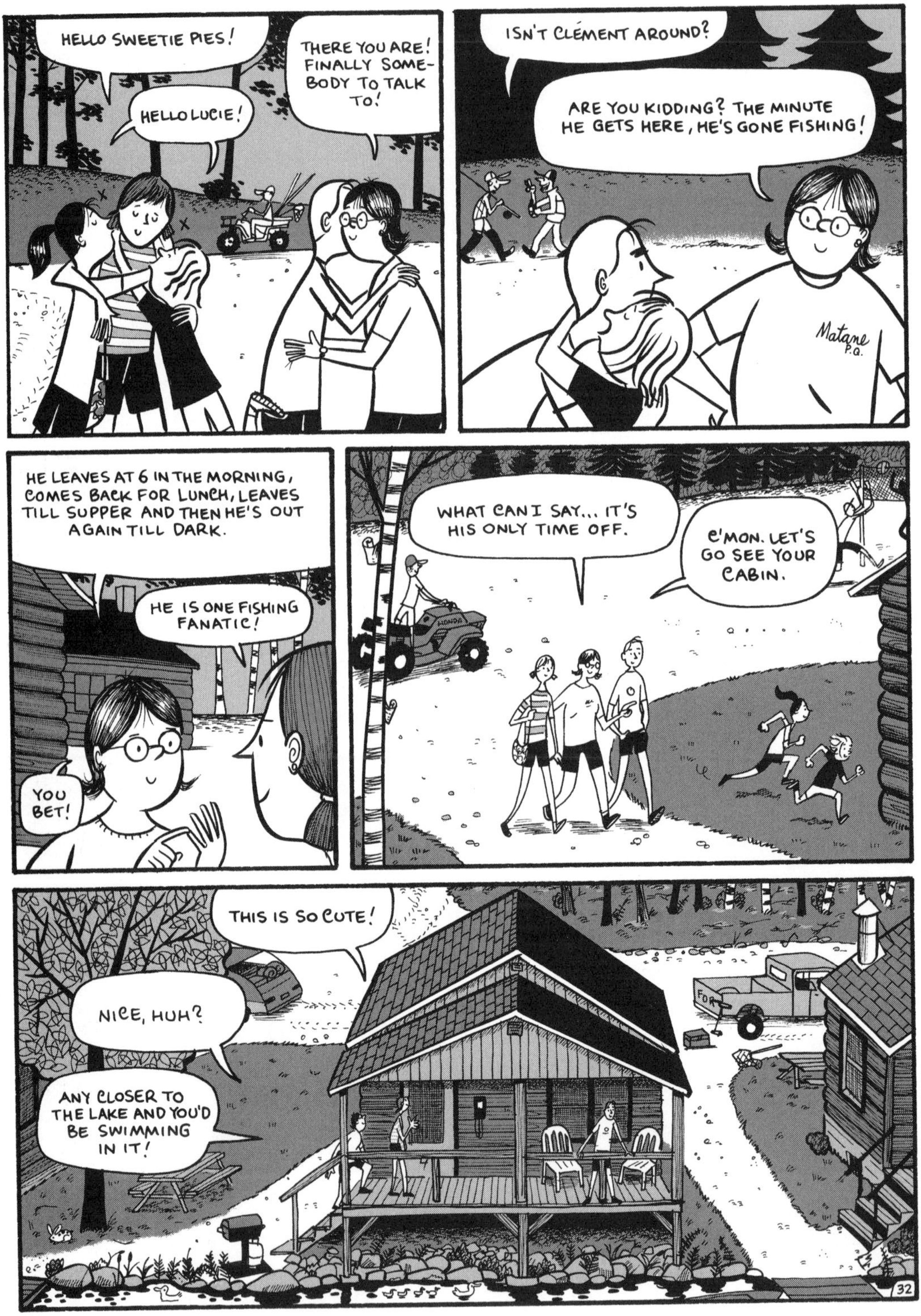
HELLO SWEETIE PIES!
HELLO LUCIE!
THERE YOU ARE! FINALLY SOMEBODY TO TALK TO!
ISN'T CLÉMENT AROUND?
ARE YOU KIDDING? THE MINUTE HE GETS HERE, HE'S GONE FISHING!
Matane P.Q.
HE LEAVES AT 6 IN THE MORNING, COMES BACK FOR LUNCH, LEAVES TILL SUPPER AND THEN HE'S OUT AGAIN TILL DARK.
HE IS ONE FISHING FANATIC!
YOU BET!
WHAT CAN I SAY... IT'S HIS ONLY TIME OFF.
C'MON. LET'S GO SEE YOUR CABIN.
HONDA
THIS IS SO CUTE!
NICE, HUH?
ANY CLOSER TO THE LAKE AND YOU'D BE SWIMMING IN IT!

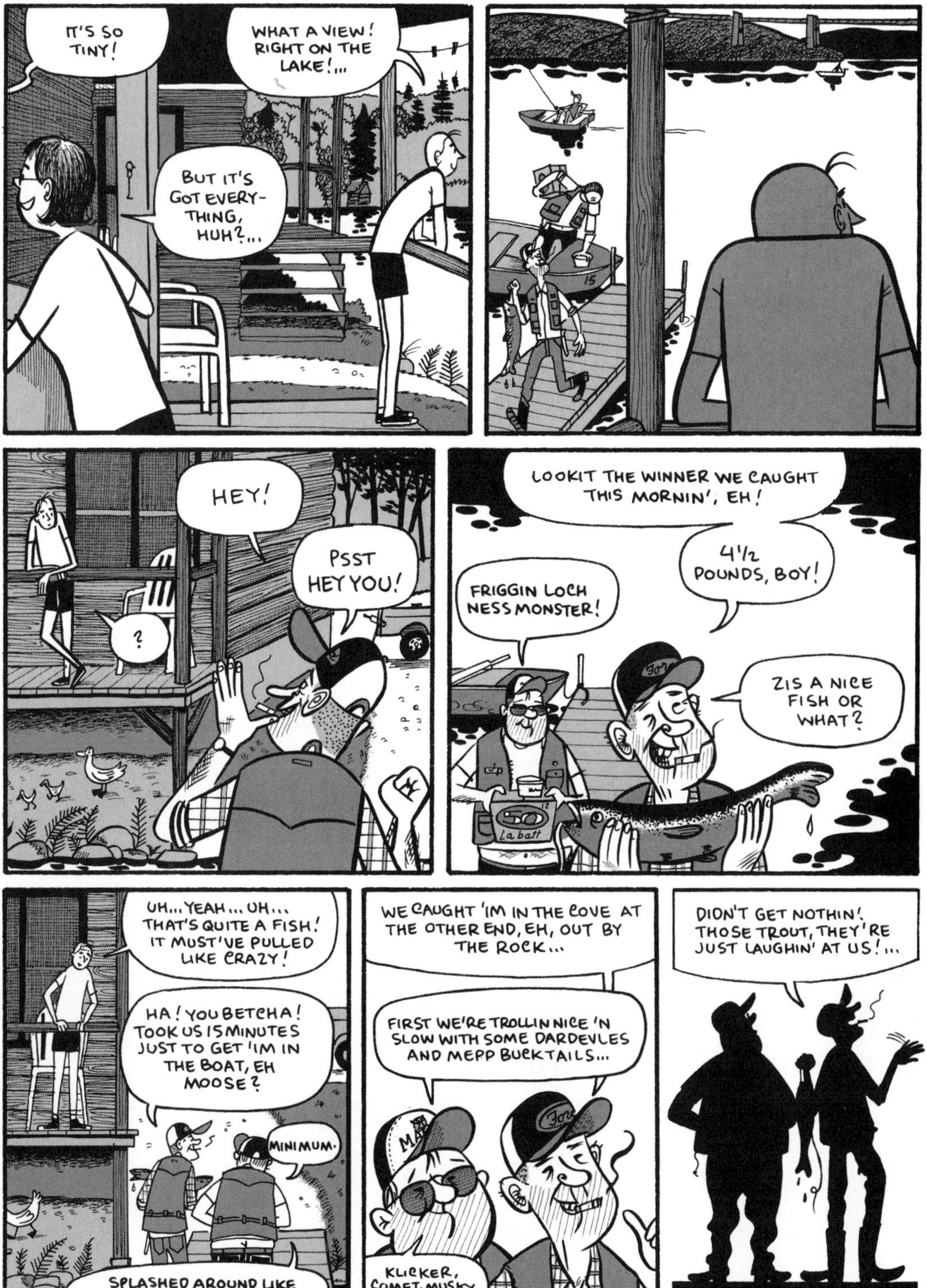
IT'S SO TINY!
WHAT A VIEW! RIGHT ON THE LAKE!...
BUT IT'S GOT EVERYTHING, HUH?...
HEY!
PSST HEY YOU!
?
LOOKIT THE WINNER WE CAUGHT THIS MORNIN', EH!
4½ POUNDS, BOY!
FRIGGIN LOCH NESS MONSTER!
ZIS A NICE FISH OR WHAT?
La batt
UH... YEAH... UH... THAT'S QUITE A FISH! IT MUST'VE PULLED LIKE CRAZY!
HA! YOU BETCHA! TOOK US 15 MINUTES JUST TO GET 'IM IN THE BOAT, EH MOOSE?
MINIMUM.
SPLASHED AROUND LIKE THE DEVIL IN HOLY WATER!
WE CAUGHT 'IM IN THE COVE AT THE OTHER END, EH, OUT BY THE ROCK...
FIRST WE'RE TROLLIN NICE 'N SLOW WITH SOME DARDEVLES AND MEPP BUCKTAILS...
KLICKER, COMET, MUSKY KILLER...
DIDN'T GET NOTHIN'. THOSE TROUT, THEY'RE JUST LAUGHIN' AT US!...

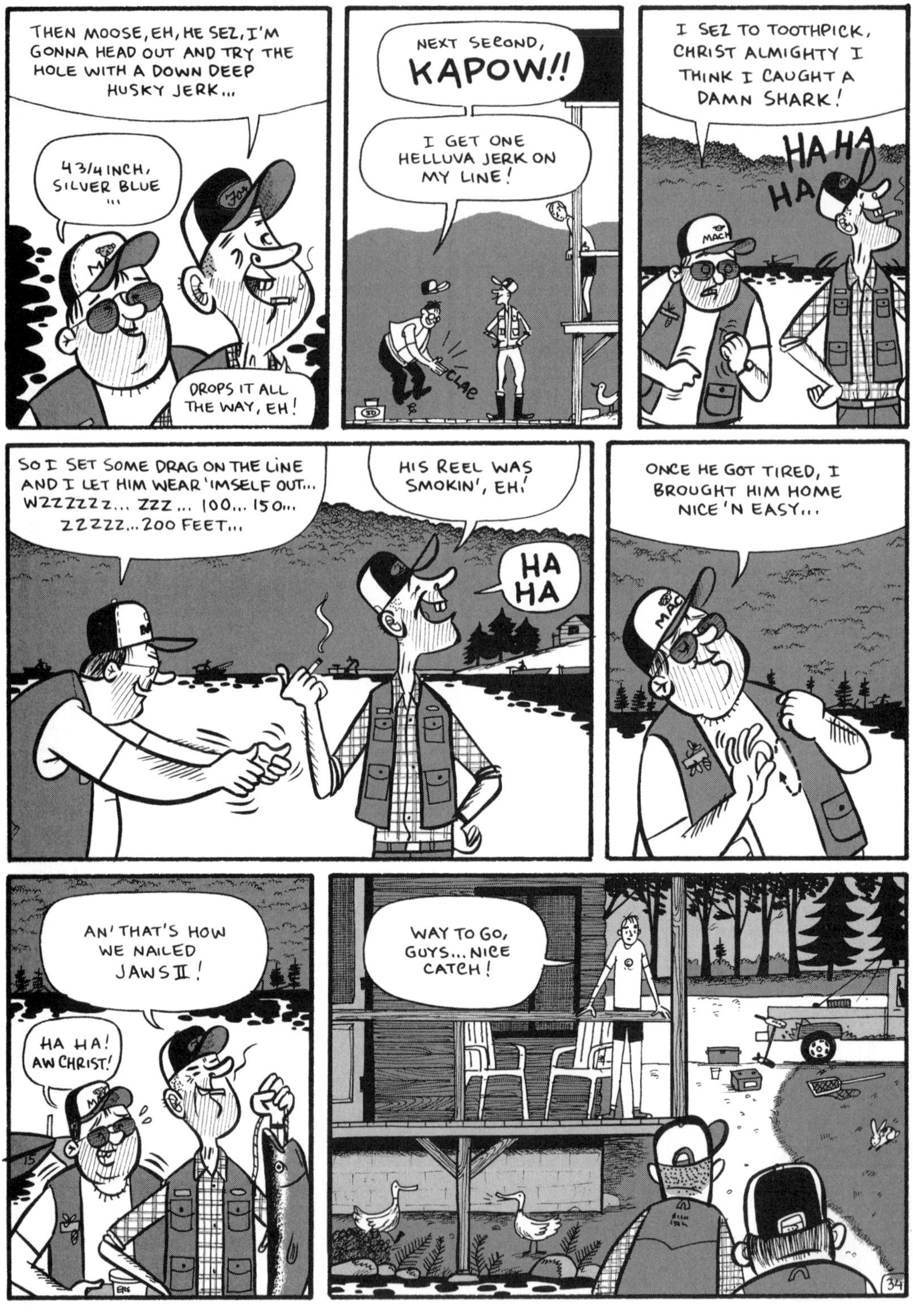
THEN MOOSE, EH, HE SEZ, I'M GONNA HEAD OUT AND TRY THE HOLE WITH A DOWN DEEP HUSKY JERK...
4 3/4 INCH, SILVER BLUE ...
DROPS IT ALL THE WAY, EH!
NEXT SECOND, KAPOW!!
I GET ONE HELLUVA JERK ON MY LINE!
CLAC
I SEZ TO TOOTHPICK, CHRIST ALMIGHTY I THINK I CAUGHT A DAMN SHARK!
HA HA HA
SO I SET SOME DRAG ON THE LINE AND I LET HIM WEAR 'IMSELF OUT... WZZZZZZ... ZZZ... 100... 150... ZZZZZ...200 FEET...
HIS REEL WAS SMOKIN', EH!
HA HA
ONCE HE GOT TIRED, I BROUGHT HIM HOME NICE 'N EASY...
AN' THAT'S HOW WE NAILED JAWS II!
HA HA! AW CHRIST!
WAY TO GO, GUYS... NICE CATCH!

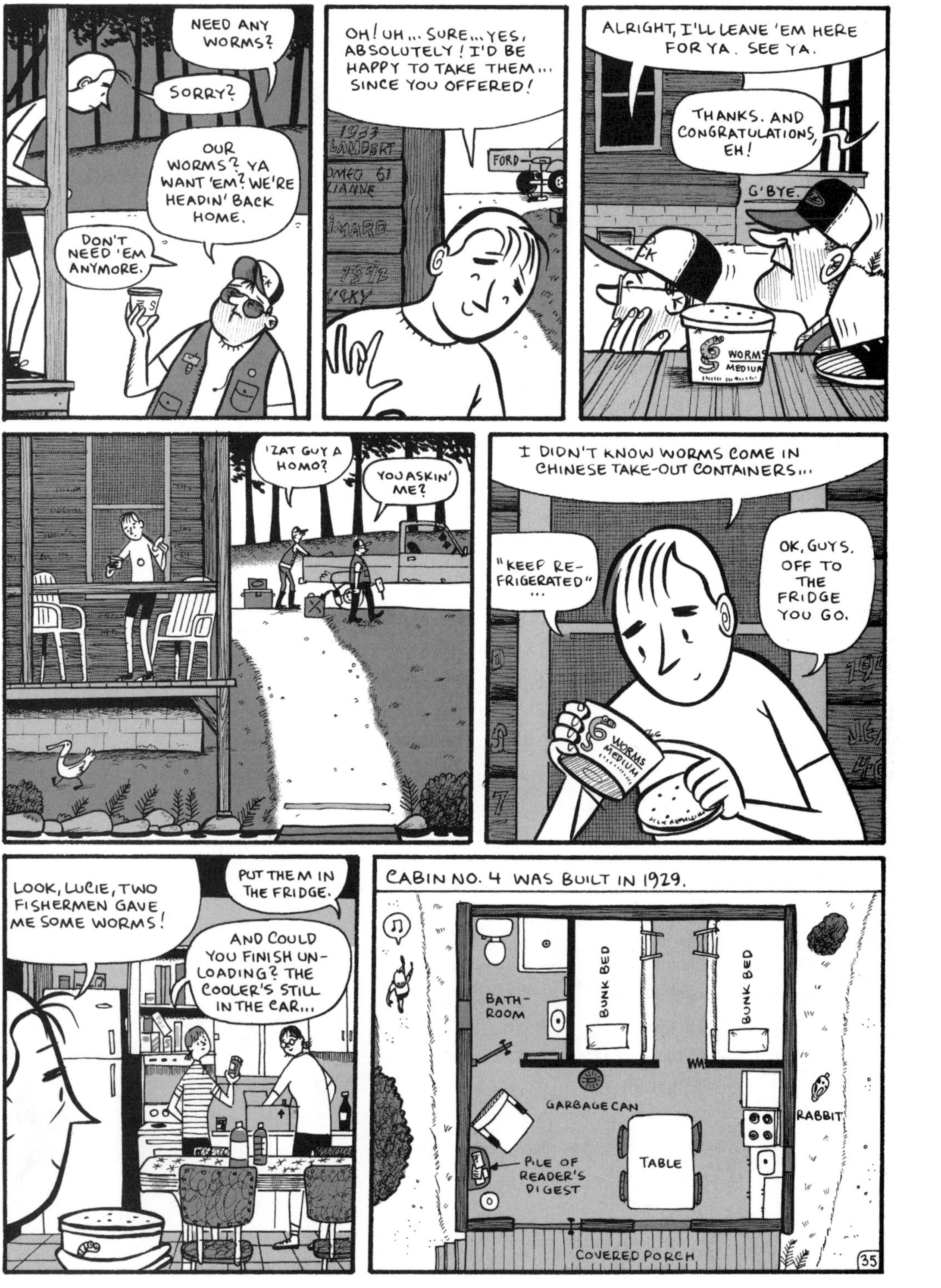
NEED ANY WORMS?
SORRY?
OUR WORMS? YA WANT 'EM? WE'RE HEADIN' BACK HOME.
DON'T NEED 'EM ANYMORE.
OH! UH... SURE... YES, ABSOLUTELY! I'D BE HAPPY TO TAKE THEM... SINCE YOU OFFERED!
FORD
ALRIGHT, I'LL LEAVE 'EM HERE FOR YA. SEE YA.
THANKS. AND CONGRATULATIONS, EH!
G'BYE.
WORMS
MEDIUM
'ZAT GUY A HOMO?
YOU ASKIN' ME?
I DIDN'T KNOW WORMS COME IN CHINESE TAKE-OUT CONTAINERS...
"KEEP RE-FRIGERATED"...
OK, GUYS, OFF TO THE FRIDGE YOU GO.
WORMS
MEDIUM
LOOK, LUCIE, TWO FISHERMEN GAVE ME SOME WORMS!
PUT THEM IN THE FRIDGE.
AND COULD YOU FINISH UN-LOADING? THE COOLER'S STILL IN THE CAR...
CABIN NO. 4 WAS BUILT IN 1929.
BATH-ROOM
BUNK BED
BUNK BED
GARBAGE CAN
RABBIT
TABLE
PILE OF READER'S DIGEST
COVERED PORCH

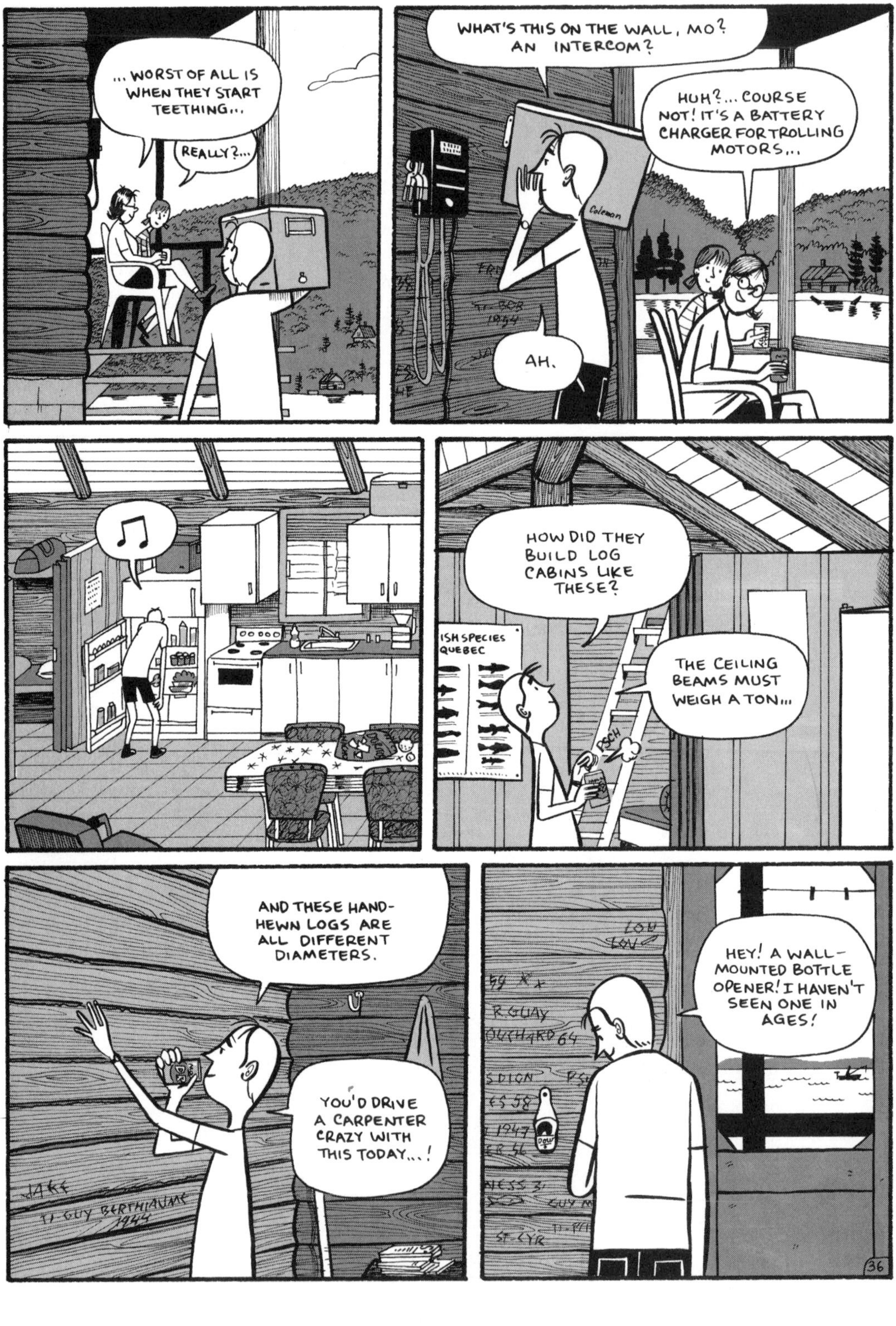

...WORST OF ALL IS WHEN THEY START TEETHING...
REALLY?...
WHAT'S THIS ON THE WALL, MO? AN INTERCOM?
HUH?... COURSE NOT! IT'S A BATTERY CHARGER FOR TROLLING MOTORS...
Coleman
AH.
HOW DID THEY BUILD LOG CABINS LIKE THESE?
ISH SPECIES QUEBEC
THE CEILING BEAMS MUST WEIGH A TON...
PSCH
AND THESE HAND-HEWN LOGS ARE ALL DIFFERENT DIAMETERS.
YOU'D DRIVE A CARPENTER CRAZY WITH THIS TODAY...!
JAKE
TI-GUY BERTHIAUME 1944
HEY! A WALL-MOUNTED BOTTLE OPENER! I HAVEN'T SEEN ONE IN AGES!
R.GUAY

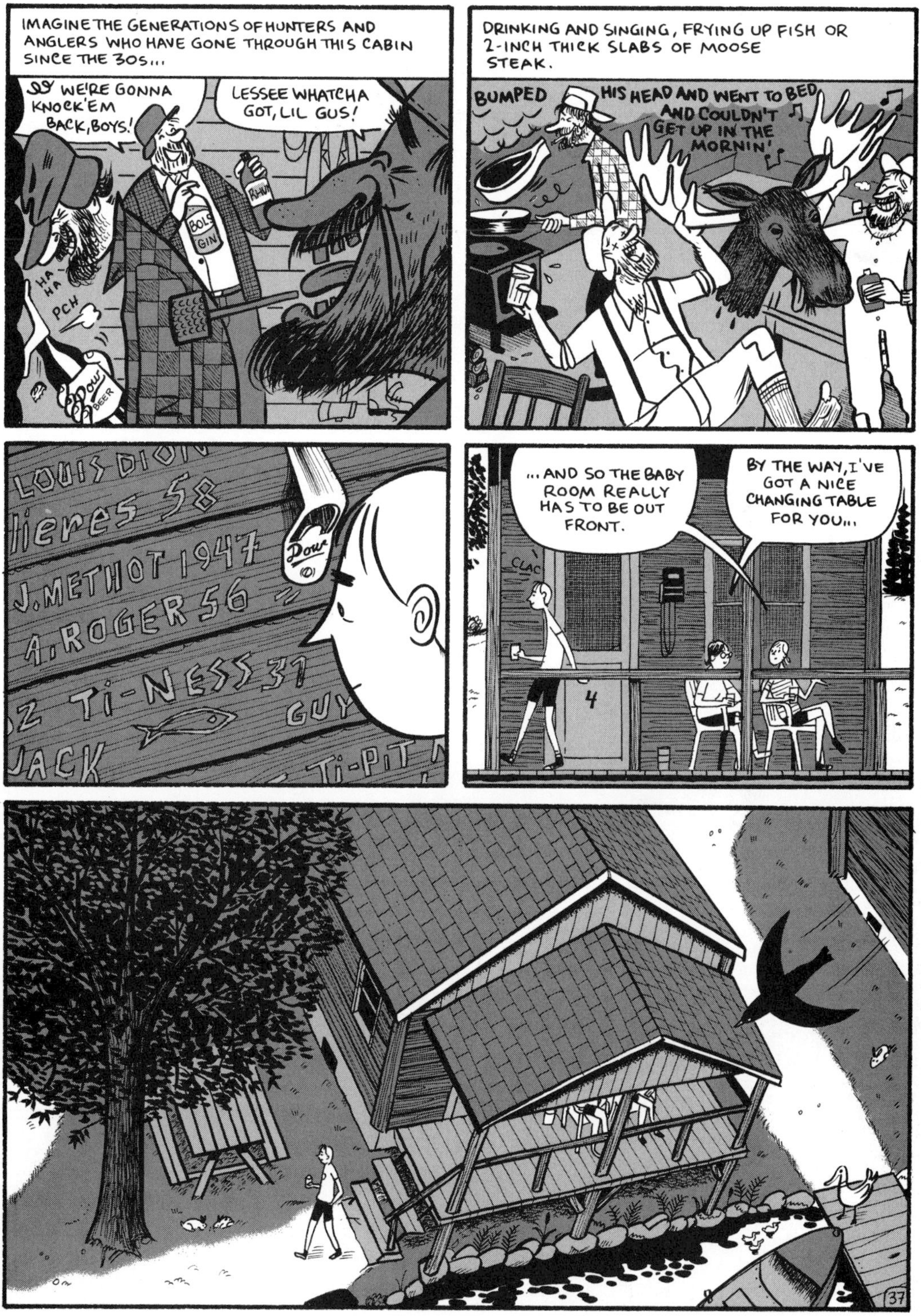
IMAGINE THE GENERATIONS OF HUNTERS AND ANGLERS WHO HAVE GONE THROUGH THIS CABIN SINCE THE 30S...
WE'RE GONNA KNOCK'EM BACK, BOYS!
LESSEE WHATCHA GOT, LIL GUS!
RHUM
BOLS GIN
HA HA
PCH
DOW BEER
DRINKING AND SINGING, FRYING UP FISH OR 2-INCH THICK SLABS OF MOOSE STEAK.
BUMPED HIS HEAD AND WENT TO BED AND COULDN'T GET UP IN THE MORNIN'
LOUIS DION
lieres 58
J. METHOT 1947
A. ROGER 56
Z Ti-NESS 37
GUY
JACK
Ti-PIT
DOW
...AND SO THE BABY ROOM REALLY HAS TO BE OUT FRONT.
BY THE WAY, I'VE GOT A NICE CHANGING TABLE FOR YOU...
CLAC
4

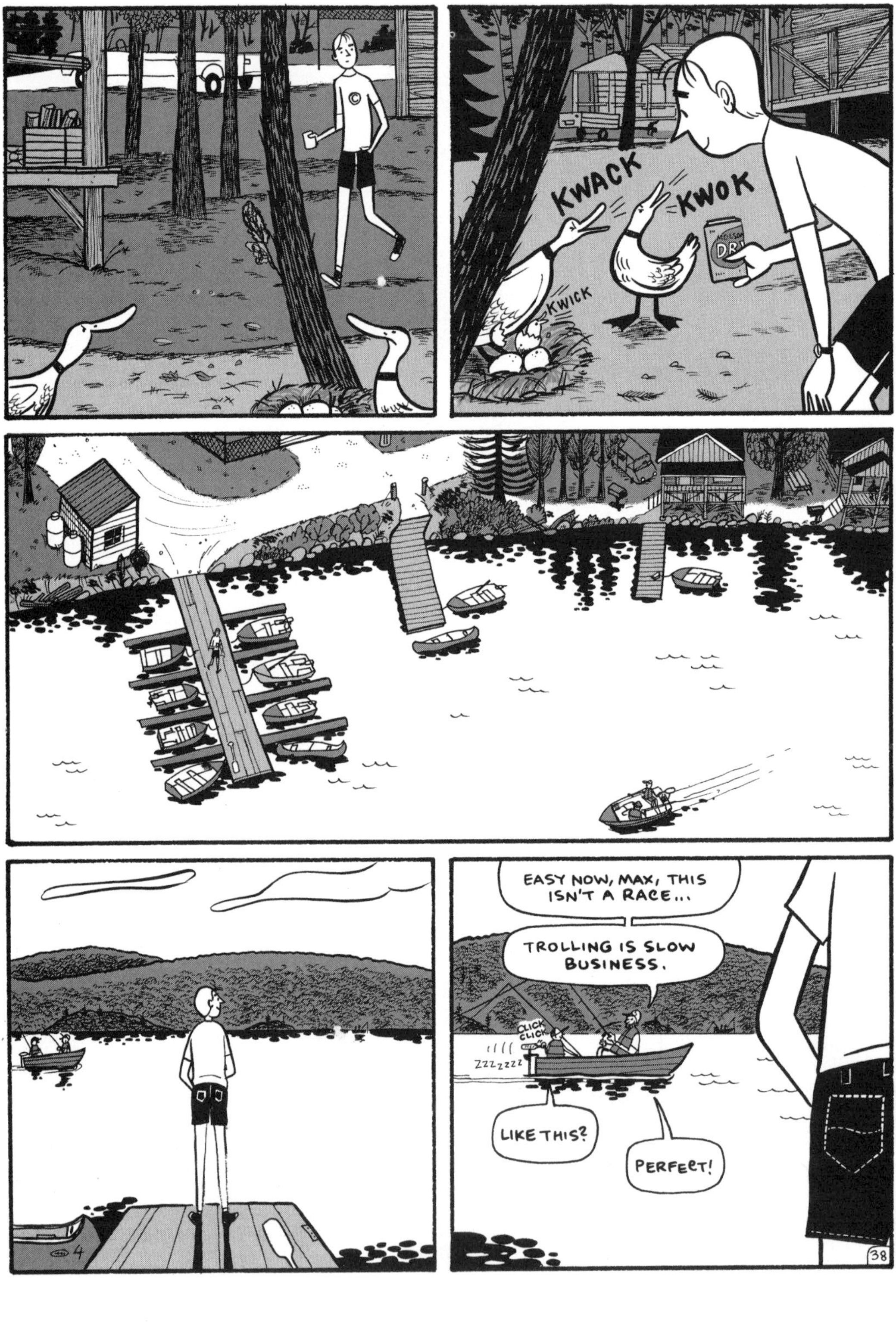
KWACK
KWOK
KWICK
EASY NOW, MAX, THIS ISN'T A RACE...
TROLLING IS SLOW BUSINESS.
CLICK CLICK
ZZZzzzz
LIKE THIS?
PERFECT!

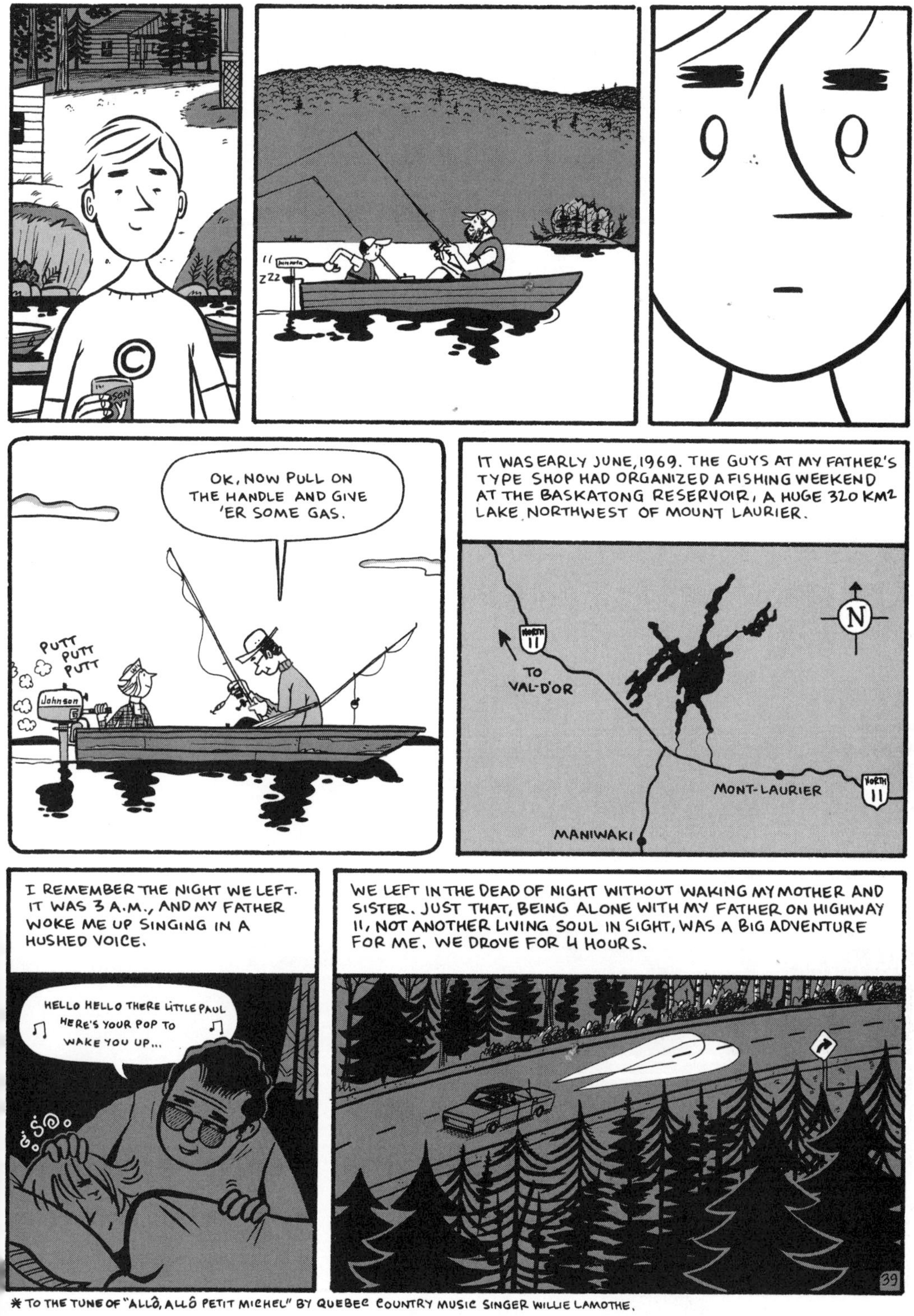
ZZZ
OK, NOW PULL ON THE HANDLE AND GIVE 'ER SOME GAS.
PUTT PUTT PUTT
Johnson
IT WAS EARLY JUNE, 1969. THE GUYS AT MY FATHER'S TYPE SHOP HAD ORGANIZED A FISHING WEEKEND AT THE BASKATONG RESERVOIR, A HUGE 320 KM2 LAKE NORTHWEST OF MOUNT LAURIER.
NORTH 11
TO VAL-D'OR
N
MONT-LAURIER
NORTH 11
MANIWAKI
I REMEMBER THE NIGHT WE LEFT. IT WAS 3 A.M., AND MY FATHER WOKE ME UP SINGING IN A HUSHED VOICE.
HELLO HELLO THERE LITTLE PAUL HERE'S YOUR POP TO WAKE YOU UP...
WE LEFT IN THE DEAD OF NIGHT WITHOUT WAKING MY MOTHER AND SISTER. JUST THAT, BEING ALONE WITH MY FATHER ON HIGHWAY 11, NOT ANOTHER LIVING SOUL IN SIGHT, WAS A BIG ADVENTURE FOR ME. WE DROVE FOR 4 HOURS.

* TO THE TUNE OF "ALLÔ, ALLÔ PETIT MICHEL" BY QUEBEC COUNTRY MUSIC SINGER WILLIE LAMOTHE.

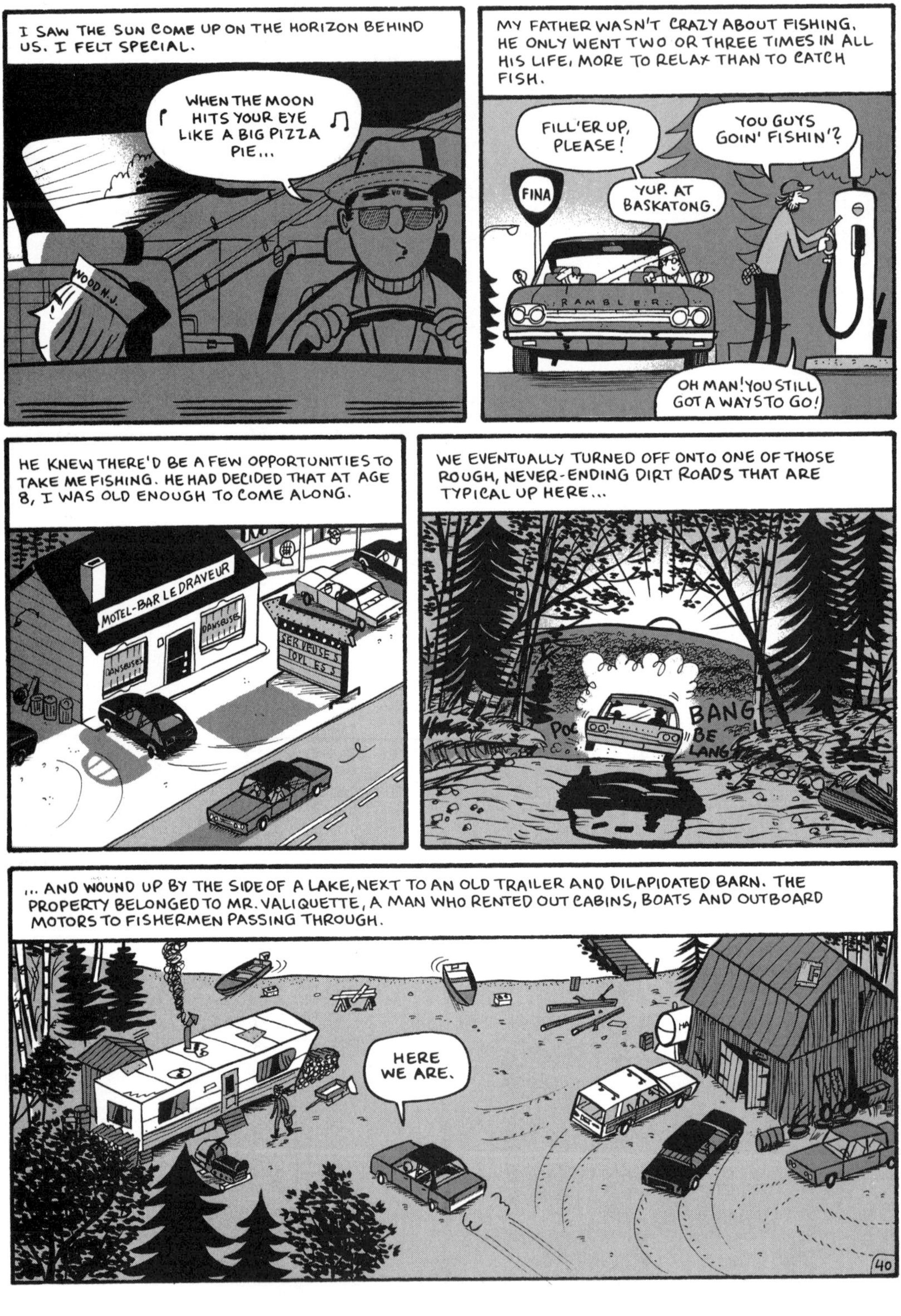
I SAW THE SUN COME UP ON THE HORIZON BEHIND US. I FELT SPECIAL.
WHEN THE MOON HITS YOUR EYE LIKE A BIG PIZZA PIE...
WOOD N.J.
MY FATHER WASN'T CRAZY ABOUT FISHING. HE ONLY WENT TWO OR THREE TIMES IN ALL HIS LIFE, MORE TO RELAX THAN TO CATCH FISH.
FINA
FILL'ER UP, PLEASE!
YOU GUYS GOIN' FISHIN'?
YUP. AT BASKATONG.
RAMBLER
OH MAN! YOU STILL GOT A WAYS TO GO!
HE KNEW THERE'D BE A FEW OPPORTUNITIES TO TAKE ME FISHING. HE HAD DECIDED THAT AT AGE 8, I WAS OLD ENOUGH TO COME ALONG.
MOTEL-BAR LE DRAVEUR
DANSEUSES
DANSEUSES
WE EVENTUALLY TURNED OFF ONTO ONE OF THOSE ROUGH, NEVER-ENDING DIRT ROADS THAT ARE TYPICAL UP HERE...
POC
BANG
BE
LANG
... AND WOUND UP BY THE SIDE OF A LAKE, NEXT TO AN OLD TRAILER AND DILAPIDATED BARN. THE PROPERTY BELONGED TO MR. VALIQUETTE, A MAN WHO RENTED OUT CABINS, BOATS AND OUTBOARD MOTORS TO FISHERMEN PASSING THROUGH.
HERE WE ARE.

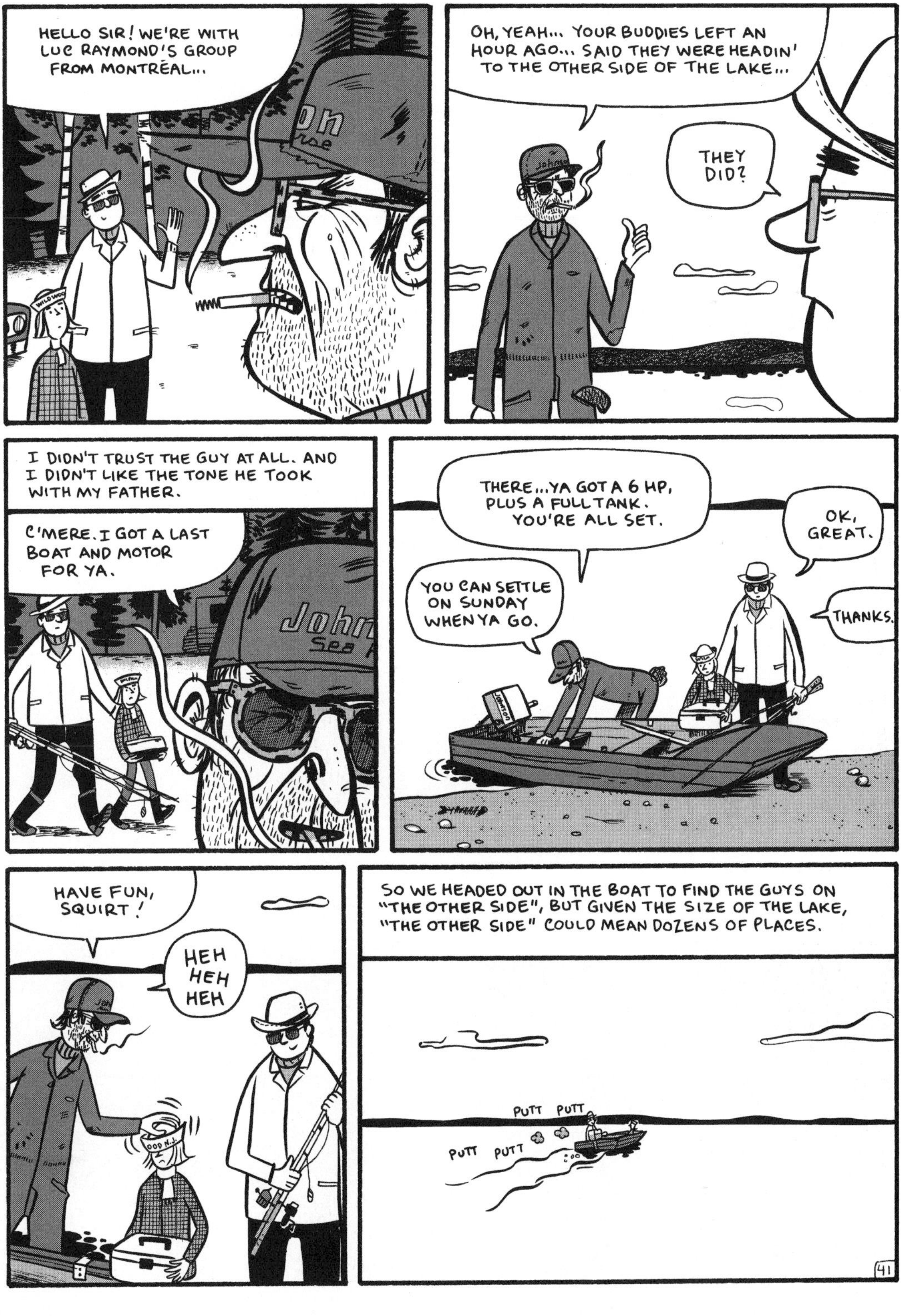
HELLO SIR! WE'RE WITH LUC RAYMOND'S GROUP FROM MONTRÉAL...
OH, YEAH... YOUR BUDDIES LEFT AN HOUR AGO... SAID THEY WERE HEADIN' TO THE OTHER SIDE OF THE LAKE...
THEY DID?
I DIDN'T TRUST THE GUY AT ALL. AND I DIDN'T LIKE THE TONE HE TOOK WITH MY FATHER.
C'MERE. I GOT A LAST BOAT AND MOTOR FOR YA.
THERE...YA GOT A 6 HP, PLUS A FULL TANK. YOU'RE ALL SET.
OK, GREAT.
YOU CAN SETTLE ON SUNDAY WHEN YA GO.
THANKS.
HAVE FUN, SQUIRT!
HEH HEH HEH
SO WE HEADED OUT IN THE BOAT TO FIND THE GUYS ON "THE OTHER SIDE", BUT GIVEN THE SIZE OF THE LAKE, "THE OTHER SIDE" COULD MEAN DOZENS OF PLACES.
PUTT PUTT
PUTT PUTT

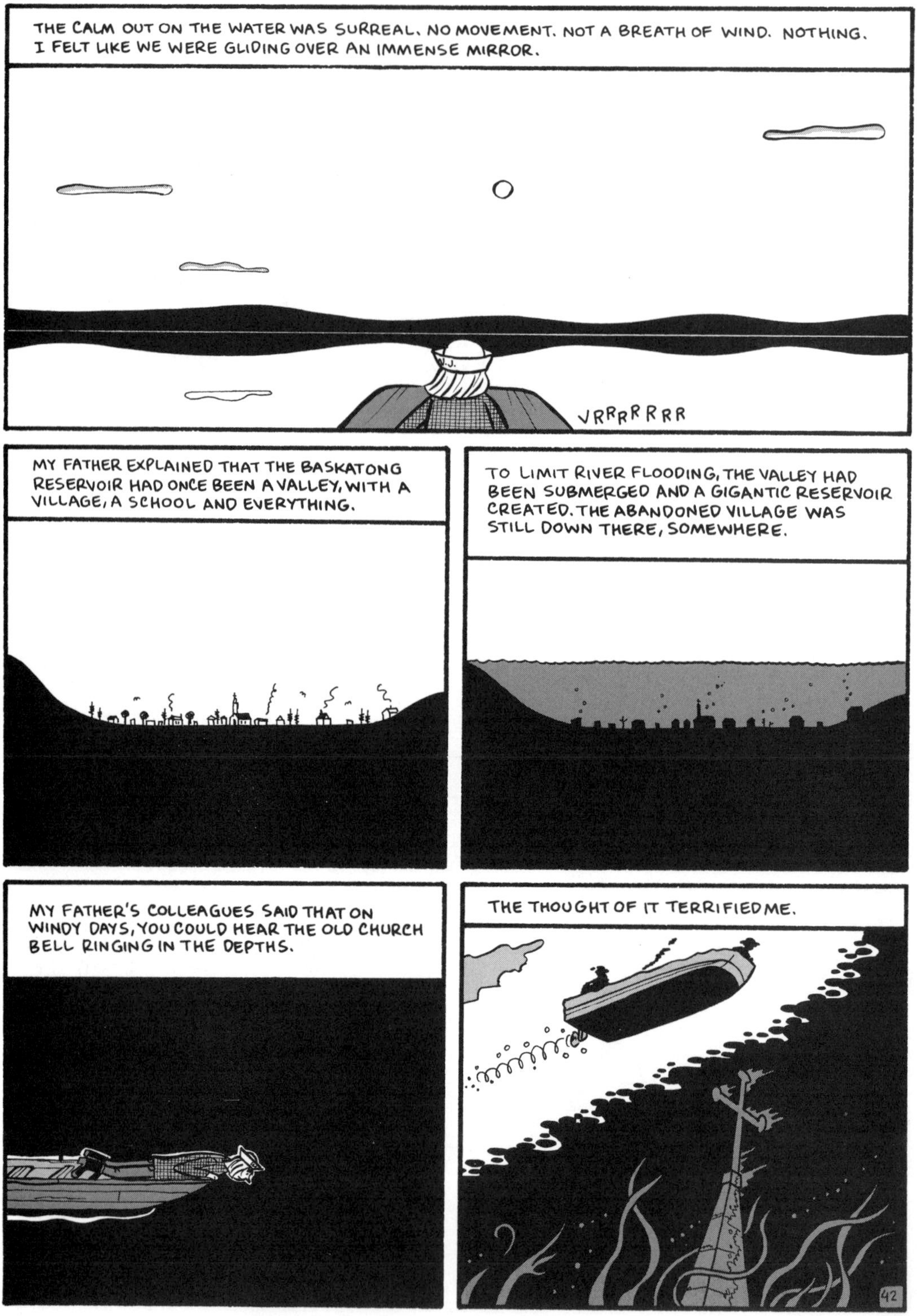
THE CALM OUT ON THE WATER WAS SURREAL. NO MOVEMENT. NOT A BREATH OF WIND. NOTHING. I FELT LIKE WE WERE GLIDING OVER AN IMMENSE MIRROR.
VRRRRRRR
MY FATHER EXPLAINED THAT THE BASKATONG RESERVOIR HAD ONCE BEEN A VALLEY, WITH A VILLAGE, A SCHOOL AND EVERYTHING.
TO LIMIT RIVER FLOODING, THE VALLEY HAD BEEN SUBMERGED AND A GIGANTIC RESERVOIR CREATED. THE ABANDONED VILLAGE WAS STILL DOWN THERE, SOMEWHERE.
MY FATHER'S COLLEAGUES SAID THAT ON WINDY DAYS, YOU COULD HEAR THE OLD CHURCH BELL RINGING IN THE DEPTHS.
THE THOUGHT OF IT TERRIFIED ME.
42

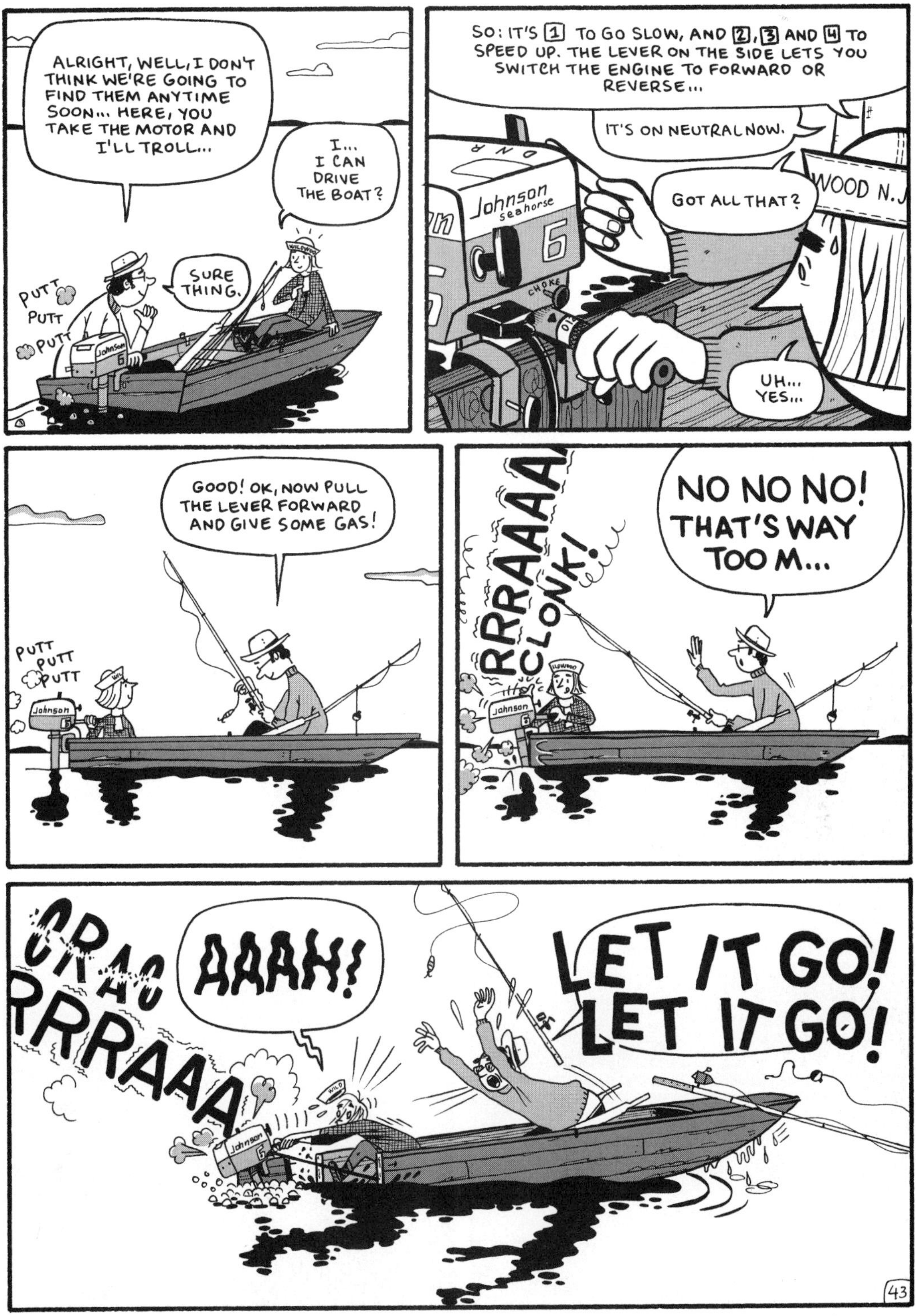
ALRIGHT, WELL, I DON'T THINK WE'RE GOING TO FIND THEM ANYTIME SOON... HERE, YOU TAKE THE MOTOR AND I'LL TROLL...
I... I CAN DRIVE THE BOAT?
SURE THING.
PUTT PUTT PUTT
Johnson
SO: IT'S 1 TO GO SLOW, AND 2, 3 AND 4 TO SPEED UP. THE LEVER ON THE SIDE LETS YOU SWITCH THE ENGINE TO FORWARD OR REVERSE...
IT'S ON NEUTRAL NOW.
GOT ALL THAT?
UH... YES...
Johnson Seahorse
CHOKE
WOOD N.J
GOOD! OK, NOW PULL THE LEVER FORWARD AND GIVE SOME GAS!
PUTT PUTT PUTT
Johnson
NO NO NO! THAT'S WAY TOO M...
RRRAAAAA
CLONK!
Johnson
CRAC
RRRAAA
AAAH!
LET IT GO! LET IT GO!
Johnson

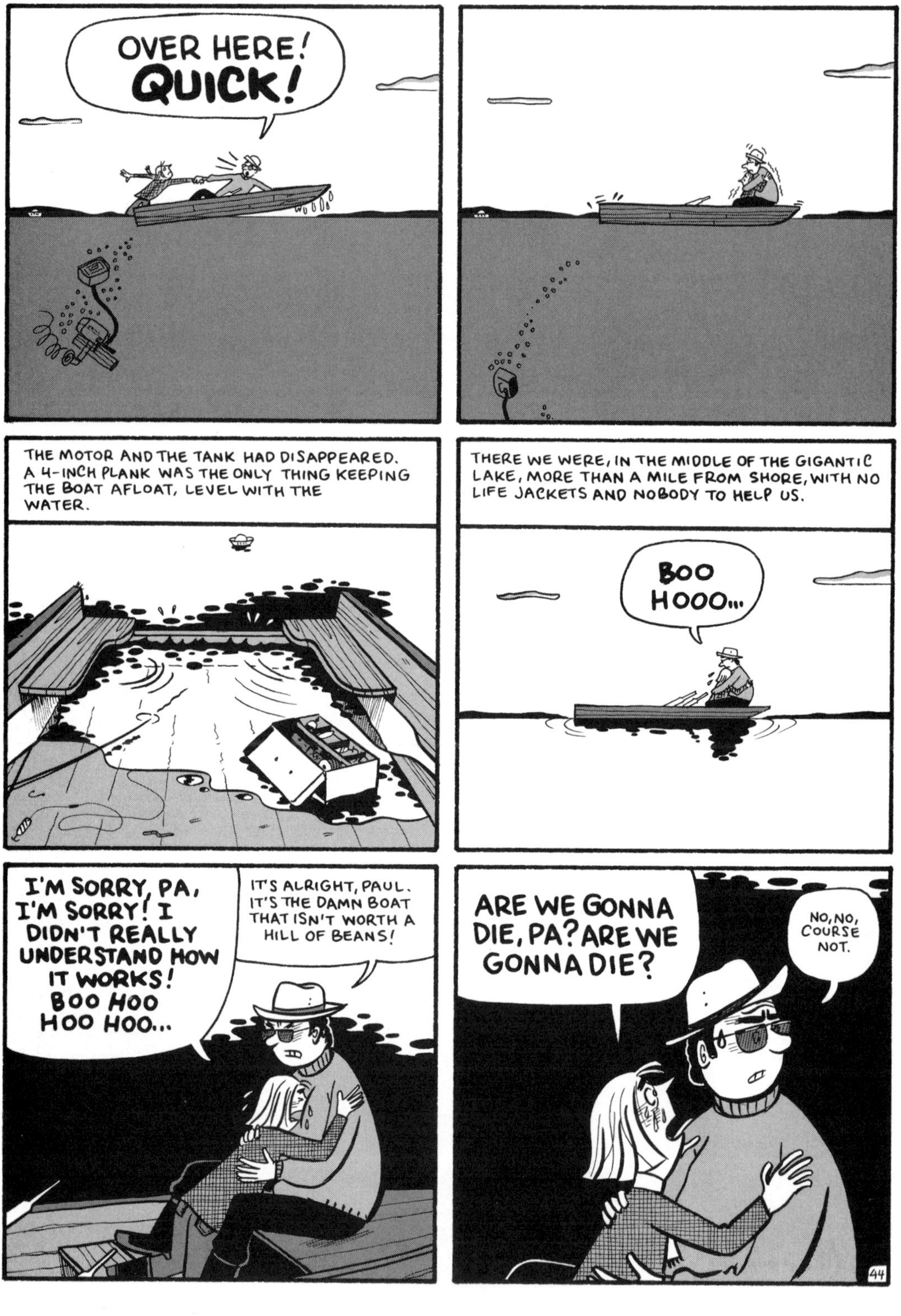

OVER HERE! QUICK!
THE MOTOR AND THE TANK HAD DISAPPEARED. A 4-INCH PLANK WAS THE ONLY THING KEEPING THE BOAT AFLOAT, LEVEL WITH THE WATER.
THERE WE WERE, IN THE MIDDLE OF THE GIGANTIC LAKE, MORE THAN A MILE FROM SHORE, WITH NO LIFE JACKETS AND NOBODY TO HELP US.
BOO HOOO...
I'M SORRY, PA, I'M SORRY! I DIDN'T REALLY UNDERSTAND HOW IT WORKS! BOO HOO HOO HOO...
IT'S ALRIGHT, PAUL. IT'S THE DAMN BOAT THAT ISN'T WORTH A HILL OF BEANS!
ARE WE GONNA DIE, PA? ARE WE GONNA DIE?
NO, NO, COURSE NOT.

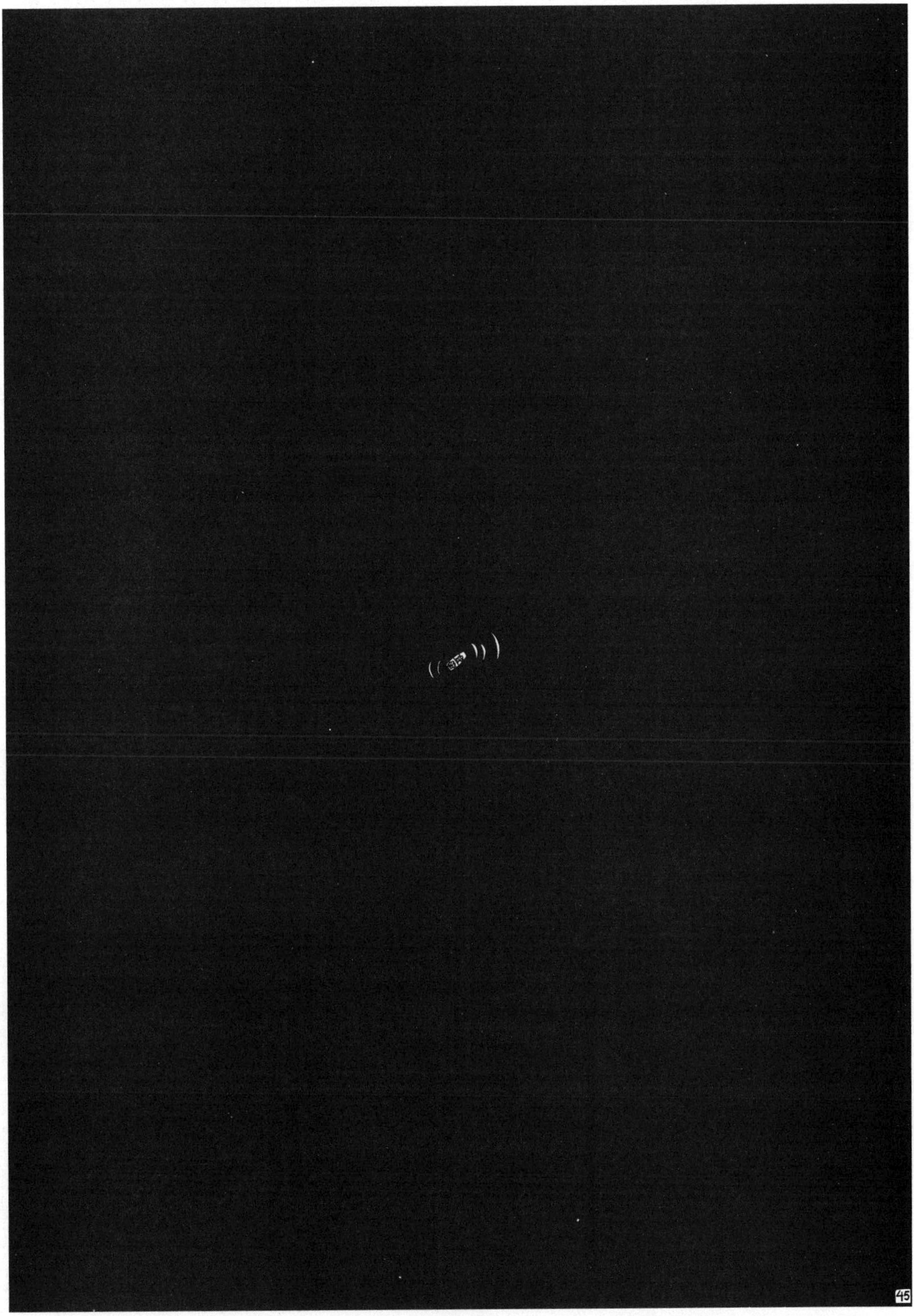

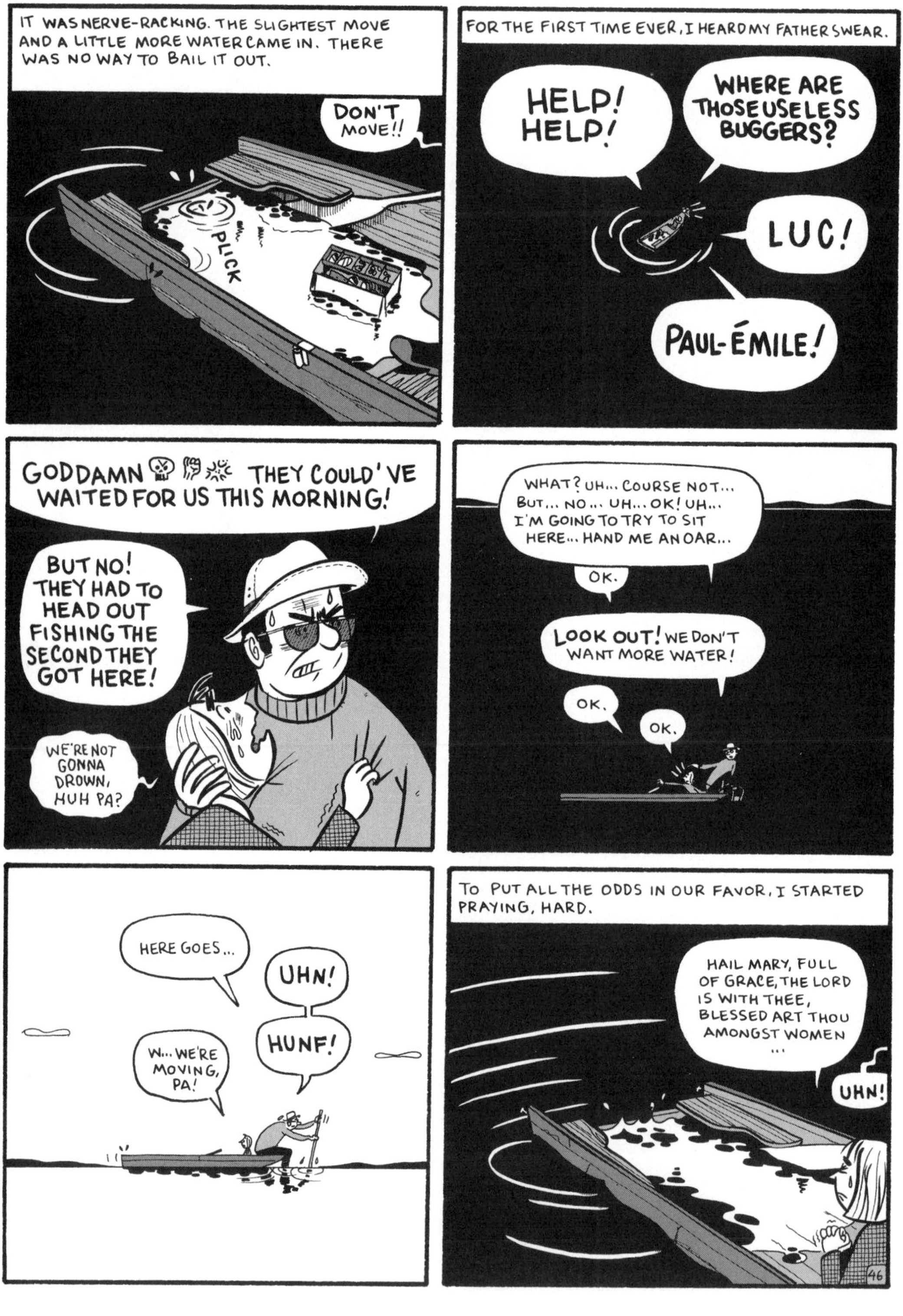
IT WAS NERVE-RACKING. THE SLIGHTEST MOVE AND A LITTLE MORE WATER CAME IN. THERE WAS NO WAY TO BAIL IT OUT.
DON'T MOVE!!
PLICK
FOR THE FIRST TIME EVER, I HEARD MY FATHER SWEAR.
HELP! HELP!
WHERE ARE THOSE USELESS BUGGERS?
LUC!
PAUL-ÉMILE!
GODDAMN THEY COULD'VE WAITED FOR US THIS MORNING!
BUT NO! THEY HAD TO HEAD OUT FISHING THE SECOND THEY GOT HERE!
WE'RE NOT GONNA DROWN, HUH PA?
WHAT? UH... COURSE NOT... BUT... NO... UH... OK! UH... I'M GOING TO TRY TO SIT HERE... HAND ME AN OAR...
OK.
LOOK OUT! WE DON'T WANT MORE WATER!
OK.
OK.
HERE GOES...
UHN!
HUNF!
W... WE'RE MOVING, PA!
TO PUT ALL THE ODDS IN OUR FAVOR, I STARTED PRAYING, HARD.
HAIL MARY, FULL OF GRACE, THE LORD IS WITH THEE, BLESSED ART THOU AMONGST WOMEN ...
UHN!
46

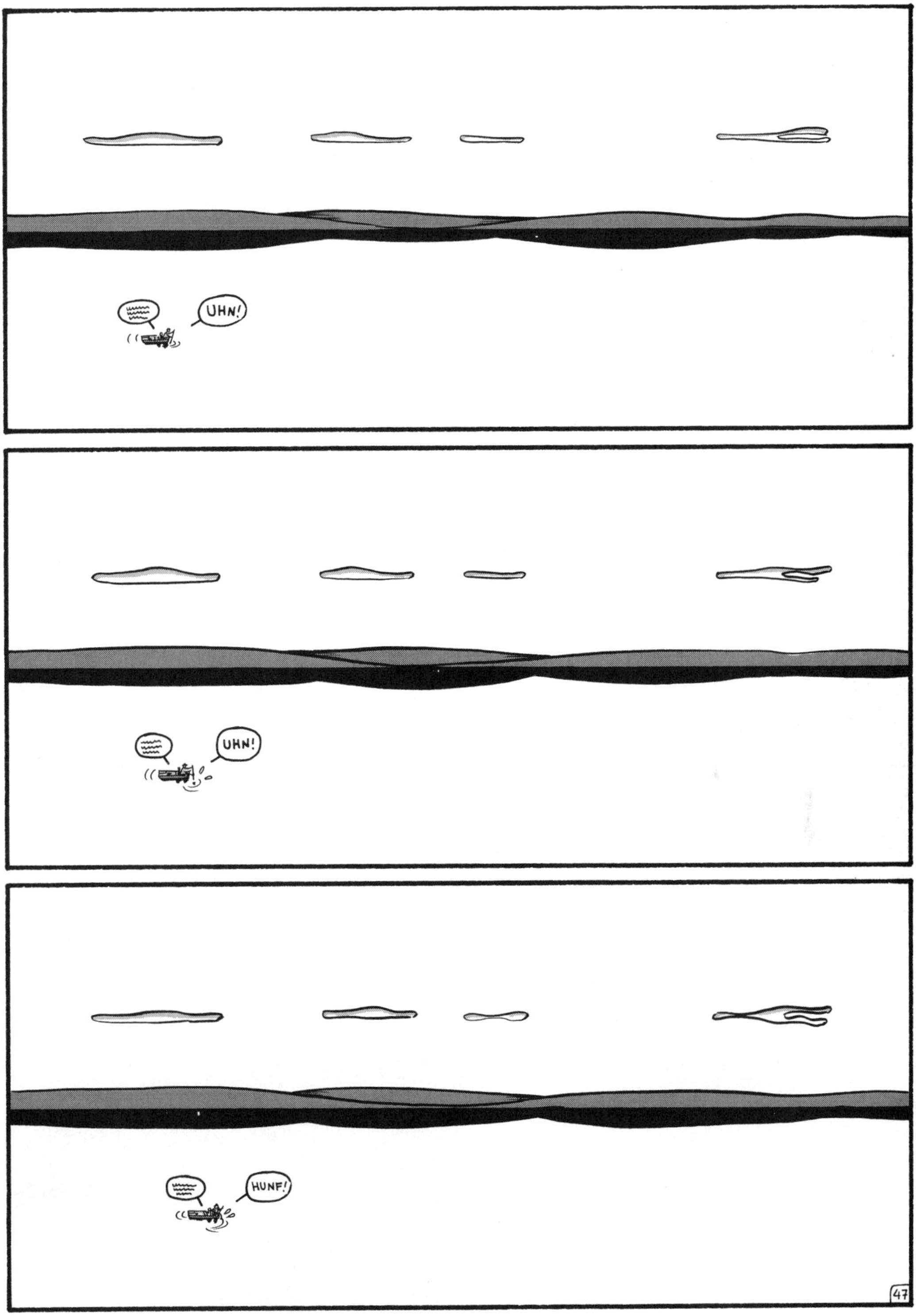
UHN!
UHN!
HUNF!

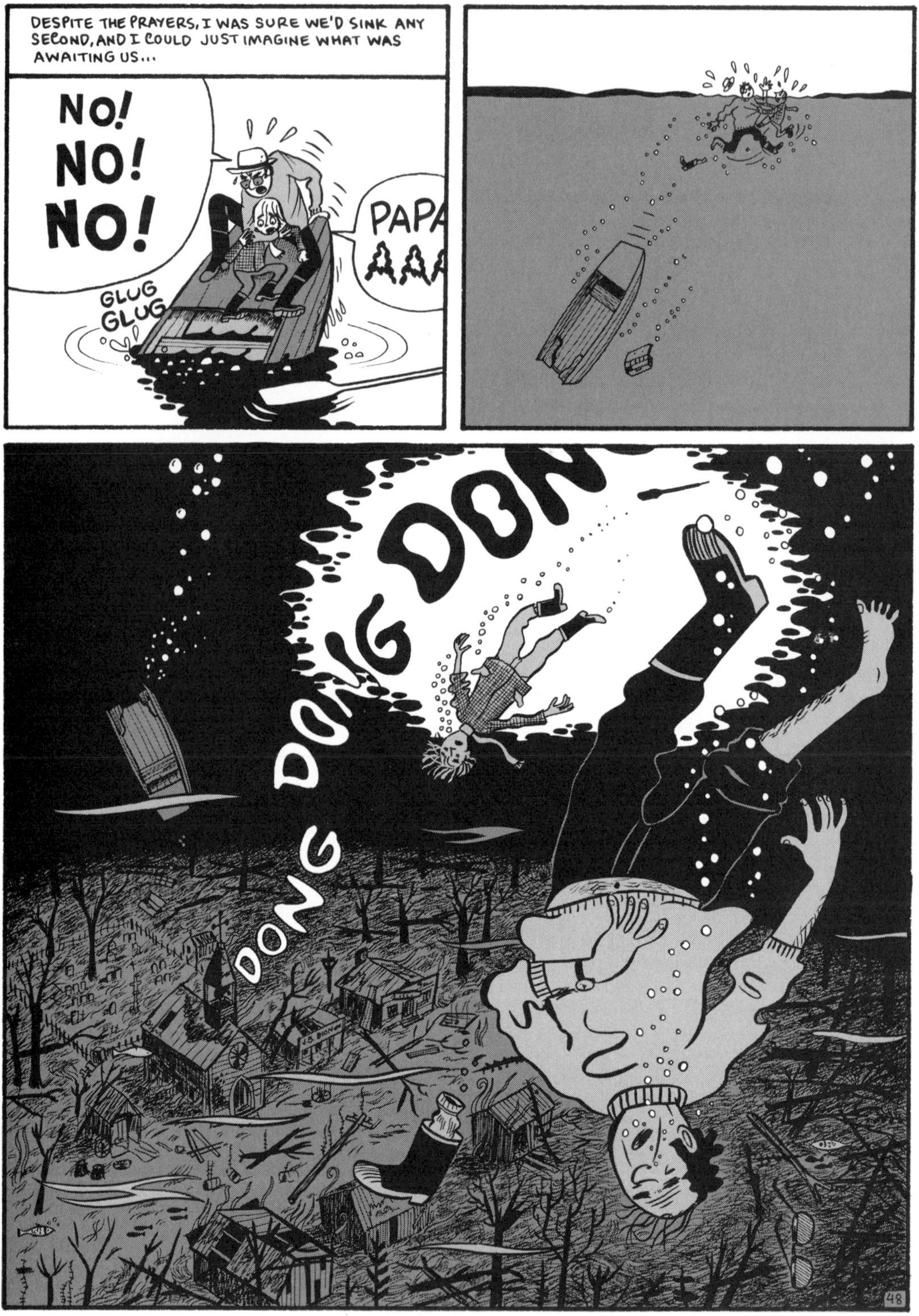
DESPITE THE PRAYERS, I WAS SURE WE'D SINK ANY SECOND, AND I COULD JUST IMAGINE WHAT WAS AWAITING US...
NO! NO! NO!
PAPA AAA
GLUG GLUG
DONG DONG DONG DON

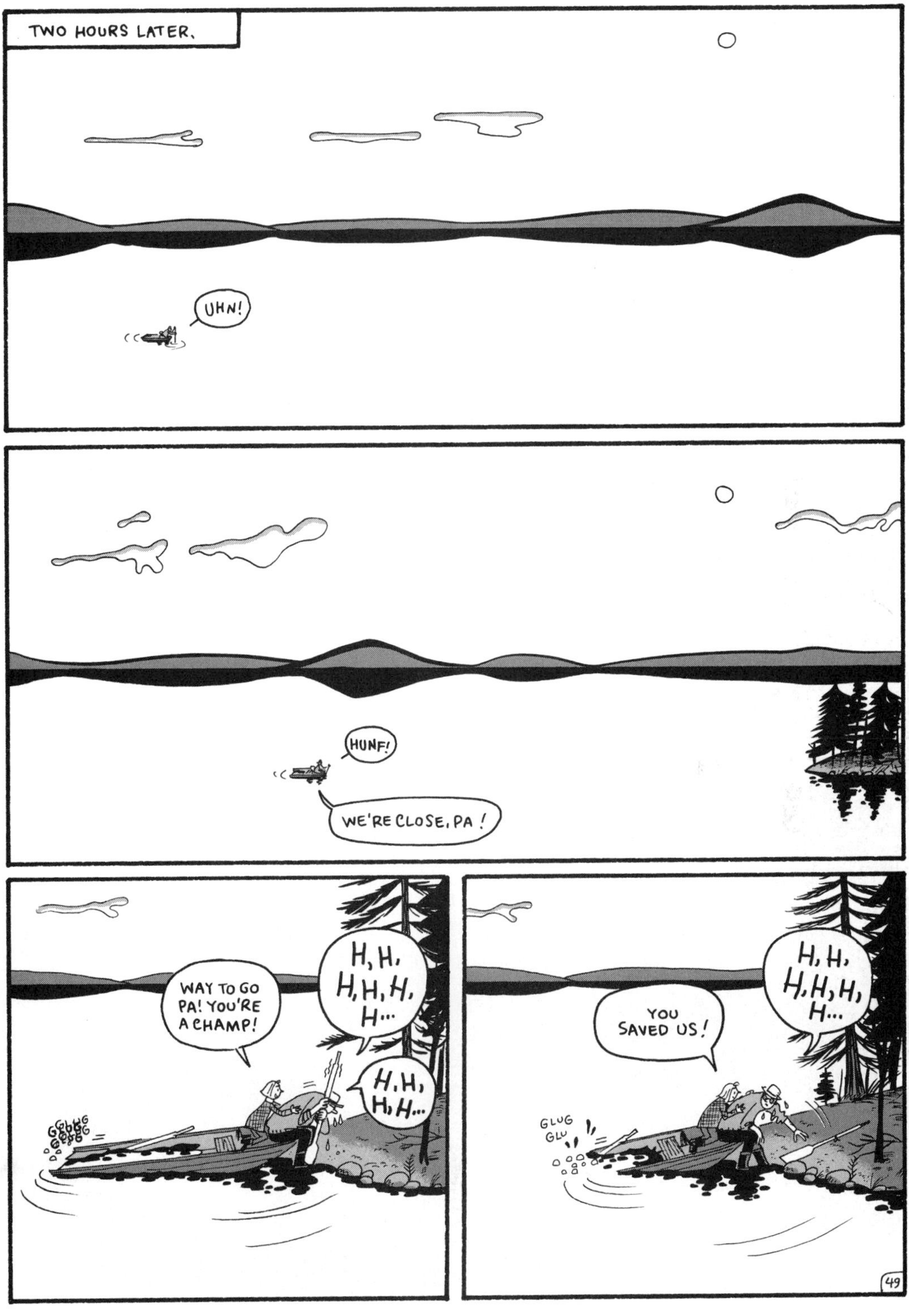
TWO HOURS LATER.
UHN!
HUNF!
WE'RE CLOSE, PA!
WAY TO GO PA! YOU'RE A CHAMP!
H, H, H, H, H, H...
H, H, H, H...
YOU SAVED US!
H, H, H, H, H, H...
GLUG GLU

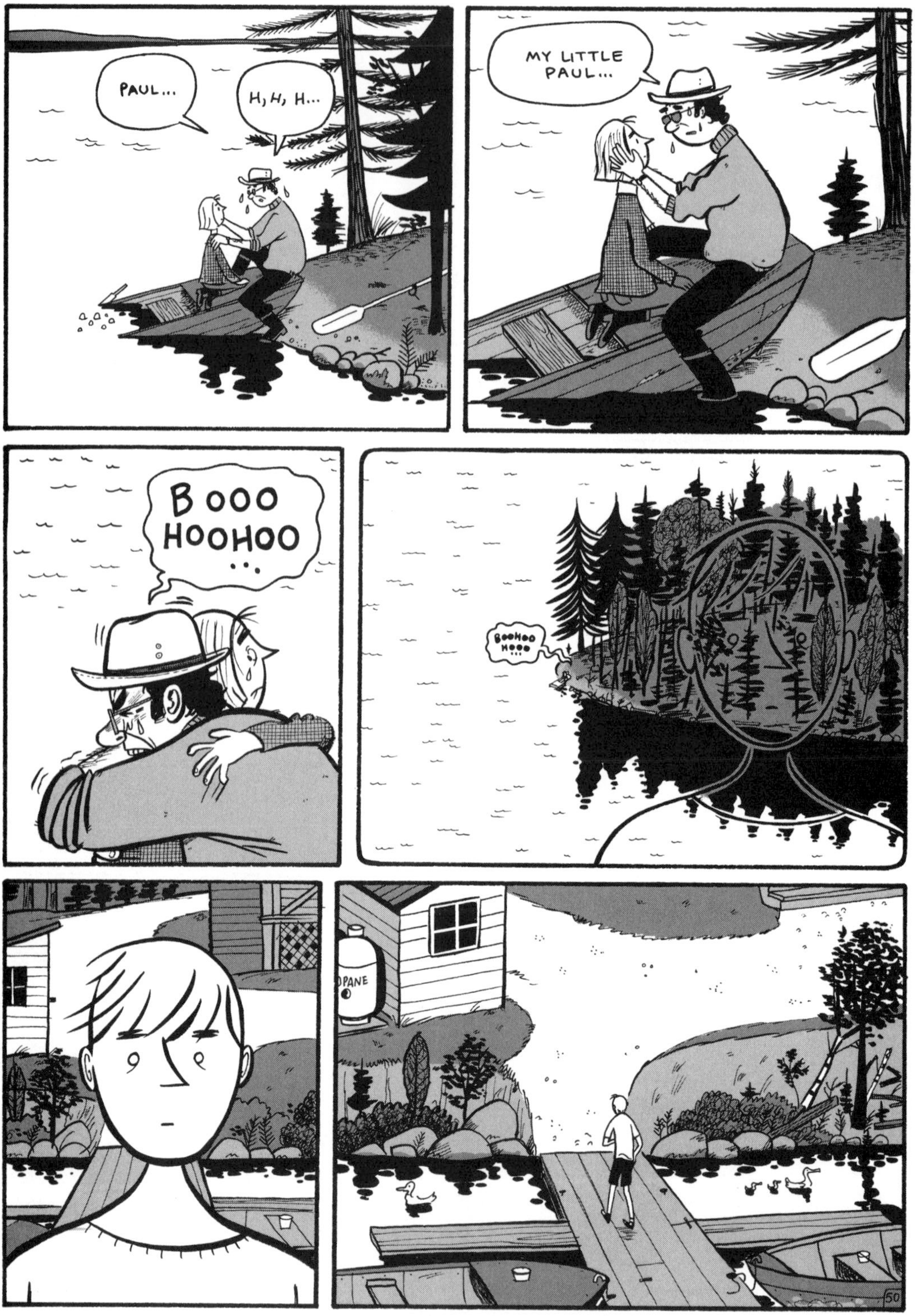
PAUL...
H, H, H...
MY LITTLE PAUL...
BOOO HOOHOO ...
BOOHOO HOOO ...
PANE

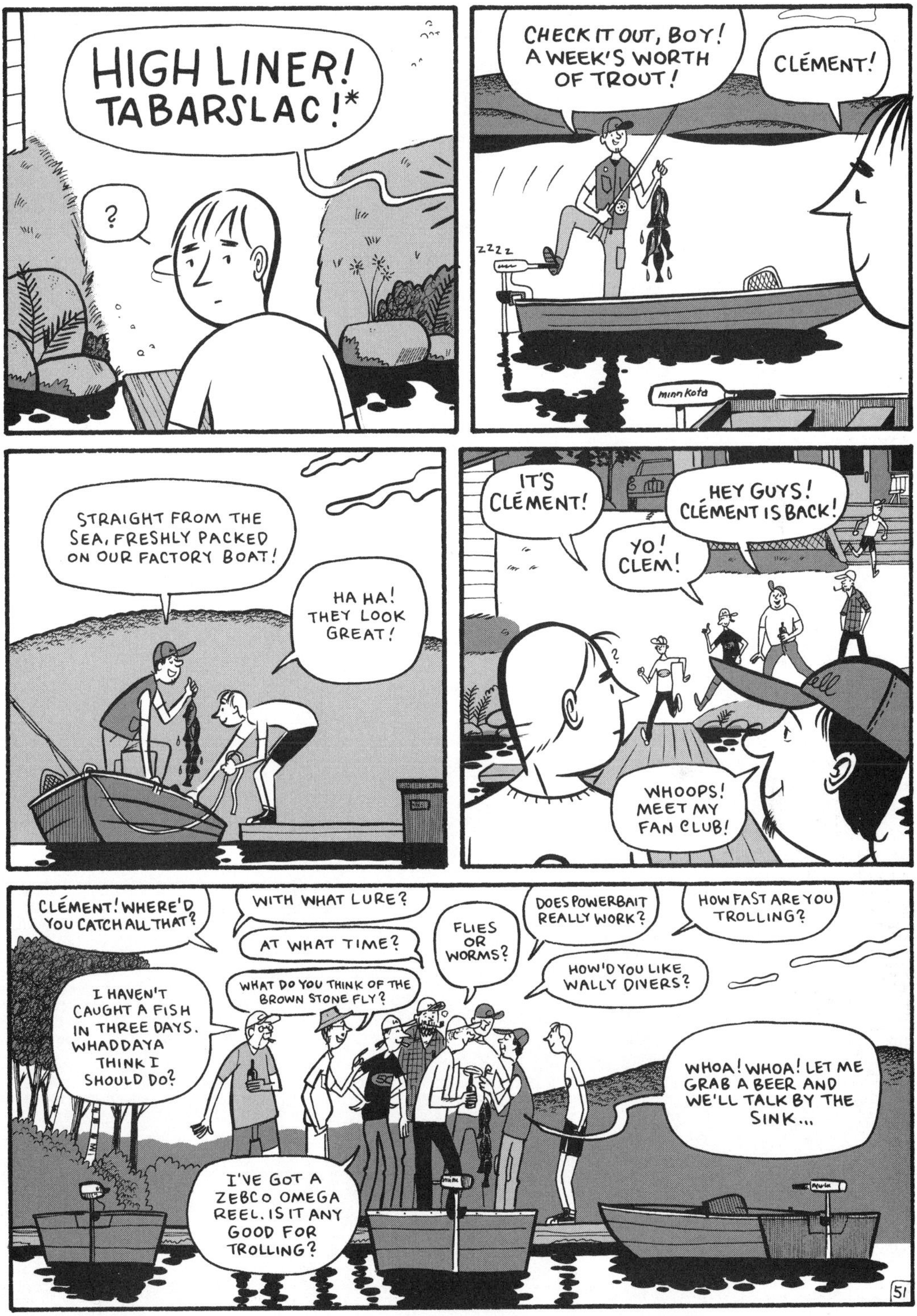
HIGH LINER! TABARSLAC!*
?
CHECK IT OUT, BOY! A WEEK'S WORTH OF TROUT!
CLÉMENT!
ZZZZ
minn kota
STRAIGHT FROM THE SEA, FRESHLY PACKED ON OUR FACTORY BOAT!
HA HA! THEY LOOK GREAT!
IT'S CLÉMENT!
HEY GUYS! CLÉMENT IS BACK!
YO! CLEM!
?
WHOOPS! MEET MY FAN CLUB!
CLÉMENT! WHERE'D YOU CATCH ALL THAT?
WITH WHAT LURE?
AT WHAT TIME?
FLIES OR WORMS?
DOES POWERBAIT REALLY WORK?
HOW FAST ARE YOU TROLLING?
HOW'D YOU LIKE WALLY DIVERS?
WHAT DO YOU THINK OF THE BROWN STONE FLY?
I HAVEN'T CAUGHT A FISH IN THREE DAYS. WHADDAYA THINK I SHOULD DO?
WHOA! WHOA! LET ME GRAB A BEER AND WE'LL TALK BY THE SINK...
I'VE GOT A ZEBCO OMEGA REEL. IS IT ANY GOOD FOR TROLLING?

*TABARSLAC: MILD VERSION OF "TABARNAC," ONE OF A NUMBER OF RELIGIOUS SWEARWORDS USED IN QUEBEC.

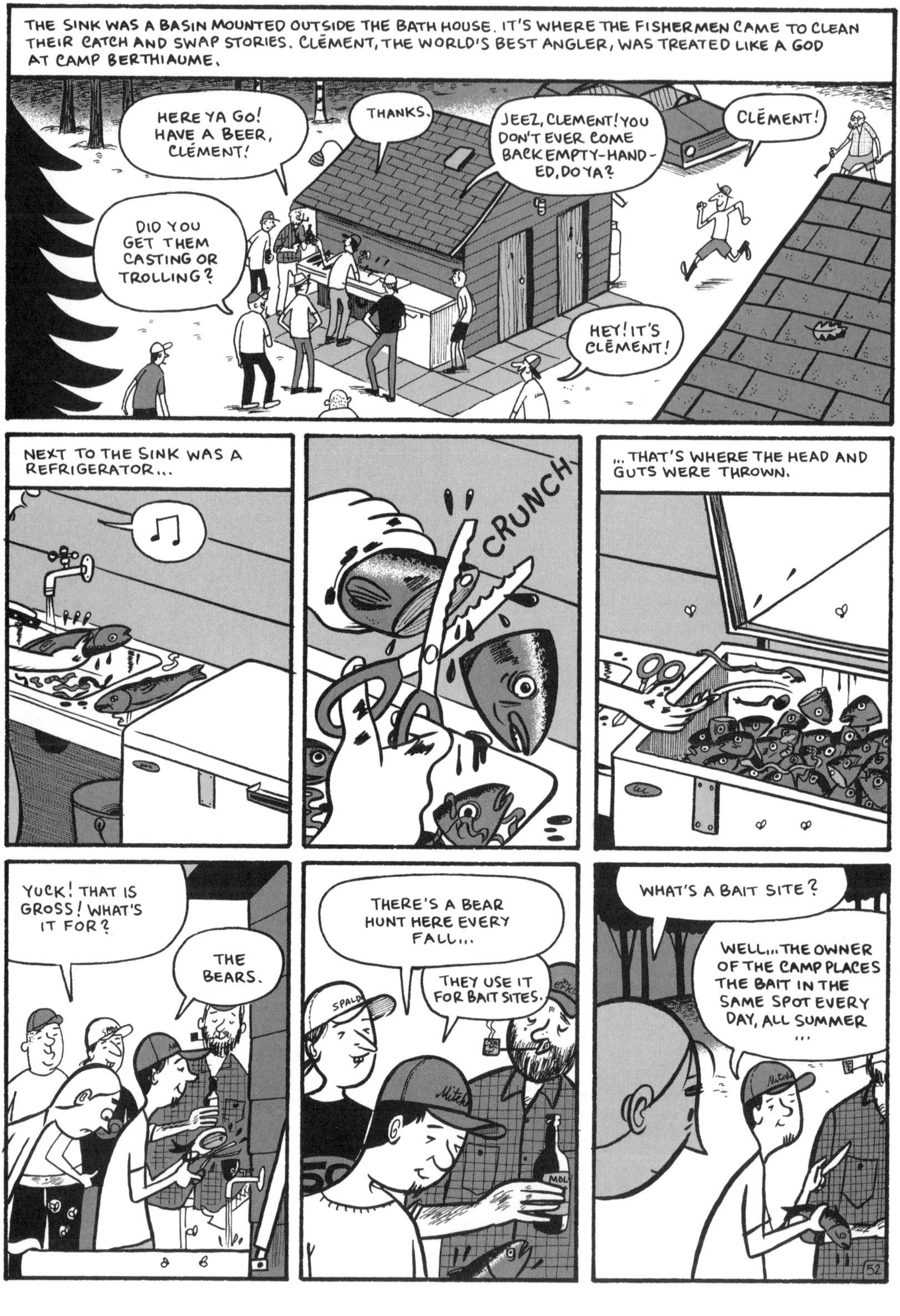
THE SINK WAS A BASIN MOUNTED OUTSIDE THE BATH HOUSE. IT'S WHERE THE FISHERMEN CAME TO CLEAN THEIR CATCH AND SWAP STORIES. CLÉMENT, THE WORLD'S BEST ANGLER, WAS TREATED LIKE A GOD AT CAMP BERTHIAUME.
HERE YA GO! HAVE A BEER, CLÉMENT!
THANKS.
JEEZ, CLEMENT! YOU DON'T EVER COME BACK EMPTY-HANDED, DO YA?
CLÉMENT!
DID YOU GET THEM CASTING OR TROLLING?
HEY! IT'S CLÉMENT!
NEXT TO THE SINK WAS A REFRIGERATOR...
♫
CRUNCH
...THAT'S WHERE THE HEAD AND GUTS WERE THROWN.
YUCK! THAT IS GROSS! WHAT'S IT FOR?
THE BEARS.
THERE'S A BEAR HUNT HERE EVERY FALL...
THEY USE IT FOR BAIT SITES.
WHAT'S A BAIT SITE?
WELL... THE OWNER OF THE CAMP PLACES THE BAIT IN THE SAME SPOT EVERY DAY, ALL SUMMER ...

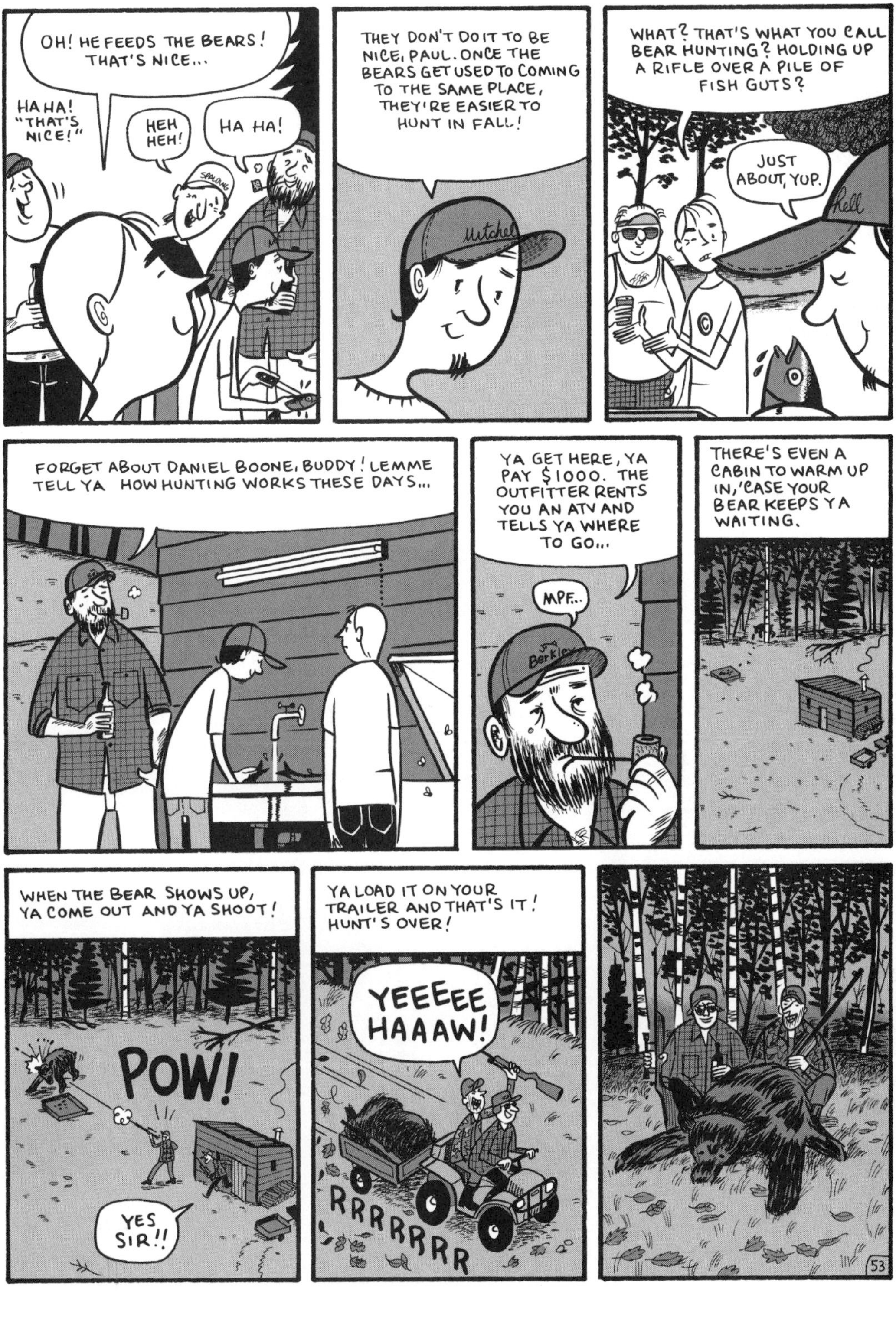
OH! HE FEEDS THE BEARS! THAT'S NICE...
HA HA! "THAT'S NICE!"
HEH HEH!
HA HA!
SPALDING
THEY DON'T DO IT TO BE NICE, PAUL. ONCE THE BEARS GET USED TO COMING TO THE SAME PLACE, THEY'RE EASIER TO HUNT IN FALL!
Mitchel
WHAT? THAT'S WHAT YOU CALL BEAR HUNTING? HOLDING UP A RIFLE OVER A PILE OF FISH GUTS?
JUST ABOUT, YUP.
FORGET ABOUT DANIEL BOONE, BUDDY! LEMME TELL YA HOW HUNTING WORKS THESE DAYS...
YA GET HERE, YA PAY $1000. THE OUTFITTER RENTS YOU AN ATV AND TELLS YA WHERE TO GO...
MPF..
Berkley
THERE'S EVEN A CABIN TO WARM UP IN, 'CASE YOUR BEAR KEEPS YA WAITING.
WHEN THE BEAR SHOWS UP, YA COME OUT AND YA SHOOT!
POW!
YES SIR!!
YA LOAD IT ON YOUR TRAILER AND THAT'S IT! HUNT'S OVER!
YEEEEEE HAAAW!
RRRRRRRRR

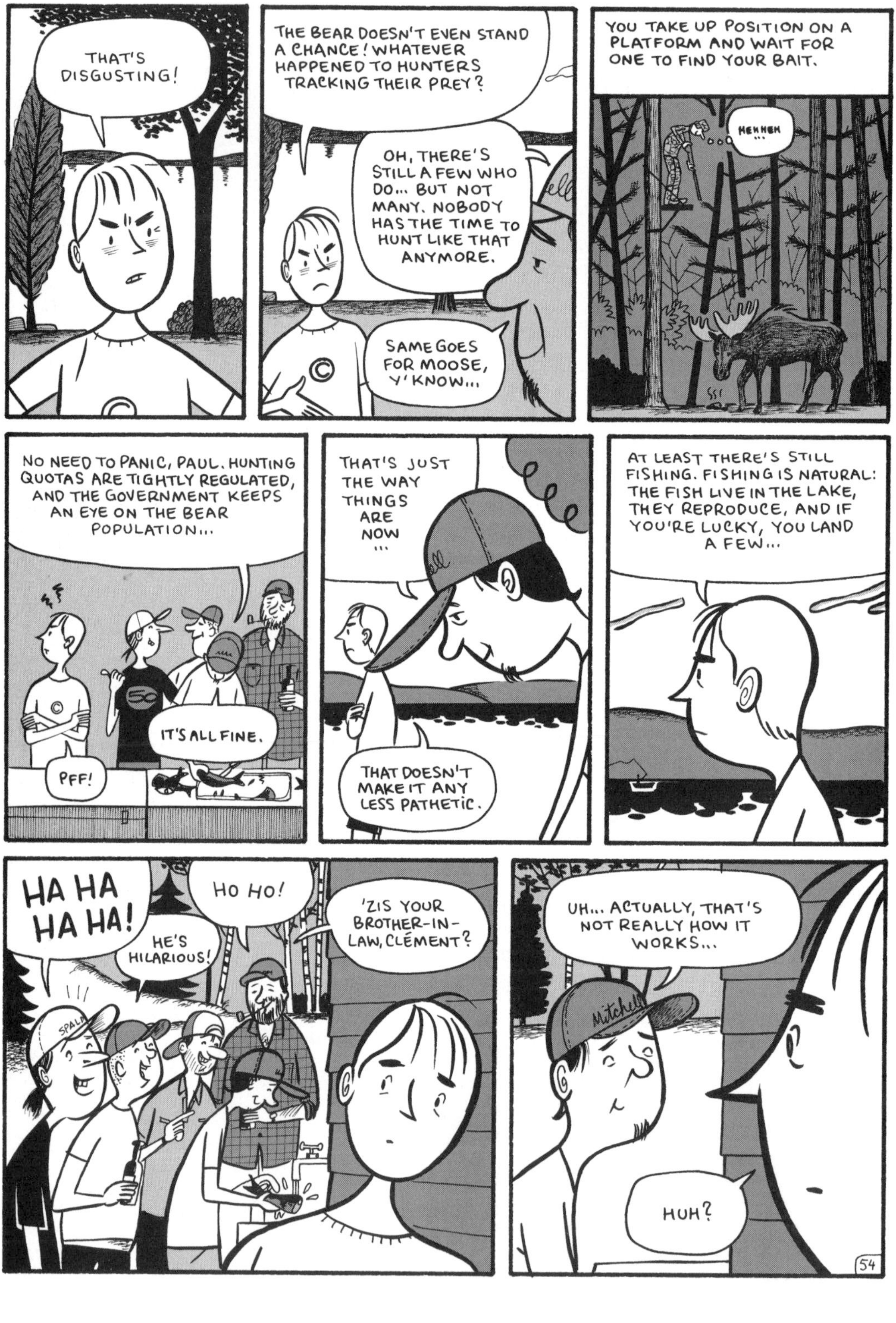
THAT'S DISGUSTING!
THE BEAR DOESN'T EVEN STAND A CHANCE! WHATEVER HAPPENED TO HUNTERS TRACKING THEIR PREY?
OH, THERE'S STILL A FEW WHO DO... BUT NOT MANY. NOBODY HAS THE TIME TO HUNT LIKE THAT ANYMORE.
SAME GOES FOR MOOSE, Y'KNOW...
YOU TAKE UP POSITION ON A PLATFORM AND WAIT FOR ONE TO FIND YOUR BAIT.
HEH HEH ...
NO NEED TO PANIC, PAUL. HUNTING QUOTAS ARE TIGHTLY REGULATED, AND THE GOVERNMENT KEEPS AN EYE ON THE BEAR POPULATION...
IT'S ALL FINE.
PFF!
THAT'S JUST THE WAY THINGS ARE NOW ...
THAT DOESN'T MAKE IT ANY LESS PATHETIC.
AT LEAST THERE'S STILL FISHING. FISHING IS NATURAL: THE FISH LIVE IN THE LAKE, THEY REPRODUCE, AND IF YOU'RE LUCKY, YOU LAND A FEW...
HA HA HA HA!
HE'S HILARIOUS!
HO HO!
'ZIS YOUR BROTHER-IN-LAW, CLÉMENT?
UH... ACTUALLY, THAT'S NOT REALLY HOW IT WORKS...
HUH?

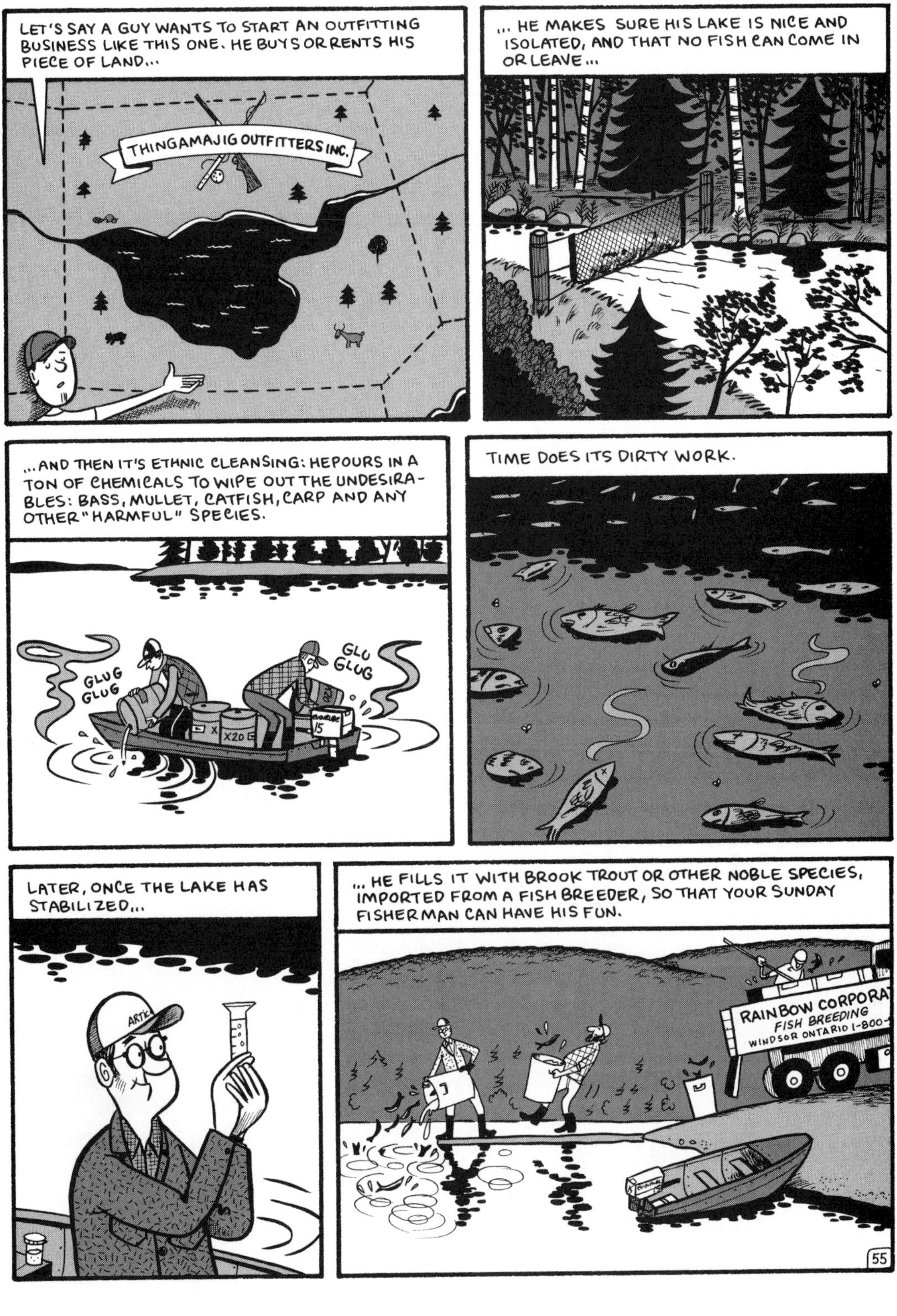
LET'S SAY A GUY WANTS TO START AN OUTFITTING BUSINESS LIKE THIS ONE. HE BUYS OR RENTS HIS PIECE OF LAND...
THINGAMAJIG OUTFITTERS INC.
... HE MAKES SURE HIS LAKE IS NICE AND ISOLATED, AND THAT NO FISH CAN COME IN OR LEAVE...
... AND THEN IT'S ETHNIC CLEANSING: HE POURS IN A TON OF CHEMICALS TO WIPE OUT THE UNDESIRABLES: BASS, MULLET, CATFISH, CARP AND ANY OTHER "HARMFUL" SPECIES.
GLUG GLUG
GLU GLUG
X20
15
TIME DOES ITS DIRTY WORK.
LATER, ONCE THE LAKE HAS STABILIZED...
... HE FILLS IT WITH BROOK TROUT OR OTHER NOBLE SPECIES, IMPORTED FROM A FISH BREEDER, SO THAT YOUR SUNDAY FISHERMAN CAN HAVE HIS FUN.
RAINBOW CORPORAT
FISH BREEDING
WINDSOR ONTARIO 1-800-

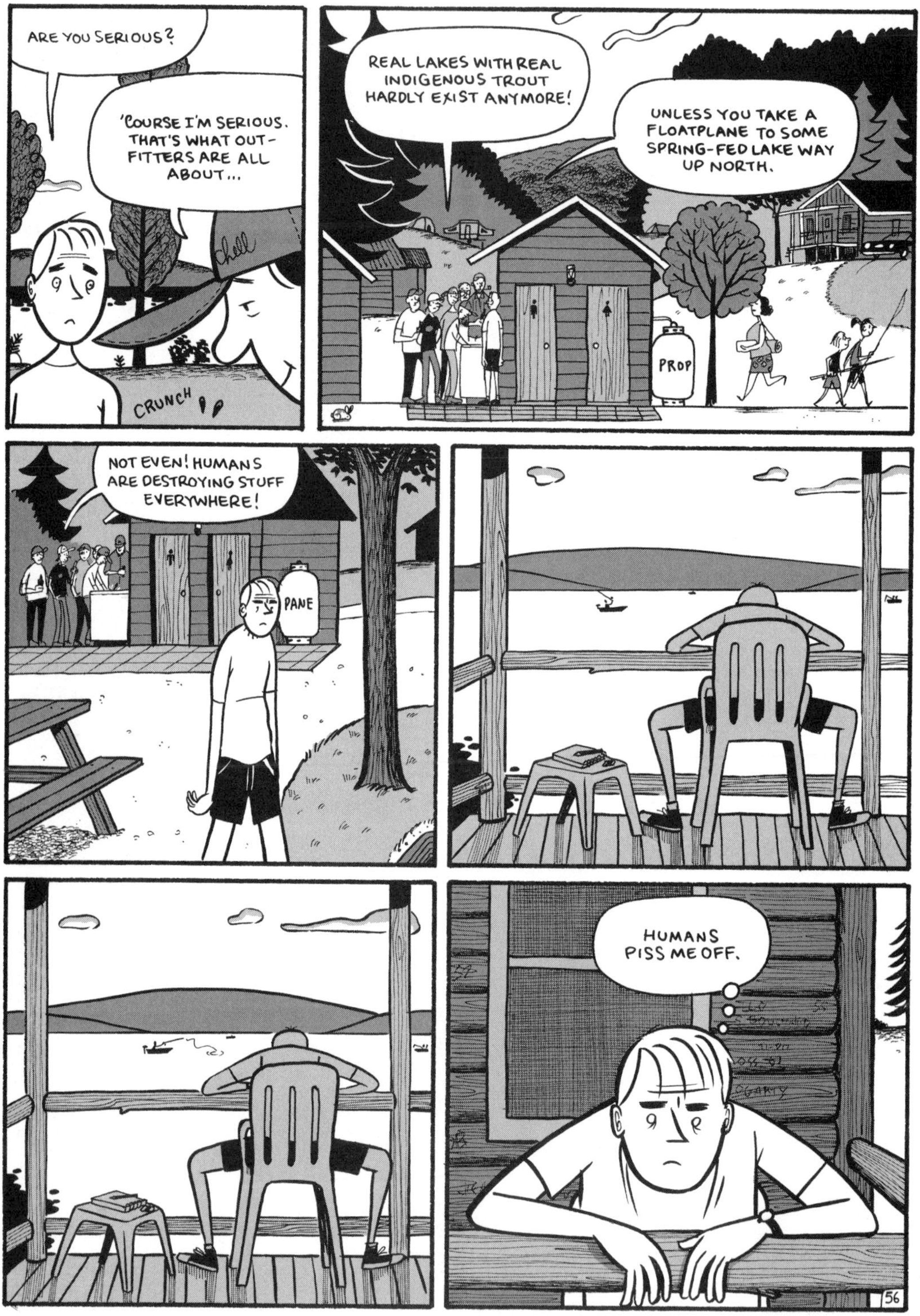
ARE YOU SERIOUS?
'COURSE I'M SERIOUS. THAT'S WHAT OUT-FITTERS ARE ALL ABOUT...
CRUNCH
REAL LAKES WITH REAL INDIGENOUS TROUT HARDLY EXIST ANYMORE!
UNLESS YOU TAKE A FLOATPLANE TO SOME SPRING-FED LAKE WAY UP NORTH.
PROP
NOT EVEN! HUMANS ARE DESTROYING STUFF EVERYWHERE!
PANE
HUMANS PISS ME OFF.

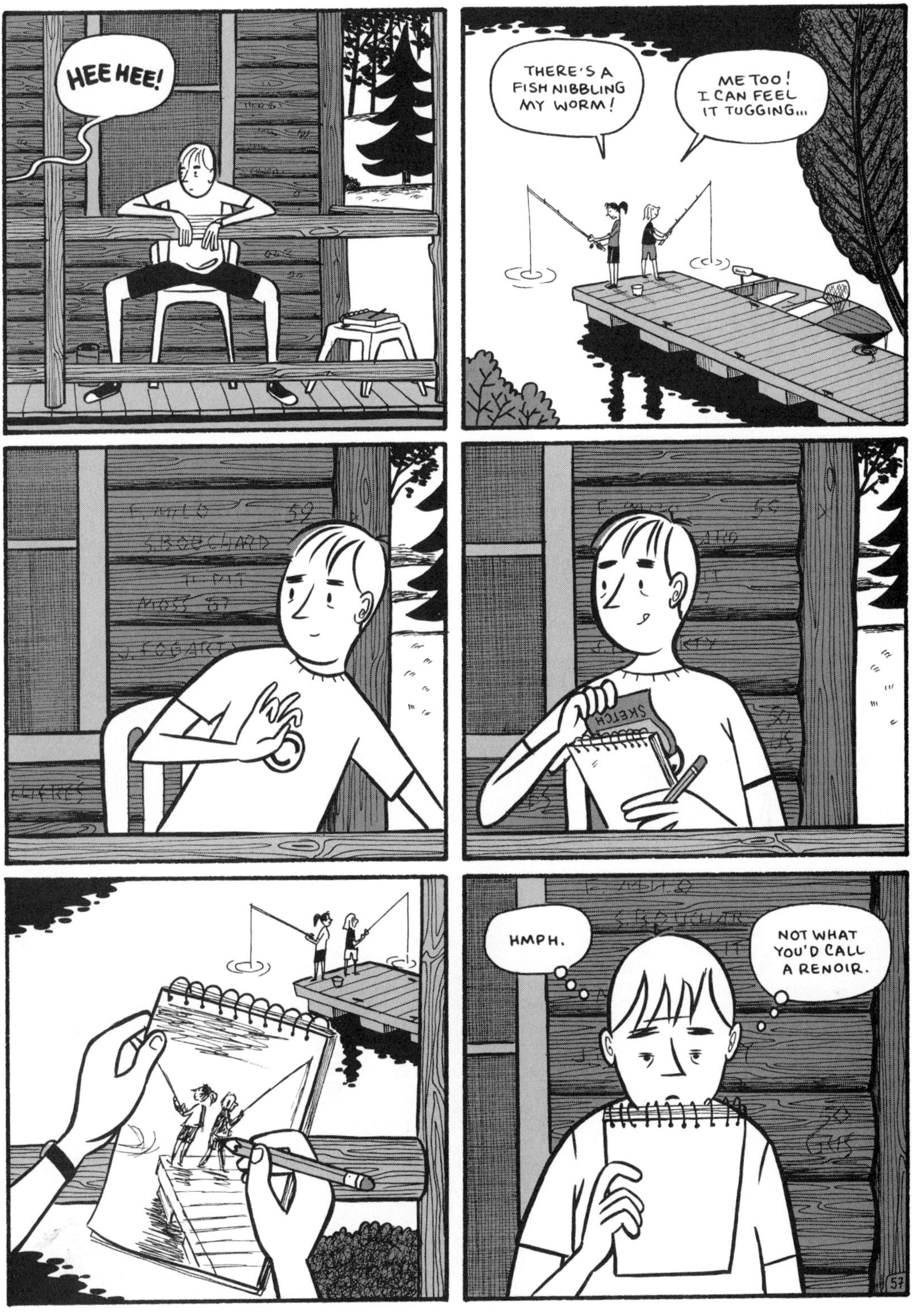
HEE HEE!
THERE'S A FISH NIBBLING MY WORM!
ME TOO! I CAN FEEL IT TUGGING...
SKETCH
HMPH.
NOT WHAT YOU'D CALL A RENOIR.

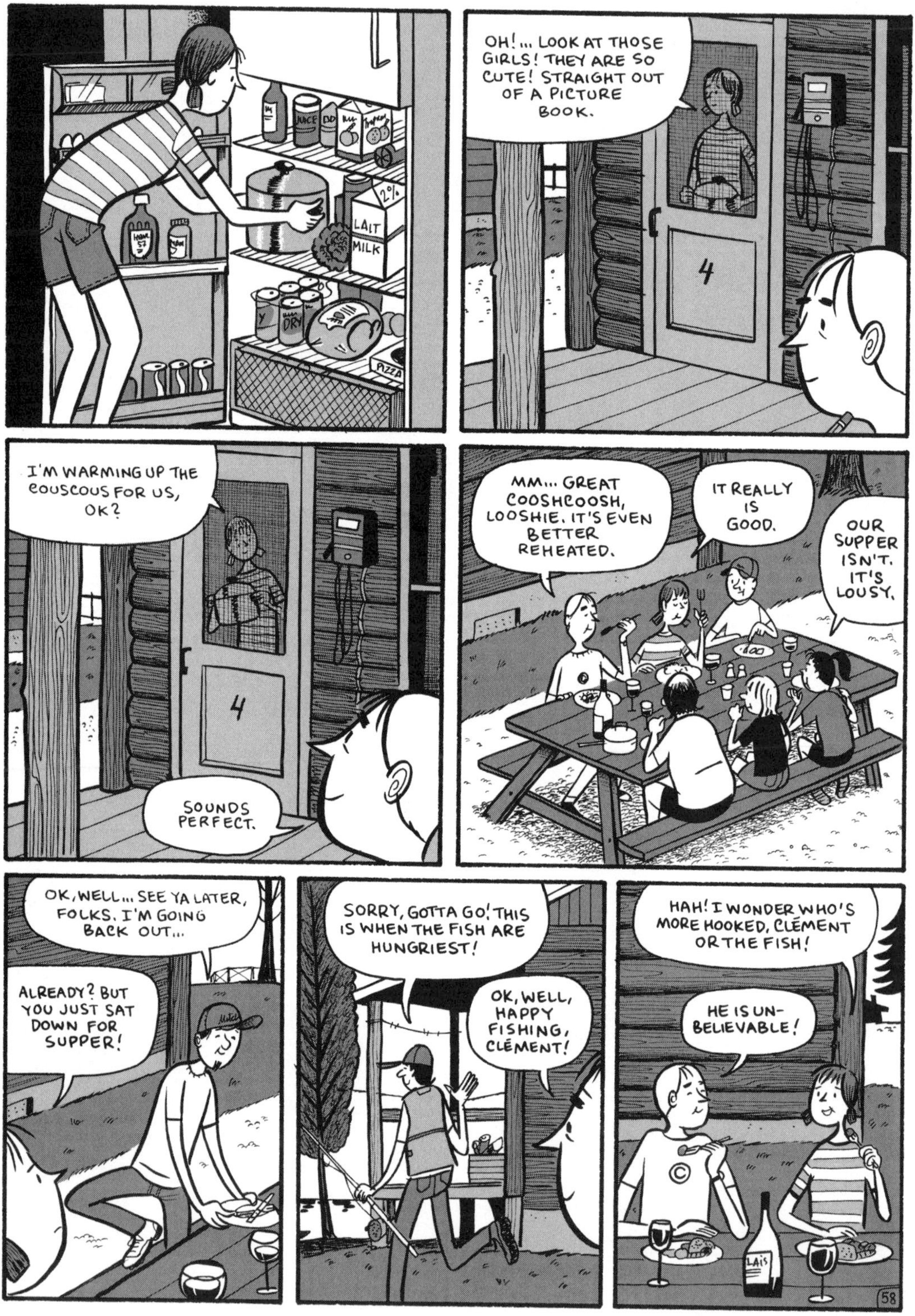

OH! ... LOOK AT THOSE GIRLS! THEY ARE SO CUTE! STRAIGHT OUT OF A PICTURE BOOK.
I'M WARMING UP THE COUSCOUS FOR US, OK?
SOUNDS PERFECT.
MM... GREAT COOSHCOOSH, LOOSHIE. IT'S EVEN BETTER REHEATED.
IT REALLY IS GOOD.
OUR SUPPER ISN'T. IT'S LOUSY.
OK, WELL... SEE YA LATER, FOLKS. I'M GOING BACK OUT...
ALREADY? BUT YOU JUST SAT DOWN FOR SUPPER!
SORRY, GOTTA GO! THIS IS WHEN THE FISH ARE HUNGRIEST!
OK, WELL, HAPPY FISHING, CLÉMENT!
HAH! I WONDER WHO'S MORE HOOKED, CLÉMENT OR THE FISH!
HE IS UNBELIEVABLE!

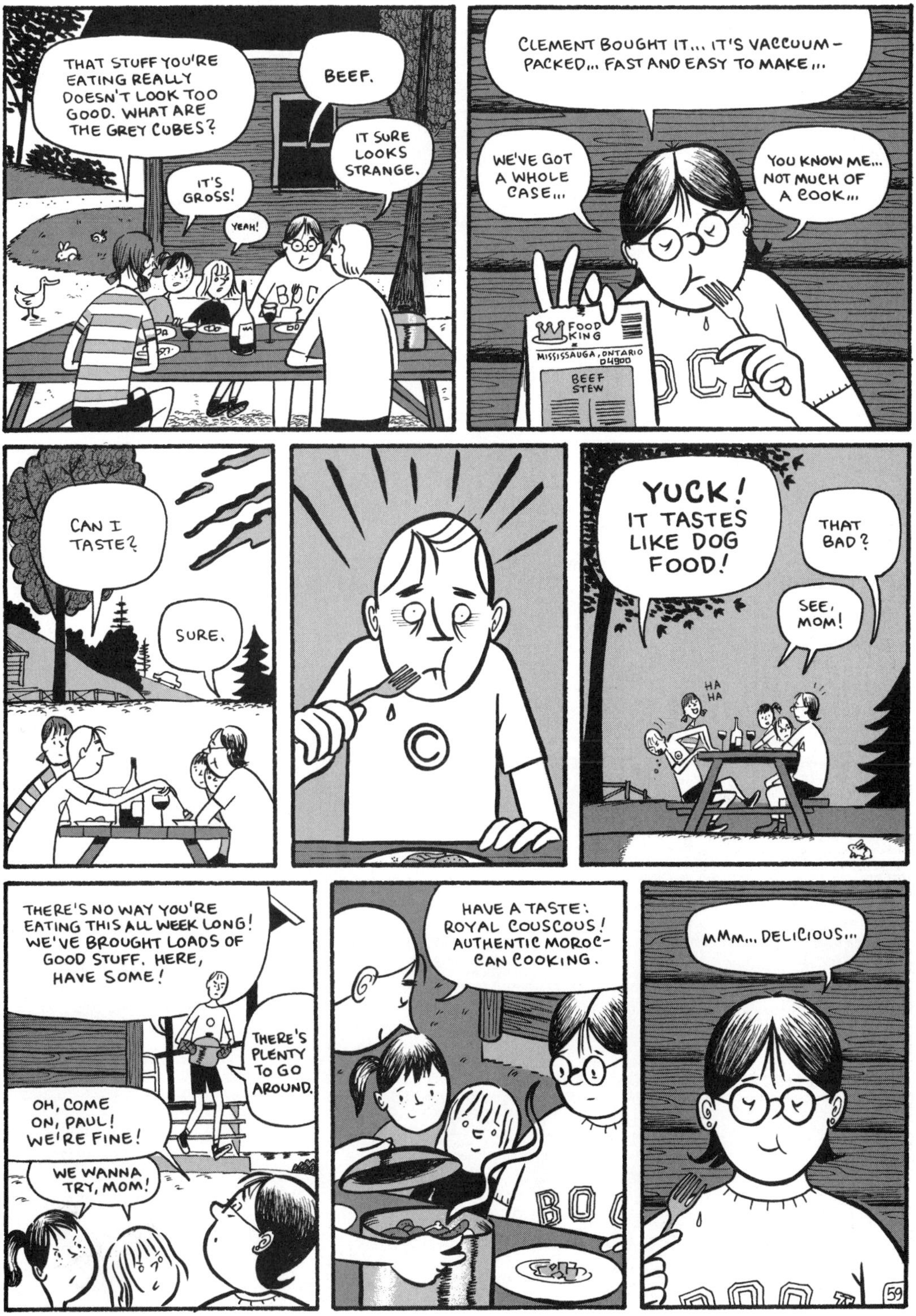

THAT STUFF YOU'RE EATING REALLY DOESN'T LOOK TOO GOOD. WHAT ARE THE GREY CUBES?
BEEF.
IT SURE LOOKS STRANGE.
IT'S GROSS!
YEAH!
CLEMENT BOUGHT IT... IT'S VACCUUM-PACKED... FAST AND EASY TO MAKE...
WE'VE GOT A WHOLE CASE...
YOU KNOW ME... NOT MUCH OF A COOK...
FOOD KING
MISSISSAUGA, ONTARIO
04900
BEEF STEW
CAN I TASTE?
SURE.
YUCK! IT TASTES LIKE DOG FOOD!
THAT BAD?
SEE, MOM!
HA HA
THERE'S NO WAY YOU'RE EATING THIS ALL WEEK LONG! WE'VE BROUGHT LOADS OF GOOD STUFF. HERE, HAVE SOME!
THERE'S PLENTY TO GO AROUND.
OH, COME ON, PAUL! WE'RE FINE!
WE WANNA TRY, MOM!
HAVE A TASTE: ROYAL COUSCOUS! AUTHENTIC MOROC-CAN COOKING.
MMM... DELICIOUS...

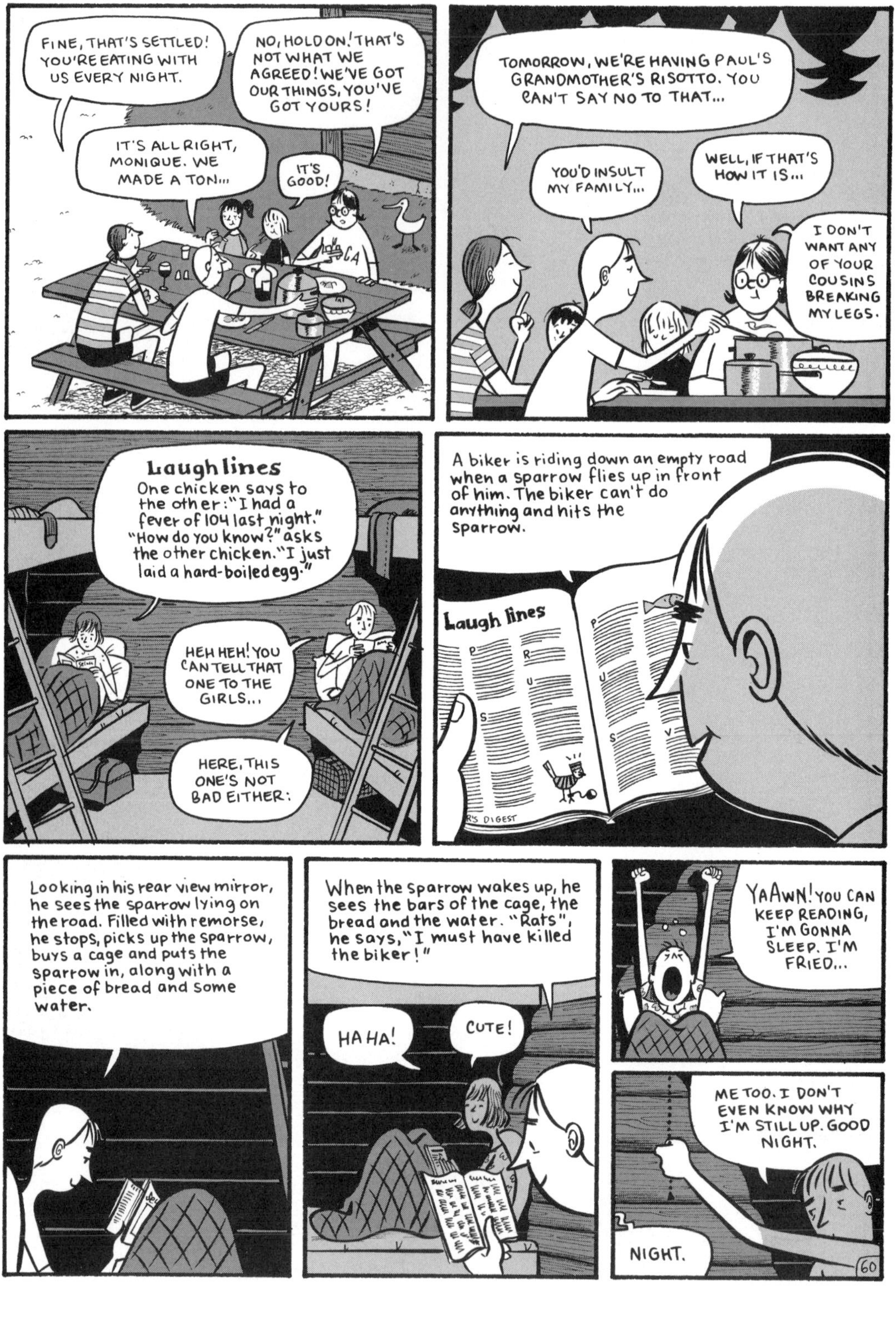
FINE, THAT'S SETTLED! YOU'RE EATING WITH US EVERY NIGHT.
NO, HOLD ON! THAT'S NOT WHAT WE AGREED! WE'VE GOT OUR THINGS, YOU'VE GOT YOURS!
IT'S ALL RIGHT, MONIQUE. WE MADE A TON...
IT'S GOOD!
TOMORROW, WE'RE HAVING PAUL'S GRANDMOTHER'S RISOTTO. YOU CAN'T SAY NO TO THAT...
YOU'D INSULT MY FAMILY...
WELL, IF THAT'S HOW IT IS...
I DON'T WANT ANY OF YOUR COUSINS BREAKING MY LEGS.
Laugh lines
One chicken says to the other: "I had a fever of 104 last night." "How do you know?" asks the other chicken. "I just laid a hard-boiled egg."
HEH HEH! YOU CAN TELL THAT ONE TO THE GIRLS...
HERE, THIS ONE'S NOT BAD EITHER:
A biker is riding down an empty road when a sparrow flies up in front of him. The biker can't do anything and hits the sparrow.
Laugh lines
R'S DIGEST
Looking in his rear view mirror, he sees the sparrow lying on the road. Filled with remorse, he stops, picks up the sparrow, buys a cage and puts the sparrow in, along with a piece of bread and some water.
When the sparrow wakes up, he sees the bars of the cage, the bread and the water. "Rats", he says, "I must have killed the biker!"
HA HA!
CUTE!
YAAWN! YOU CAN KEEP READING, I'M GONNA SLEEP. I'M FRIED...
ME TOO. I DON'T EVEN KNOW WHY I'M STILL UP. GOOD NIGHT.
NIGHT.

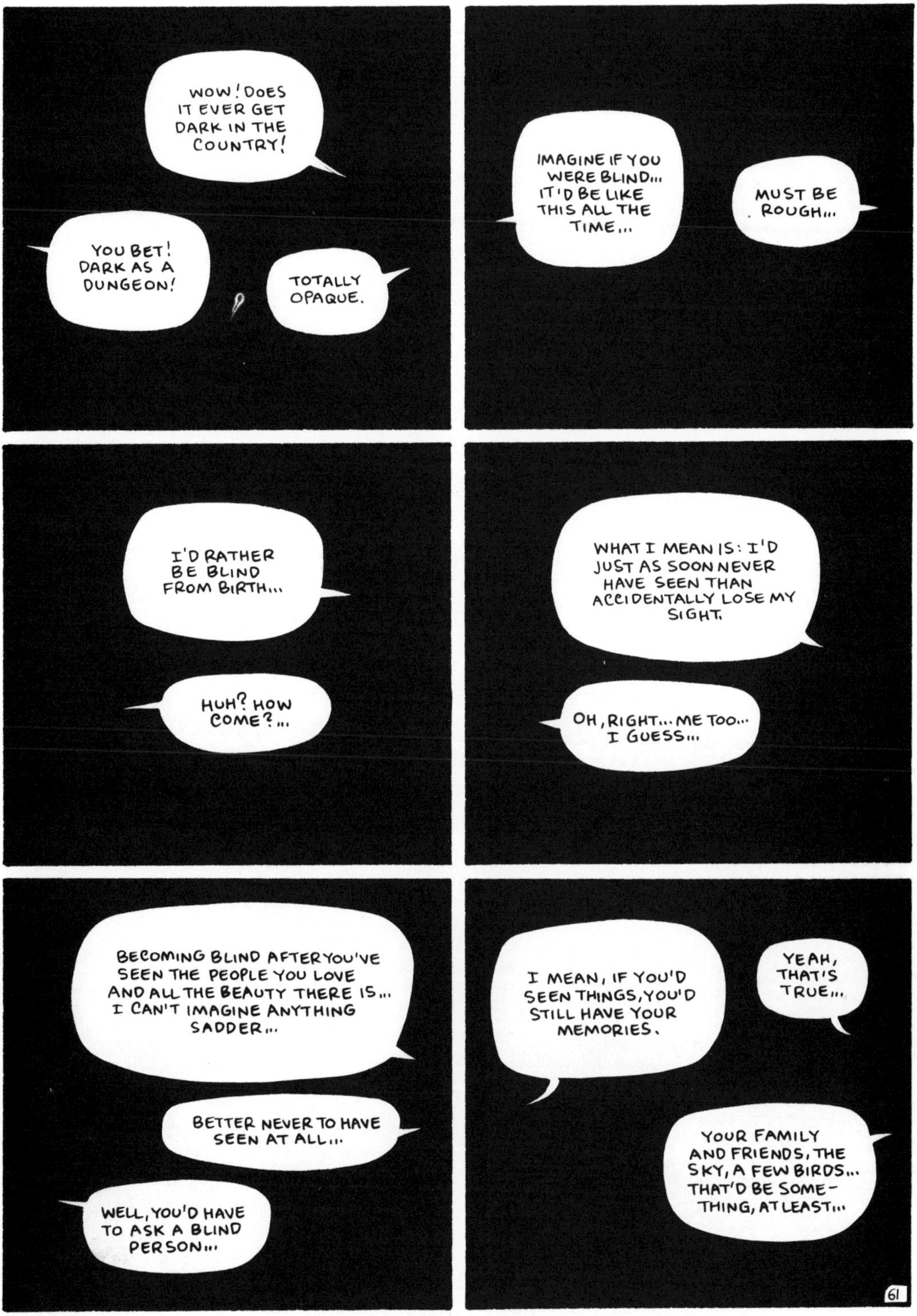
WOW! DOES IT EVER GET DARK IN THE COUNTRY!
YOU BET! DARK AS A DUNGEON!
TOTALLY OPAQUE.
IMAGINE IF YOU WERE BLIND... IT'D BE LIKE THIS ALL THE TIME...
MUST BE ROUGH...
I'D RATHER BE BLIND FROM BIRTH...
HUH? HOW COME?...
WHAT I MEAN IS: I'D JUST AS SOON NEVER HAVE SEEN THAN ACCIDENTALLY LOSE MY SIGHT.
OH, RIGHT... ME TOO... I GUESS...
BECOMING BLIND AFTER YOU'VE SEEN THE PEOPLE YOU LOVE AND ALL THE BEAUTY THERE IS... I CAN'T IMAGINE ANYTHING SADDER...
BETTER NEVER TO HAVE SEEN AT ALL...
WELL, YOU'D HAVE TO ASK A BLIND PERSON...
I MEAN, IF YOU'D SEEN THINGS, YOU'D STILL HAVE YOUR MEMORIES.
YEAH, THAT'S TRUE...
YOUR FAMILY AND FRIENDS, THE SKY, A FEW BIRDS... THAT'D BE SOME-THING, AT LEAST...

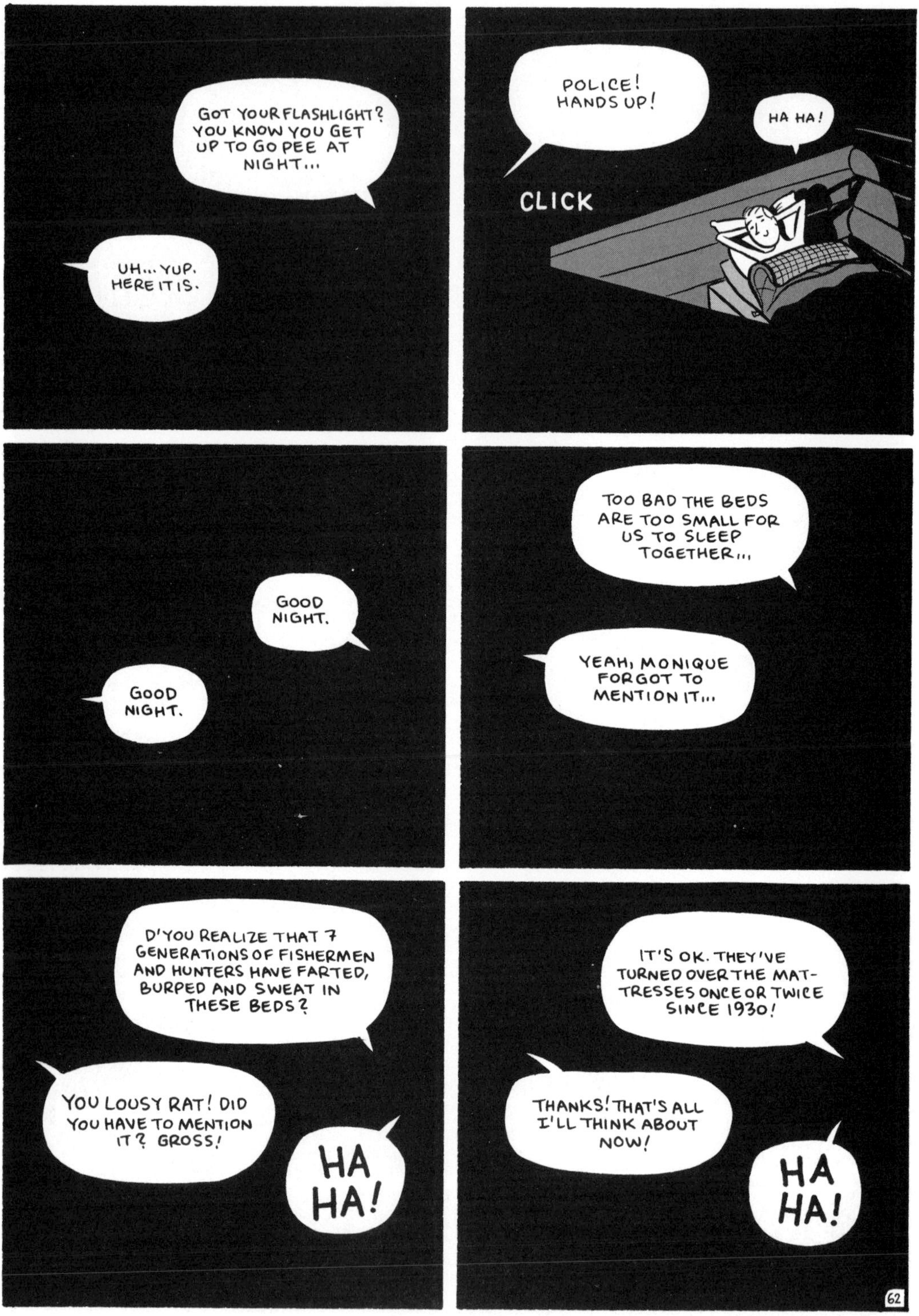
GOT YOUR FLASHLIGHT? YOU KNOW YOU GET UP TO GO PEE AT NIGHT...
UH... YUP. HERE IT IS.
POLICE! HANDS UP!
HA HA!
CLICK
GOOD NIGHT.
GOOD NIGHT.
TOO BAD THE BEDS ARE TOO SMALL FOR US TO SLEEP TOGETHER...
YEAH, MONIQUE FORGOT TO MENTION IT...
D'YOU REALIZE THAT 7 GENERATIONS OF FISHERMEN AND HUNTERS HAVE FARTED, BURPED AND SWEAT IN THESE BEDS?
YOU LOUSY RAT! DID YOU HAVE TO MENTION IT? GROSS!
HA HA!
IT'S OK. THEY'VE TURNED OVER THE MAT-TRESSES ONCE OR TWICE SINCE 1930!
THANKS! THAT'S ALL I'LL THINK ABOUT NOW!
HA HA!

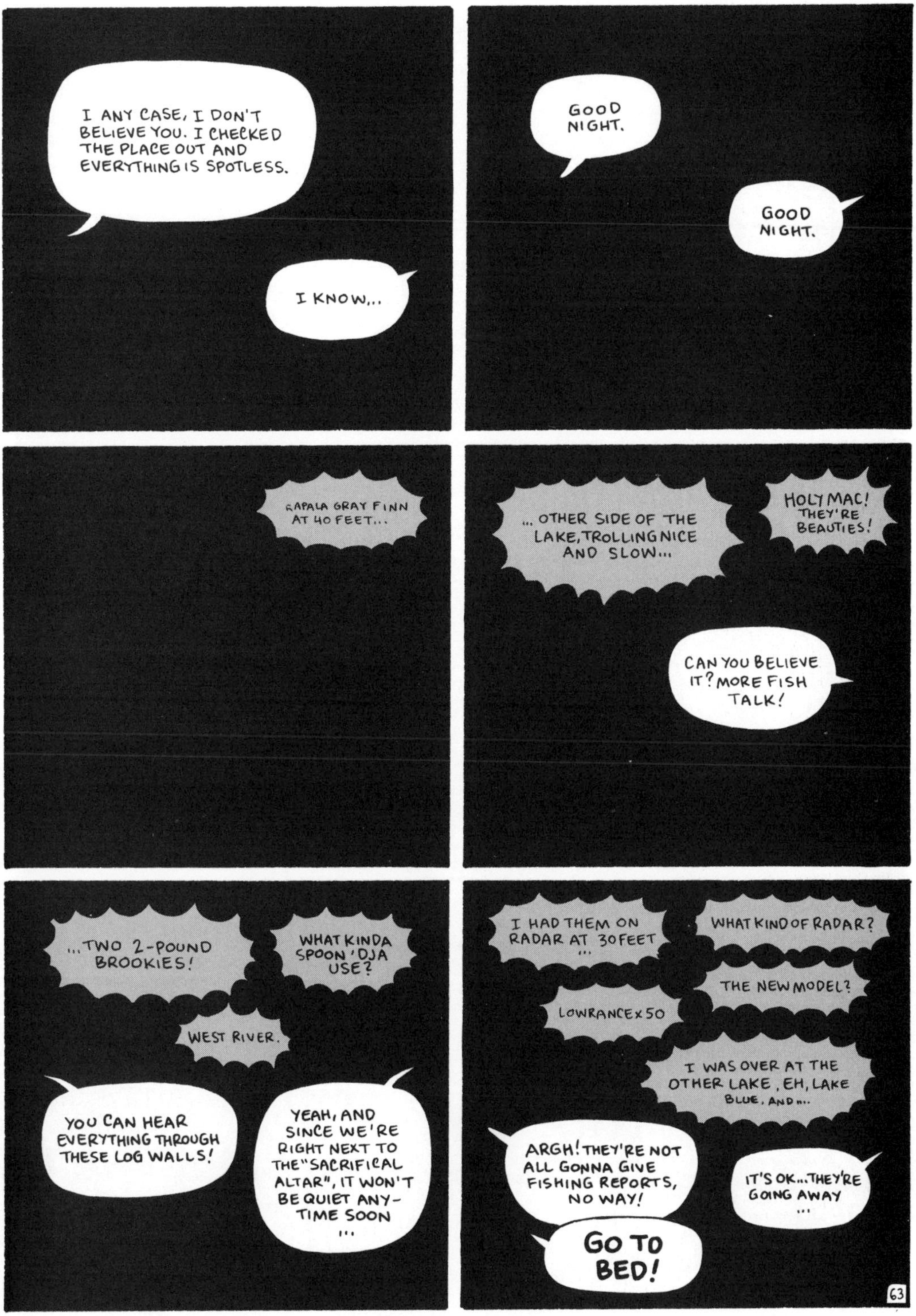
I ANY CASE, I DON'T BELIEVE YOU. I CHECKED THE PLACE OUT AND EVERYTHING IS SPOTLESS.
I KNOW...
GOOD NIGHT.
GOOD NIGHT.
RAPALA GRAY FINN AT 40 FEET...
... OTHER SIDE OF THE LAKE, TROLLING NICE AND SLOW...
HOLY MAC! THEY'RE BEAUTIES!
CAN YOU BELIEVE IT? MORE FISH TALK!
... TWO 2-POUND BROOKIES!
WHAT KINDA SPOON 'DJA USE?
WEST RIVER.
YOU CAN HEAR EVERYTHING THROUGH THESE LOG WALLS!
YEAH, AND SINCE WE'RE RIGHT NEXT TO THE "SACRIFICAL ALTAR", IT WON'T BE QUIET ANY-TIME SOON ...
I HAD THEM ON RADAR AT 30 FEET ...
WHAT KIND OF RADAR?
THE NEW MODEL?
LOWRANCE X50
I WAS OVER AT THE OTHER LAKE, EH, LAKE BLUE. AND...
ARGH! THEY'RE NOT ALL GONNA GIVE FISHING REPORTS, NO WAY!
IT'S OK... THEY'RE GOING AWAY ...
GO TO BED!
63

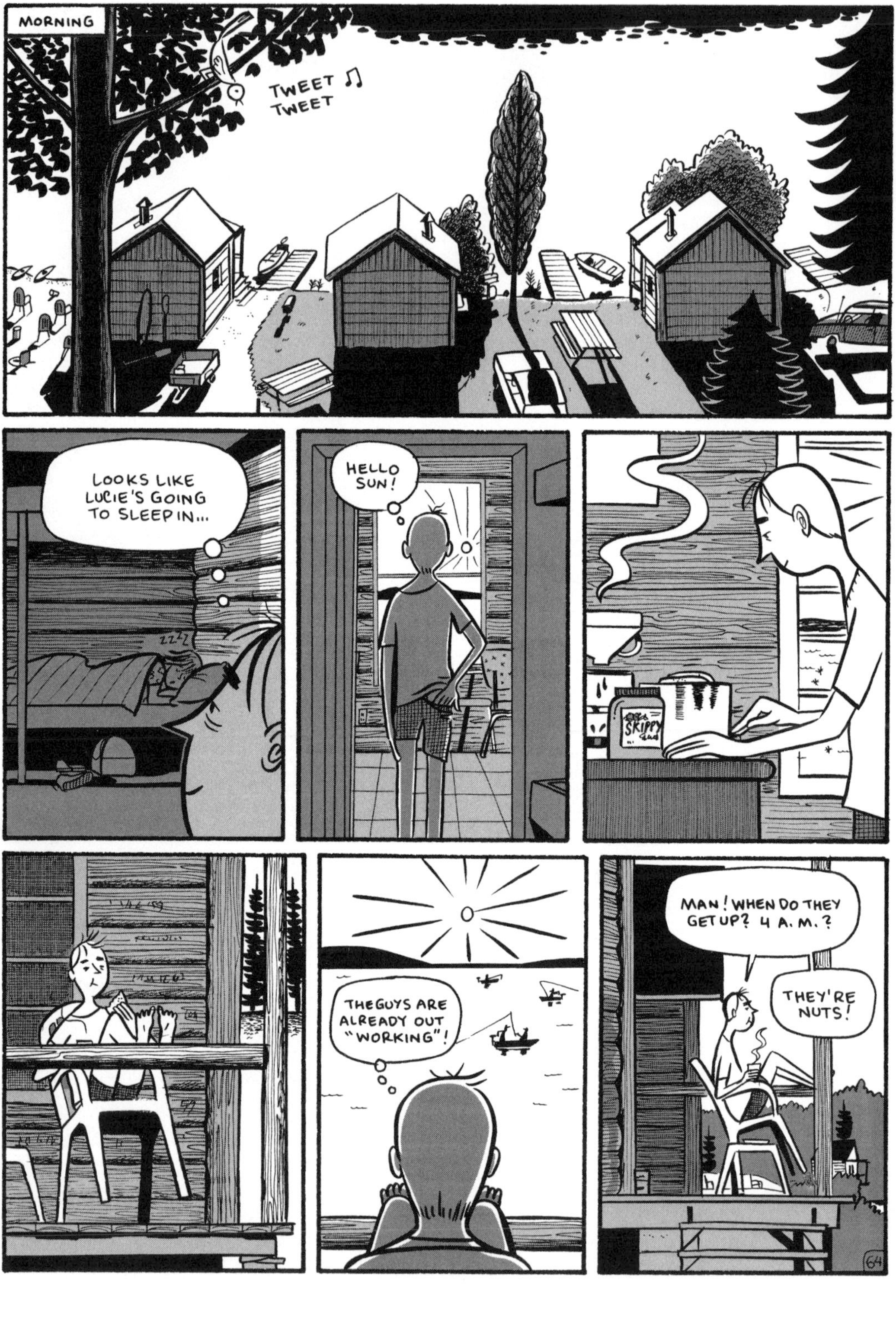
MORNING
TWEET ♫ TWEET
LOOKS LIKE LUCIE'S GOING TO SLEEP IN...
ZZZ
HELLO SUN!
SKIPPY
THE GUYS ARE ALREADY OUT "WORKING"!
MAN! WHEN DO THEY GET UP? 4 A.M.?
THEY'RE NUTS!

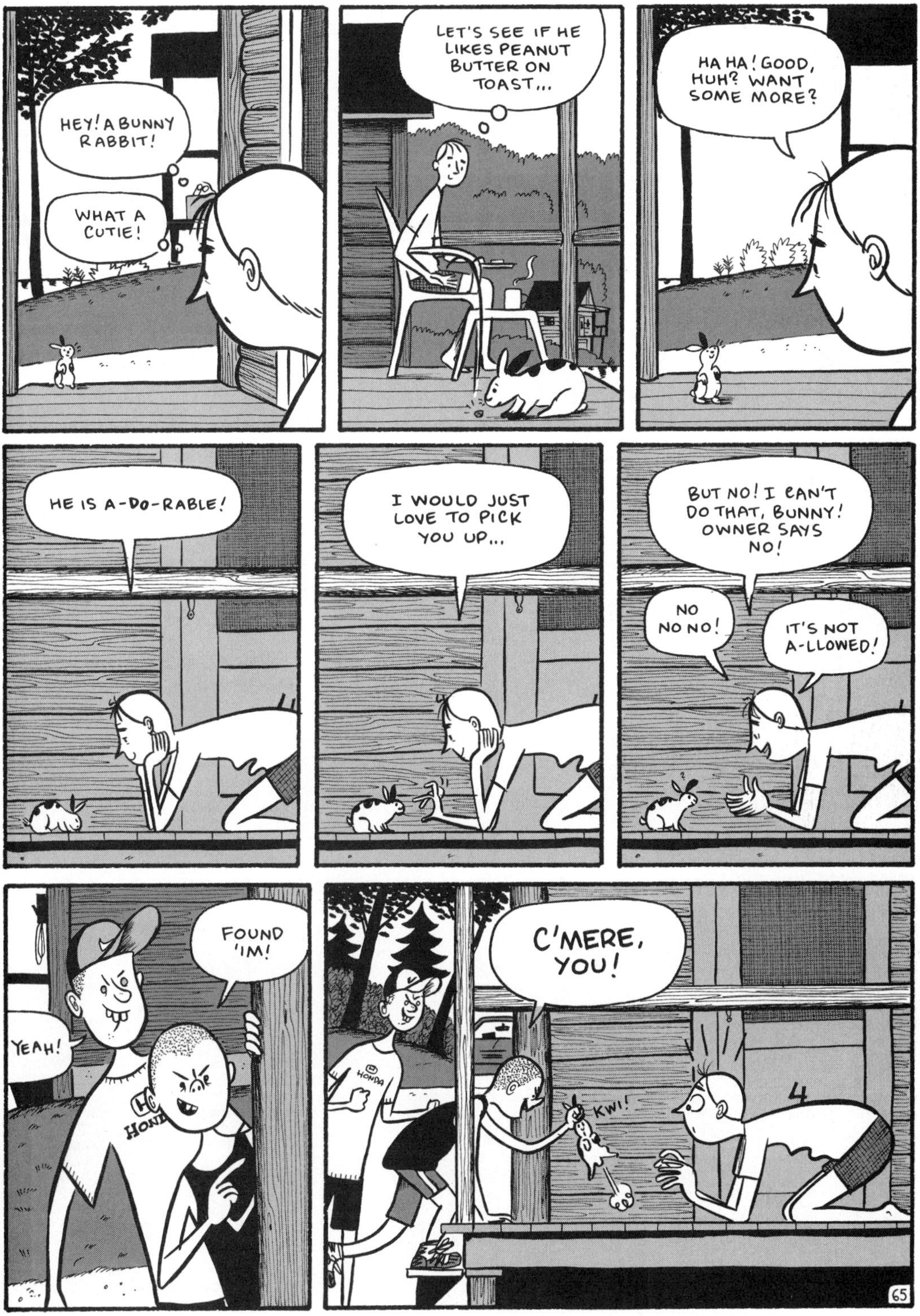
HEY! A BUNNY RABBIT!
WHAT A CUTIE!
LET'S SEE IF HE LIKES PEANUT BUTTER ON TOAST...
HA HA! GOOD, HUH? WANT SOME MORE?
HE IS A-DO-RABLE!
I WOULD JUST LOVE TO PICK YOU UP...
BUT NO! I CAN'T DO THAT, BUNNY! OWNER SAYS NO!
NO NO NO!
IT'S NOT A-LLOWED!
FOUND 'IM!
YEAH!
HONDA
C'MERE, YOU!
HONDA
KWI!

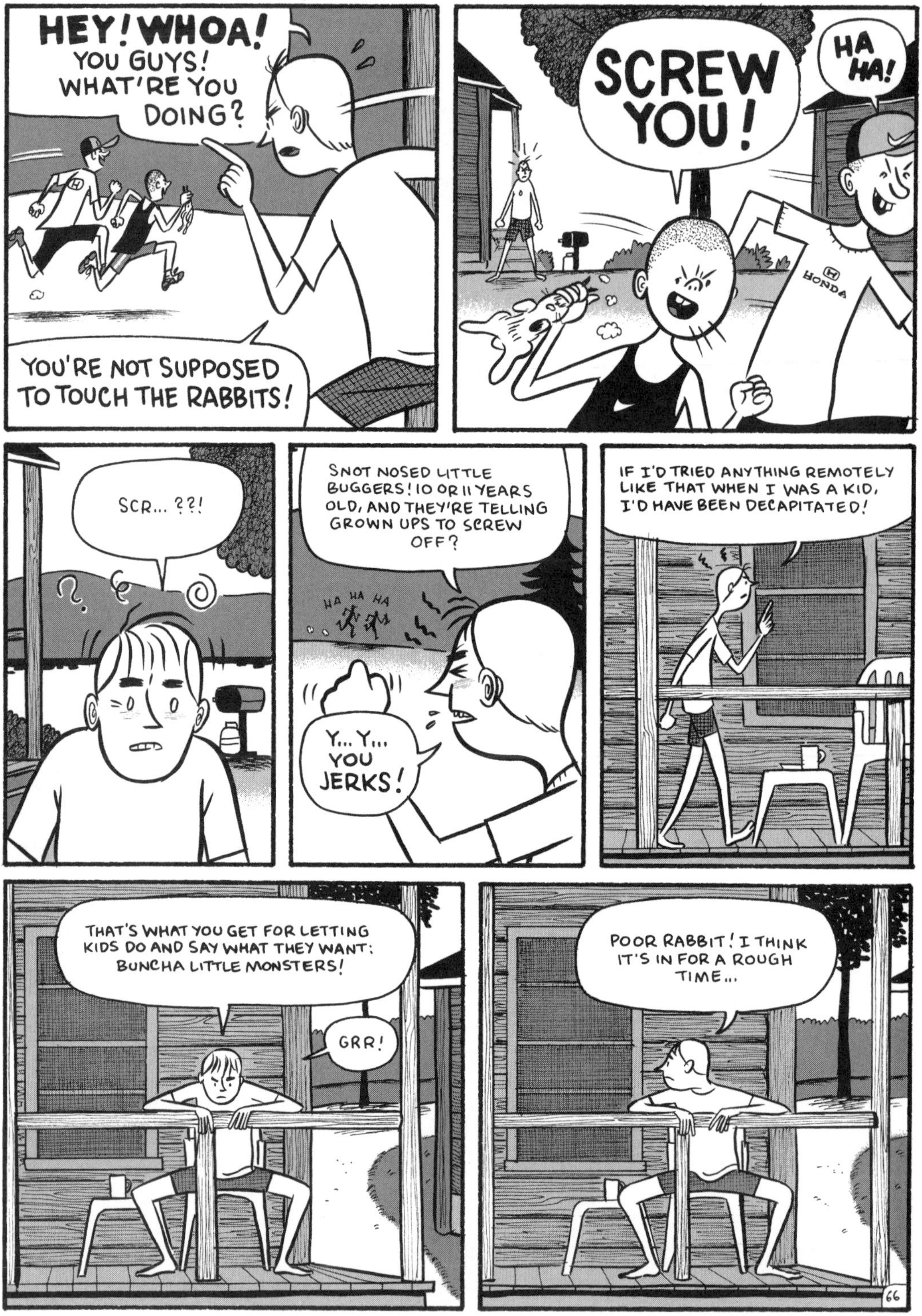
HEY! WHOA! YOU GUYS! WHAT'RE YOU DOING?
YOU'RE NOT SUPPOSED TO TOUCH THE RABBITS!
SCREW YOU!
HA HA!
HONDA
SCR... ??!
SNOT NOSED LITTLE BUGGERS! 10 OR 11 YEARS OLD, AND THEY'RE TELLING GROWN UPS TO SCREW OFF?
HA HA HA
Y... Y... YOU JERKS!
IF I'D TRIED ANYTHING REMOTELY LIKE THAT WHEN I WAS A KID, I'D HAVE BEEN DECAPITATED!
THAT'S WHAT YOU GET FOR LETTING KIDS DO AND SAY WHAT THEY WANT: BUNCHA LITTLE MONSTERS!
GRR!
POOR RABBIT! I THINK IT'S IN FOR A ROUGH TIME...

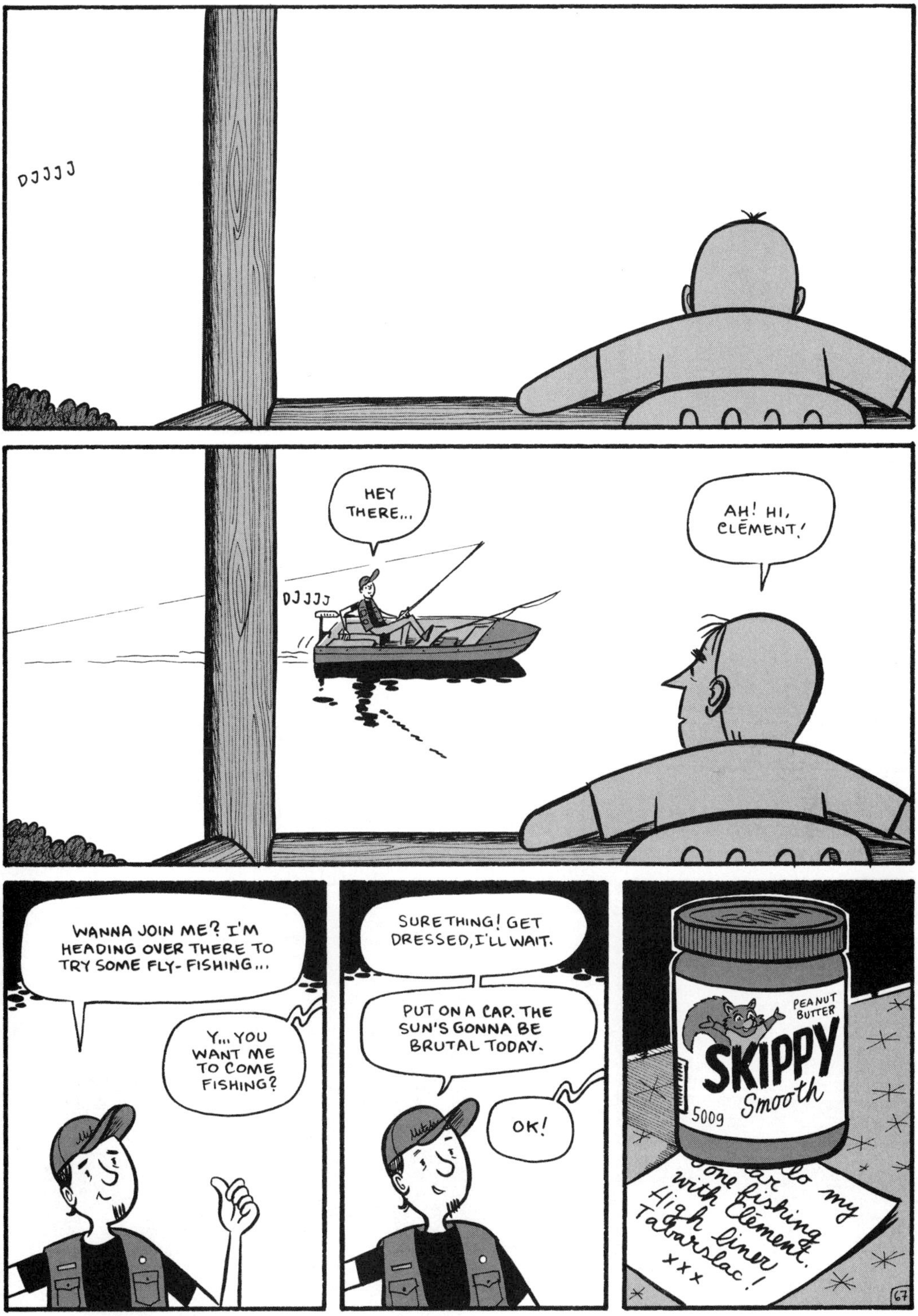
DJJJJ
HEY THERE...
DJJJJ
AH! HI, CLÉMENT!
WANNA JOIN ME? I'M HEADING OVER THERE TO TRY SOME FLY-FISHING...
Y... YOU WANT ME TO COME FISHING?
SURE THING! GET DRESSED, I'LL WAIT.
PUT ON A CAP. THE SUN'S GONNA BE BRUTAL TODAY.
OK!
PEANUT BUTTER
SKIPPY
Smooth
500g
one fishing
with Clément.
High liner
Tabarslac!
xxx

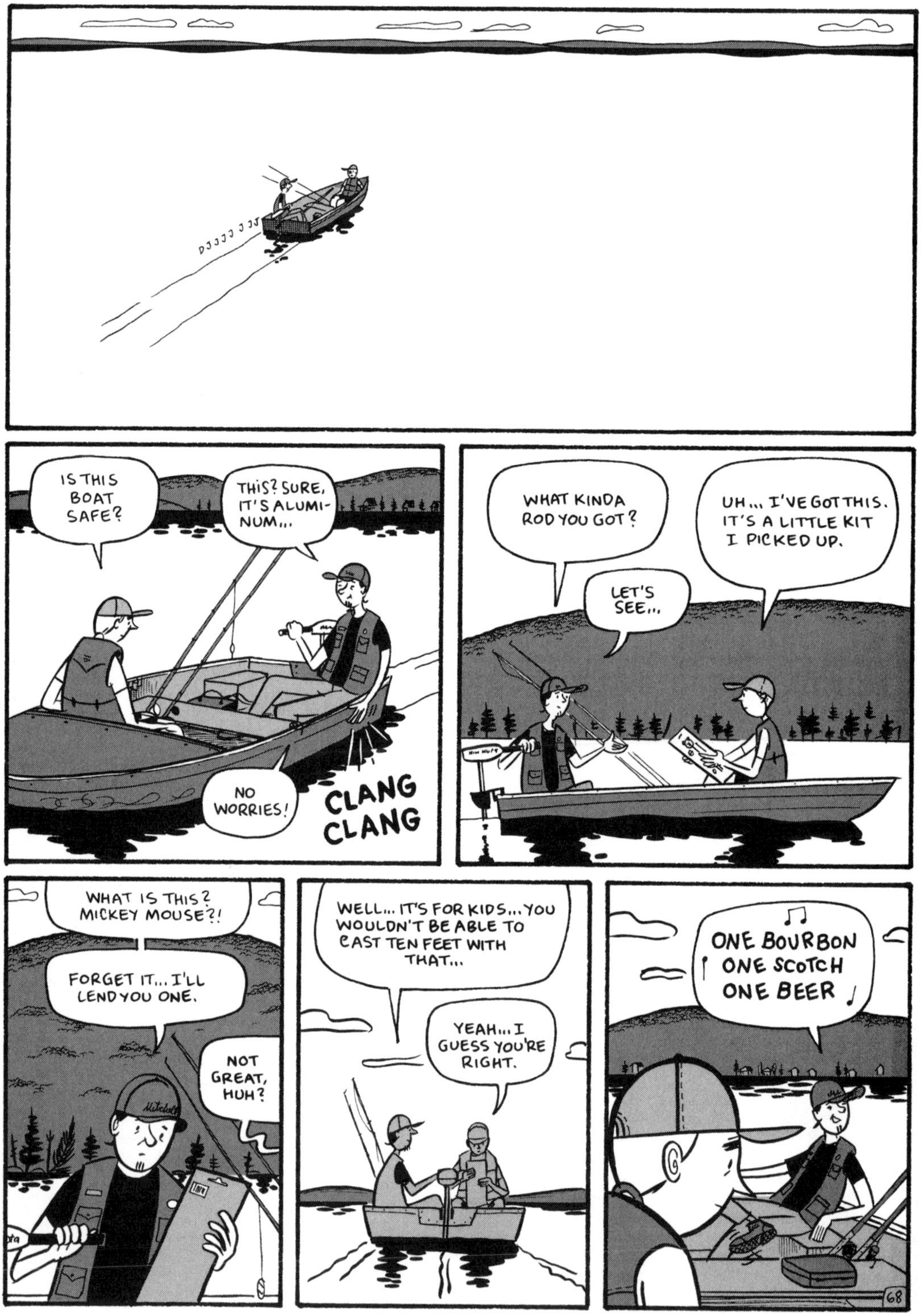
DJJJJ JJJ
IS THIS BOAT SAFE?
THIS? SURE, IT'S ALUMI-NUM...
NO WORRIES!
CLANG CLANG
WHAT KINDA ROD YOU GOT?
UH... I'VE GOT THIS. IT'S A LITTLE KIT I PICKED UP.
LET'S SEE...
WHAT IS THIS? MICKEY MOUSE?!
FORGET IT... I'LL LEND YOU ONE.
NOT GREAT, HUH?
WELL... IT'S FOR KIDS... YOU WOULDN'T BE ABLE TO CAST TEN FEET WITH THAT...
YEAH... I GUESS YOU'RE RIGHT.
ONE BOURBON ONE SCOTCH ONE BEER
68

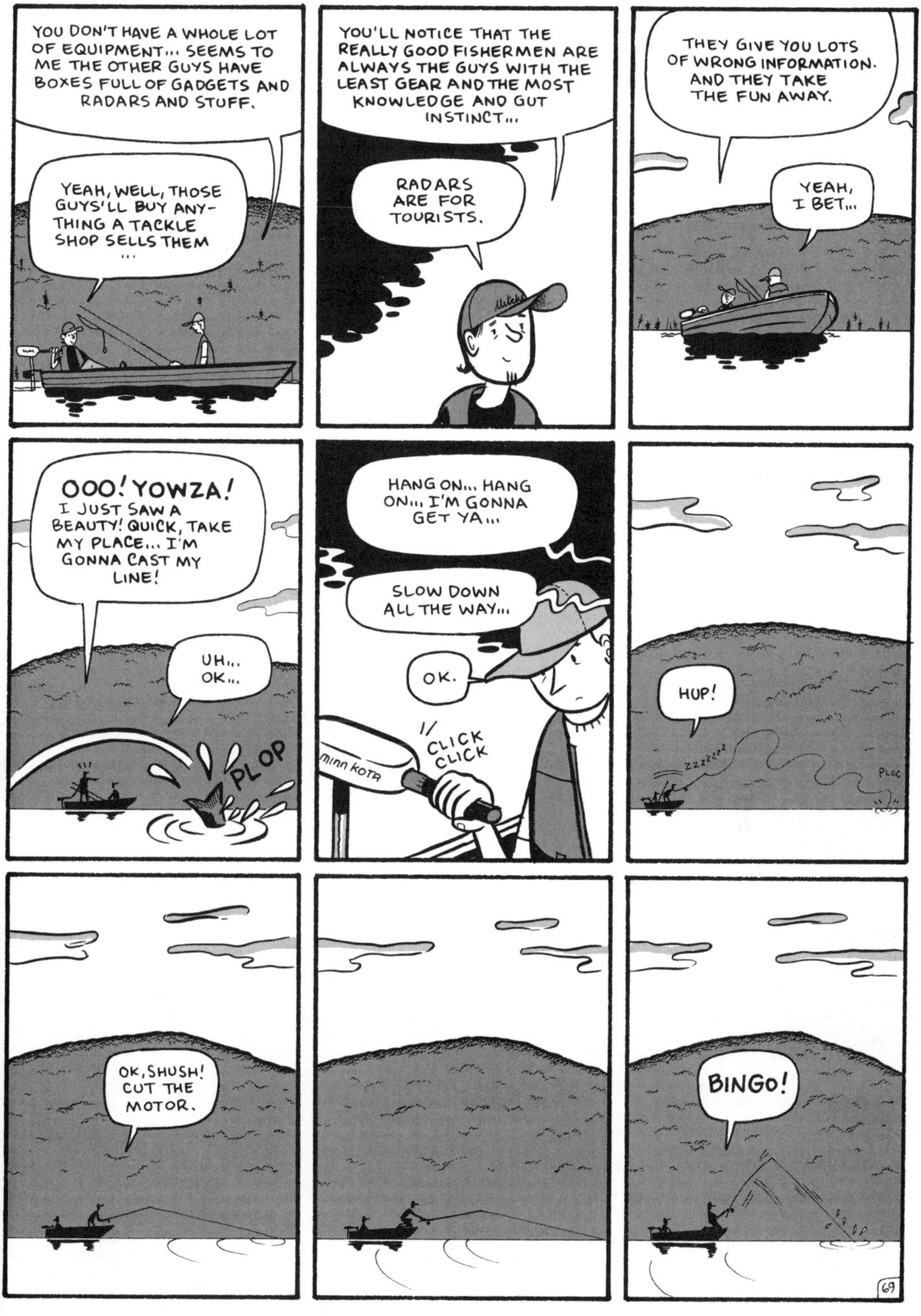
YOU DON'T HAVE A WHOLE LOT OF EQUIPMENT... SEEMS TO ME THE OTHER GUYS HAVE BOXES FULL OF GADGETS AND RADARS AND STUFF.
YEAH, WELL, THOSE GUYS'LL BUY ANYTHING A TACKLE SHOP SELLS THEM ...
YOU'LL NOTICE THAT THE REALLY GOOD FISHERMEN ARE ALWAYS THE GUYS WITH THE LEAST GEAR AND THE MOST KNOWLEDGE AND GUT INSTINCT...
RADARS ARE FOR TOURISTS.
THEY GIVE YOU LOTS OF WRONG INFORMATION. AND THEY TAKE THE FUN AWAY.
YEAH, I BET...
OOO! YOWZA! I JUST SAW A BEAUTY! QUICK, TAKE MY PLACE... I'M GONNA CAST MY LINE!
UH... OK...
PLOP
HANG ON... HANG ON... I'M GONNA GET YA...
SLOW DOWN ALL THE WAY...
OK.
CLICK CLICK
MINN KOTA
HUP!
ZZZZZZZ
PLOC
OK, SHUSH! CUT THE MOTOR.
BINGO!

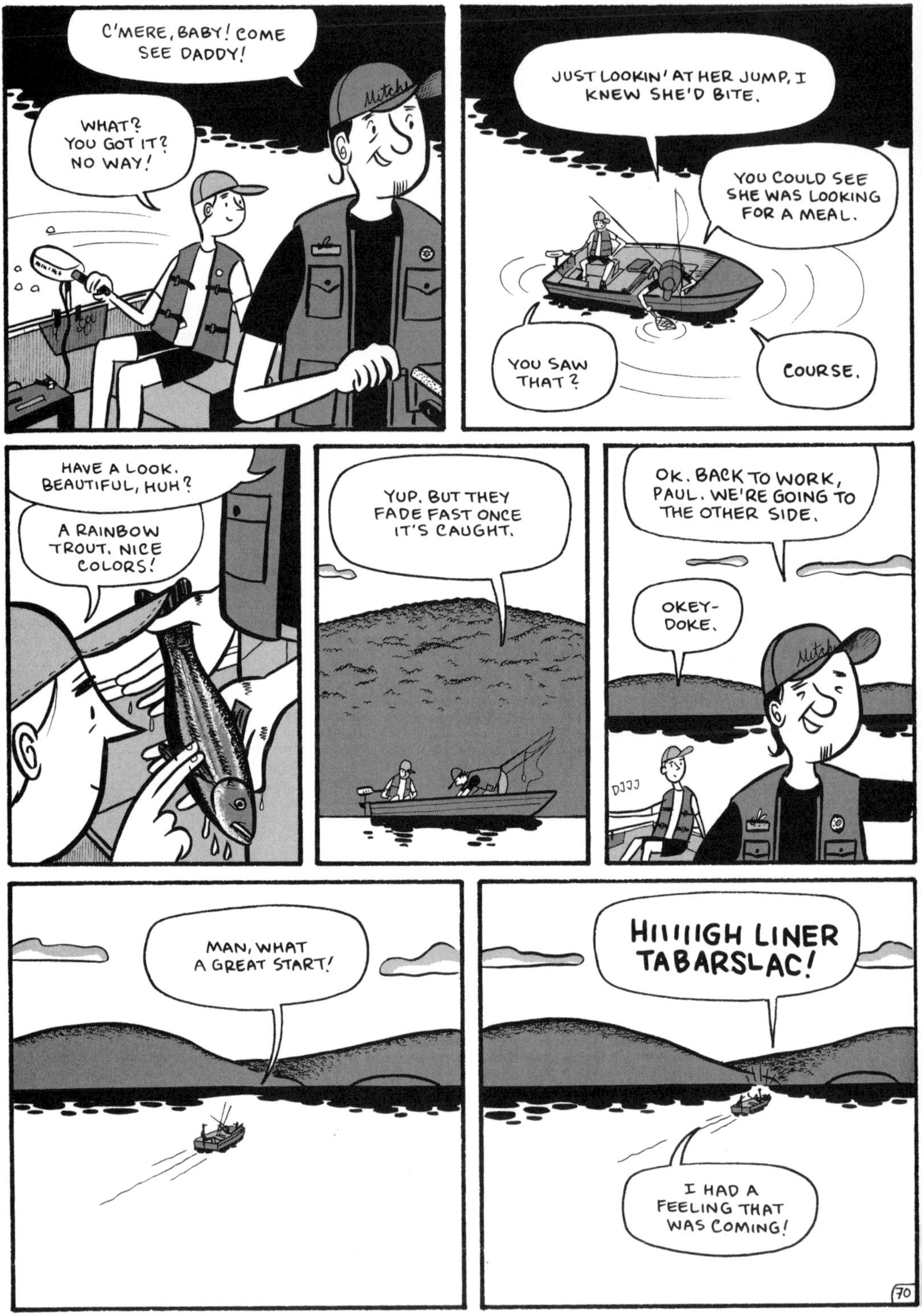
C'MERE, BABY! COME SEE DADDY!
WHAT? YOU GOT IT? NO WAY!
JUST LOOKIN' AT HER JUMP, I KNEW SHE'D BITE.
YOU COULD SEE SHE WAS LOOKING FOR A MEAL.
YOU SAW THAT?
COURSE.
HAVE A LOOK. BEAUTIFUL, HUH?
A RAINBOW TROUT. NICE COLORS!
YUP. BUT THEY FADE FAST ONCE IT'S CAUGHT.
OK. BACK TO WORK, PAUL. WE'RE GOING TO THE OTHER SIDE.
OKEY-DOKE.
DJJJ
MAN, WHAT A GREAT START!
HIIIIIGH LINER TABARSLAC!
I HAD A FEELING THAT WAS COMING!

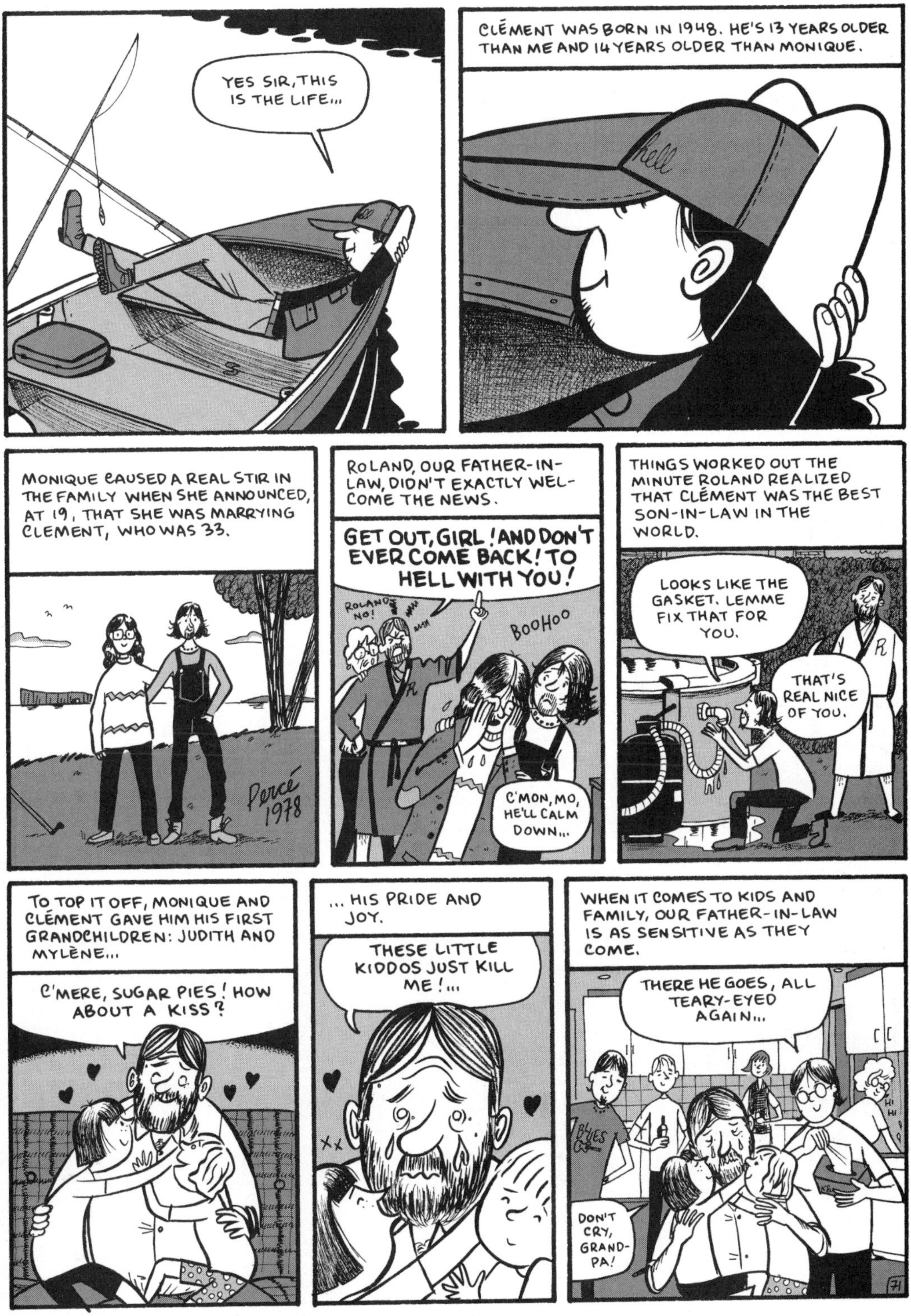
YES SIR, THIS IS THE LIFE...
CLÉMENT WAS BORN IN 1948. HE'S 13 YEARS OLDER THAN ME AND 14 YEARS OLDER THAN MONIQUE.
MONIQUE CAUSED A REAL STIR IN THE FAMILY WHEN SHE ANNOUNCED, AT 19, THAT SHE WAS MARRYING CLEMENT, WHO WAS 33.
Percé 1978
ROLAND, OUR FATHER-IN-LAW, DIDN'T EXACTLY WELCOME THE NEWS.
GET OUT, GIRL! AND DON'T EVER COME BACK! TO HELL WITH YOU!
ROLAND, NO!
BOOHOO
C'MON, MO, HE'LL CALM DOWN...
THINGS WORKED OUT THE MINUTE ROLAND REALIZED THAT CLÉMENT WAS THE BEST SON-IN-LAW IN THE WORLD.
LOOKS LIKE THE GASKET. LEMME FIX THAT FOR YOU.
THAT'S REAL NICE OF YOU.
TO TOP IT OFF, MONIQUE AND CLÉMENT GAVE HIM HIS FIRST GRANDCHILDREN: JUDITH AND MYLÈNE...
C'MERE, SUGAR PIES! HOW ABOUT A KISS?
... HIS PRIDE AND JOY.
THESE LITTLE KIDDOS JUST KILL ME!...
WHEN IT COMES TO KIDS AND FAMILY, OUR FATHER-IN-LAW IS AS SENSITIVE AS THEY COME.
THERE HE GOES, ALL TEARY-EYED AGAIN...
BLUES
HI HI
DON'T CRY, GRANDPA!

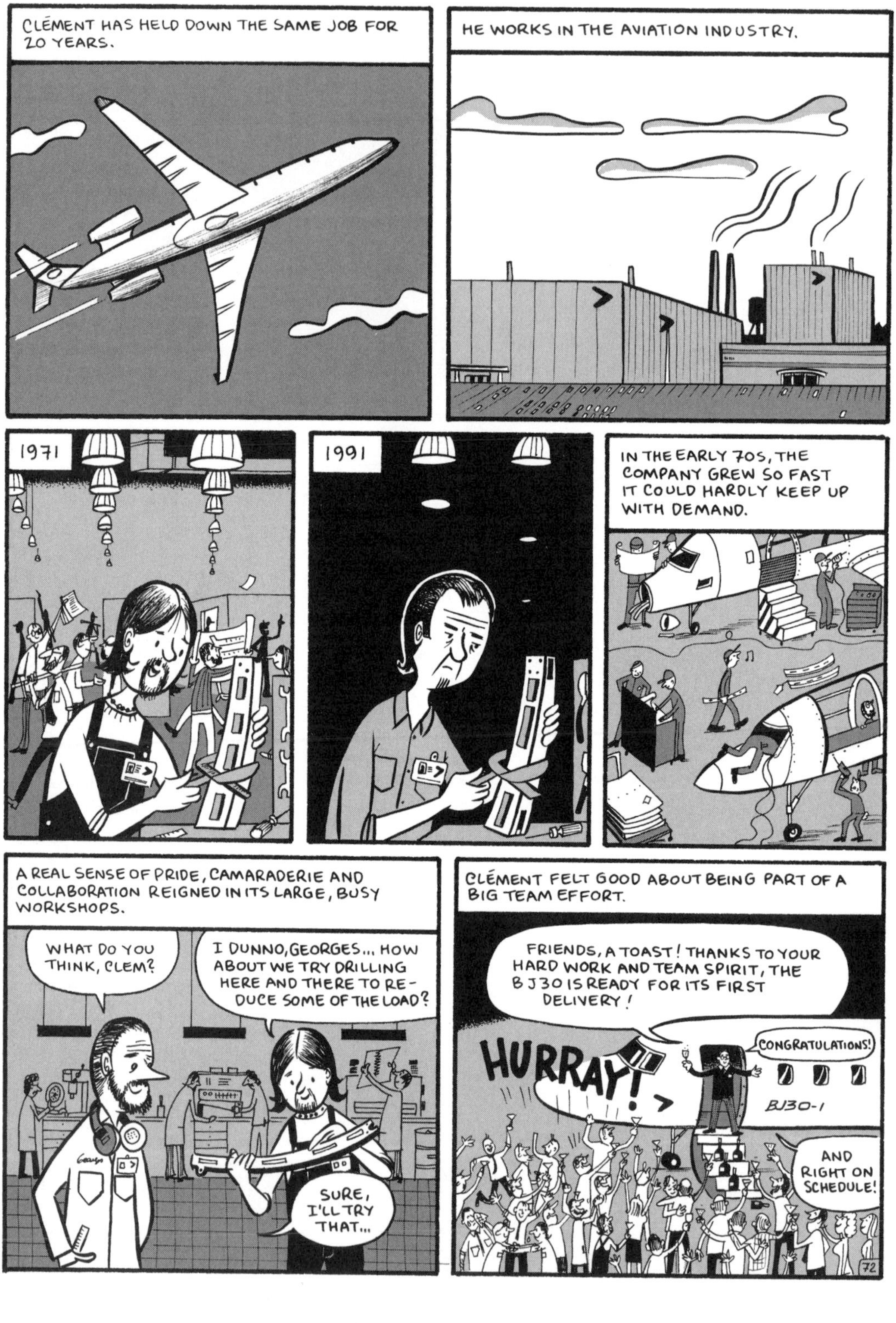

CLÉMENT HAS HELD DOWN THE SAME JOB FOR 20 YEARS.
HE WORKS IN THE AVIATION INDUSTRY.
1971
1991
IN THE EARLY 70S, THE COMPANY GREW SO FAST IT COULD HARDLY KEEP UP WITH DEMAND.
A REAL SENSE OF PRIDE, CAMARADERIE AND COLLABORATION REIGNED IN ITS LARGE, BUSY WORKSHOPS.
WHAT DO YOU THINK, CLEM?
I DUNNO, GEORGES... HOW ABOUT WE TRY DRILLING HERE AND THERE TO REDUCE SOME OF THE LOAD?
SURE, I'LL TRY THAT...
CLÉMENT FELT GOOD ABOUT BEING PART OF A BIG TEAM EFFORT.
FRIENDS, A TOAST! THANKS TO YOUR HARD WORK AND TEAM SPIRIT, THE BJ30 IS READY FOR ITS FIRST DELIVERY!
CONGRATULATIONS!
HURRAY!
BJ30-1
AND RIGHT ON SCHEDULE!

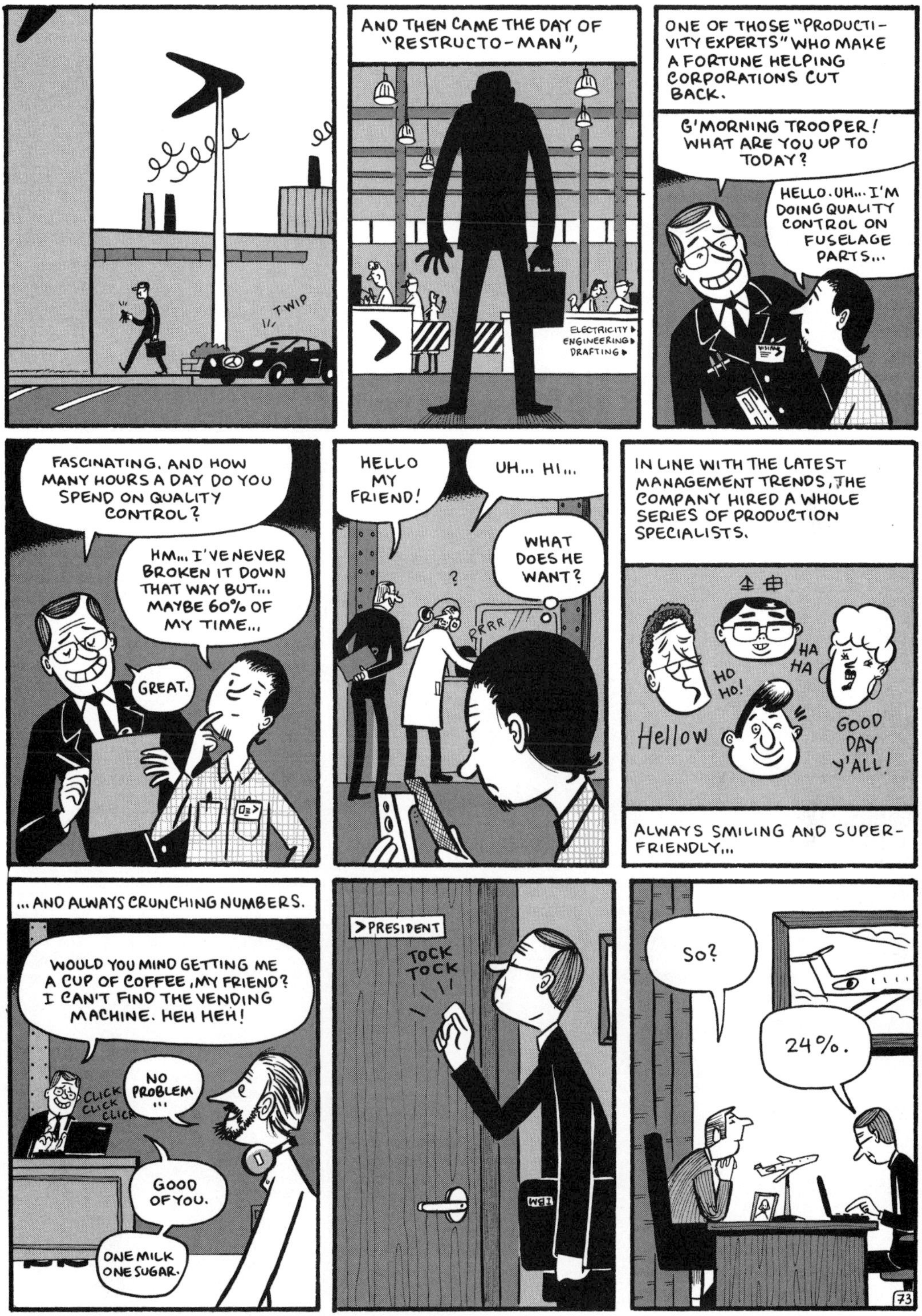
TWIP
AND THEN CAME THE DAY OF "RESTRUCTO-MAN",
ELECTRICITY ▸
ENGINEERING ▸
DRAFTING ▸
ONE OF THOSE "PRODUCTIVITY EXPERTS" WHO MAKE A FORTUNE HELPING CORPORATIONS CUT BACK.
G'MORNING TROOPER! WHAT ARE YOU UP TO TODAY?
HELLO. UH... I'M DOING QUALITY CONTROL ON FUSELAGE PARTS...
FASCINATING. AND HOW MANY HOURS A DAY DO YOU SPEND ON QUALITY CONTROL?
HM... I'VE NEVER BROKEN IT DOWN THAT WAY BUT... MAYBE 60% OF MY TIME...
GREAT.
HELLO MY FRIEND!
UH... HI...
WHAT DOES HE WANT?
?
RRRR
IN LINE WITH THE LATEST MANAGEMENT TRENDS, THE COMPANY HIRED A WHOLE SERIES OF PRODUCTION SPECIALISTS.
HO HO!
HA HA
Hellow
GOOD DAY Y'ALL!
ALWAYS SMILING AND SUPER-FRIENDLY...
... AND ALWAYS CRUNCHING NUMBERS.
WOULD YOU MIND GETTING ME A CUP OF COFFEE, MY FRIEND? I CAN'T FIND THE VENDING MACHINE. HEH HEH!
CLICK CLICK CLICK
NO PROBLEM ...
GOOD OF YOU.
ONE MILK ONE SUGAR.
> PRESIDENT
TOCK TOCK
SO?
24%.

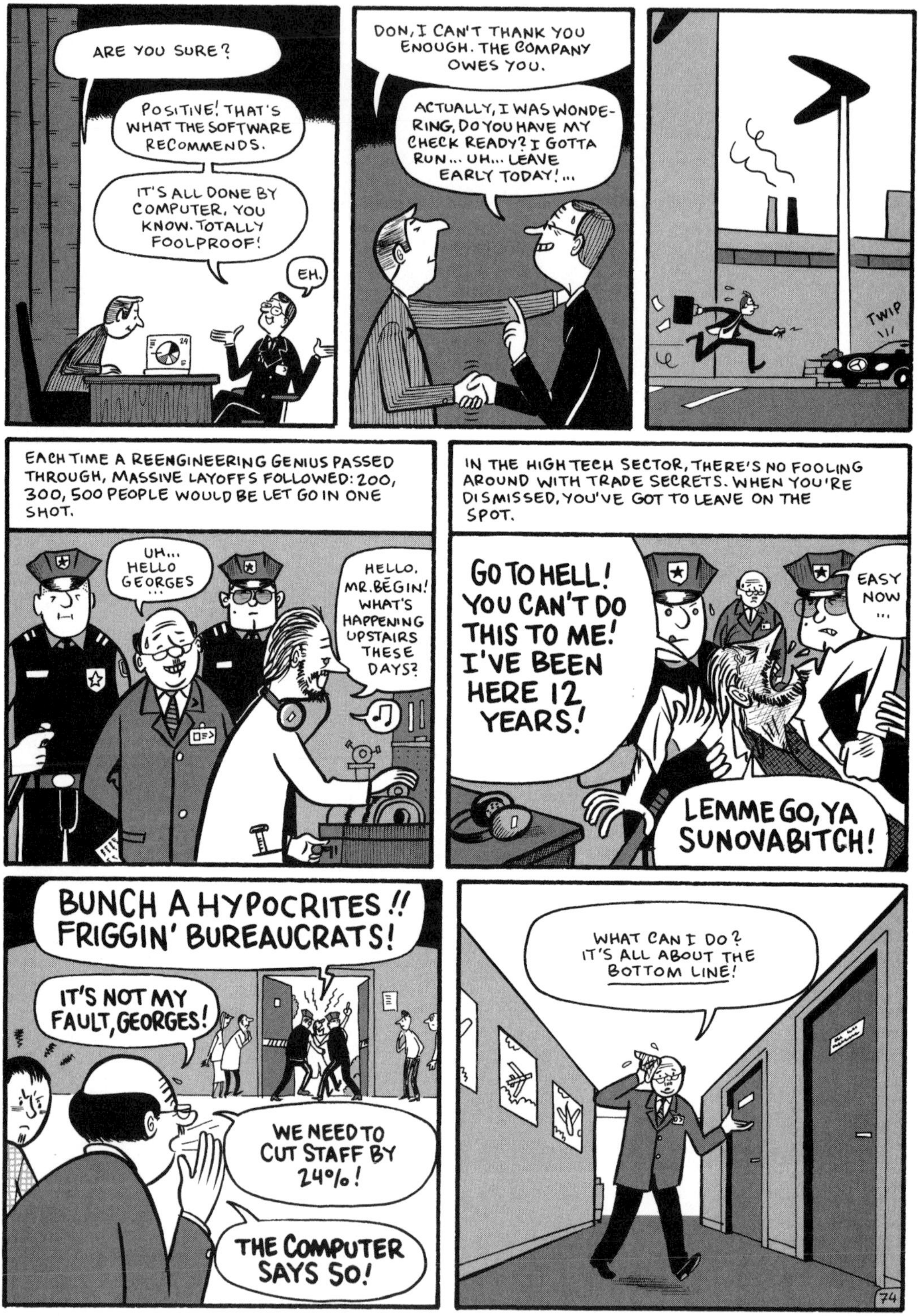

ARE YOU SURE?
POSITIVE! THAT'S WHAT THE SOFTWARE RECOMMENDS.
IT'S ALL DONE BY COMPUTER, YOU KNOW. TOTALLY FOOLPROOF!
EH.
DON, I CAN'T THANK YOU ENOUGH. THE COMPANY OWES YOU.
ACTUALLY, I WAS WONDERING, DO YOU HAVE MY CHECK READY? I GOTTA RUN... UH... LEAVE EARLY TODAY!...
TWIP
EACH TIME A REENGINEERING GENIUS PASSED THROUGH, MASSIVE LAYOFFS FOLLOWED: 200, 300, 500 PEOPLE WOULD BE LET GO IN ONE SHOT.
UH... HELLO GEORGES ...
HELLO, MR. BÉGIN! WHAT'S HAPPENING UPSTAIRS THESE DAYS?
IN THE HIGH TECH SECTOR, THERE'S NO FOOLING AROUND WITH TRADE SECRETS. WHEN YOU'RE DISMISSED, YOU'VE GOT TO LEAVE ON THE SPOT.
GO TO HELL! YOU CAN'T DO THIS TO ME! I'VE BEEN HERE 12 YEARS!
EASY NOW ...
LEMME GO, YA SUNOVABITCH!
BUNCH A HYPOCRITES!! FRIGGIN' BUREAUCRATS!
IT'S NOT MY FAULT, GEORGES!
WE NEED TO CUT STAFF BY 24%!
THE COMPUTER SAYS SO!
WHAT CAN I DO? IT'S ALL ABOUT THE BOTTOM LINE!

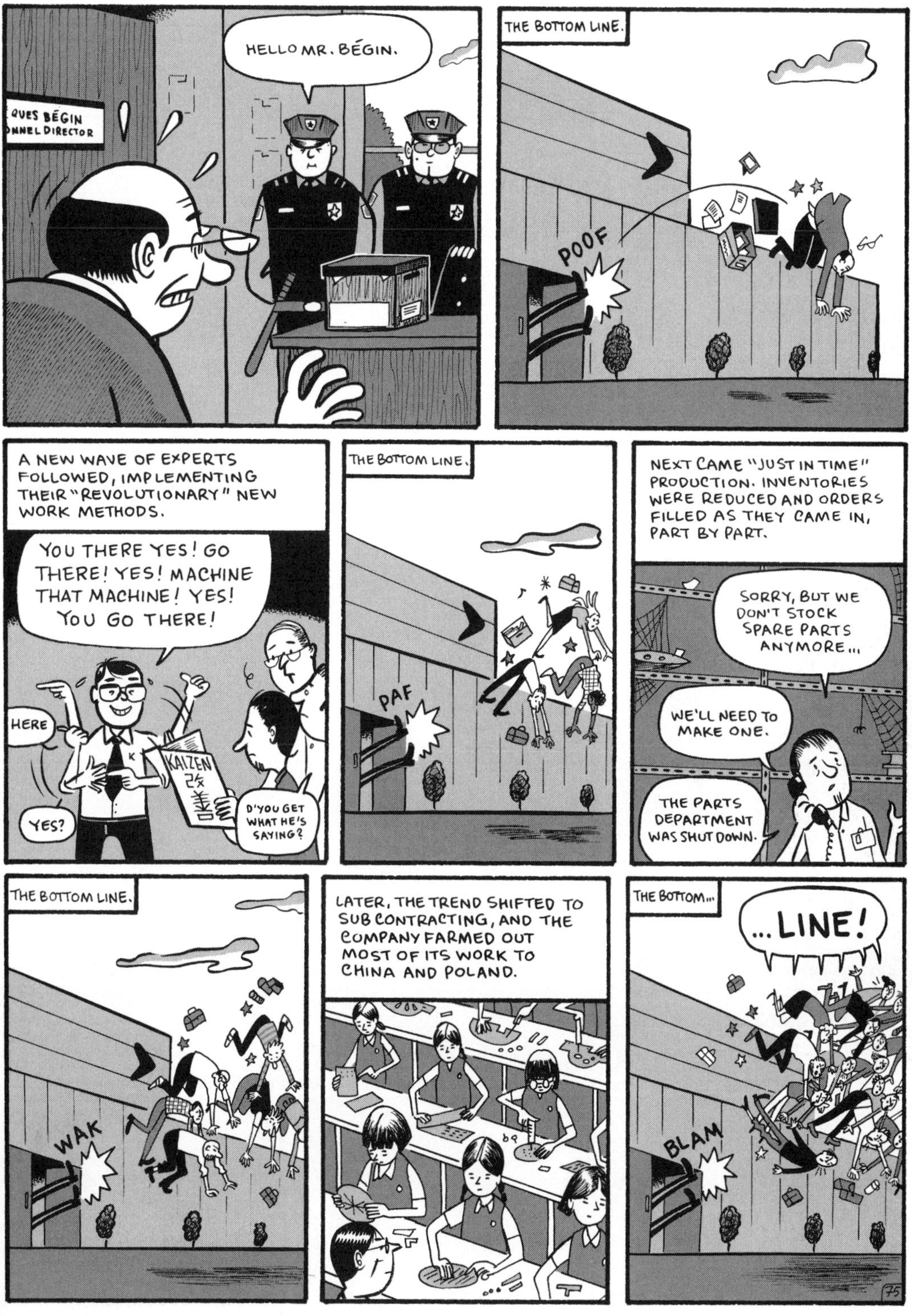
…QUES BÉGIN
…NNEL DIRECTOR
HELLO MR. BÉGIN.
THE BOTTOM LINE.
POOF
A NEW WAVE OF EXPERTS FOLLOWED, IMPLEMENTING THEIR "REVOLUTIONARY" NEW WORK METHODS.
YOU THERE YES! GO THERE! YES! MACHINE THAT MACHINE! YES! YOU GO THERE!
HERE
YES?
KAIZEN
改善
D'YOU GET WHAT HE'S SAYING?
THE BOTTOM LINE.
PAF
NEXT CAME "JUST IN TIME" PRODUCTION. INVENTORIES WERE REDUCED AND ORDERS FILLED AS THEY CAME IN, PART BY PART.
SORRY, BUT WE DON'T STOCK SPARE PARTS ANYMORE...
WE'LL NEED TO MAKE ONE.
THE PARTS DEPARTMENT WAS SHUT DOWN.
THE BOTTOM LINE.
WAK
LATER, THE TREND SHIFTED TO SUBCONTRACTING, AND THE COMPANY FARMED OUT MOST OF ITS WORK TO CHINA AND POLAND.
THE BOTTOM...
...LINE!
BLAM

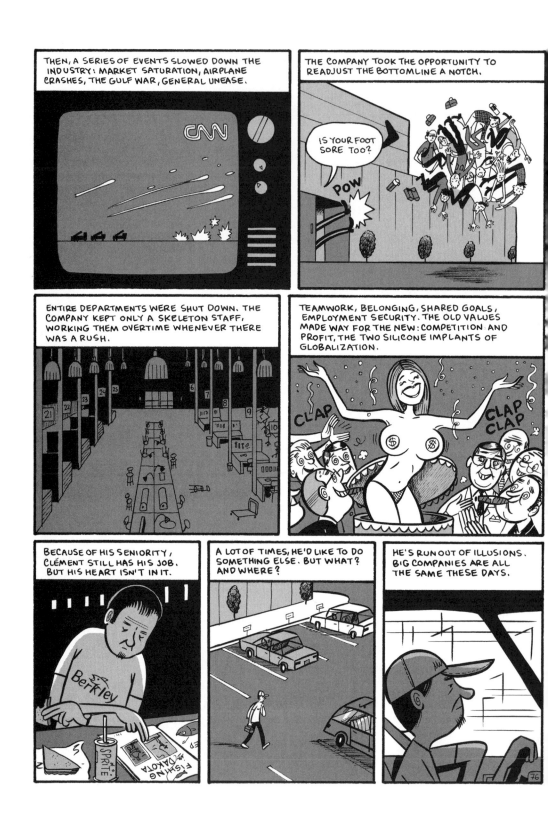

THEN, A SERIES OF EVENTS SLOWED DOWN THE INDUSTRY: MARKET SATURATION, AIRPLANE CRASHES, THE GULF WAR, GENERAL UNEASE.

THE COMPANY TOOK THE OPPORTUNITY TO READJUST THE BOTTOMLINE A NOTCH.

IS YOUR FOOT SORE TOO?

POW

ENTIRE DEPARTMENTS WERE SHUT DOWN. THE COMPANY KEPT ONLY A SKELETON STAFF, WORKING THEM OVERTIME WHENEVER THERE WAS A RUSH.

TEAMWORK, BELONGING, SHARED GOALS, EMPLOYMENT SECURITY. THE OLD VALUES MADE WAY FOR THE NEW: COMPETITION AND PROFIT, THE TWO SILICONE IMPLANTS OF GLOBALIZATION.

CLAP

CLAP CLAP

BECAUSE OF HIS SENIORITY, CLÉMENT STILL HAS HIS JOB, BUT HIS HEART ISN'T IN IT.

Berkley

A LOT OF TIMES, HE'D LIKE TO DO SOMETHING ELSE. BUT WHAT? AND WHERE?

HE'S RUN OUT OF ILLUSIONS. BIG COMPANIES ARE ALL THE SAME THESE DAYS.

76

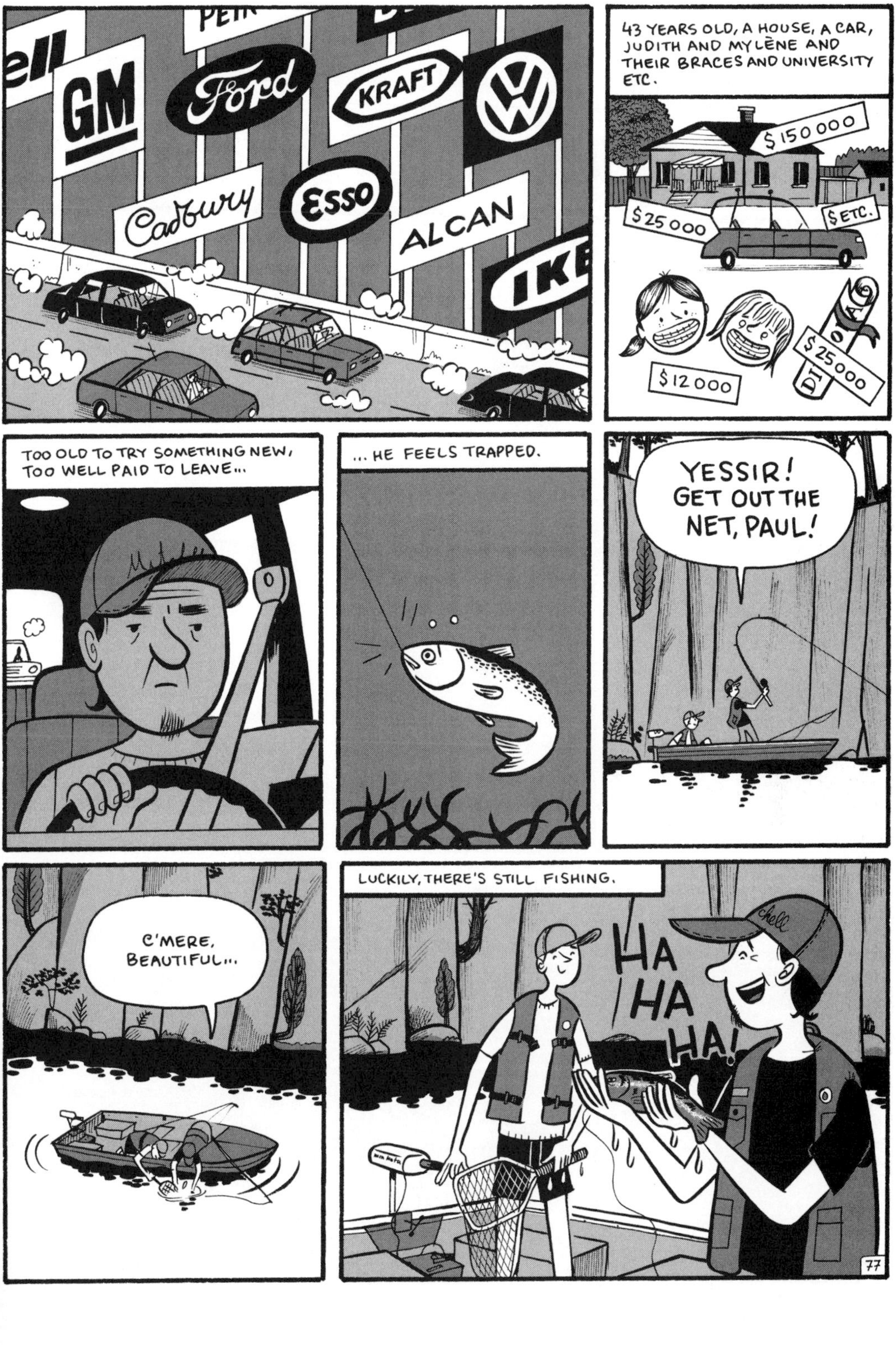
GM
Ford
KRAFT
Cadbury
ESSO
ALCAN
43 YEARS OLD, A HOUSE, A CAR, JUDITH AND MYLÈNE AND THEIR BRACES AND UNIVERSITY ETC.
$150 000
$25 000
$ ETC.
$12 000
$25 000
TOO OLD TO TRY SOMETHING NEW, TOO WELL PAID TO LEAVE...
... HE FEELS TRAPPED.
YESSIR! GET OUT THE NET, PAUL!
C'MERE, BEAUTIFUL...
LUCKILY, THERE'S STILL FISHING.
HA HA HA!

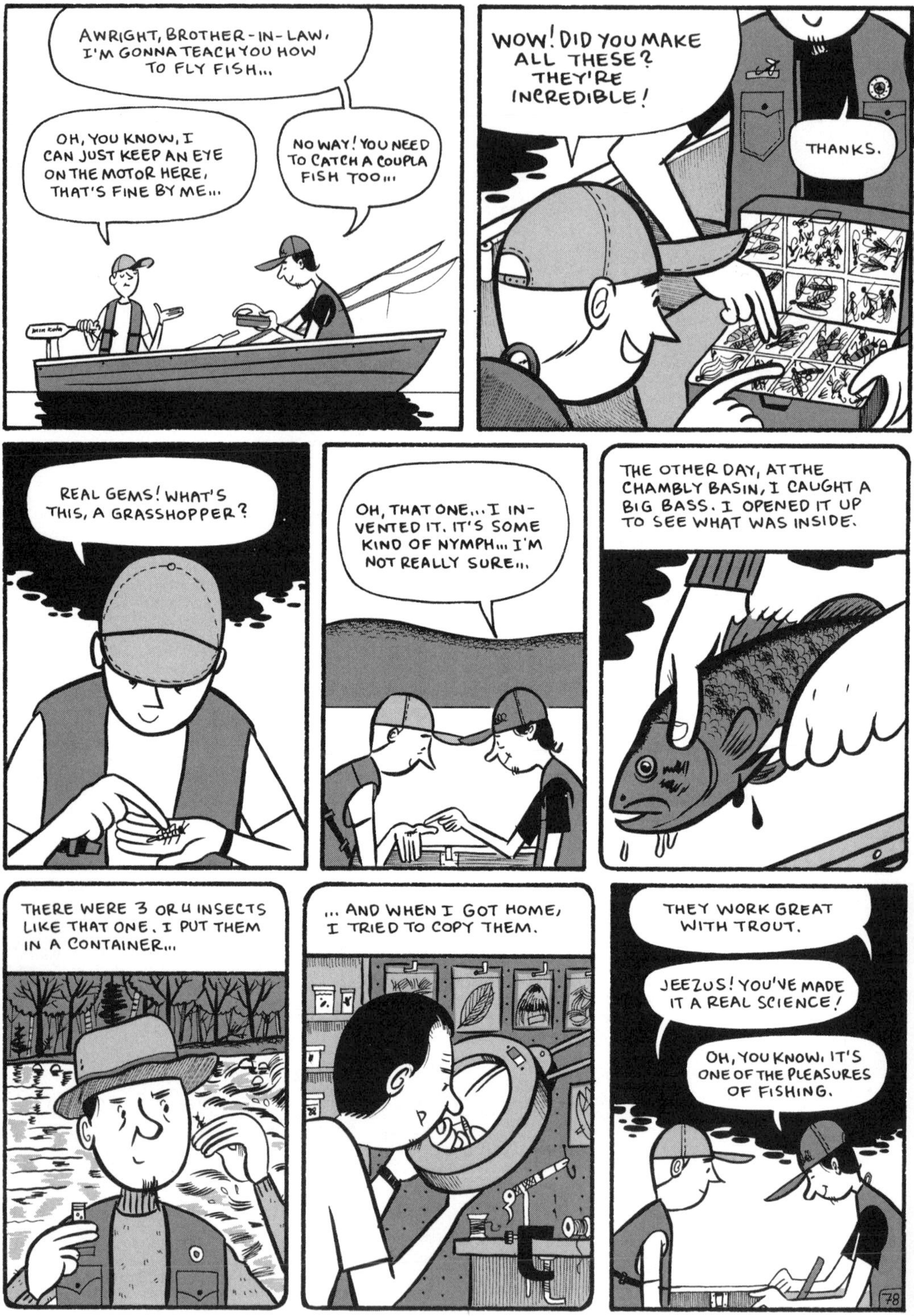
AWRIGHT, BROTHER-IN-LAW, I'M GONNA TEACH YOU HOW TO FLY FISH...
OH, YOU KNOW, I CAN JUST KEEP AN EYE ON THE MOTOR HERE, THAT'S FINE BY ME...
NO WAY! YOU NEED TO CATCH A COUPLA FISH TOO...
WOW! DID YOU MAKE ALL THESE? THEY'RE INCREDIBLE!
THANKS.
REAL GEMS! WHAT'S THIS, A GRASSHOPPER?
OH, THAT ONE... I IN-VENTED IT. IT'S SOME KIND OF NYMPH... I'M NOT REALLY SURE...
THE OTHER DAY, AT THE CHAMBLY BASIN, I CAUGHT A BIG BASS. I OPENED IT UP TO SEE WHAT WAS INSIDE.
THERE WERE 3 OR 4 INSECTS LIKE THAT ONE. I PUT THEM IN A CONTAINER...
... AND WHEN I GOT HOME, I TRIED TO COPY THEM.
THEY WORK GREAT WITH TROUT.
JEEZUS! YOU'VE MADE IT A REAL SCIENCE!
OH, YOU KNOW, IT'S ONE OF THE PLEASURES OF FISHING.
78

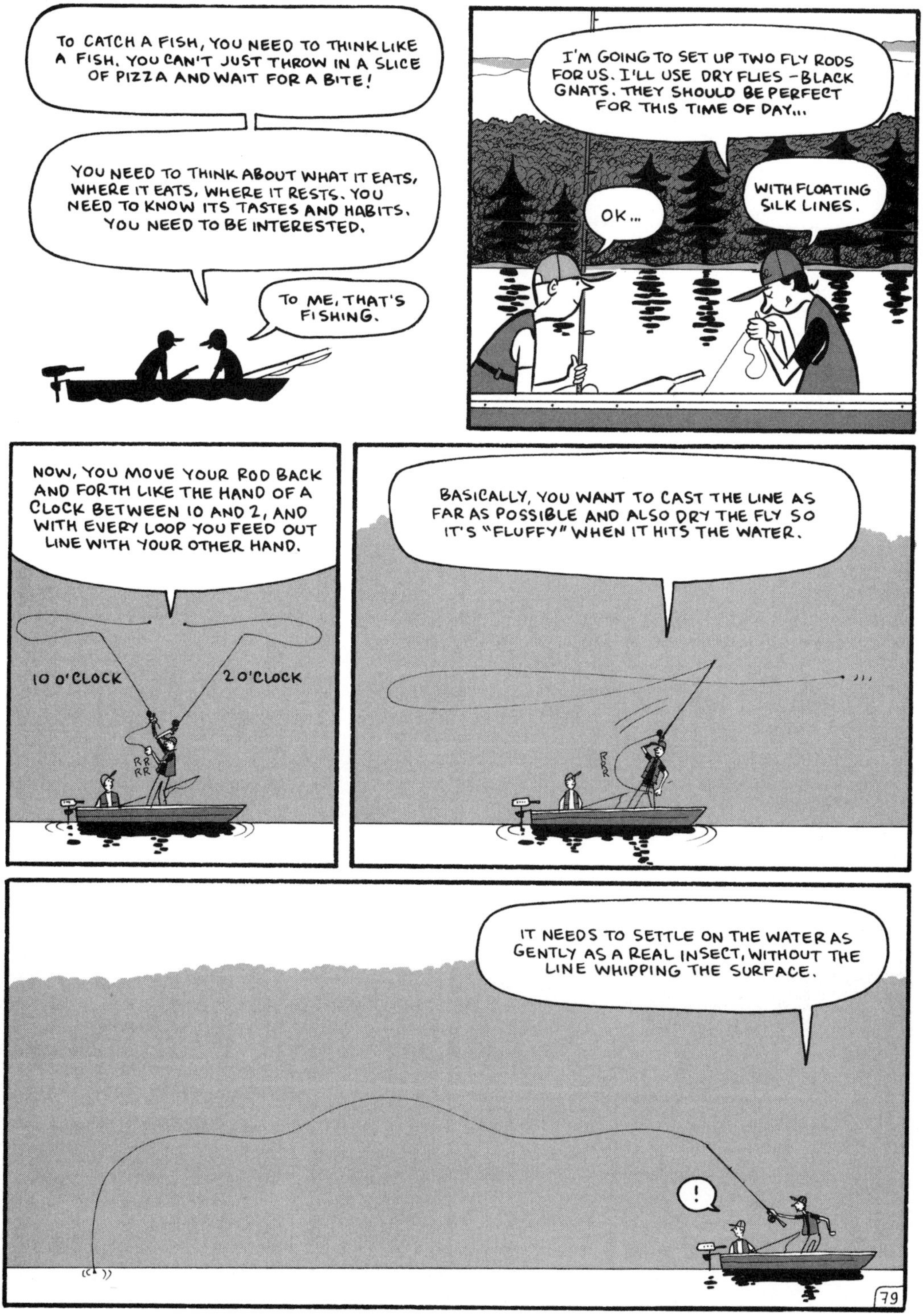
TO CATCH A FISH, YOU NEED TO THINK LIKE A FISH. YOU CAN'T JUST THROW IN A SLICE OF PIZZA AND WAIT FOR A BITE!
YOU NEED TO THINK ABOUT WHAT IT EATS, WHERE IT EATS, WHERE IT RESTS. YOU NEED TO KNOW ITS TASTES AND HABITS. YOU NEED TO BE INTERESTED.
TO ME, THAT'S FISHING.
I'M GOING TO SET UP TWO FLY RODS FOR US. I'LL USE DRY FLIES - BLACK GNATS. THEY SHOULD BE PERFECT FOR THIS TIME OF DAY...
OK...
WITH FLOATING SILK LINES.
NOW, YOU MOVE YOUR ROD BACK AND FORTH LIKE THE HAND OF A CLOCK BETWEEN 10 AND 2, AND WITH EVERY LOOP YOU FEED OUT LINE WITH YOUR OTHER HAND.
10 O'CLOCK
2 O'CLOCK
RR RR
BASICALLY, YOU WANT TO CAST THE LINE AS FAR AS POSSIBLE AND ALSO DRY THE FLY SO IT'S "FLUFFY" WHEN IT HITS THE WATER.
RRR
IT NEEDS TO SETTLE ON THE WATER AS GENTLY AS A REAL INSECT, WITHOUT THE LINE WHIPPING THE SURFACE.
!

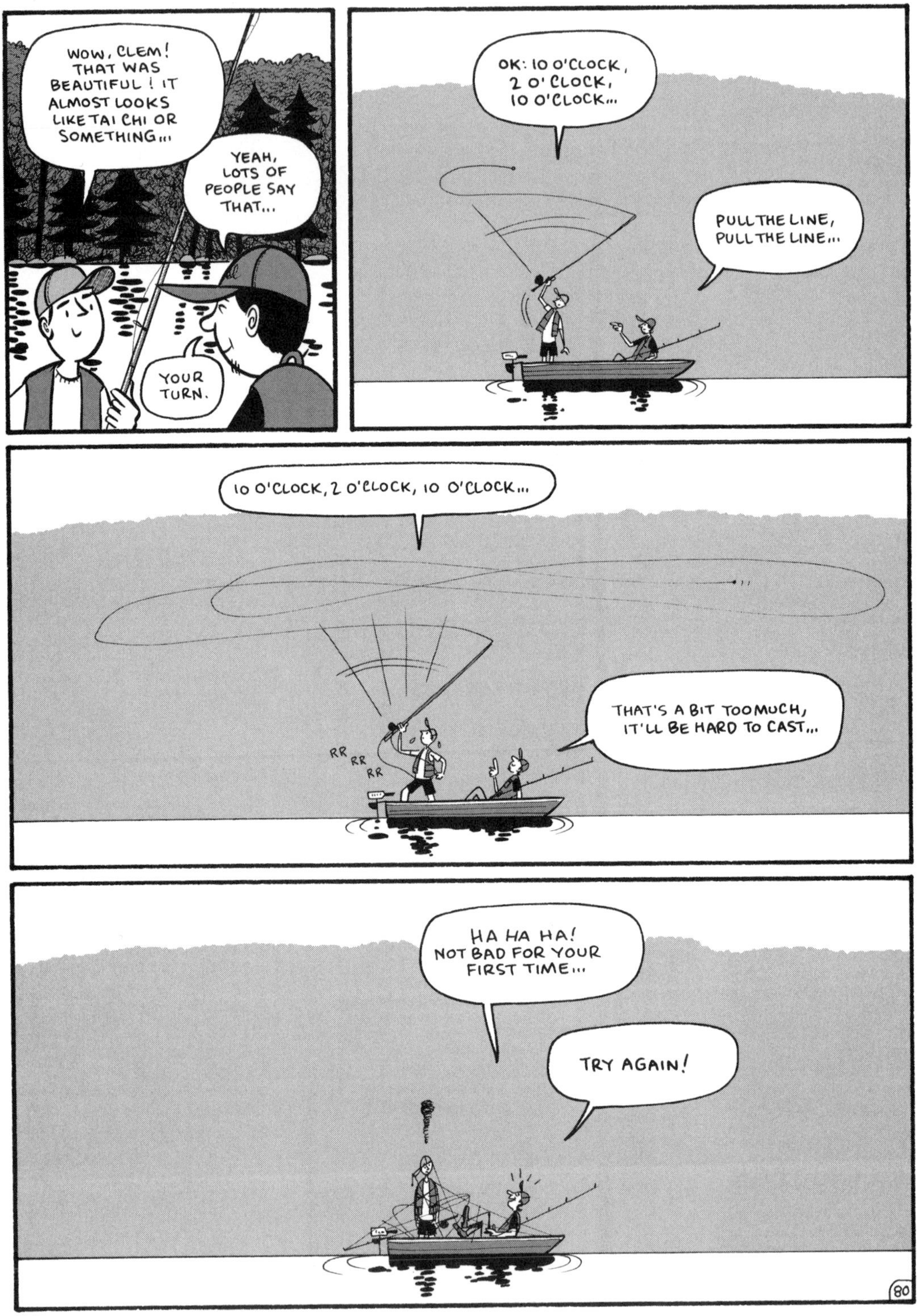
WOW, CLEM! THAT WAS BEAUTIFUL! IT ALMOST LOOKS LIKE TAI CHI OR SOMETHING...
YEAH, LOTS OF PEOPLE SAY THAT...
YOUR TURN.
OK: 10 O'CLOCK, 2 O'CLOCK, 10 O'CLOCK...
PULL THE LINE, PULL THE LINE...
10 O'CLOCK, 2 O'CLOCK, 10 O'CLOCK...
THAT'S A BIT TOO MUCH, IT'LL BE HARD TO CAST...
RR RR RR
HA HA HA! NOT BAD FOR YOUR FIRST TIME...
TRY AGAIN!

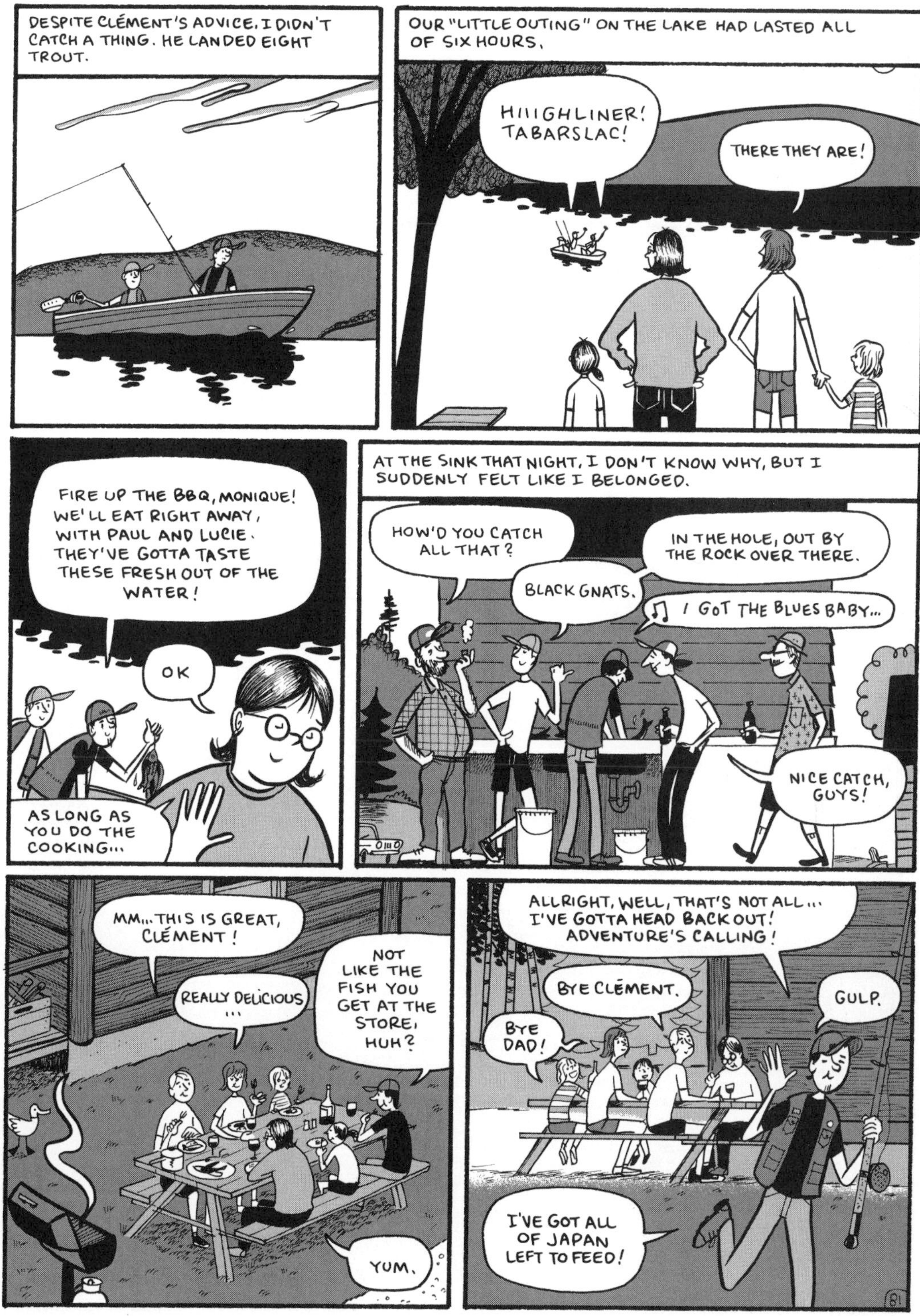
DESPITE CLÉMENT'S ADVICE, I DIDN'T CATCH A THING. HE LANDED EIGHT TROUT.
OUR "LITTLE OUTING" ON THE LAKE HAD LASTED ALL OF SIX HOURS.
HIIIGHLINER! TABARSLAC!
THERE THEY ARE!
FIRE UP THE BBQ, MONIQUE! WE'LL EAT RIGHT AWAY, WITH PAUL AND LUCIE. THEY'VE GOTTA TASTE THESE FRESH OUT OF THE WATER!
OK
AS LONG AS YOU DO THE COOKING...
AT THE SINK THAT NIGHT, I DON'T KNOW WHY, BUT I SUDDENLY FELT LIKE I BELONGED.
HOW'D YOU CATCH ALL THAT?
BLACK GNATS.
IN THE HOLE, OUT BY THE ROCK OVER THERE.
♫ I GOT THE BLUES BABY...
NICE CATCH, GUYS!
MM... THIS IS GREAT, CLÉMENT!
REALLY DELICIOUS...
NOT LIKE THE FISH YOU GET AT THE STORE, HUH?
YUM.
ALLRIGHT, WELL, THAT'S NOT ALL... I'VE GOTTA HEAD BACK OUT! ADVENTURE'S CALLING!
BYE CLÉMENT.
BYE DAD!
GULP.
I'VE GOT ALL OF JAPAN LEFT TO FEED!

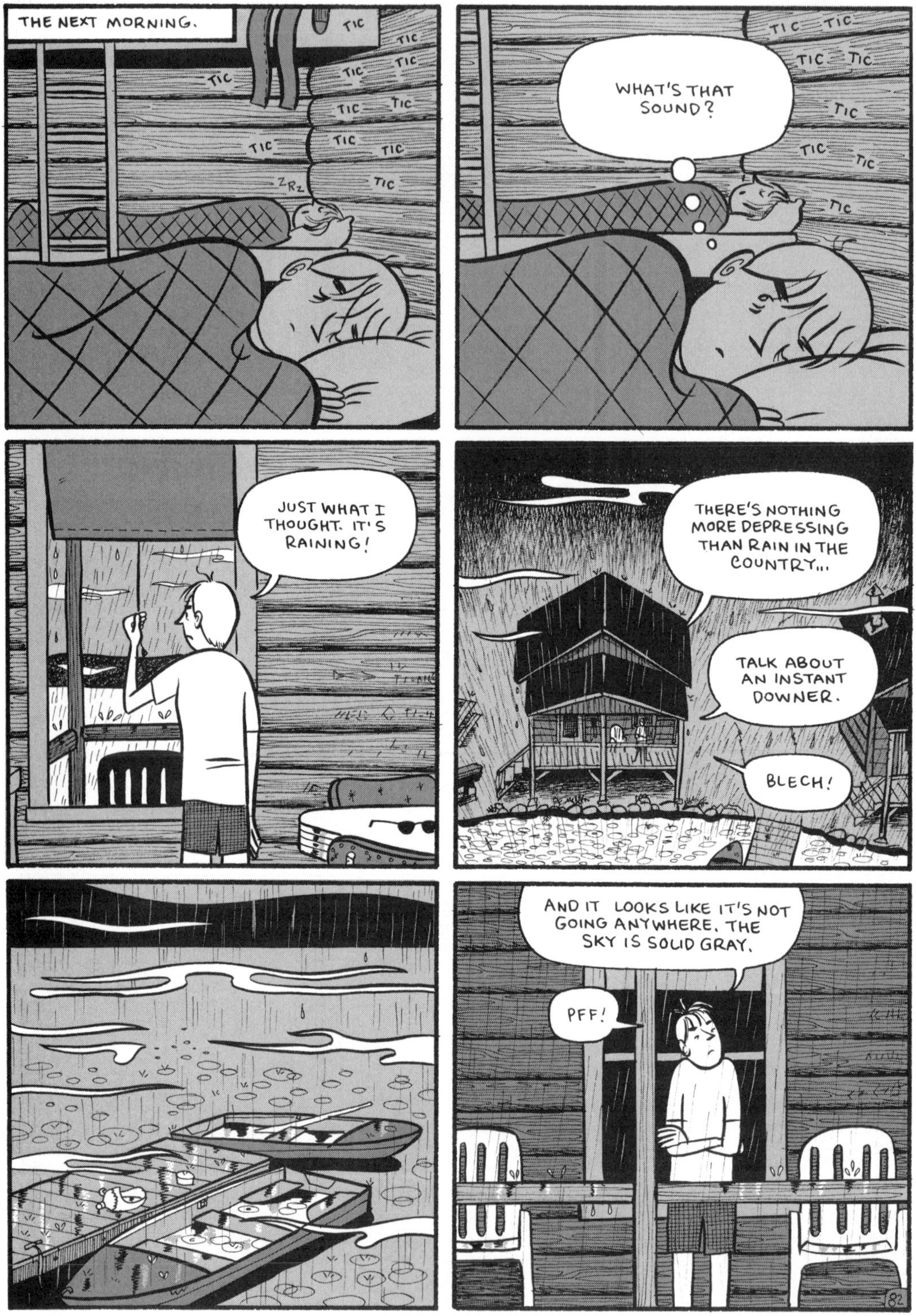
THE NEXT MORNING.
TIC TIC TIC TIC TIC TIC TIC TIC TIC TIC TIC
ZRZ
WHAT'S THAT SOUND?
TIC TIC TIC TIC TIC TIC TIC TIC
JUST WHAT I THOUGHT. IT'S RAINING!
THERE'S NOTHING MORE DEPRESSING THAN RAIN IN THE COUNTRY...
TALK ABOUT AN INSTANT DOWNER.
BLECH!
AND IT LOOKS LIKE IT'S NOT GOING ANYWHERE. THE SKY IS SOLID GRAY.
PFF!
82

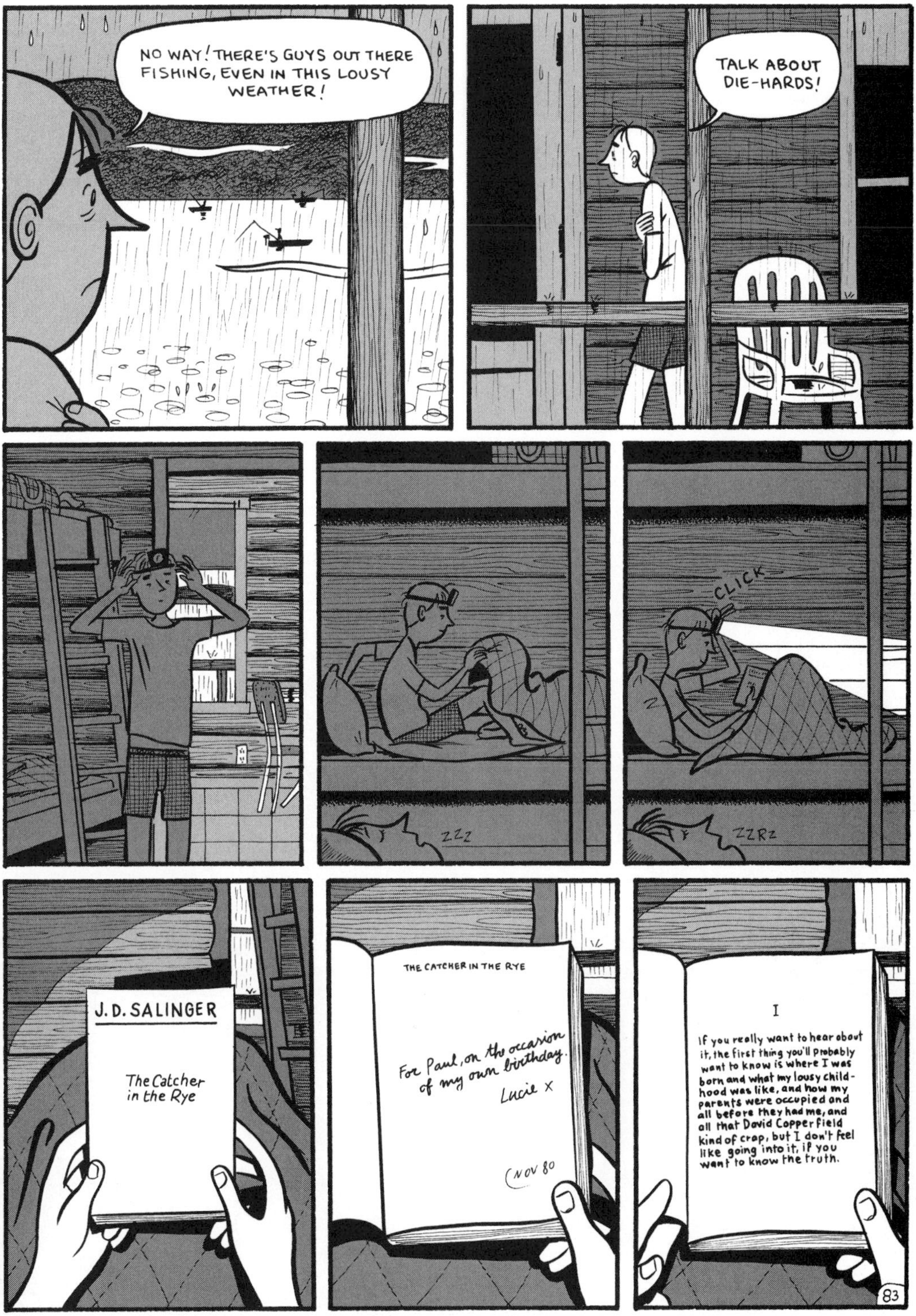
NO WAY! THERE'S GUYS OUT THERE FISHING, EVEN IN THIS LOUSY WEATHER!
TALK ABOUT DIE-HARDS!
ZZZ
CLICK
ZZRZ
J. D. SALINGER
The Catcher in the Rye
THE CATCHER IN THE RYE
For Paul, on the occasion of my own birthday.
Lucie x
NOV 80
I
If you really want to hear about it, the first thing you'll probably want to know is where I was born and what my lousy childhood was like, and how my parents were occupied and all before they had me, and all that David Copperfield kind of crap, but I don't feel like going into it, if you want to know the truth.
83

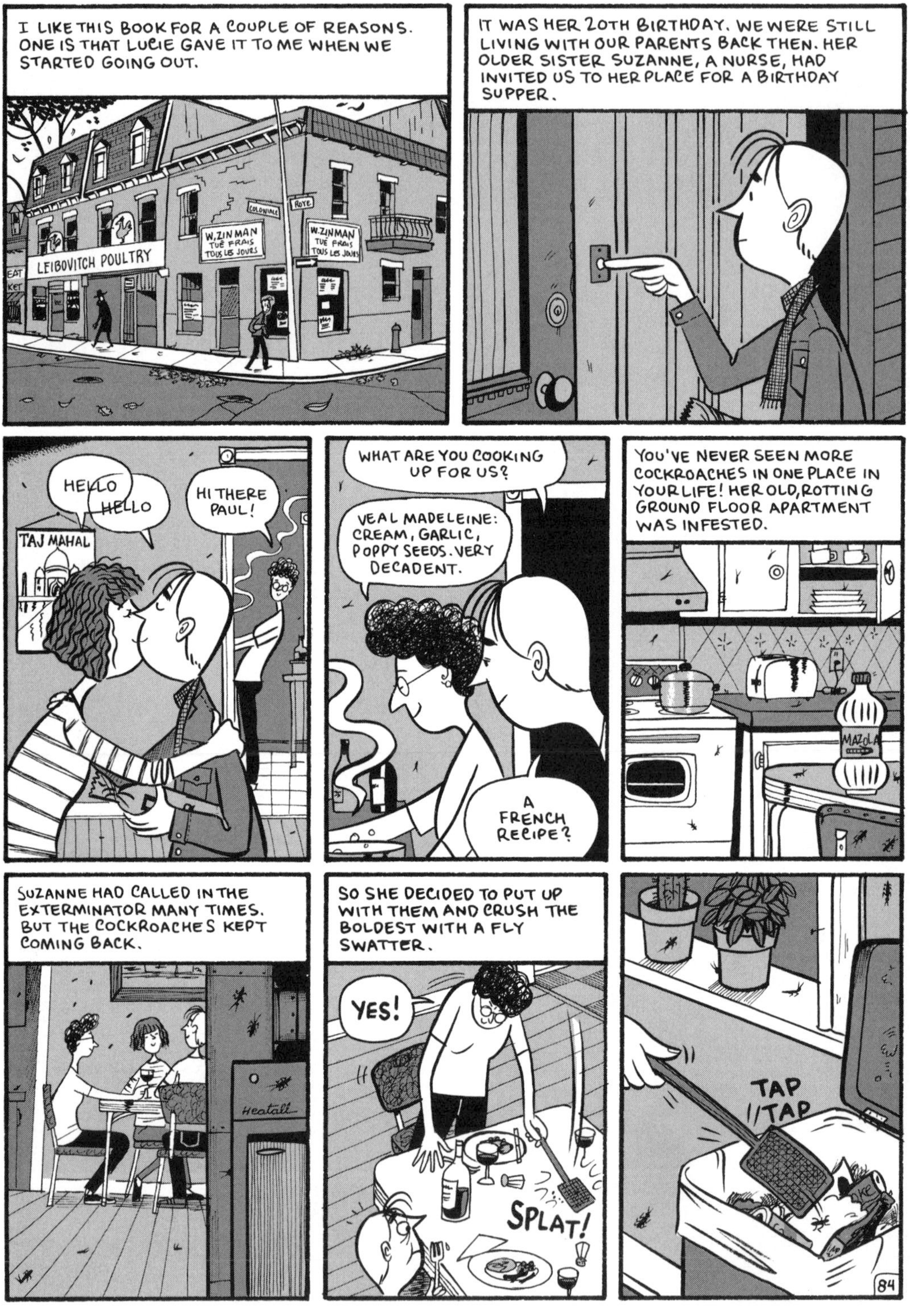
I LIKE THIS BOOK FOR A COUPLE OF REASONS. ONE IS THAT LUCIE GAVE IT TO ME WHEN WE STARTED GOING OUT.
COLONIALE
ROYE
LEIBOVITCH POULTRY
W. ZINMAN TUÉ FRAIS TOUS LES JOURS
W. ZINMAN TUÉ FRAIS TOUS LES JOURS
IT WAS HER 20TH BIRTHDAY. WE WERE STILL LIVING WITH OUR PARENTS BACK THEN. HER OLDER SISTER SUZANNE, A NURSE, HAD INVITED US TO HER PLACE FOR A BIRTHDAY SUPPER.
HELLO
HELLO
HI THERE PAUL!
TAJ MAHAL
WHAT ARE YOU COOKING UP FOR US?
VEAL MADELEINE: CREAM, GARLIC, POPPY SEEDS. VERY DECADENT.
A FRENCH RECIPE?
YOU'VE NEVER SEEN MORE COCKROACHES IN ONE PLACE IN YOUR LIFE! HER OLD, ROTTING GROUND FLOOR APARTMENT WAS INFESTED.
MAZOLA
SUZANNE HAD CALLED IN THE EXTERMINATOR MANY TIMES. BUT THE COCKROACHES KEPT COMING BACK.
Heatall
SO SHE DECIDED TO PUT UP WITH THEM AND CRUSH THE BOLDEST WITH A FLY SWATTER.
YES!
SPLAT!
TAP TAP
84

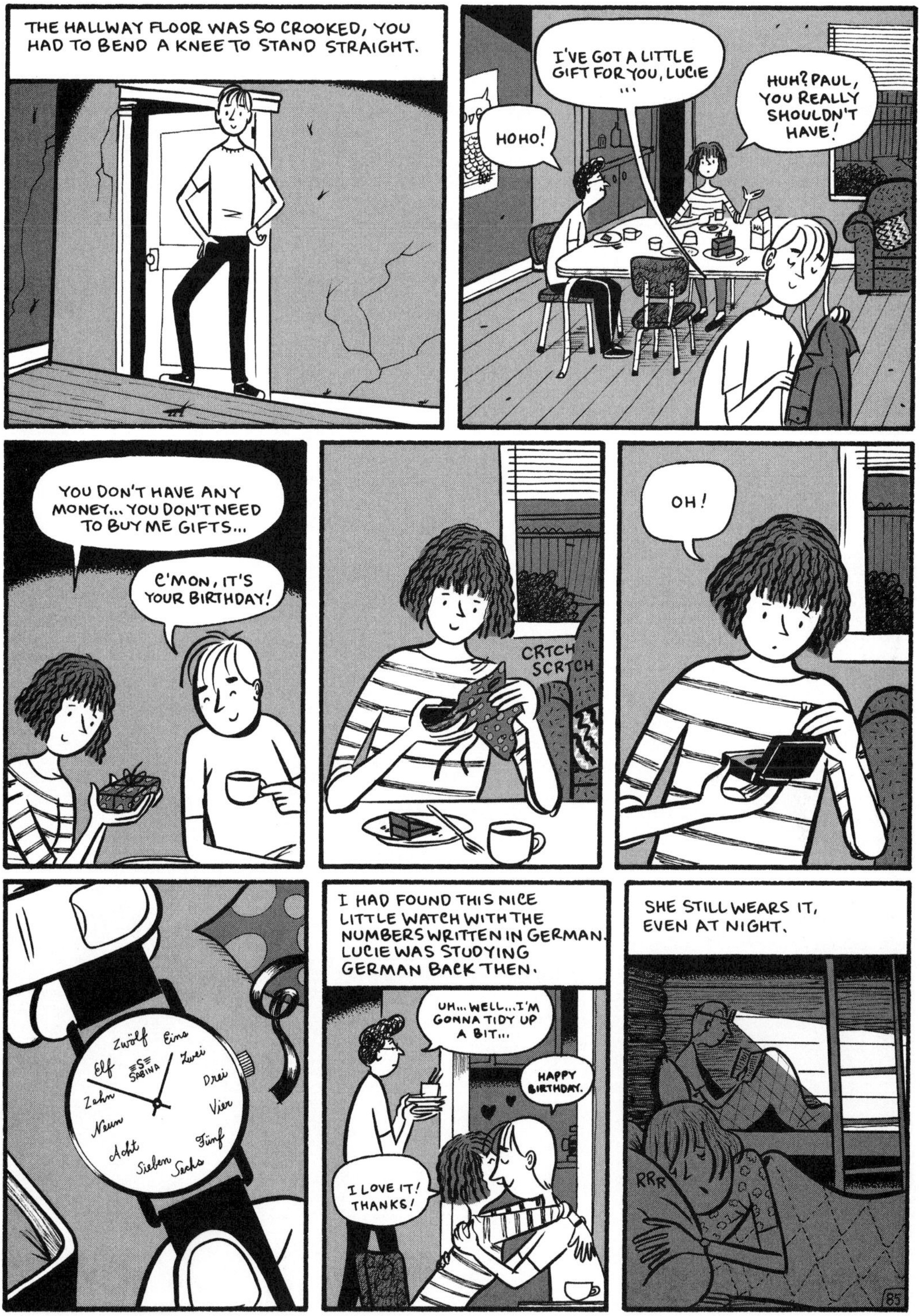
THE HALLWAY FLOOR WAS SO CROOKED, YOU HAD TO BEND A KNEE TO STAND STRAIGHT.
I'VE GOT A LITTLE GIFT FOR YOU, LUCIE ...
HOHO!
HUH? PAUL, YOU REALLY SHOULDN'T HAVE!
YOU DON'T HAVE ANY MONEY... YOU DON'T NEED TO BUY ME GIFTS...
C'MON, IT'S YOUR BIRTHDAY!
CRTCH SCRTCH
OH!
Zwölf
Eins
Elf
S SABINA
Zwei
Drei
Zehn
Vier
Neun
Fünf
Acht
Sieben
Sechs
I HAD FOUND THIS NICE LITTLE WATCH WITH THE NUMBERS WRITTEN IN GERMAN. LUCIE WAS STUDYING GERMAN BACK THEN.
UH... WELL... I'M GONNA TIDY UP A BIT...
HAPPY BIRTHDAY.
I LOVE IT! THANKS!
SHE STILL WEARS IT, EVEN AT NIGHT.
RRR

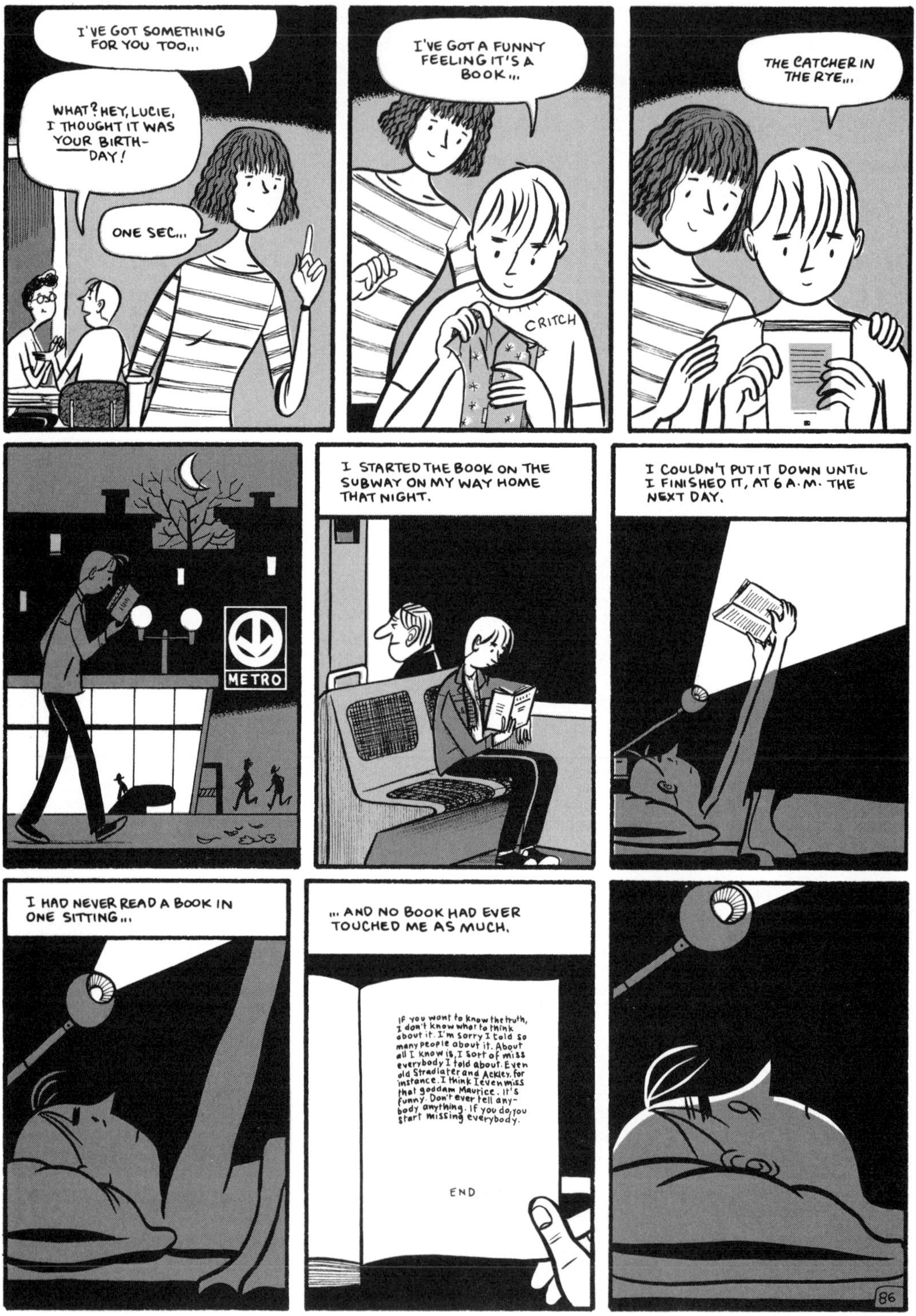
I'VE GOT SOMETHING FOR YOU TOO...
WHAT? HEY, LUCIE, I THOUGHT IT WAS YOUR BIRTH-DAY!
ONE SEC...
I'VE GOT A FUNNY FEELING IT'S A BOOK...
CRITCH
THE CATCHER IN THE RYE...
METRO
I STARTED THE BOOK ON THE SUBWAY ON MY WAY HOME THAT NIGHT.
I COULDN'T PUT IT DOWN UNTIL I FINISHED IT, AT 6 A.M. THE NEXT DAY.
I HAD NEVER READ A BOOK IN ONE SITTING...
... AND NO BOOK HAD EVER TOUCHED ME AS MUCH.
If you want to know the truth, I don't know what to think about it. I'm sorry I told so many people about it. About all I know is, I sort of miss everybody I told about. Even old Stradlater and Ackley, for instance. I think I even miss that goddam Maurice. It's funny. Don't ever tell anybody anything. If you do, you start missing everybody.
END

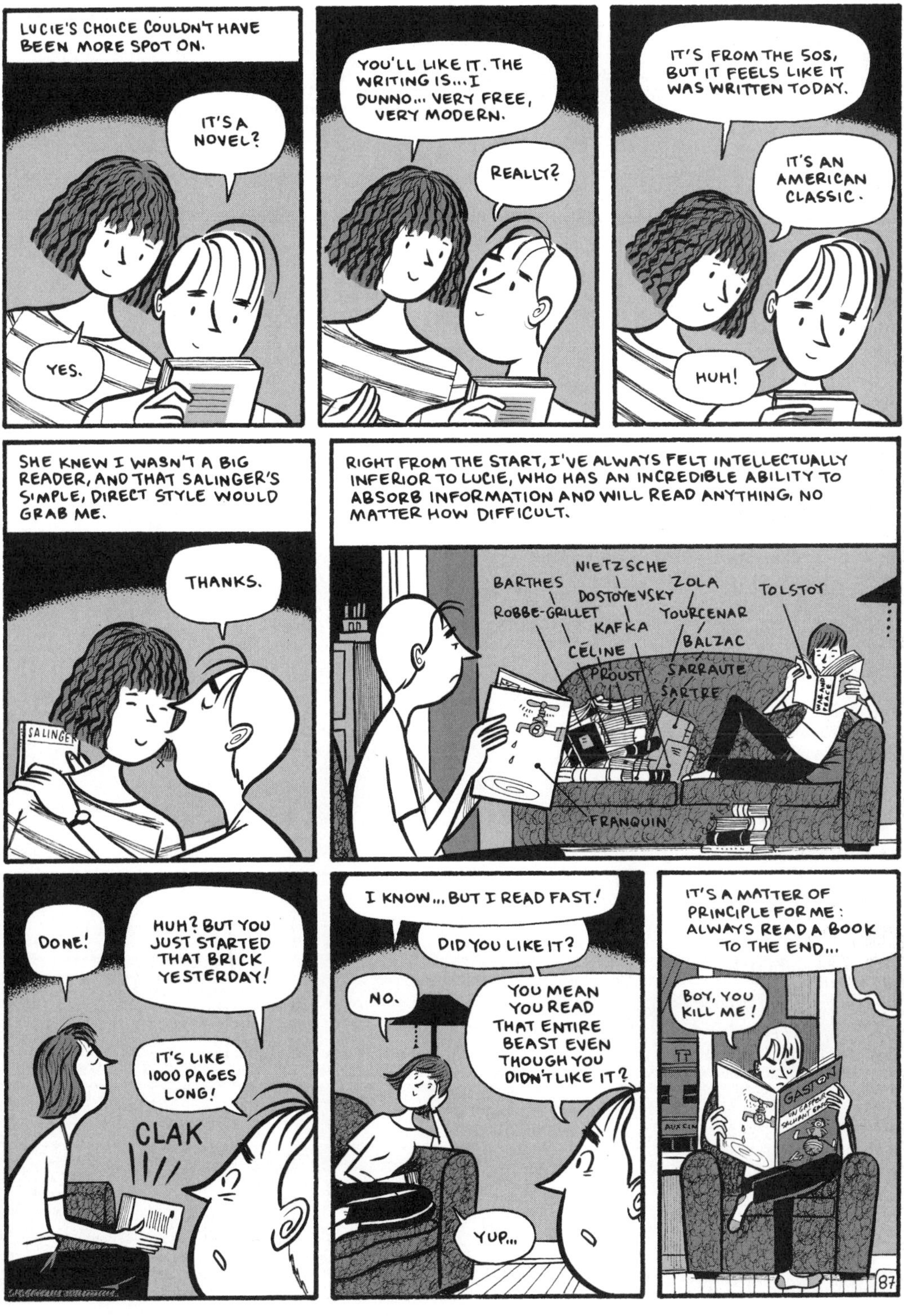

LUCIE'S CHOICE COULDN'T HAVE BEEN MORE SPOT ON.
IT'S A NOVEL?
YES.
YOU'LL LIKE IT. THE WRITING IS... I DUNNO... VERY FREE, VERY MODERN.
REALLY?
IT'S FROM THE 50S, BUT IT FEELS LIKE IT WAS WRITTEN TODAY.
IT'S AN AMERICAN CLASSIC.
HUH!
SHE KNEW I WASN'T A BIG READER, AND THAT SALINGER'S SIMPLE, DIRECT STYLE WOULD GRAB ME.
THANKS.
SALINGER
RIGHT FROM THE START, I'VE ALWAYS FELT INTELLECTUALLY INFERIOR TO LUCIE, WHO HAS AN INCREDIBLE ABILITY TO ABSORB INFORMATION AND WILL READ ANYTHING, NO MATTER HOW DIFFICULT.
NIETZSCHE
BARTHES
DOSTOYEVSKY
ZOLA
TOLSTOY
ROBBE-GRILLET
YOURCENAR
KAFKA
BALZAC
CÉLINE
PROUST
SARRAUTE
SARTRE
WAR AND PEACE
FRANQUIN
DONE!
HUH? BUT YOU JUST STARTED THAT BRICK YESTERDAY!
IT'S LIKE 1000 PAGES LONG!
CLAK
I KNOW... BUT I READ FAST!
DID YOU LIKE IT?
NO.
YOU MEAN YOU READ THAT ENTIRE BEAST EVEN THOUGH YOU DIDN'T LIKE IT?
YUP...
IT'S A MATTER OF PRINCIPLE FOR ME: ALWAYS READ A BOOK TO THE END...
BOY, YOU KILL ME!
GASTON

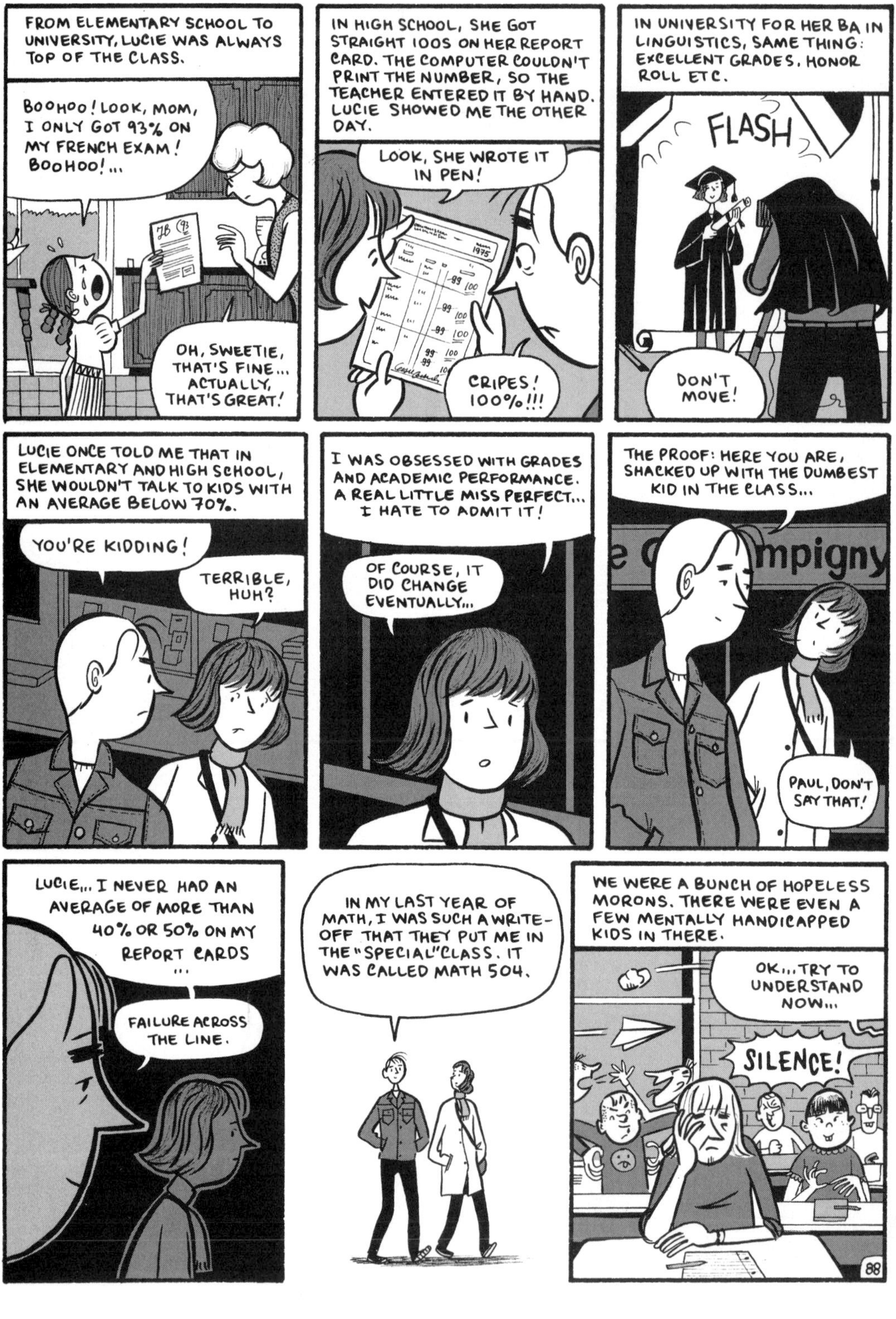
FROM ELEMENTARY SCHOOL TO UNIVERSITY, LUCIE WAS ALWAYS TOP OF THE CLASS.
BOOHOO! LOOK, MOM, I ONLY GOT 93% ON MY FRENCH EXAM! BOOHOO!...
OH, SWEETIE, THAT'S FINE... ACTUALLY, THAT'S GREAT!
IN HIGH SCHOOL, SHE GOT STRAIGHT 100S ON HER REPORT CARD. THE COMPUTER COULDN'T PRINT THE NUMBER, SO THE TEACHER ENTERED IT BY HAND. LUCIE SHOWED ME THE OTHER DAY.
LOOK, SHE WROTE IT IN PEN!
CRIPES! 100%!!!
IN UNIVERSITY FOR HER BA IN LINGUISTICS, SAME THING: EXCELLENT GRADES, HONOR ROLL ETC.
FLASH
DON'T MOVE!
LUCIE ONCE TOLD ME THAT IN ELEMENTARY AND HIGH SCHOOL, SHE WOULDN'T TALK TO KIDS WITH AN AVERAGE BELOW 70%.
YOU'RE KIDDING!
TERRIBLE, HUH?
I WAS OBSESSED WITH GRADES AND ACADEMIC PERFORMANCE. A REAL LITTLE MISS PERFECT... I HATE TO ADMIT IT!
OF COURSE, IT DID CHANGE EVENTUALLY...
THE PROOF: HERE YOU ARE, SHACKED UP WITH THE DUMBEST KID IN THE CLASS...
PAUL, DON'T SAY THAT!
LUCIE... I NEVER HAD AN AVERAGE OF MORE THAN 40% OR 50% ON MY REPORT CARDS ...
FAILURE ACROSS THE LINE.
IN MY LAST YEAR OF MATH, I WAS SUCH A WRITE-OFF THAT THEY PUT ME IN THE "SPECIAL" CLASS. IT WAS CALLED MATH 504.
WE WERE A BUNCH OF HOPELESS MORONS. THERE WERE EVEN A FEW MENTALLY HANDICAPPED KIDS IN THERE.
OK... TRY TO UNDERSTAND NOW...
SILENCE!
88

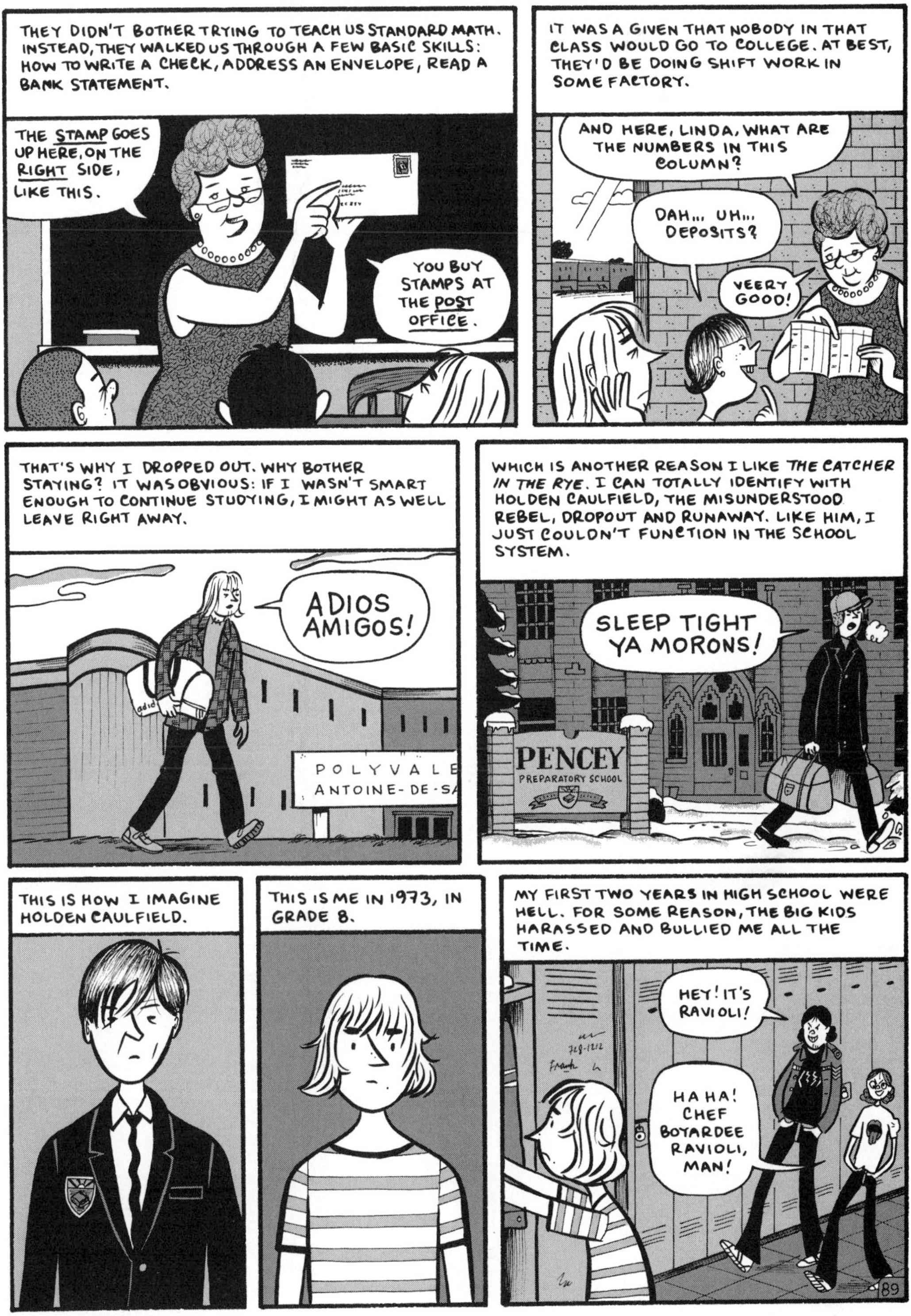
THEY DIDN'T BOTHER TRYING TO TEACH US STANDARD MATH. INSTEAD, THEY WALKED US THROUGH A FEW BASIC SKILLS: HOW TO WRITE A CHECK, ADDRESS AN ENVELOPE, READ A BANK STATEMENT.
THE STAMP GOES UP HERE, ON THE RIGHT SIDE, LIKE THIS.
YOU BUY STAMPS AT THE POST OFFICE.
IT WAS A GIVEN THAT NOBODY IN THAT CLASS WOULD GO TO COLLEGE. AT BEST, THEY'D BE DOING SHIFT WORK IN SOME FACTORY.
AND HERE, LINDA, WHAT ARE THE NUMBERS IN THIS COLUMN?
DAH... UH... DEPOSITS?
VEERY GOOD!
THAT'S WHY I DROPPED OUT. WHY BOTHER STAYING? IT WAS OBVIOUS: IF I WASN'T SMART ENOUGH TO CONTINUE STUDYING, I MIGHT AS WELL LEAVE RIGHT AWAY.
ADIOS AMIGOS!
POLYVALE
ANTOINE-DE-SA
WHICH IS ANOTHER REASON I LIKE *THE CATCHER IN THE RYE*. I CAN TOTALLY IDENTIFY WITH HOLDEN CAULFIELD, THE MISUNDERSTOOD REBEL, DROPOUT AND RUNAWAY. LIKE HIM, I JUST COULDN'T FUNCTION IN THE SCHOOL SYSTEM.
SLEEP TIGHT YA MORONS!
PENCEY
PREPARATORY SCHOOL
THIS IS HOW I IMAGINE HOLDEN CAULFIELD.
THIS IS ME IN 1973, IN GRADE 8.
MY FIRST TWO YEARS IN HIGH SCHOOL WERE HELL. FOR SOME REASON, THE BIG KIDS HARASSED AND BULLIED ME ALL THE TIME.
HEY! IT'S RAVIOLI!
HA HA! CHEF BOYARDEE RAVIOLI, MAN!

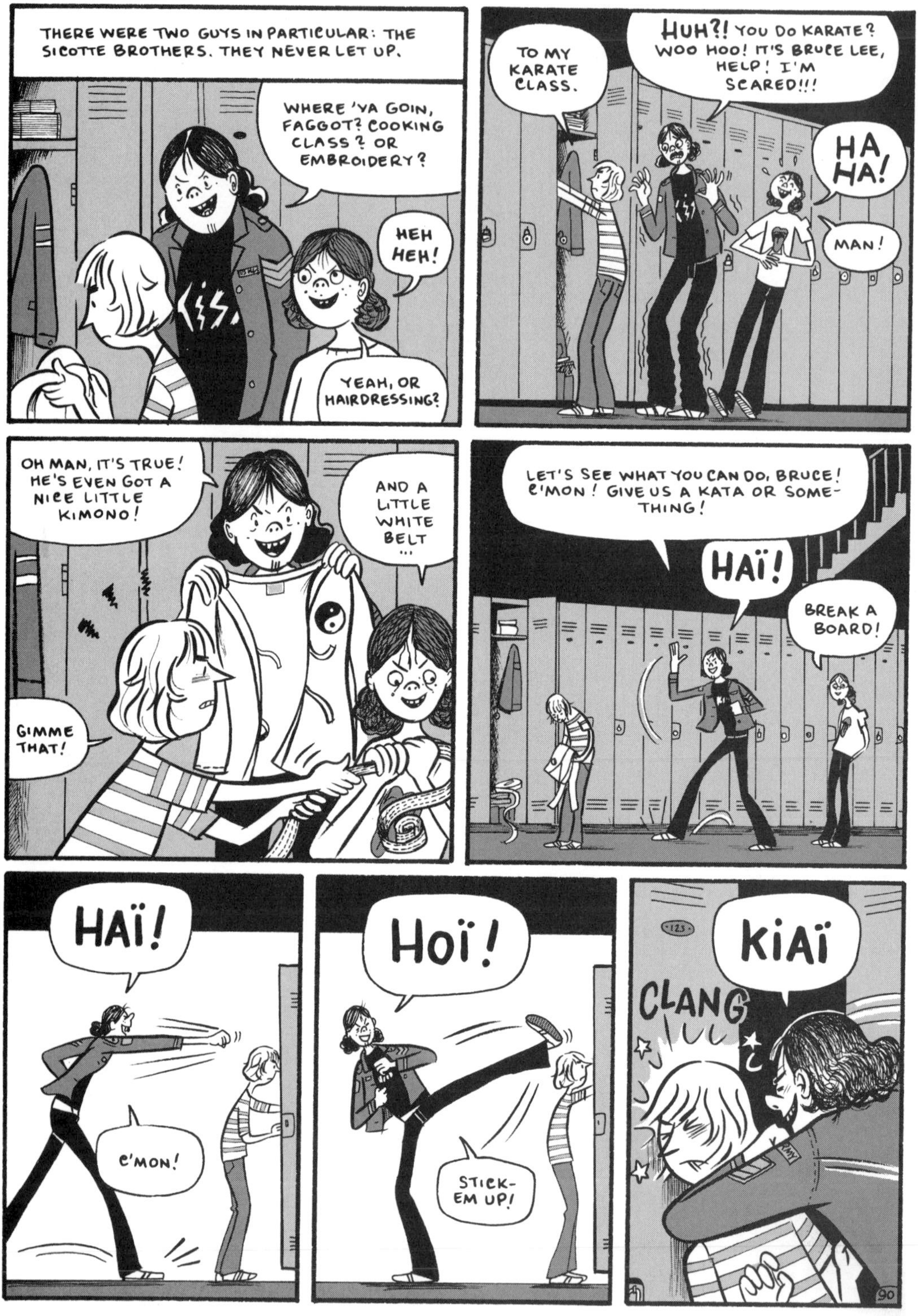
THERE WERE TWO GUYS IN PARTICULAR: THE SICOTTE BROTHERS. THEY NEVER LET UP.
WHERE 'YA GOIN, FAGGOT? COOKING CLASS? OR EMBROIDERY?
HEH HEH!
YEAH, OR HAIRDRESSING?
TO MY KARATE CLASS.
HUH?! YOU DO KARATE? WOO HOO! IT'S BRUCE LEE, HELP! I'M SCARED!!!
HA HA!
MAN!
OH MAN, IT'S TRUE! HE'S EVEN GOT A NICE LITTLE KIMONO!
AND A LITTLE WHITE BELT ...
GIMME THAT!
LET'S SEE WHAT YOU CAN DO, BRUCE! C'MON! GIVE US A KATA OR SOMETHING!
HAÏ!
BREAK A BOARD!
HAÏ!
C'MON!
HOÏ!
STICK-EM UP!
KIAÏ
CLANG

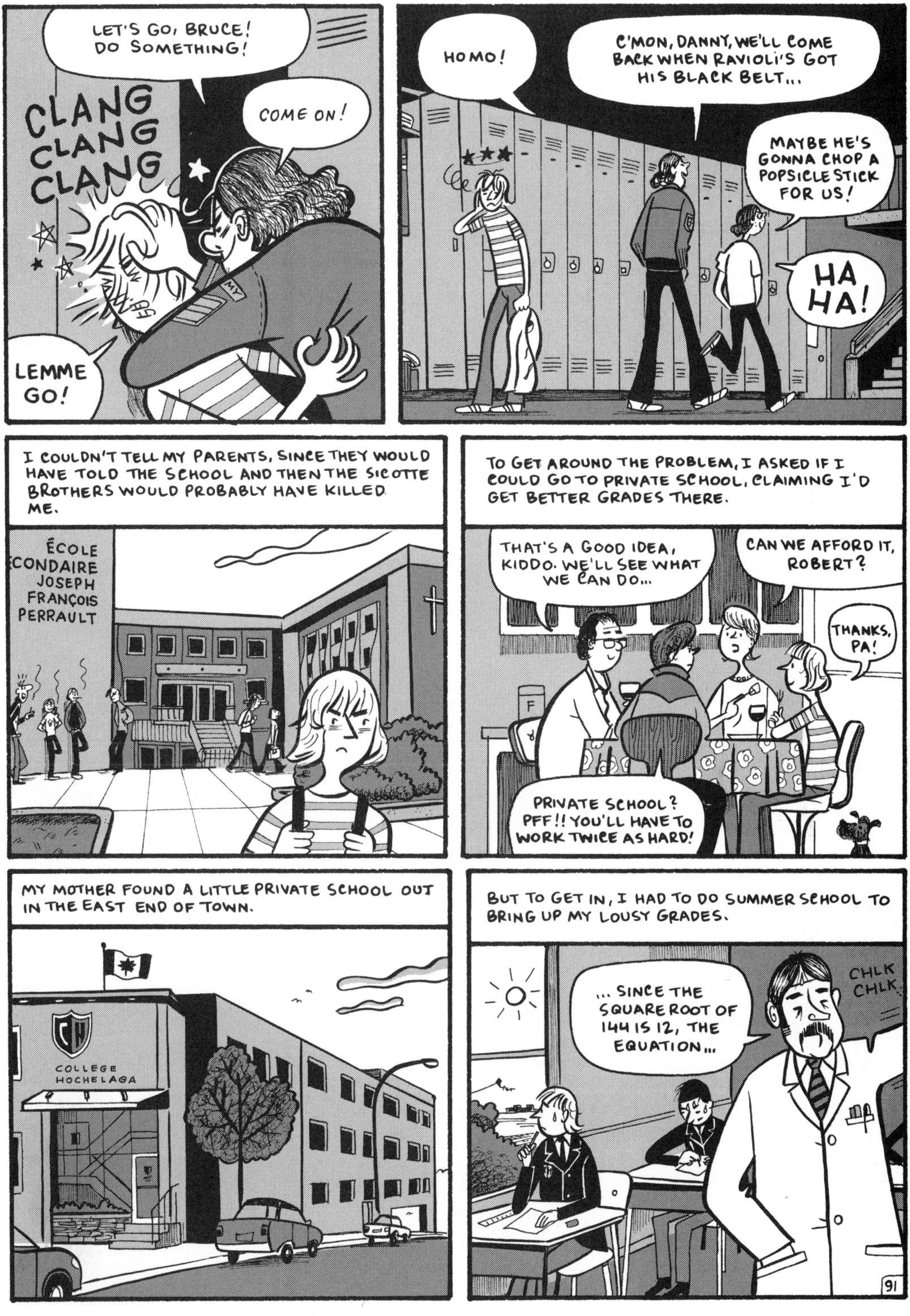
LET'S GO, BRUCE! DO SOMETHING!
COME ON!
CLANG CLANG CLANG
LEMME GO!
HOMO!
C'MON, DANNY, WE'LL COME BACK WHEN RAVIOLI'S GOT HIS BLACK BELT...
MAYBE HE'S GONNA CHOP A POPSICLE STICK FOR US!
HA HA!
I COULDN'T TELL MY PARENTS, SINCE THEY WOULD HAVE TOLD THE SCHOOL AND THEN THE SICOTTE BROTHERS WOULD PROBABLY HAVE KILLED ME.
ÉCOLE
CONDAIRE
JOSEPH
FRANÇOIS
PERRAULT
TO GET AROUND THE PROBLEM, I ASKED IF I COULD GO TO PRIVATE SCHOOL, CLAIMING I'D GET BETTER GRADES THERE.
THAT'S A GOOD IDEA, KIDDO. WE'LL SEE WHAT WE CAN DO...
CAN WE AFFORD IT, ROBERT?
THANKS, PA!
PRIVATE SCHOOL? PFF!! YOU'LL HAVE TO WORK TWICE AS HARD!
MY MOTHER FOUND A LITTLE PRIVATE SCHOOL OUT IN THE EAST END OF TOWN.
COLLEGE
HOCHELAGA
BUT TO GET IN, I HAD TO DO SUMMER SCHOOL TO BRING UP MY LOUSY GRADES.
... SINCE THE SQUARE ROOT OF 144 IS 12, THE EQUATION...
CHLK CHLK

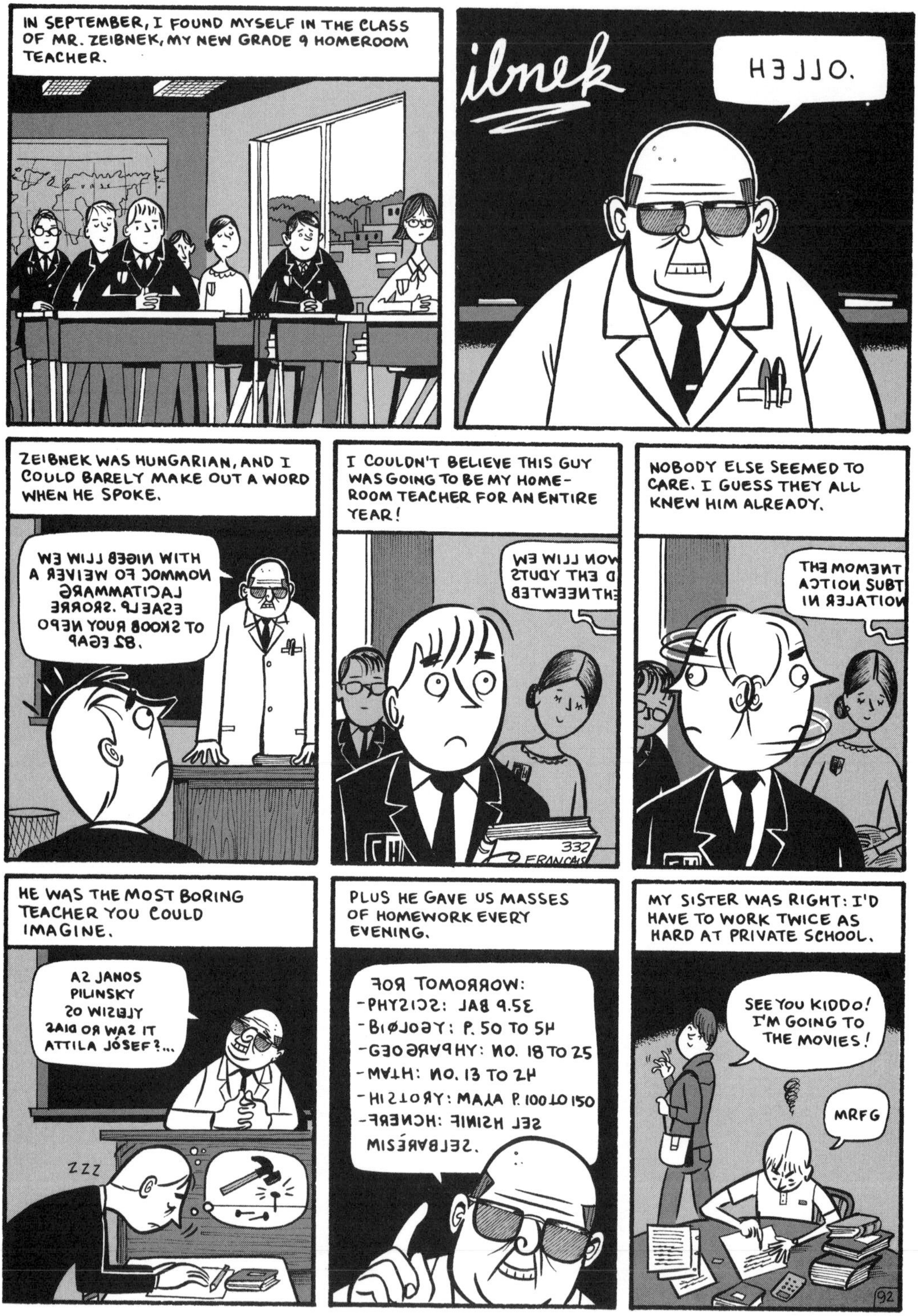

IN SEPTEMBER, I FOUND MYSELF IN THE CLASS OF MR. ZEIBNEK, MY NEW GRADE 9 HOMEROOM TEACHER.
ibnek
HELLO.
ZEIBNEK WAS HUNGARIAN, AND I COULD BARELY MAKE OUT A WORD WHEN HE SPOKE.
WE WILL BEGIN WITH A REVIEW OF COMMON GRAMMATICAL ERRORS. PLEASE OPEN YOUR BOOKS TO PAGE 28.
I COULDN'T BELIEVE THIS GUY WAS GOING TO BE MY HOMEROOM TEACHER FOR AN ENTIRE YEAR!
WE WILL NOW STUDY THE D BETWEEN THE
332 FRANCAIS
NOBODY ELSE SEEMED TO CARE. I GUESS THEY ALL KNEW HIM ALREADY.
THE MOMENT ACTION SUBT IN RELATION
HE WAS THE MOST BORING TEACHER YOU COULD IMAGINE.
AS JANOS PILINSKY SO WISELY SAID OR WAS IT ATTILA JÓSEF?...
ZZZ
PLUS HE GAVE US MASSES OF HOMEWORK EVERY EVENING.
FOR TOMORROW:
-PHYSICS: LAB 9.53
-BIOLOGY: P. 50 TO 54
-GEOGRAPHY: NO. 18 TO 25
-MATH: NO. 13 TO 24
-HISTORY: MAYA P. 100 TO 150
-FRENCH: FINISH LES MISÉRABLES.
MY SISTER WAS RIGHT: I'D HAVE TO WORK TWICE AS HARD AT PRIVATE SCHOOL.
SEE YOU KIDDO! I'M GOING TO THE MOVIES!
MRFG

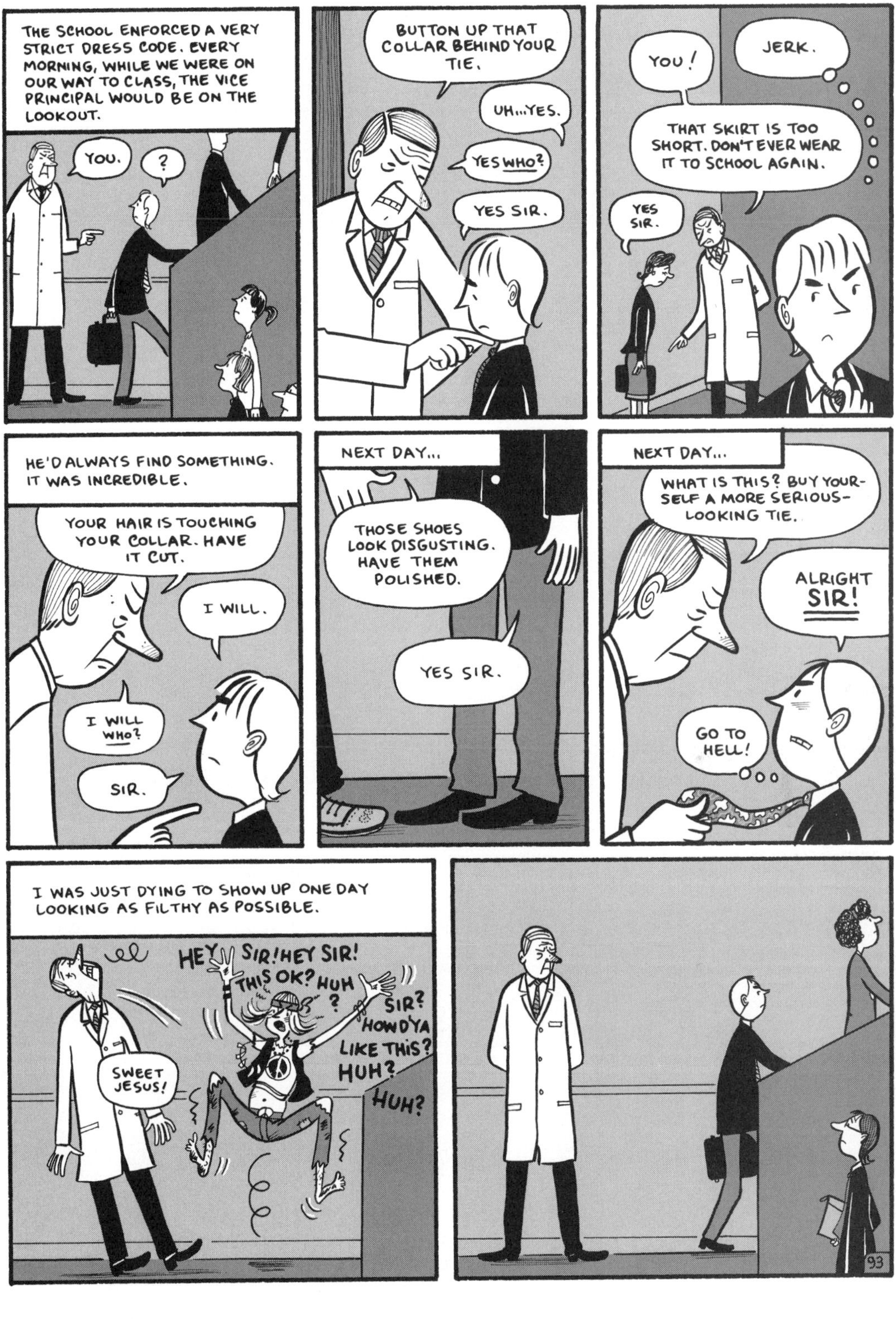
THE SCHOOL ENFORCED A VERY STRICT DRESS CODE. EVERY MORNING, WHILE WE WERE ON OUR WAY TO CLASS, THE VICE PRINCIPAL WOULD BE ON THE LOOKOUT.
YOU.
?
BUTTON UP THAT COLLAR BEHIND YOUR TIE.
UH...YES.
YES WHO?
YES SIR.
YOU!
JERK.
THAT SKIRT IS TOO SHORT. DON'T EVER WEAR IT TO SCHOOL AGAIN.
YES SIR.
HE'D ALWAYS FIND SOMETHING. IT WAS INCREDIBLE.
YOUR HAIR IS TOUCHING YOUR COLLAR. HAVE IT CUT.
I WILL.
I WILL WHO?
SIR.
NEXT DAY...
THOSE SHOES LOOK DISGUSTING. HAVE THEM POLISHED.
YES SIR.
NEXT DAY...
WHAT IS THIS? BUY YOURSELF A MORE SERIOUS-LOOKING TIE.
ALRIGHT SIR!
GO TO HELL!
I WAS JUST DYING TO SHOW UP ONE DAY LOOKING AS FILTHY AS POSSIBLE.
HEY SIR! HEY SIR! THIS OK? HUH? SIR? HOW'D'YA LIKE THIS? HUH? HUH?
SWEET JESUS!

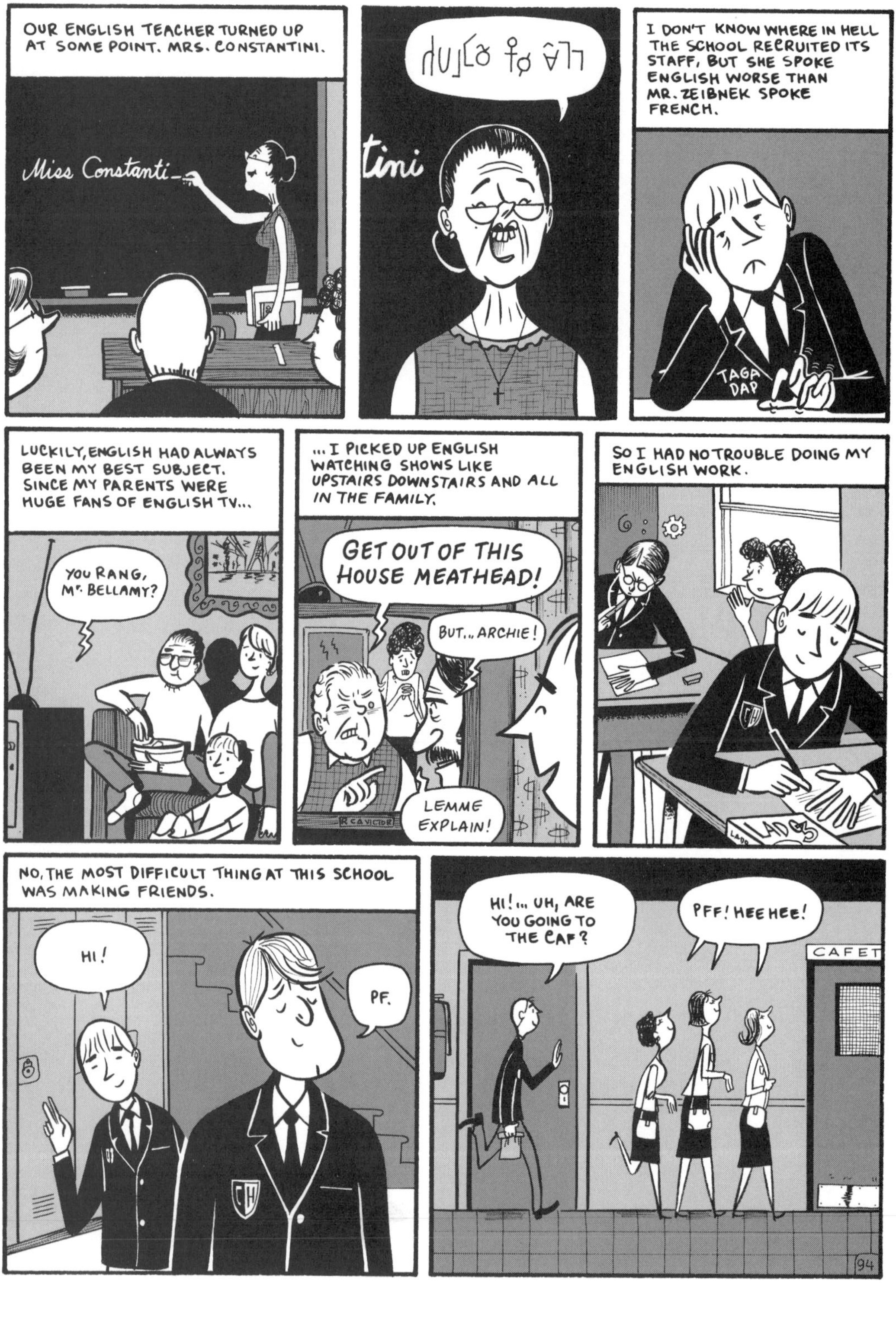

OUR ENGLISH TEACHER TURNED UP AT SOME POINT. MRS. CONSTANTINI.
Miss Constanti_
tini
I DON'T KNOW WHERE IN HELL THE SCHOOL RECRUITED ITS STAFF, BUT SHE SPOKE ENGLISH WORSE THAN MR. ZEIBNEK SPOKE FRENCH.
TAGA DAP
LUCKILY, ENGLISH HAD ALWAYS BEEN MY BEST SUBJECT. SINCE MY PARENTS WERE HUGE FANS OF ENGLISH TV...
YOU RANG, Mr. BELLAMY?
...I PICKED UP ENGLISH WATCHING SHOWS LIKE UPSTAIRS DOWNSTAIRS AND ALL IN THE FAMILY.
GET OUT OF THIS HOUSE MEATHEAD!
BUT... ARCHIE!
LEMME EXPLAIN!
RCA VICTOR
SO I HAD NO TROUBLE DOING MY ENGLISH WORK.
LAD
NO, THE MOST DIFFICULT THING AT THIS SCHOOL WAS MAKING FRIENDS.
HI!
PF.
HI! ... UH, ARE YOU GOING TO THE CAF?
PFF! HEE HEE!
CAFET

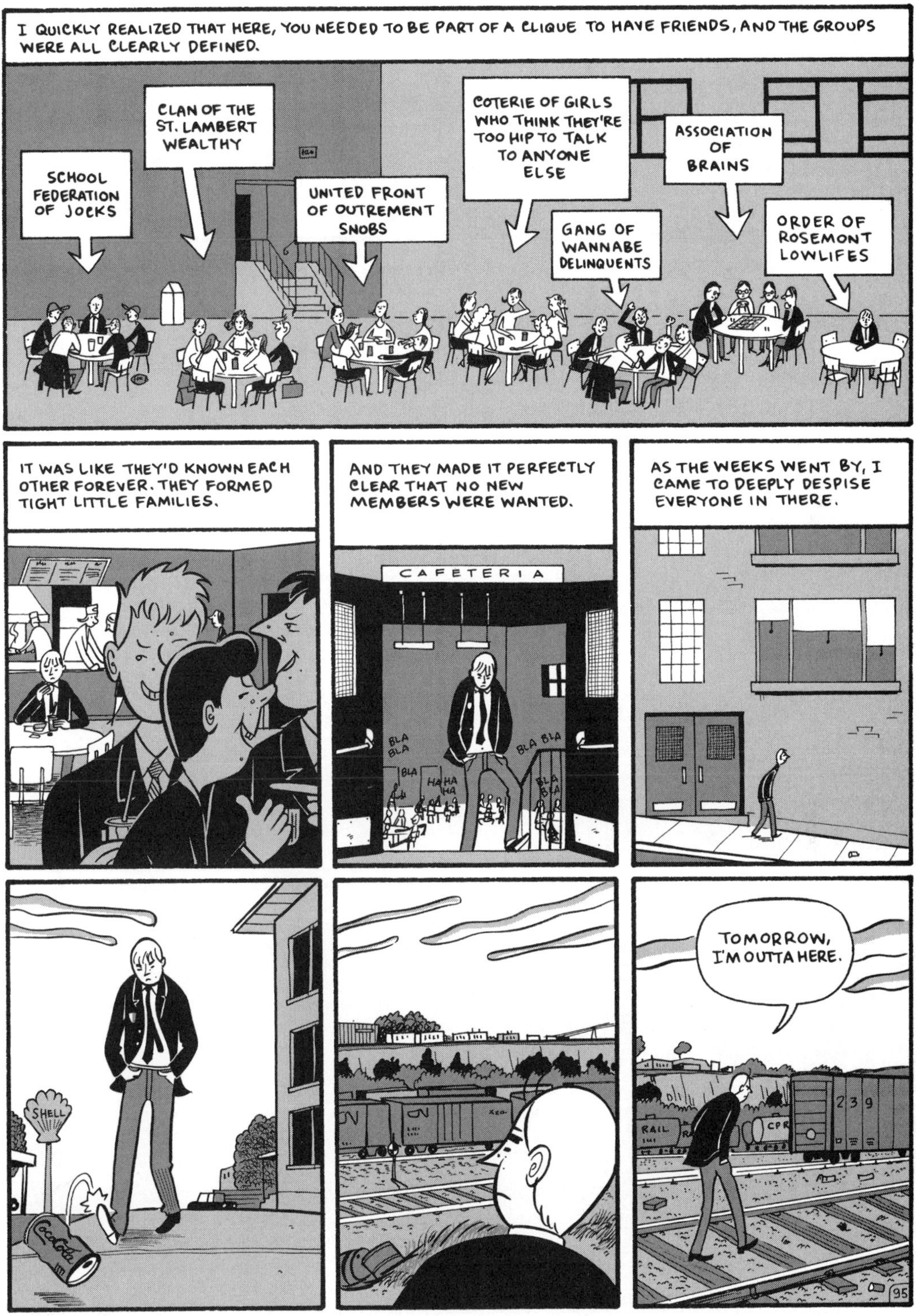
I QUICKLY REALIZED THAT HERE, YOU NEEDED TO BE PART OF A CLIQUE TO HAVE FRIENDS, AND THE GROUPS WERE ALL CLEARLY DEFINED.
SCHOOL FEDERATION OF JOCKS
CLAN OF THE ST. LAMBERT WEALTHY
UNITED FRONT OF OUTREMENT SNOBS
COTERIE OF GIRLS WHO THINK THEY'RE TOO HIP TO TALK TO ANYONE ELSE
GANG OF WANNABE DELINQUENTS
ASSOCIATION OF BRAINS
ORDER OF ROSEMONT LOWLIFES
IT WAS LIKE THEY'D KNOWN EACH OTHER FOREVER. THEY FORMED TIGHT LITTLE FAMILIES.
AND THEY MADE IT PERFECTLY CLEAR THAT NO NEW MEMBERS WERE WANTED.
CAFETERIA
BLA BLA
BLA
HA HA
BLA BLA
BLA BLA
AS THE WEEKS WENT BY, I CAME TO DEEPLY DESPISE EVERYONE IN THERE.
SHELL
Coca-Cola
TOMORROW, I'M OUTTA HERE.
RAIL
CPR
239

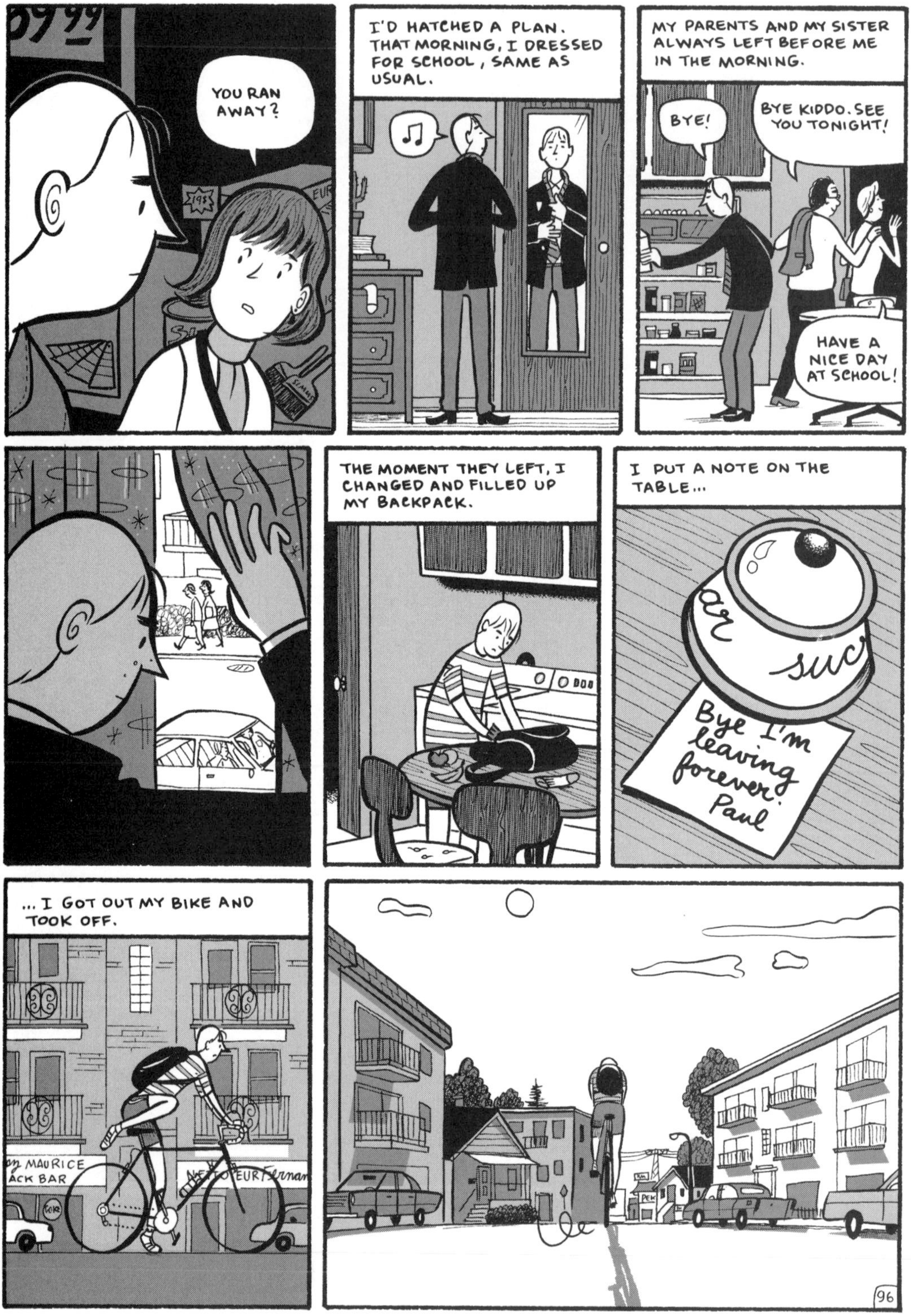
YOU RAN AWAY?
I'D HATCHED A PLAN. THAT MORNING, I DRESSED FOR SCHOOL, SAME AS USUAL.
♫
MY PARENTS AND MY SISTER ALWAYS LEFT BEFORE ME IN THE MORNING.
BYE!
BYE KIDDO. SEE YOU TONIGHT!
HAVE A NICE DAY AT SCHOOL!
THE MOMENT THEY LEFT, I CHANGED AND FILLED UP MY BACKPACK.
I PUT A NOTE ON THE TABLE...
Bye I'm leaving forever! Paul
... I GOT OUT MY BIKE AND TOOK OFF.
MAURICE

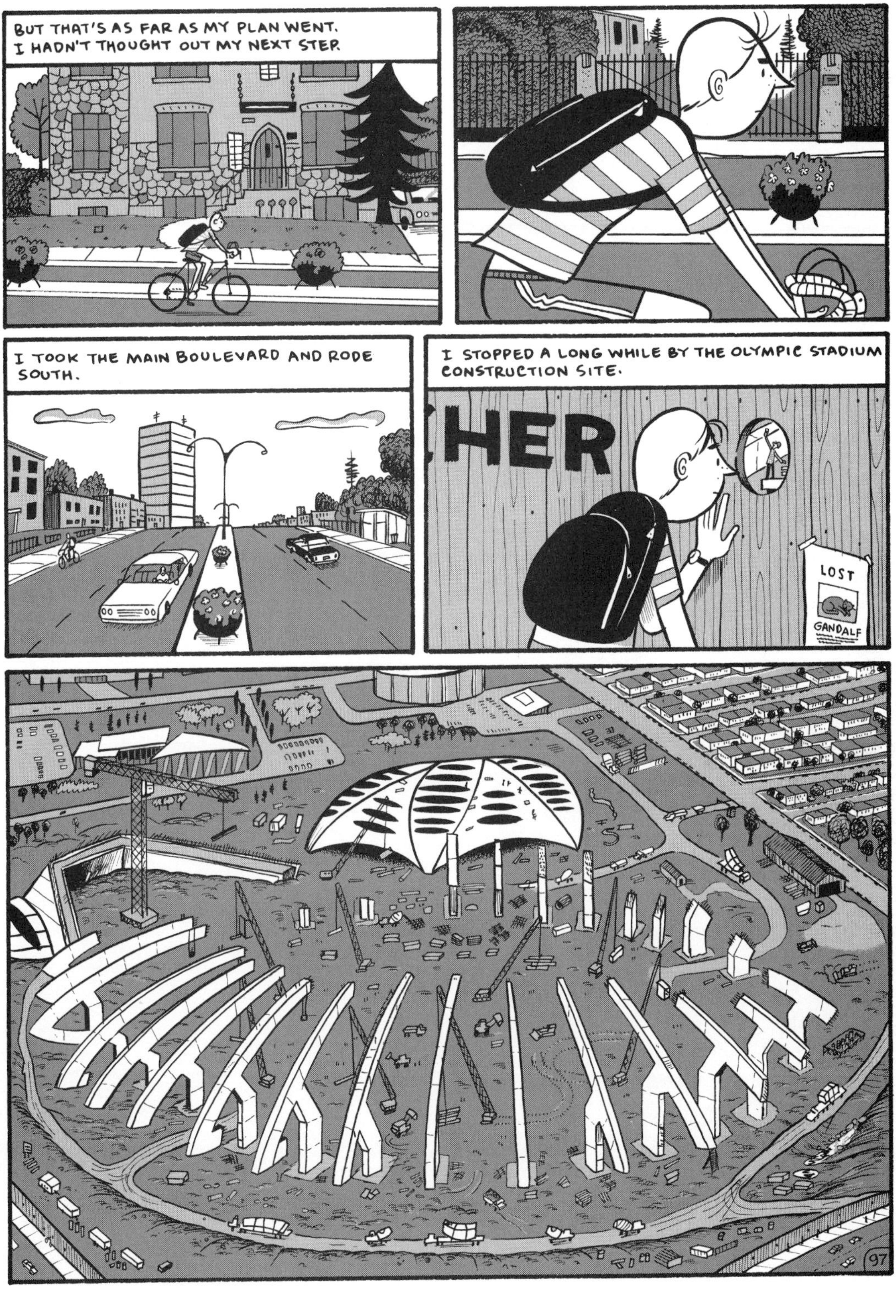
BUT THAT'S AS FAR AS MY PLAN WENT. I HADN'T THOUGHT OUT MY NEXT STEP.
I TOOK THE MAIN BOULEVARD AND RODE SOUTH.
I STOPPED A LONG WHILE BY THE OLYMPIC STADIUM CONSTRUCTION SITE.
HER
LOST
GANDALF

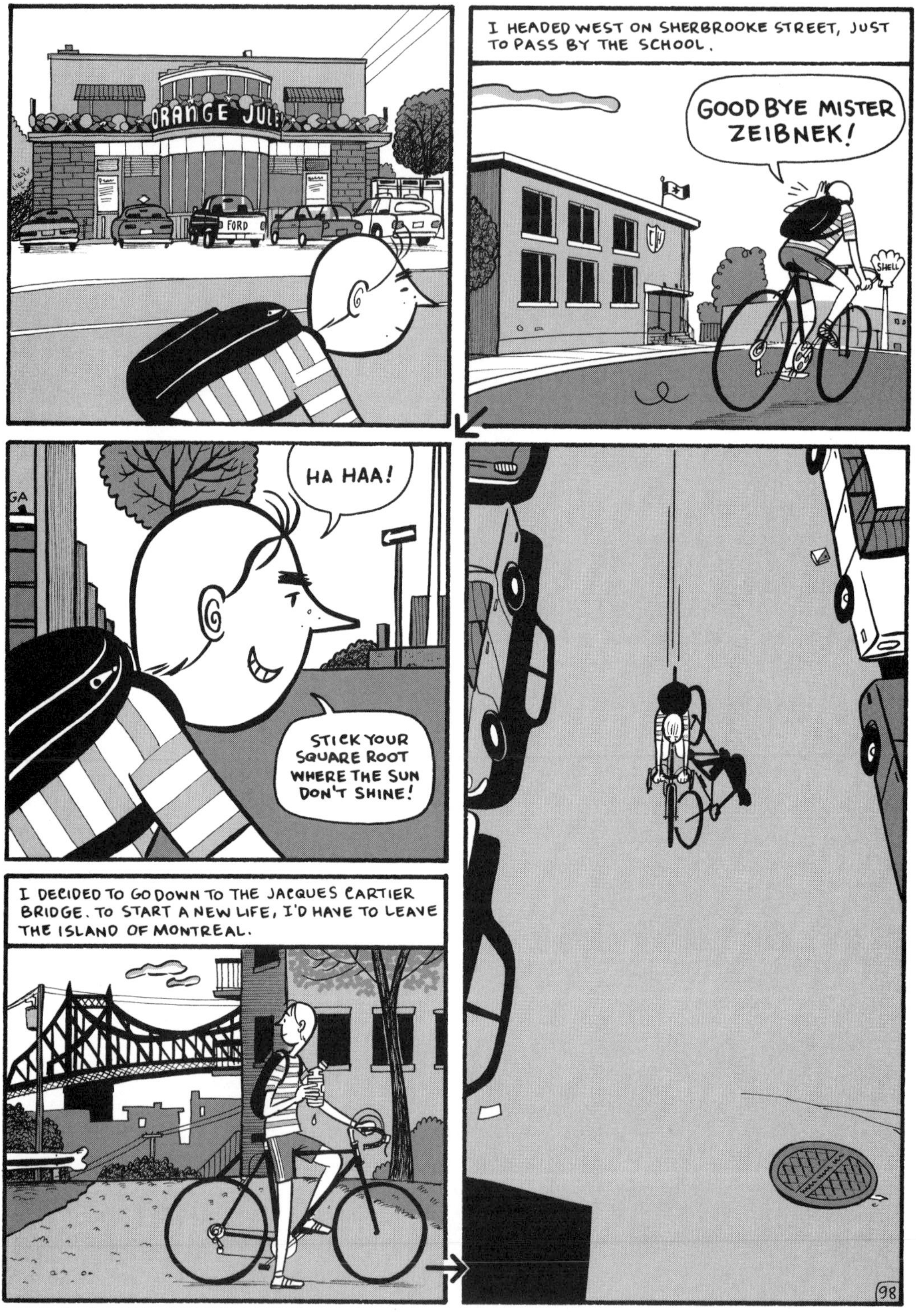
I HEADED WEST ON SHERBROOKE STREET, JUST TO PASS BY THE SCHOOL.
GOOD BYE MISTER ZEIBNEK!
HA HAA!
STICK YOUR SQUARE ROOT WHERE THE SUN DON'T SHINE!
I DECIDED TO GO DOWN TO THE JACQUES CARTIER BRIDGE. TO START A NEW LIFE, I'D HAVE TO LEAVE THE ISLAND OF MONTREAL.

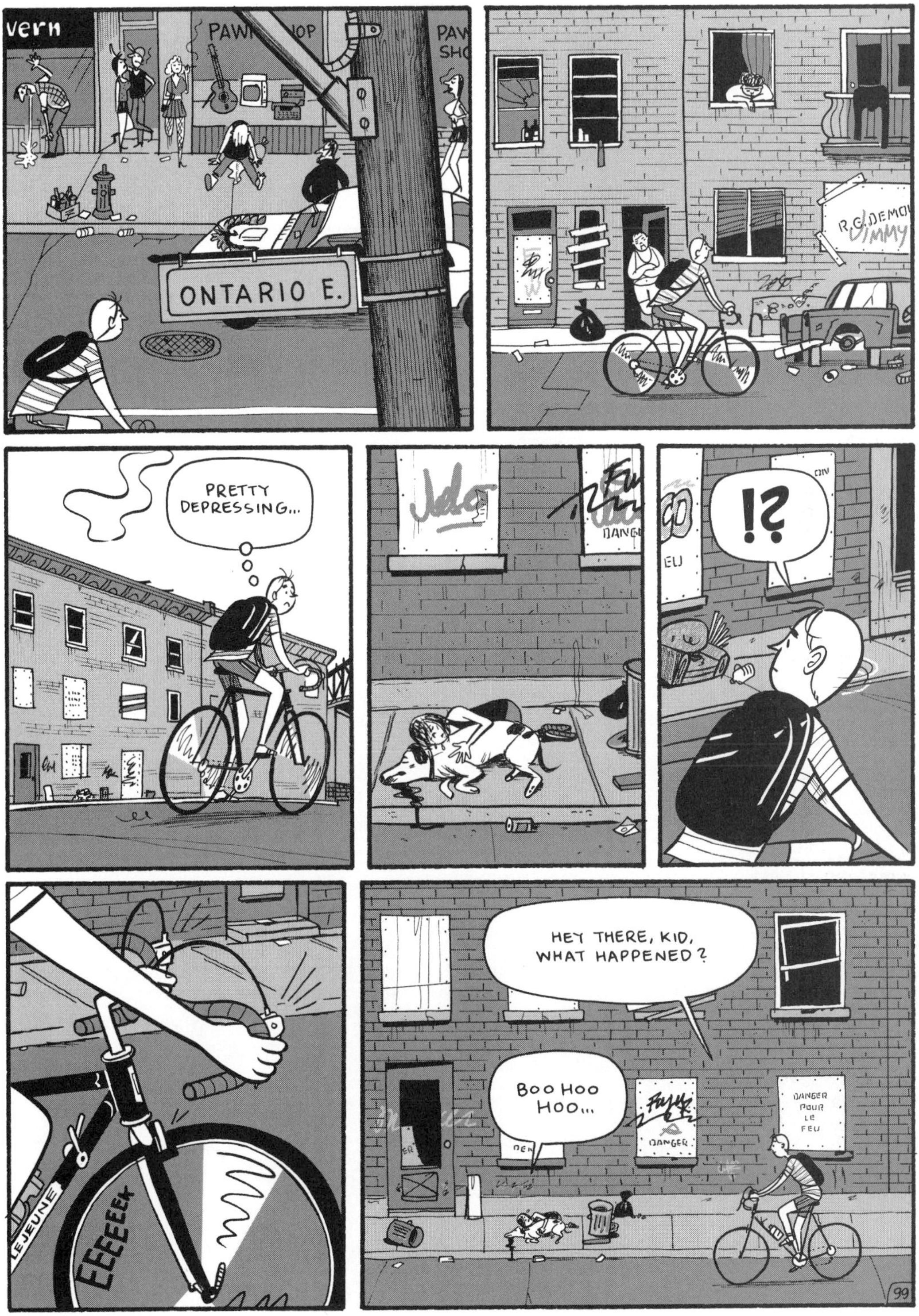
vern
PAWN SHOP
ONTARIO E.
R.G. DEMO
PRETTY DEPRESSING...
DANGER
!?
EEEEEEK
LEJEUNE
HEY THERE, KID, WHAT HAPPENED?
BOO HOO HOO...
DANGER
DANGER POUR LE FEU

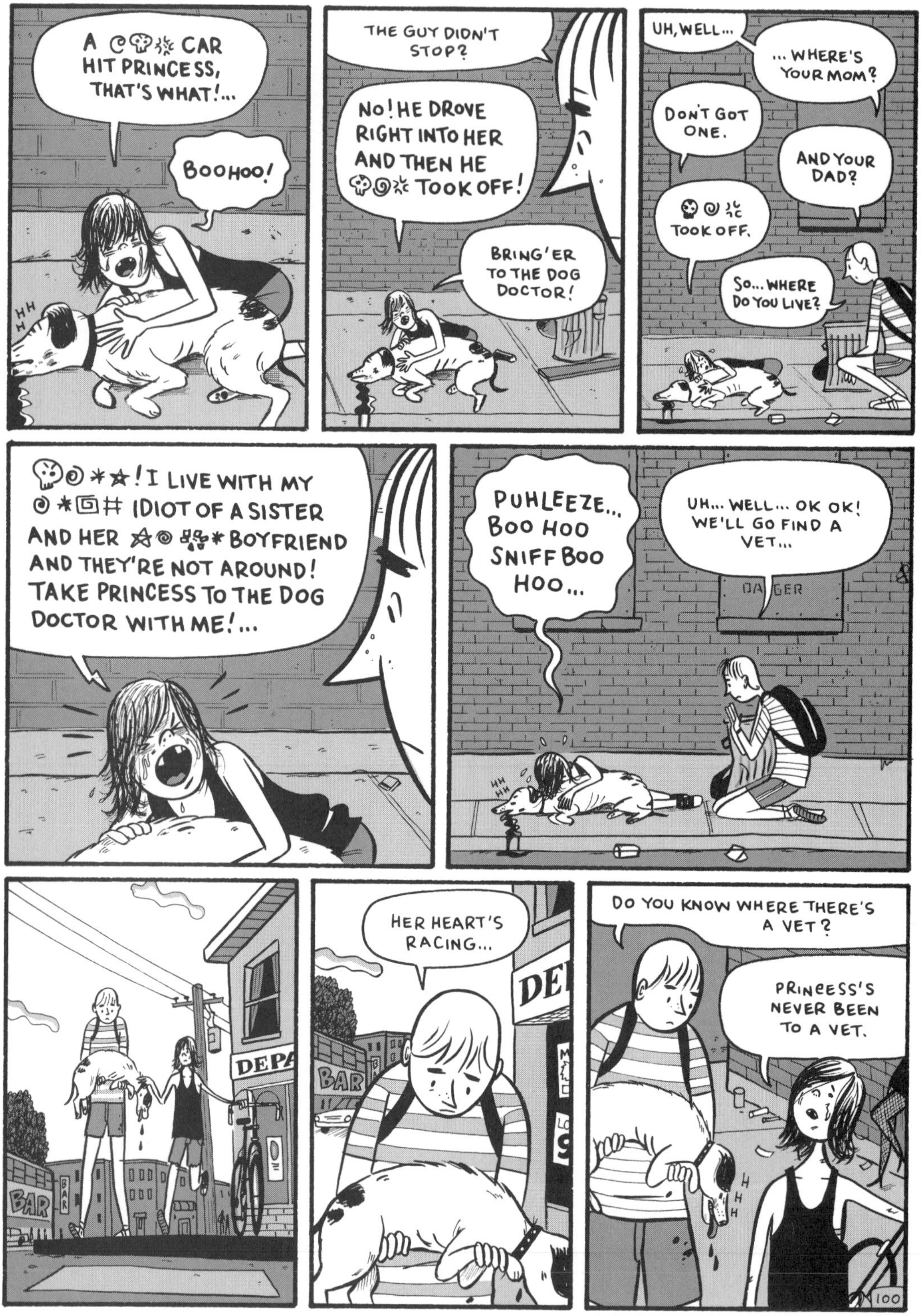
A @💀⁂ CAR HIT PRINCESS, THAT'S WHAT!...
BOOHOO!
HH H
THE GUY DIDN'T STOP?
NO! HE DROVE RIGHT INTO HER AND THEN HE 💀@⁂ TOOK OFF!
BRING'ER TO THE DOG DOCTOR!
UH, WELL...
... WHERE'S YOUR MOM?
DON'T GOT ONE.
AND YOUR DAD?
💀@⁂ TOOK OFF.
SO... WHERE DO YOU LIVE?
💀@*☆! I LIVE WITH MY @*▣# IDIOT OF A SISTER AND HER ☆@⁂* BOYFRIEND AND THEY'RE NOT AROUND! TAKE PRINCESS TO THE DOG DOCTOR WITH ME!...
PUHLEEZE... BOO HOO SNIFF BOO HOO...
UH... WELL... OK OK! WE'LL GO FIND A VET...
DA GER
HH HH
DEPA
BAR
BAR
HER HEART'S RACING...
DE
BAR
DO YOU KNOW WHERE THERE'S A VET?
PRINCESS'S NEVER BEEN TO A VET.
HHH

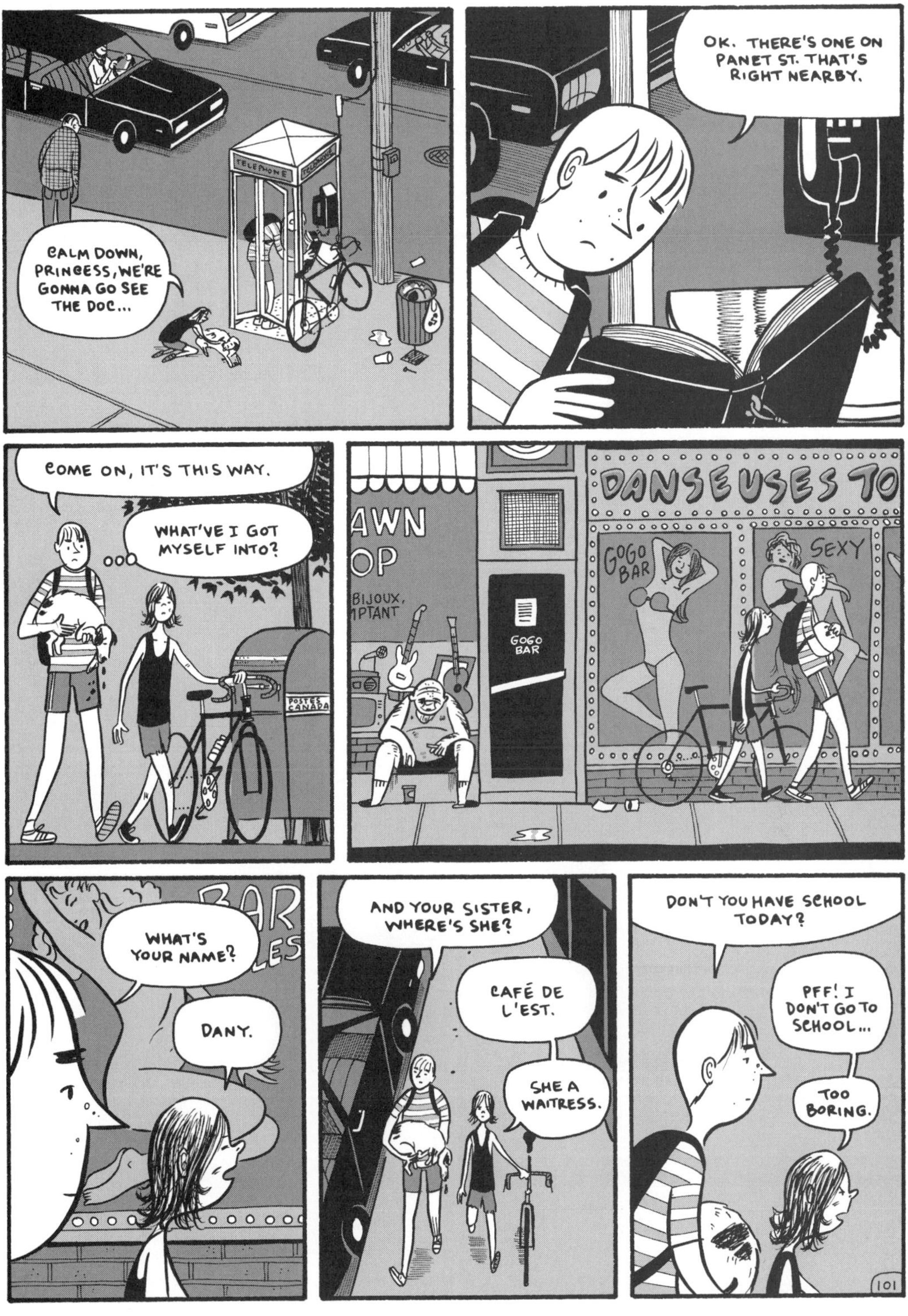
TELEPHONE
TÉLÉPHONE
CALM DOWN, PRINCESS, WE'RE GONNA GO SEE THE DOC...
OK. THERE'S ONE ON PANET ST. THAT'S RIGHT NEARBY.
COME ON, IT'S THIS WAY.
WHAT'VE I GOT MYSELF INTO?
POSTES CANADA
AWN
OP
BIJOUX,
MPTANT
GOGO BAR
DANSEUSES TO
GOGO BAR
SEXY
WHAT'S YOUR NAME?
DANY.
AND YOUR SISTER, WHERE'S SHE?
CAFÉ DE L'EST.
SHE A WAITRESS.
DON'T YOU HAVE SCHOOL TODAY?
PFF! I DON'T GO TO SCHOOL...
TOO BORING.

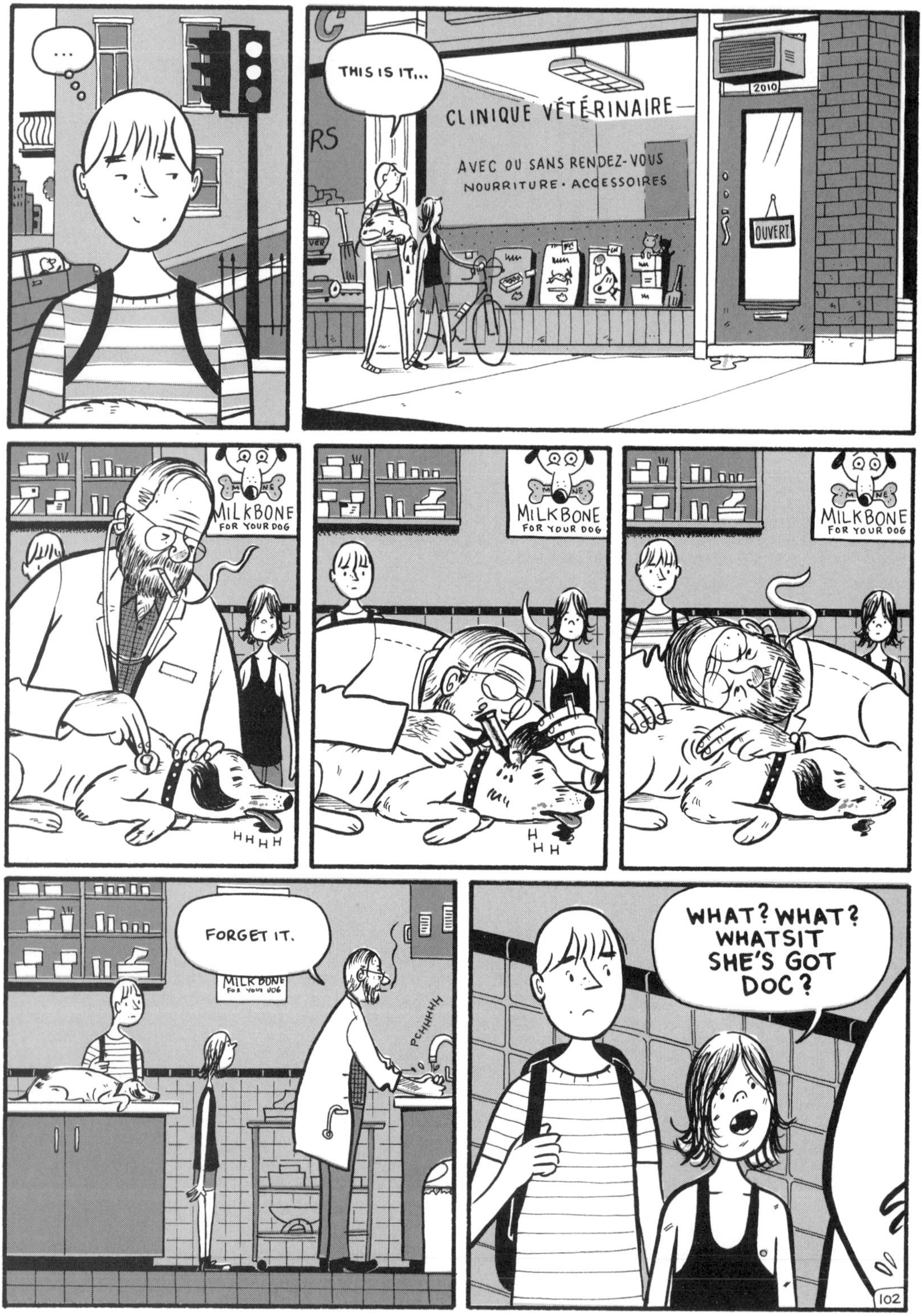
...
THIS IS IT...
CLINIQUE VÉTÉRINAIRE
AVEC OU SANS RENDEZ-VOUS
NOURRITURE • ACCESSOIRES
2010
OUVERT
MILKBONE FOR YOUR DOG
HHHH
MILKBONE FOR YOUR DOG
HHH
MILKBONE FOR YOUR DOG
FORGET IT.
MILKBONE FOR YOUR DOG
PCHHHHH
WHAT? WHAT? WHATSIT SHE'S GOT DOC?

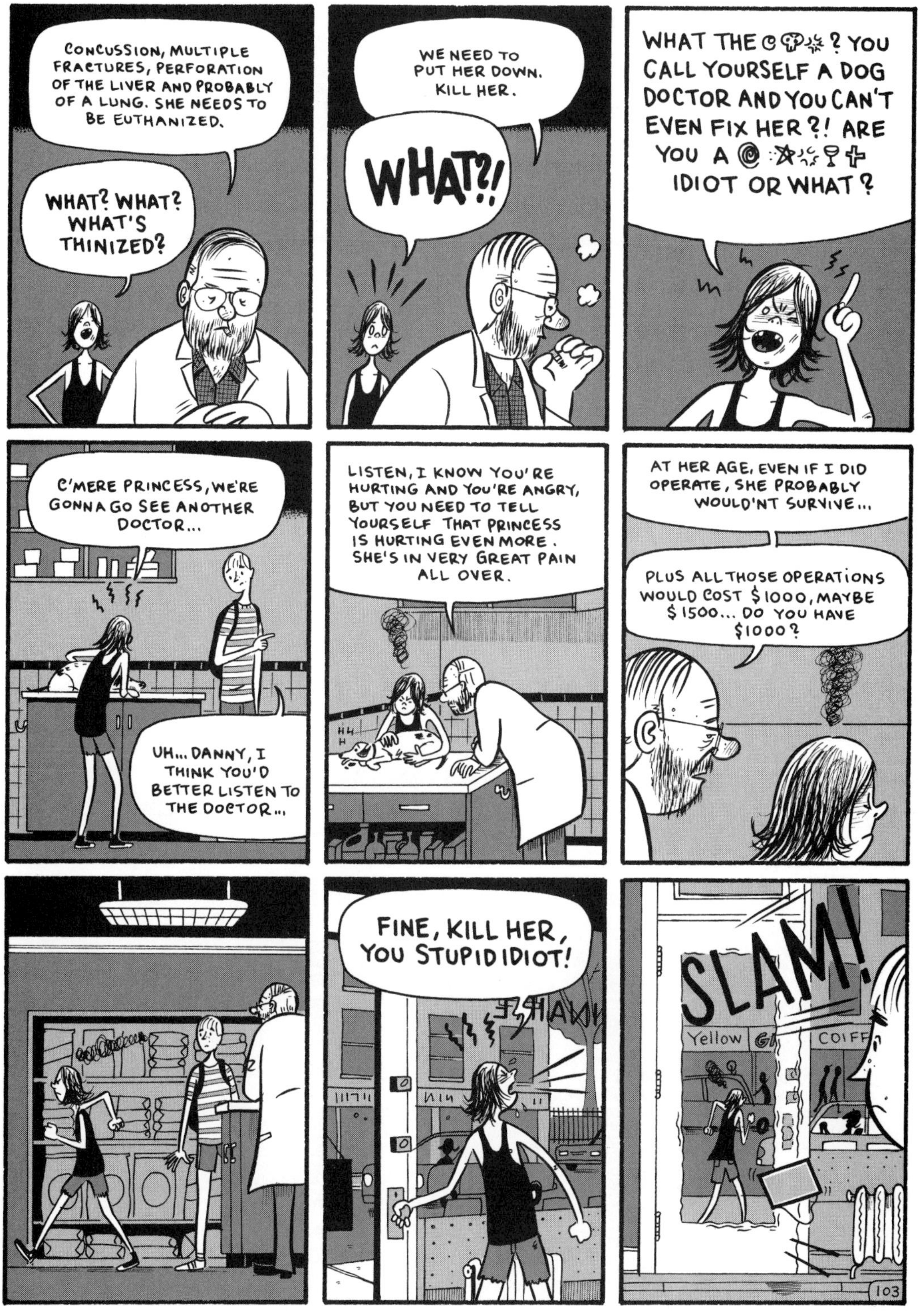
CONCUSSION, MULTIPLE FRACTURES, PERFORATION OF THE LIVER AND PROBABLY OF A LUNG. SHE NEEDS TO BE EUTHANIZED.
WHAT? WHAT? WHAT'S THINIZED?
WE NEED TO PUT HER DOWN. KILL HER.
WHAT?!
WHAT THE @☠*? YOU CALL YOURSELF A DOG DOCTOR AND YOU CAN'T EVEN FIX HER?! ARE YOU A @*★*†✝ IDIOT OR WHAT?
C'MERE PRINCESS, WE'RE GONNA GO SEE ANOTHER DOCTOR...
UH... DANNY, I THINK YOU'D BETTER LISTEN TO THE DOCTOR...
LISTEN, I KNOW YOU'RE HURTING AND YOU'RE ANGRY, BUT YOU NEED TO TELL YOURSELF THAT PRINCESS IS HURTING EVEN MORE. SHE'S IN VERY GREAT PAIN ALL OVER.
AT HER AGE, EVEN IF I DID OPERATE, SHE PROBABLY WOULD'NT SURVIVE...
PLUS ALL THOSE OPERATIONS WOULD COST $1000, MAYBE $1500... DO YOU HAVE $1000?
FINE, KILL HER, YOU STUPID IDIOT!
SLAM!
Yellow
COIFF

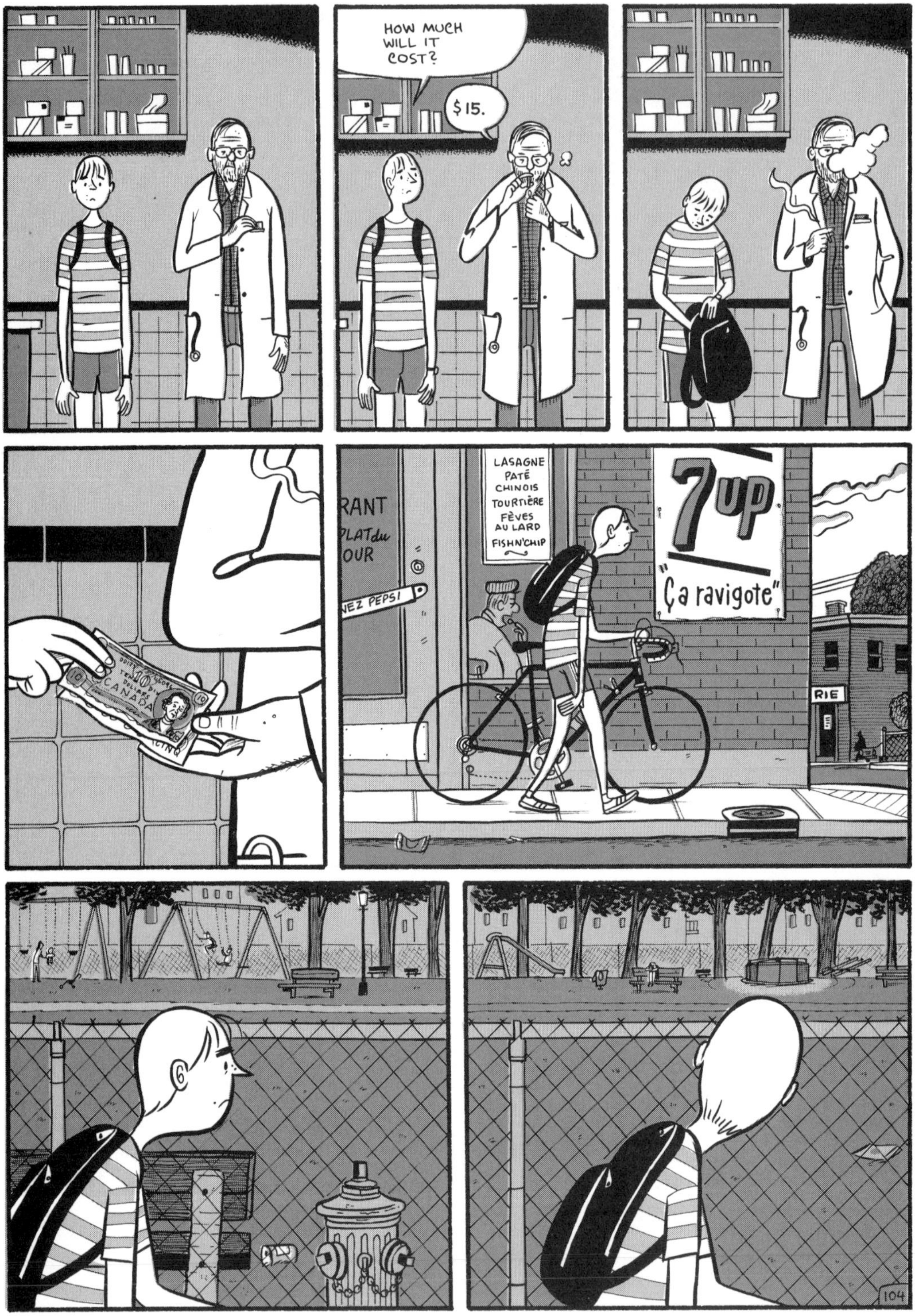
HOW MUCH WILL IT COST?
$15.
CANADA
RANT
PLAT du
OUR
NEZ PEPSI
LASAGNE
PATÉ CHINOIS
TOURTIÈRE
FÈVES AU LARD
FISHN'CHIP
7up
"Ça ravigote"
RIE

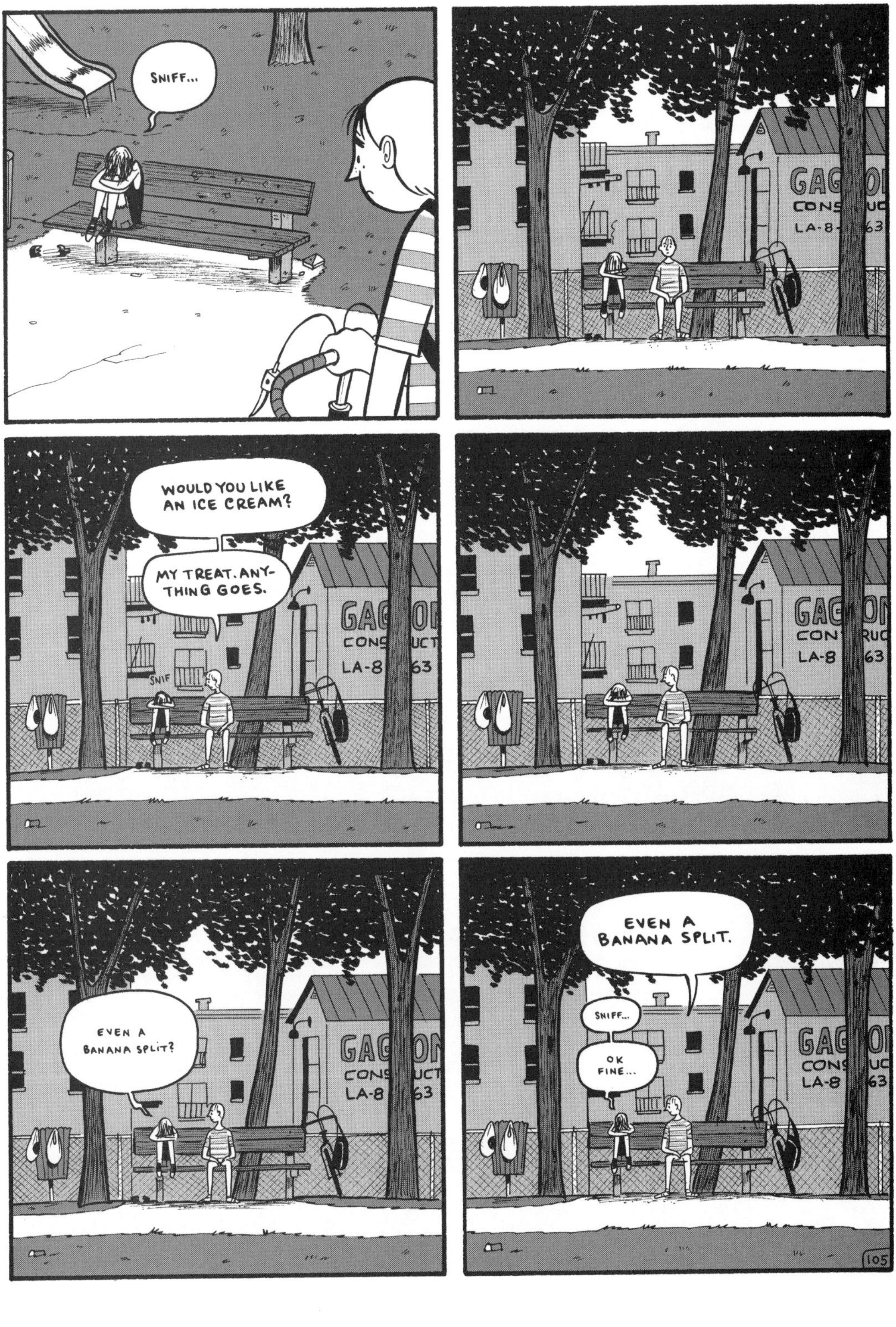
SNIFF...
WOULD YOU LIKE AN ICE CREAM?
MY TREAT. ANYTHING GOES.
SNIF
EVEN A BANANA SPLIT?
EVEN A BANANA SPLIT.
SNIFF...
OK FINE...

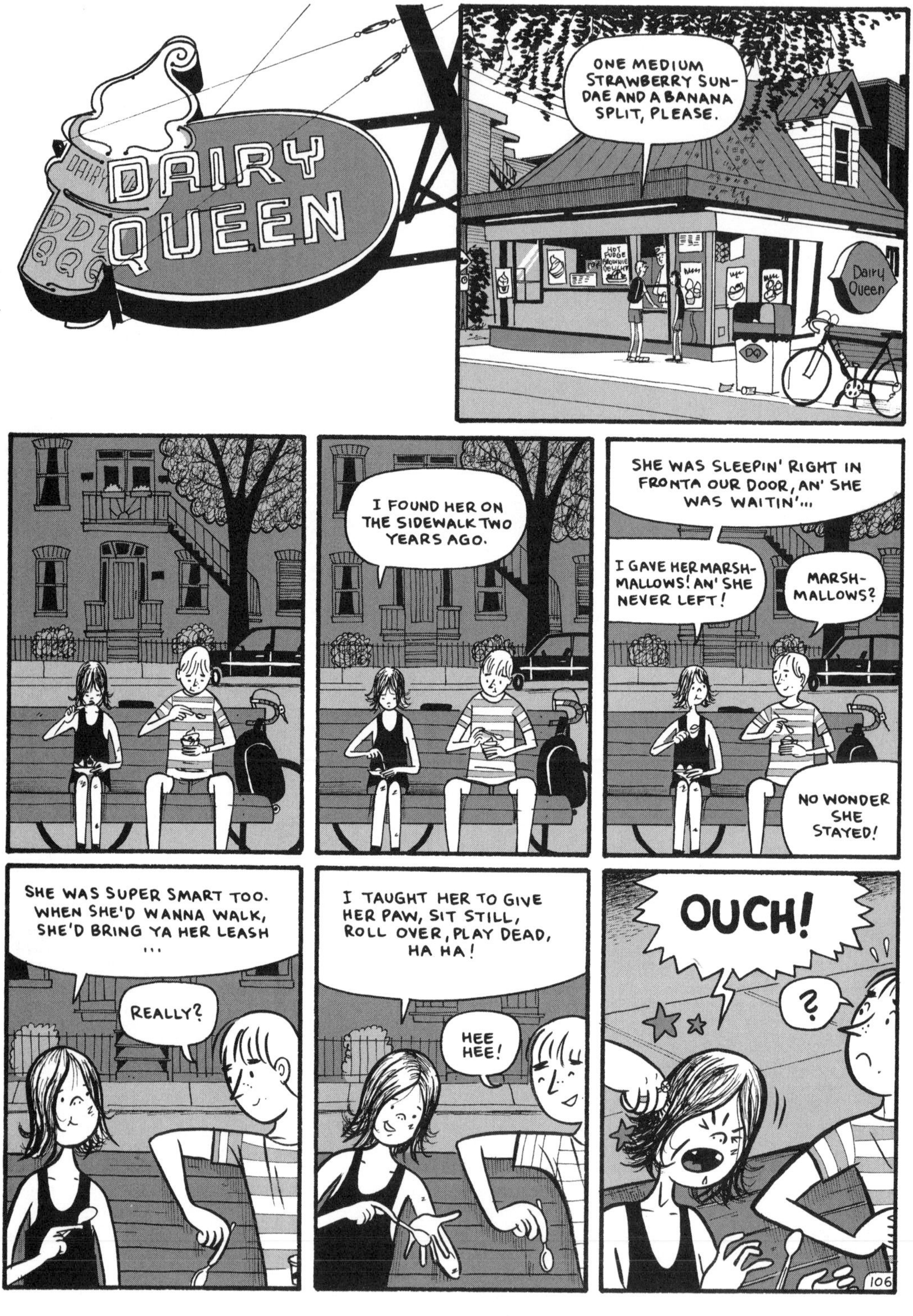

DAIRY QUEEN
ONE MEDIUM STRAWBERRY SUNDAE AND A BANANA SPLIT, PLEASE.
Dairy Queen
I FOUND HER ON THE SIDEWALK TWO YEARS AGO.
SHE WAS SLEEPIN' RIGHT IN FRONTA OUR DOOR, AN' SHE WAS WAITIN'...
I GAVE HER MARSHMALLOWS! AN' SHE NEVER LEFT!
MARSHMALLOWS?
NO WONDER SHE STAYED!
SHE WAS SUPER SMART TOO. WHEN SHE'D WANNA WALK, SHE'D BRING YA HER LEASH ...
REALLY?
I TAUGHT HER TO GIVE HER PAW, SIT STILL, ROLL OVER, PLAY DEAD, HA HA!
HEE HEE!
OUCH!
?

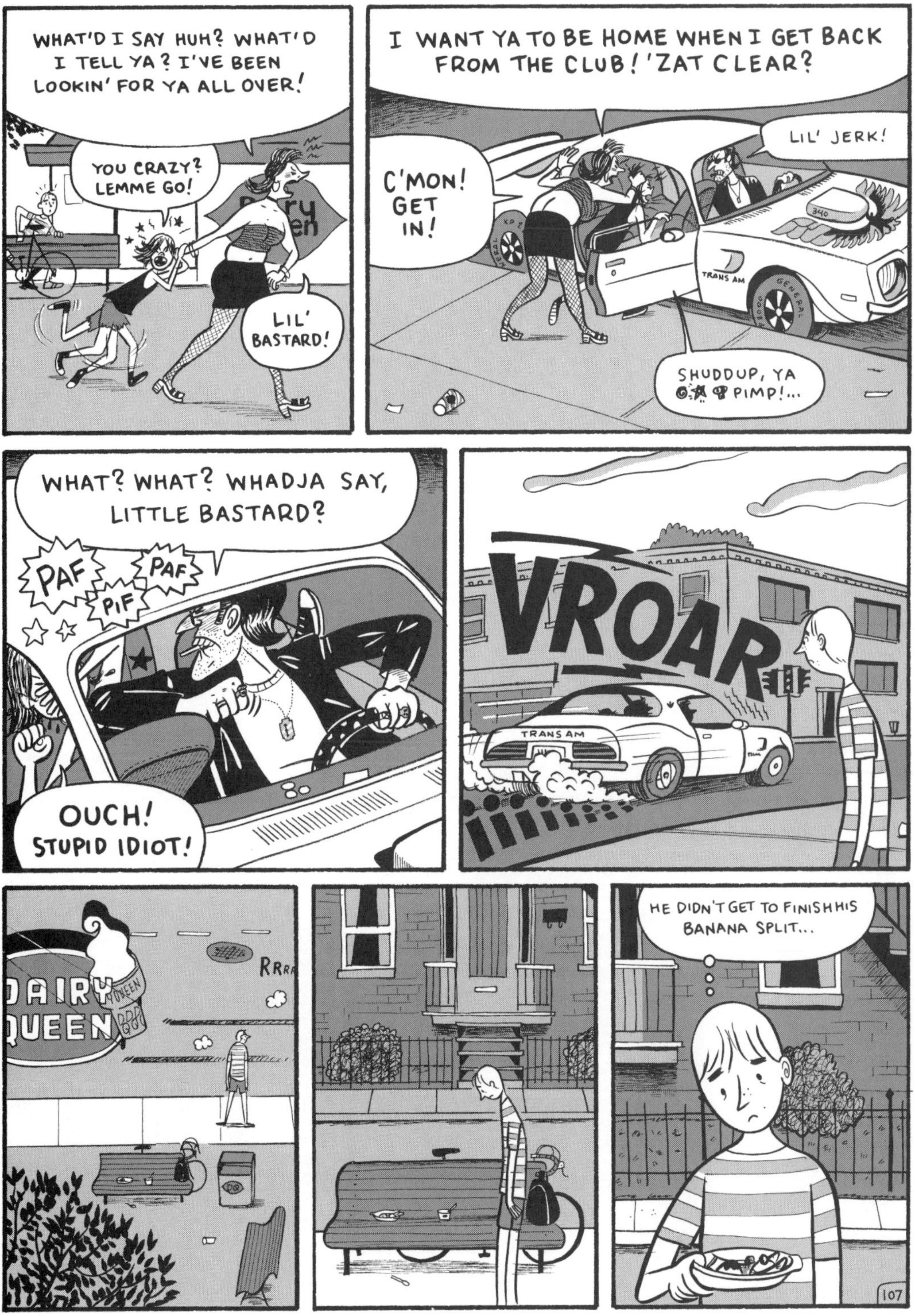
WHAT'D I SAY HUH? WHAT'D I TELL YA? I'VE BEEN LOOKIN' FOR YA ALL OVER!
YOU CRAZY? LEMME GO!
LIL' BASTARD!
I WANT YA TO BE HOME WHEN I GET BACK FROM THE CLUB! 'ZAT CLEAR?
C'MON! GET IN!
LIL' JERK!
TRANS AM
SHUDDUP, YA PIMP!...
WHAT? WHAT? WHADJA SAY, LITTLE BASTARD?
PAF
PIF
PAF
OUCH! STUPID IDIOT!
VROAR
TRANS AM
DAIRY QUEEN
RRRR
HE DIDN'T GET TO FINISH HIS BANANA SPLIT...

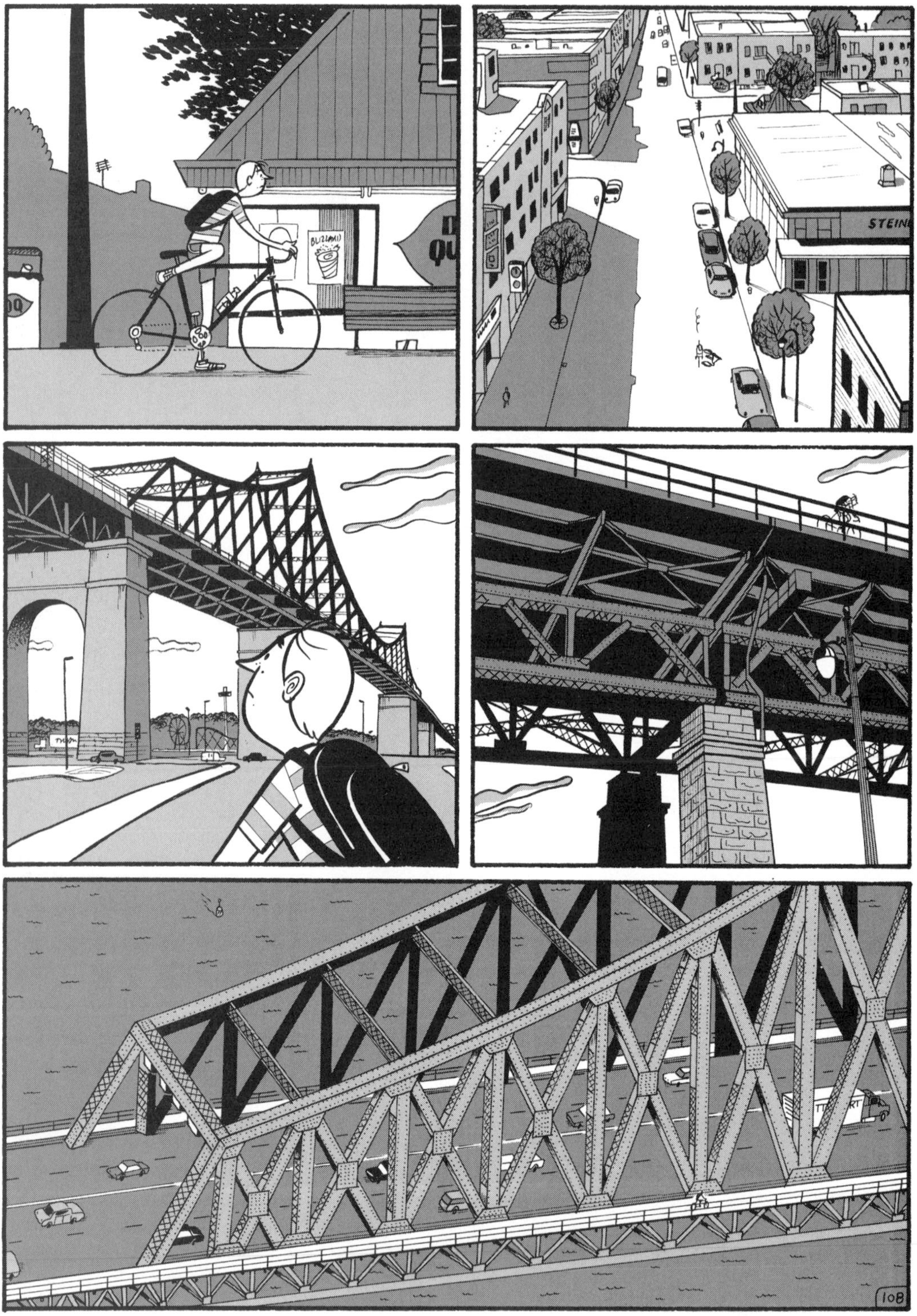
STEIN

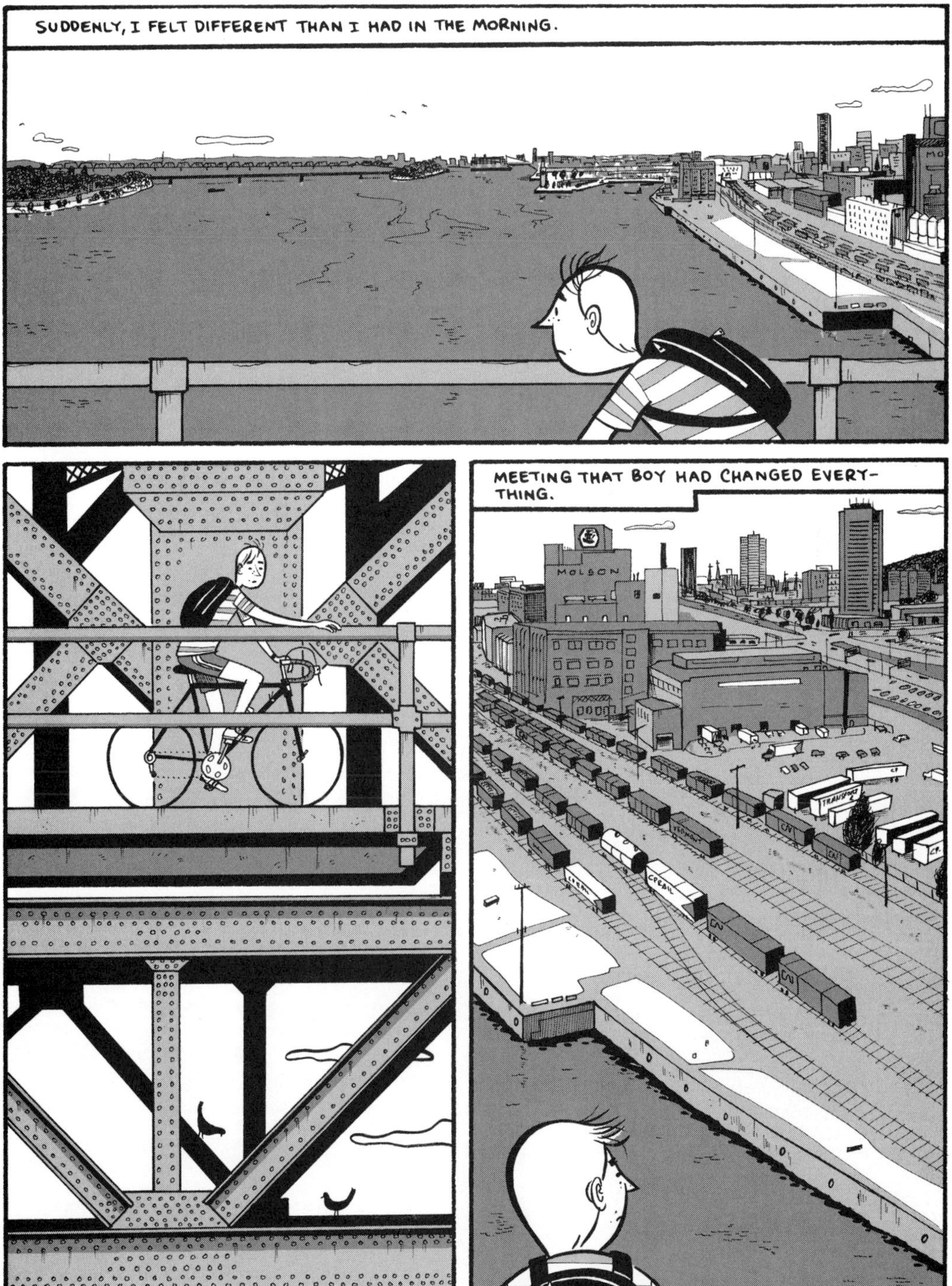
SUDDENLY, I FELT DIFFERENT THAN I HAD IN THE MORNING.
MEETING THAT BOY HAD CHANGED EVERY-THING.
MOLSON

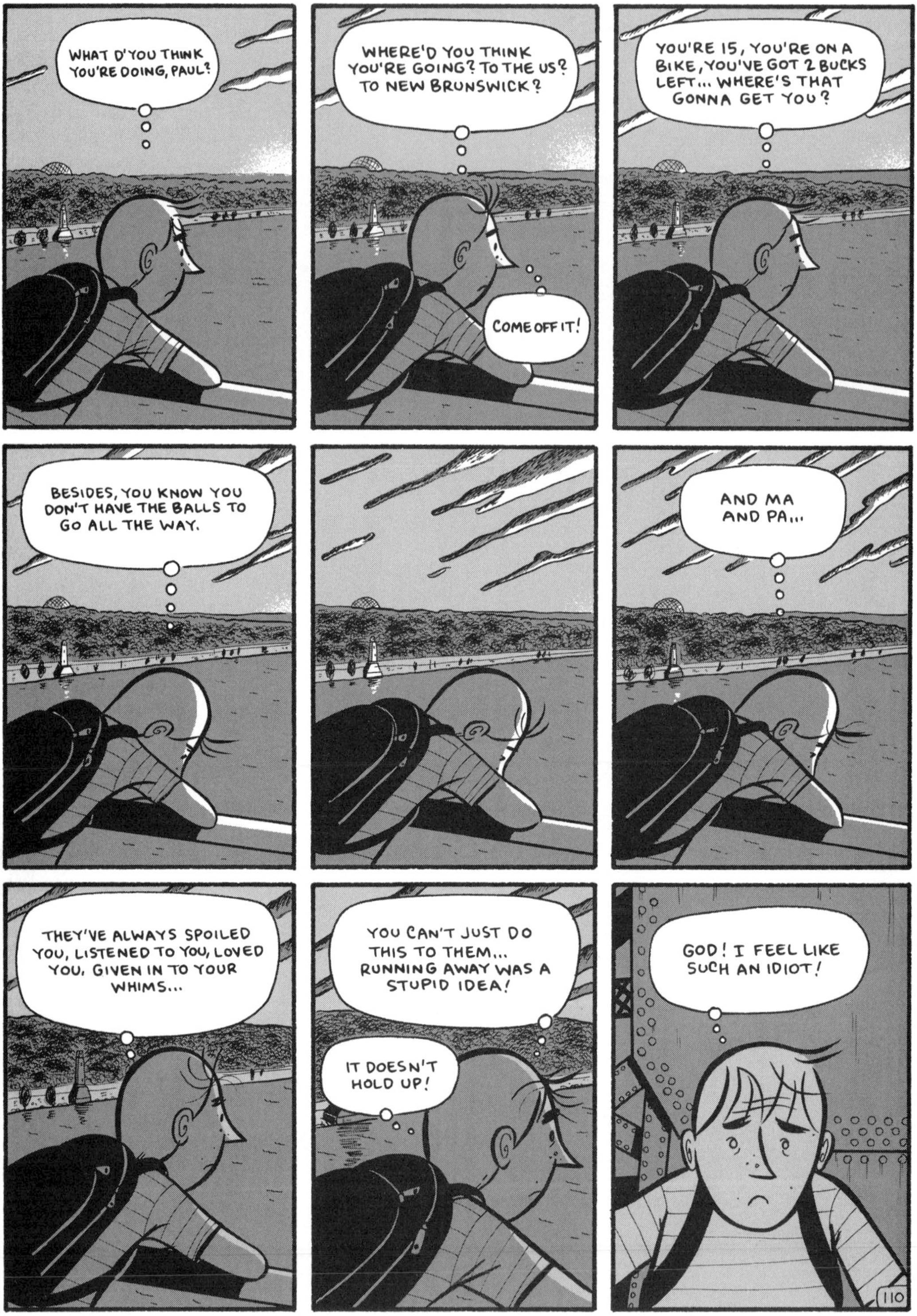
WHAT D'YOU THINK YOU'RE DOING, PAUL?
WHERE'D YOU THINK YOU'RE GOING? TO THE US? TO NEW BRUNSWICK?
COME OFF IT!
YOU'RE 15, YOU'RE ON A BIKE, YOU'VE GOT 2 BUCKS LEFT... WHERE'S THAT GONNA GET YOU?
BESIDES, YOU KNOW YOU DON'T HAVE THE BALLS TO GO ALL THE WAY.
AND MA AND PA...
THEY'VE ALWAYS SPOILED YOU, LISTENED TO YOU, LOVED YOU, GIVEN IN TO YOUR WHIMS...
YOU CAN'T JUST DO THIS TO THEM... RUNNING AWAY WAS A STUPID IDEA!
IT DOESN'T HOLD UP!
GOD! I FEEL LIKE SUCH AN IDIOT!

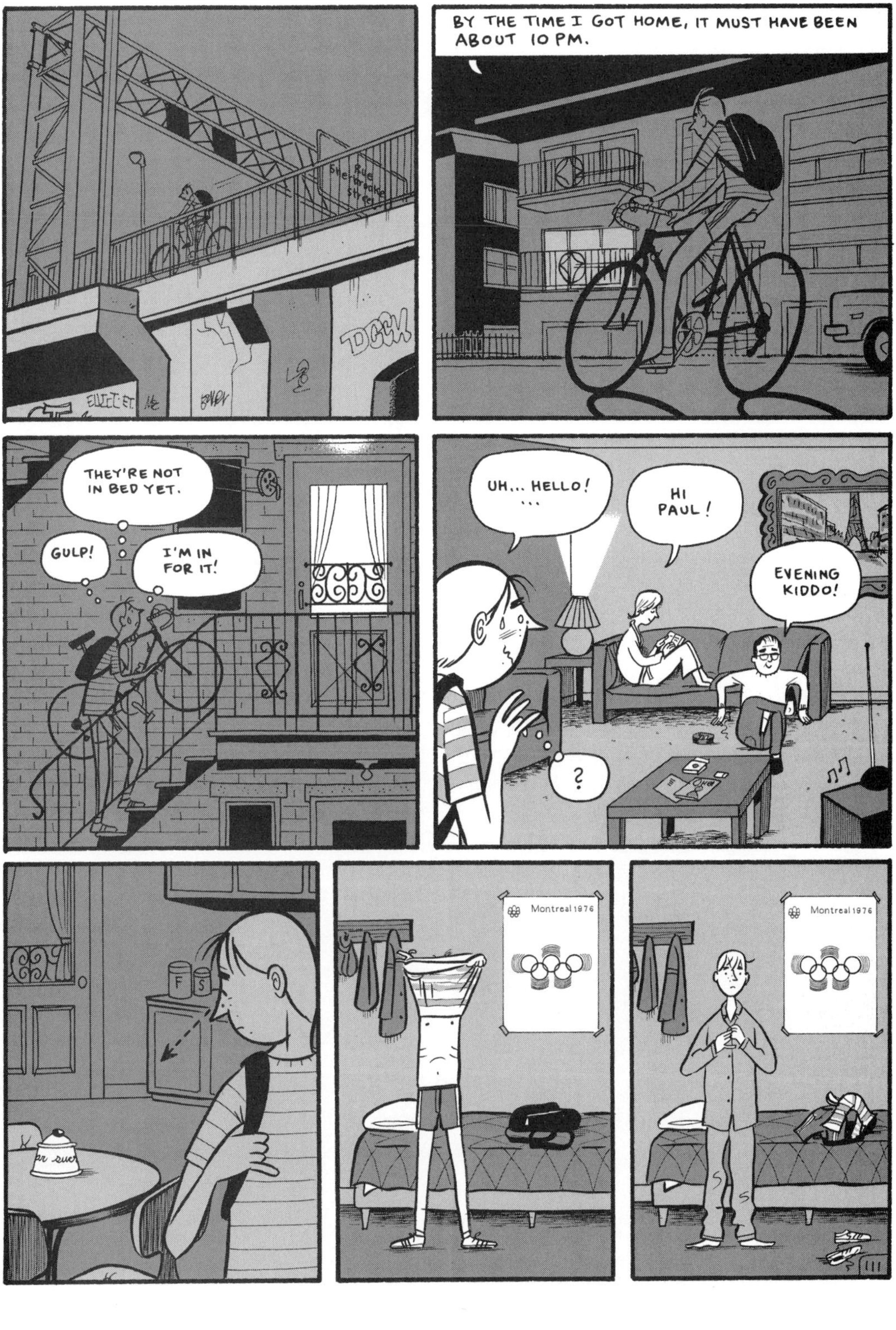
Rue Sherbrooke Street
BY THE TIME I GOT HOME, IT MUST HAVE BEEN ABOUT 10 PM.
THEY'RE NOT IN BED YET.
GULP!
I'M IN FOR IT!
UH... HELLO! ...
HI PAUL!
EVENING KIDDO!
?
Montreal 1976
Montreal 1976

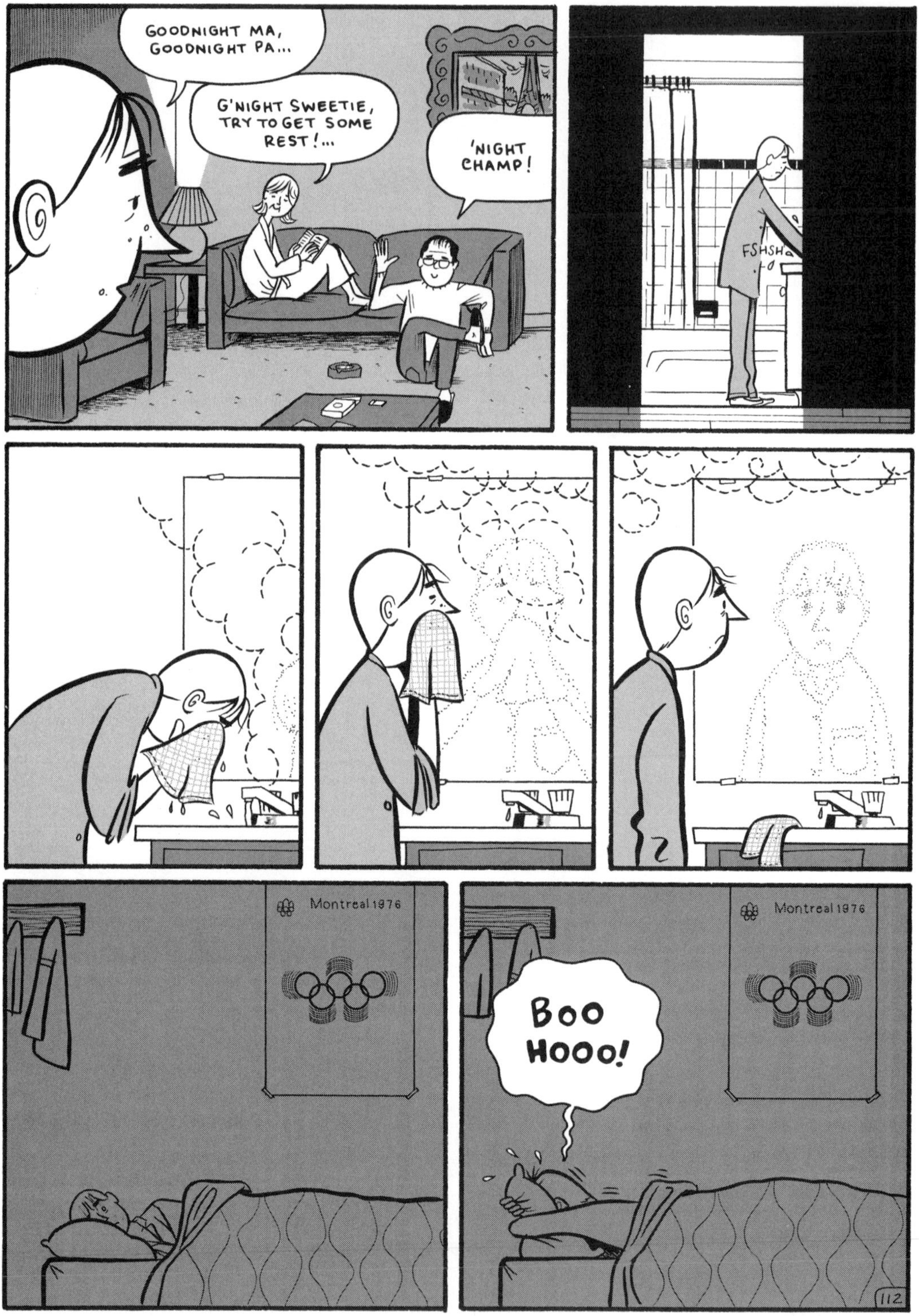
GOODNIGHT MA, GOODNIGHT PA...
G'NIGHT SWEETIE, TRY TO GET SOME REST!...
'NIGHT CHAMP!
FSHSHA
Montreal 1976
Montreal 1976
BOO HOOO!

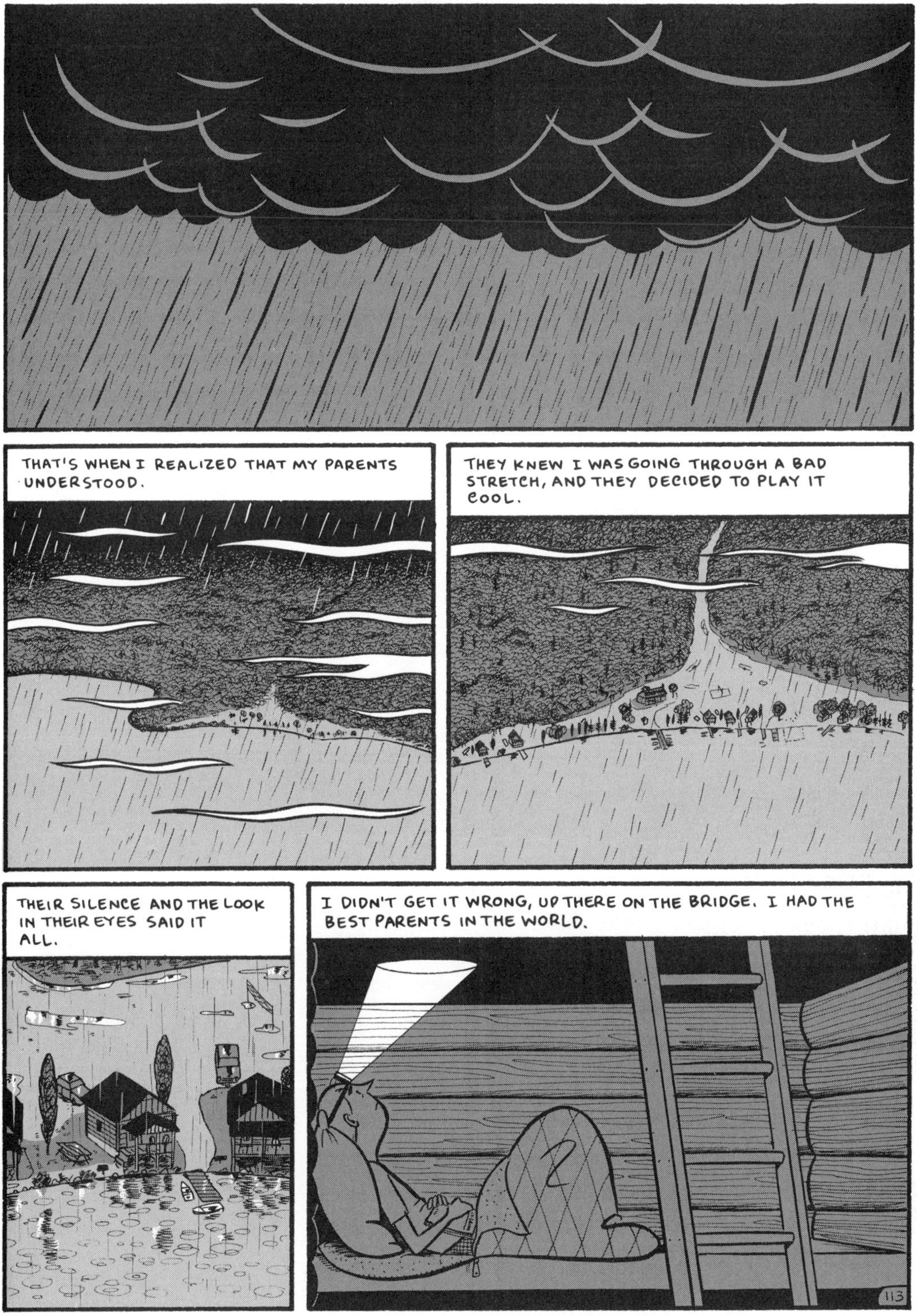
THAT'S WHEN I REALIZED THAT MY PARENTS UNDERSTOOD.
THEY KNEW I WAS GOING THROUGH A BAD STRETCH, AND THEY DECIDED TO PLAY IT COOL.
THEIR SILENCE AND THE LOOK IN THEIR EYES SAID IT ALL.
I DIDN'T GET IT WRONG, UP THERE ON THE BRIDGE. I HAD THE BEST PARENTS IN THE WORLD.
113

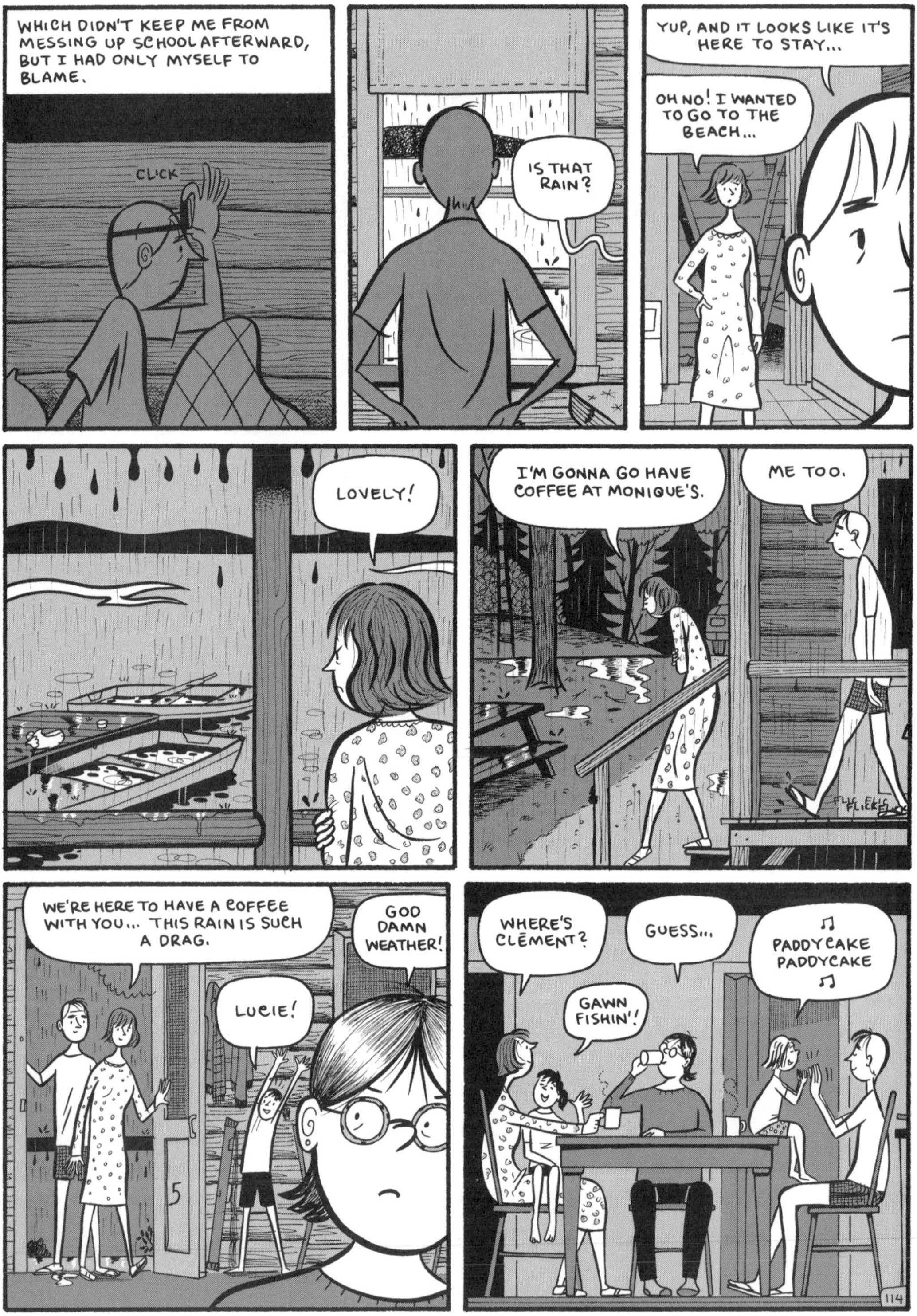
WHICH DIDN'T KEEP ME FROM MESSING UP SCHOOL AFTERWARD, BUT I HAD ONLY MYSELF TO BLAME.
CLICK
IS THAT RAIN?
YUP, AND IT LOOKS LIKE IT'S HERE TO STAY...
OH NO! I WANTED TO GO TO THE BEACH...
LOVELY!
I'M GONNA GO HAVE COFFEE AT MONIQUE'S.
ME TOO.
FLIC FLIC FLICK FLICK
WE'RE HERE TO HAVE A COFFEE WITH YOU... THIS RAIN IS SUCH A DRAG.
GOD DAMN WEATHER!
LUCIE!
5
WHERE'S CLÉMENT?
GUESS...
GAWN FISHIN'!
♫ PADDYCAKE PADDYCAKE ♫

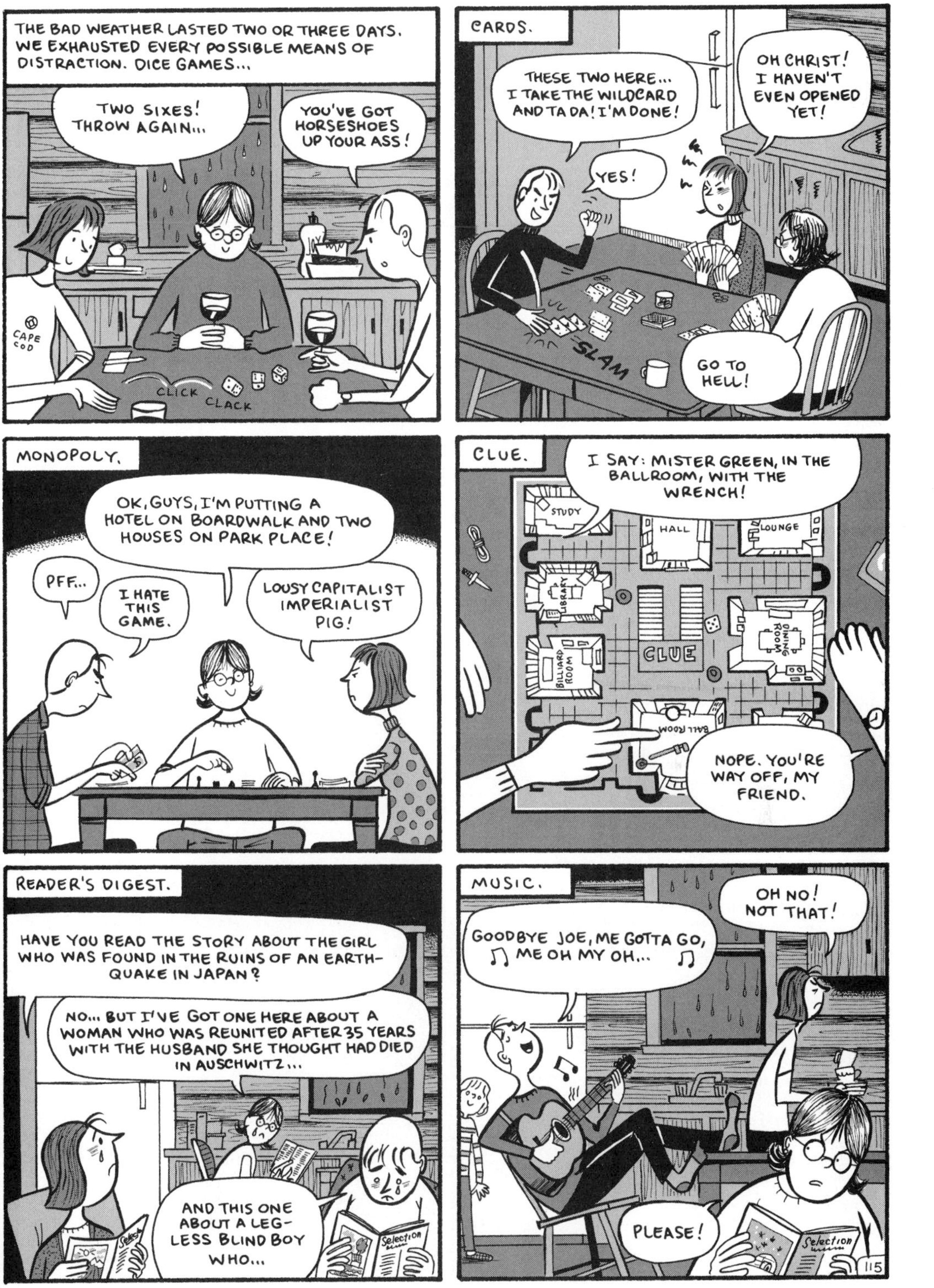
THE BAD WEATHER LASTED TWO OR THREE DAYS. WE EXHAUSTED EVERY POSSIBLE MEANS OF DISTRACTION. DICE GAMES...
TWO SIXES! THROW AGAIN...
YOU'VE GOT HORSESHOES UP YOUR ASS!
CAPE COD
CLICK
CLACK
CARDS.
THESE TWO HERE... I TAKE THE WILDCARD AND TA DA! I'M DONE!
OH CHRIST! I HAVEN'T EVEN OPENED YET!
YES!
SLAM
GO TO HELL!
MONOPOLY.
OK, GUYS, I'M PUTTING A HOTEL ON BOARDWALK AND TWO HOUSES ON PARK PLACE!
PFF...
I HATE THIS GAME.
LOUSY CAPITALIST IMPERIALIST PIG!
CLUE.
I SAY: MISTER GREEN, IN THE BALLROOM, WITH THE WRENCH!
STUDY
HALL
LOUNGE
LIBRARY
DINING ROOM
CLUE
BILLIARD ROOM
BALL ROOM
NOPE. YOU'RE WAY OFF, MY FRIEND.
READER'S DIGEST.
HAVE YOU READ THE STORY ABOUT THE GIRL WHO WAS FOUND IN THE RUINS OF AN EARTHQUAKE IN JAPAN?
NO... BUT I'VE GOT ONE HERE ABOUT A WOMAN WHO WAS REUNITED AFTER 35 YEARS WITH THE HUSBAND SHE THOUGHT HAD DIED IN AUSCHWITZ...
Selection
AND THIS ONE ABOUT A LEGLESS BLIND BOY WHO...
Selection
MUSIC.
OH NO! NOT THAT!
GOODBYE JOE, ME GOTTA GO, ♫ ME OH MY OH... ♫
PLEASE!
Selection

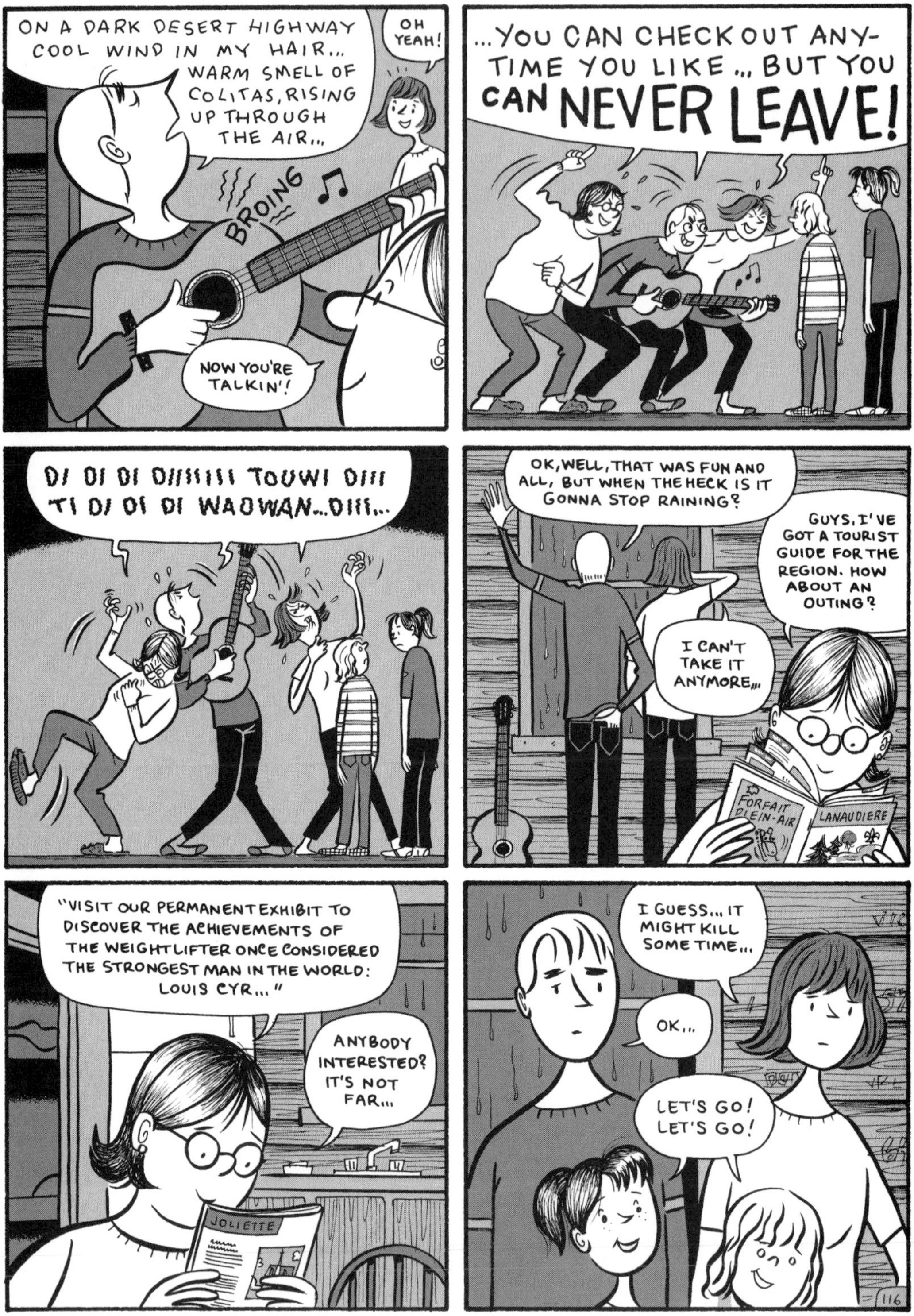
ON A DARK DESERT HIGHWAY
COOL WIND IN MY HAIR...
WARM SMELL OF COLITAS, RISING UP THROUGH THE AIR...
OH YEAH!
BROING
NOW YOU'RE TALKIN'!
...YOU CAN CHECK OUT ANY-TIME YOU LIKE... BUT YOU CAN NEVER LEAVE!
DI DI DI DI!!!!!! TOUWI DIII
TI DI DI DI WAOWAN...DIII...
OK, WELL, THAT WAS FUN AND ALL, BUT WHEN THE HECK IS IT GONNA STOP RAINING?
GUYS, I'VE GOT A TOURIST GUIDE FOR THE REGION. HOW ABOUT AN OUTING?
I CAN'T TAKE IT ANYMORE...
FORFAIT PLEIN-AIR
LANAUDIERE
"VISIT OUR PERMANENT EXHIBIT TO DISCOVER THE ACHIEVEMENTS OF THE WEIGHTLIFTER ONCE CONSIDERED THE STRONGEST MAN IN THE WORLD: LOUIS CYR..."
ANYBODY INTERESTED? IT'S NOT FAR...
JOLIETTE
I GUESS... IT MIGHT KILL SOME TIME...
OK...
LET'S GO! LET'S GO!

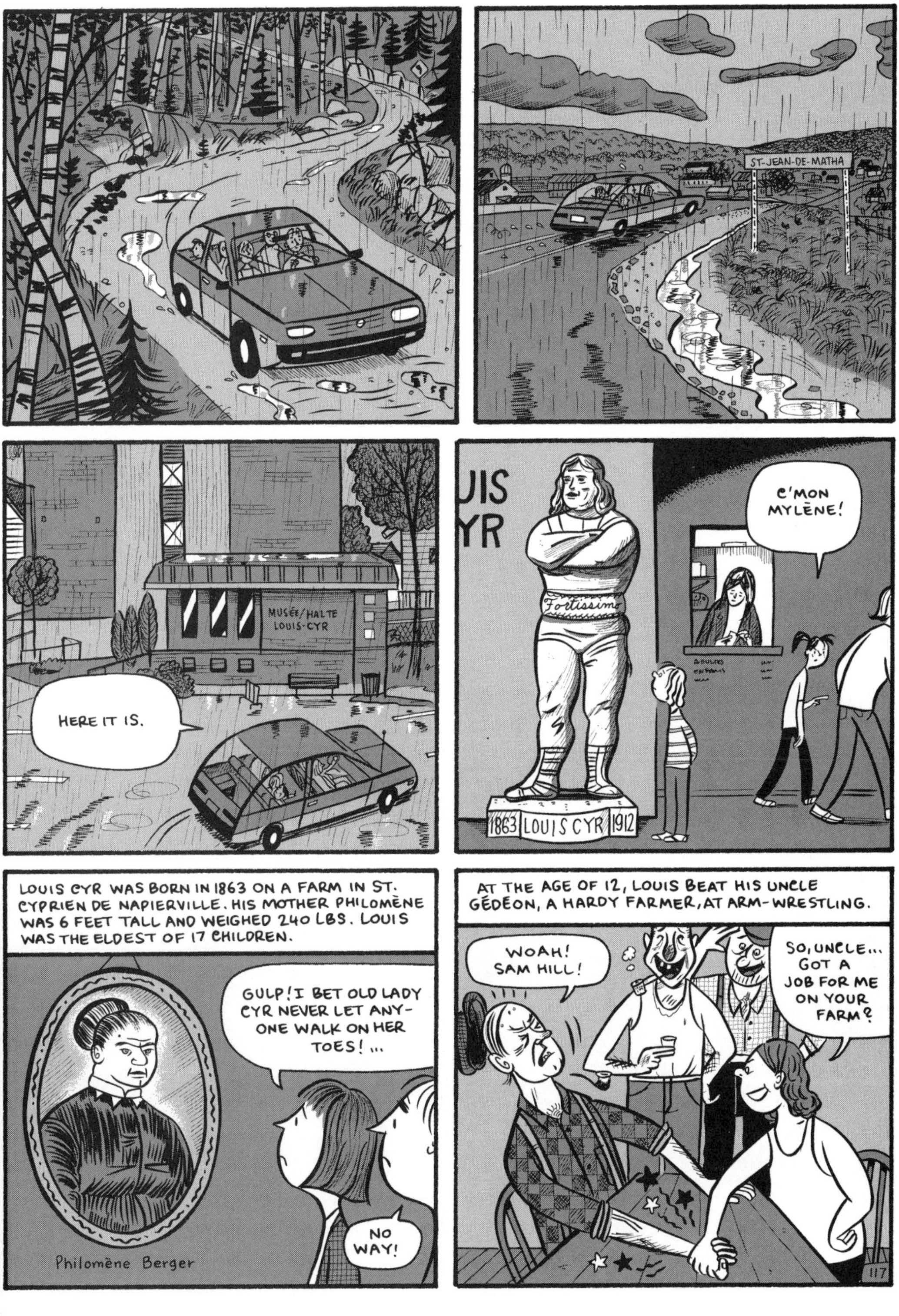
ST-JEAN-DE-MATHA
MUSÉE/HALTE LOUIS-CYR
HERE IT IS.
UIS
YR
Fortissimo
1863 LOUIS CYR 1912
C'MON MYLÈNE!
LOUIS CYR WAS BORN IN 1863 ON A FARM IN ST. CYPRIEN DE NAPIERVILLE. HIS MOTHER PHILOMÈNE WAS 6 FEET TALL AND WEIGHED 240 LBS. LOUIS WAS THE ELDEST OF 17 CHILDREN.
GULP! I BET OLD LADY CYR NEVER LET ANY-ONE WALK ON HER TOES! ...
NO WAY!
Philomène Berger
AT THE AGE OF 12, LOUIS BEAT HIS UNCLE GÉDEON, A HARDY FARMER, AT ARM-WRESTLING.
WOAH! SAM HILL!
SO, UNCLE... GOT A JOB FOR ME ON YOUR FARM?

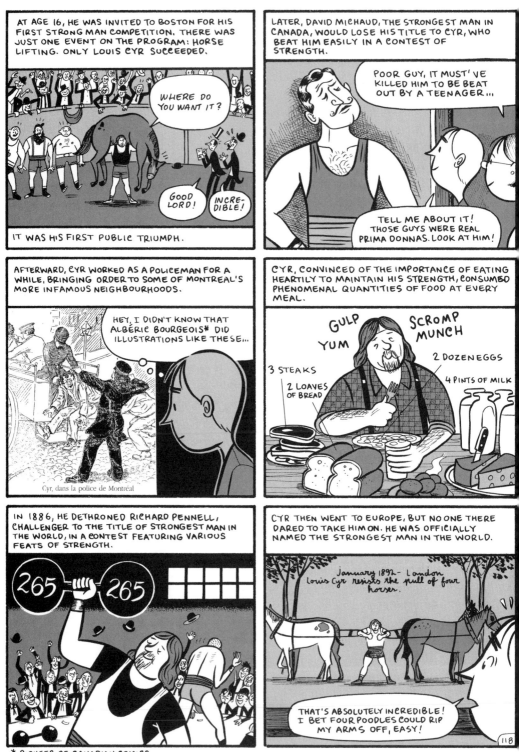

AT AGE 16, HE WAS INVITED TO BOSTON FOR HIS FIRST STRONG MAN COMPETITION. THERE WAS JUST ONE EVENT ON THE PROGRAM: HORSE LIFTING. ONLY LOUIS CYR SUCCEEDED.

WHERE DO YOU WANT IT?

GOOD LORD!

INCRE-DIBLE!

IT WAS HIS FIRST PUBLIC TRIUMPH.

LATER, DAVID MICHAUD, THE STRONGEST MAN IN CANADA, WOULD LOSE HIS TITLE TO CYR, WHO BEAT HIM EASILY IN A CONTEST OF STRENGTH.

POOR GUY, IT MUST'VE KILLED HIM TO BE BEAT OUT BY A TEENAGER...

TELL ME ABOUT IT! THOSE GUYS WERE REAL PRIMA DONNAS. LOOK AT HIM!

AFTERWARD, CYR WORKED AS A POLICEMAN FOR A WHILE, BRINGING ORDER TO SOME OF MONTREAL'S MORE INFAMOUS NEIGHBOURHOODS.

HEY, I DIDN'T KNOW THAT ALBÉRIC BOURGEOIS* DID ILLUSTRATIONS LIKE THESE...

Cyr, dans la police de Montréal

CYR, CONVINCED OF THE IMPORTANCE OF EATING HEARTILY TO MAINTAIN HIS STRENGTH, CONSUMED PHENOMENAL QUANTITIES OF FOOD AT EVERY MEAL.

GULP
YUM
SCROMP
MUNCH

3 STEAKS

2 LOAVES OF BREAD

2 DOZEN EGGS

4 PINTS OF MILK

IN 1886, HE DETHRONED RICHARD PENNELL, CHALLENGER TO THE TITLE OF STRONGEST MAN IN THE WORLD, IN A CONTEST FEATURING VARIOUS FEATS OF STRENGTH.

265   265

CYR THEN WENT TO EUROPE, BUT NO ONE THERE DARED TO TAKE HIM ON. HE WAS OFFICIALLY NAMED THE STRONGEST MAN IN THE WORLD.

January 1892 - London Louis Cyr resists the pull of four horses.

THAT'S ABSOLUTELY INCREDIBLE! I BET FOUR POODLES COULD RIP MY ARMS OFF, EASY!

118

* PIONEER OF CANADIAN COMICS

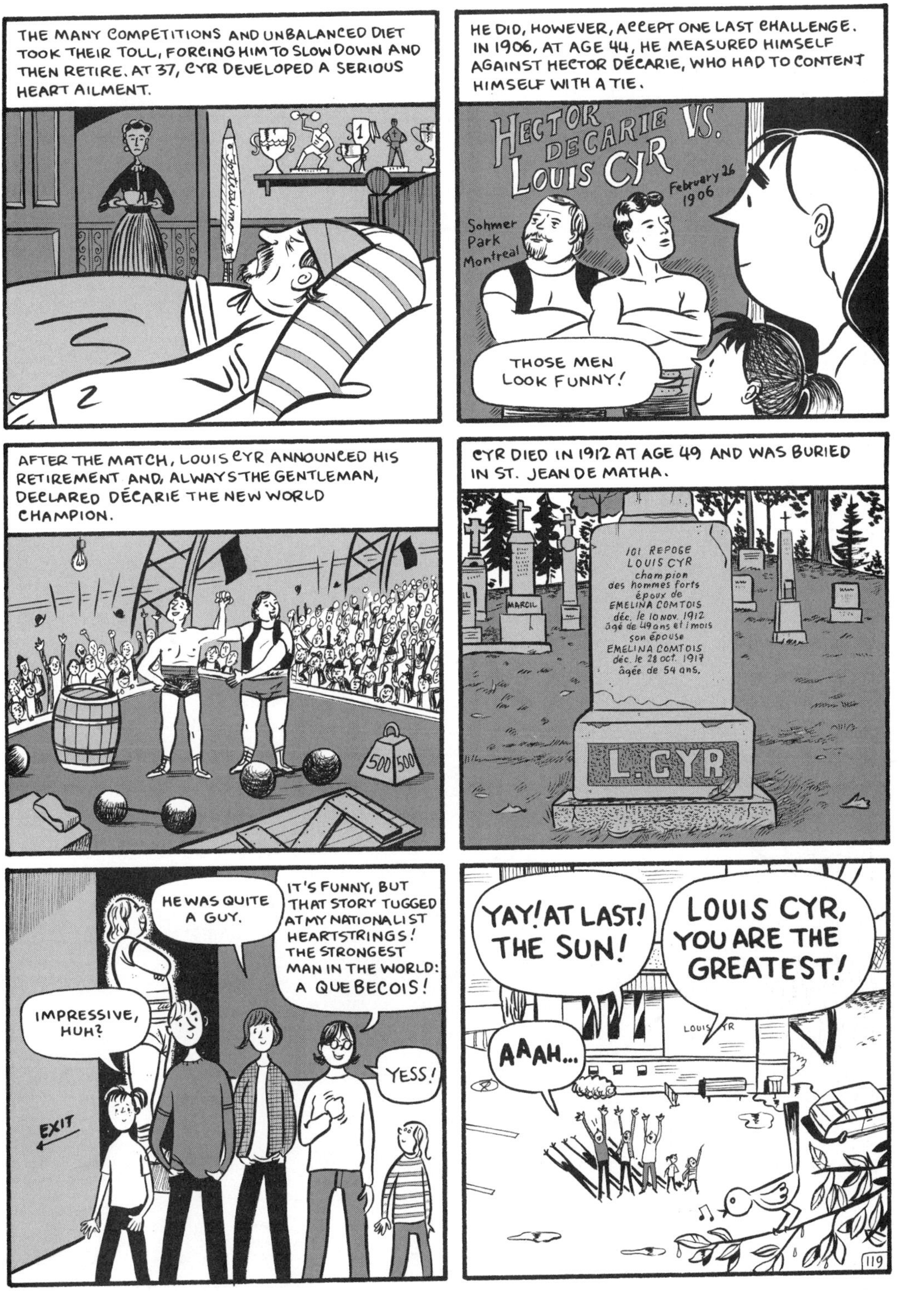
THE MANY COMPETITIONS AND UNBALANCED DIET TOOK THEIR TOLL, FORCING HIM TO SLOW DOWN AND THEN RETIRE. AT 37, CYR DEVELOPED A SERIOUS HEART AILMENT.
Z
HE DID, HOWEVER, ACCEPT ONE LAST CHALLENGE. IN 1906, AT AGE 44, HE MEASURED HIMSELF AGAINST HECTOR DÉCARIE, WHO HAD TO CONTENT HIMSELF WITH A TIE.
HECTOR DECARIE VS. LOUIS CYR
February 26 1906
Sohmer Park Montreal
THOSE MEN LOOK FUNNY!
AFTER THE MATCH, LOUIS CYR ANNOUNCED HIS RETIREMENT AND, ALWAYS THE GENTLEMAN, DECLARED DÉCARIE THE NEW WORLD CHAMPION.
500 500
CYR DIED IN 1912 AT AGE 49 AND WAS BURIED IN ST. JEAN DE MATHA.
MARCIL
ICI REPOSE LOUIS CYR champion des hommes forts époux de EMELINA COMTOIS déc. le 10 nov. 1912 âgé de 49 ans et 1 mois son épouse EMELINA COMTOIS déc. le 28 oct. 1917 âgée de 54 ans.
L. CYR
HE WAS QUITE A GUY.
IT'S FUNNY, BUT THAT STORY TUGGED AT MY NATIONALIST HEARTSTRINGS! THE STRONGEST MAN IN THE WORLD: A QUEBECOIS!
IMPRESSIVE, HUH?
YESS!
EXIT
YAY! AT LAST! THE SUN!
LOUIS CYR, YOU ARE THE GREATEST!
AAAH...

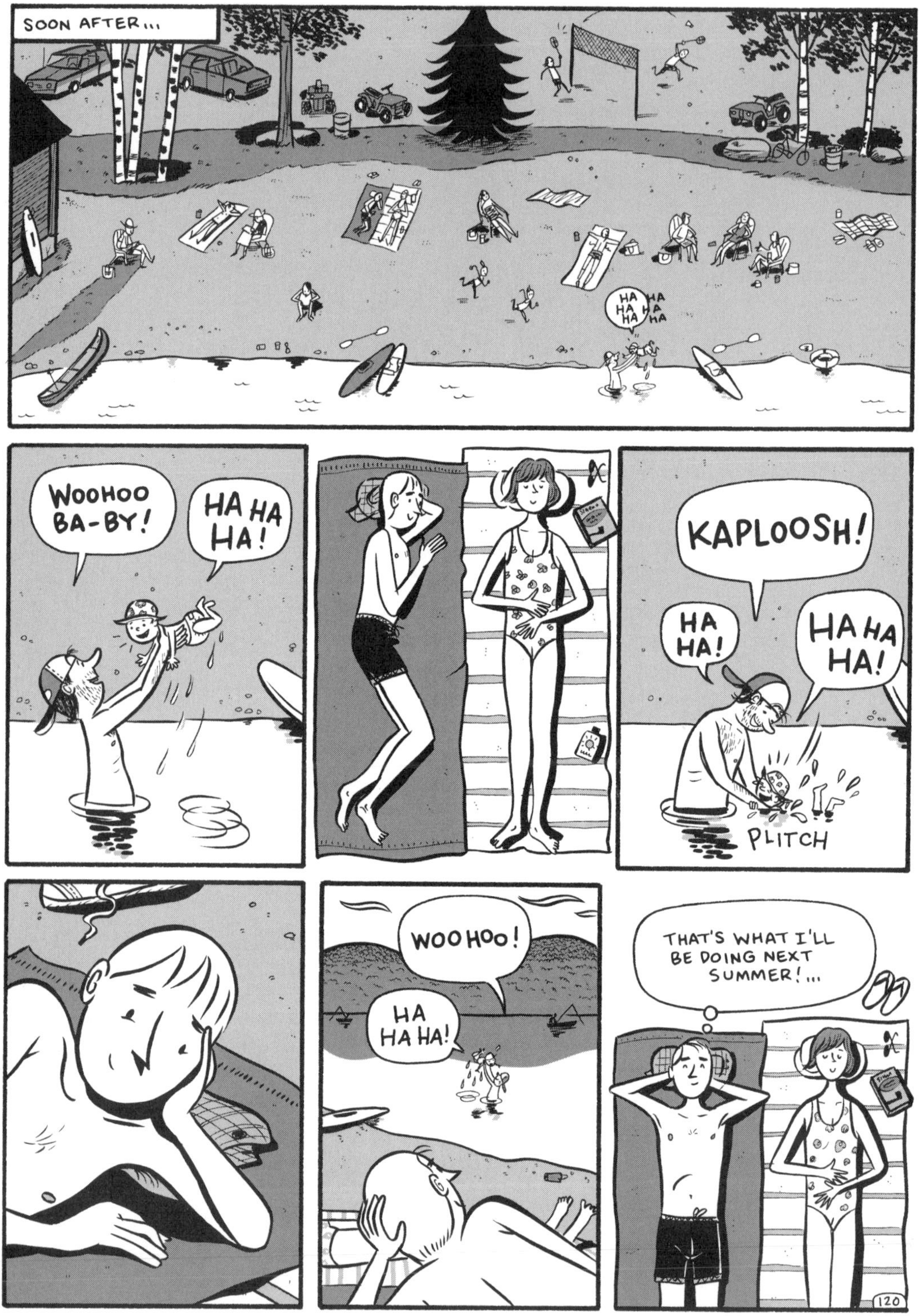
SOON AFTER...
HA HA HA HA HA HA HA HA
WOOHOO BA-BY!
HA HA HA!
KAPLOOSH!
HA HA!
HA HA HA!
PLITCH
WOO HOO!
HA HA HA!
THAT'S WHAT I'LL BE DOING NEXT SUMMER!...

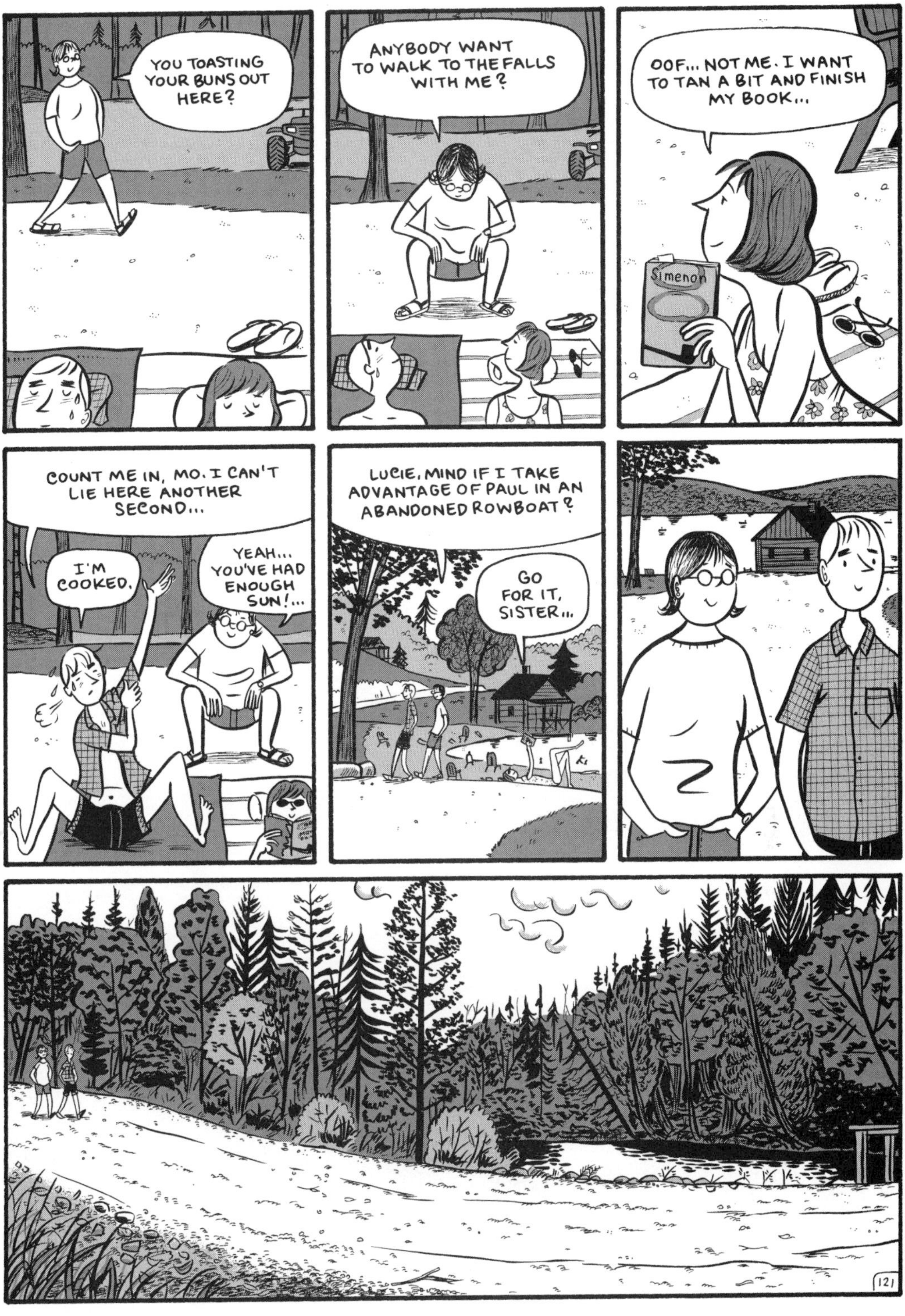
YOU TOASTING YOUR BUNS OUT HERE?
ANYBODY WANT TO WALK TO THE FALLS WITH ME?
OOF... NOT ME. I WANT TO TAN A BIT AND FINISH MY BOOK...
Simenon
COUNT ME IN, MO. I CAN'T LIE HERE ANOTHER SECOND...
I'M COOKED.
YEAH... YOU'VE HAD ENOUGH SUN!...
LUCIE, MIND IF I TAKE ADVANTAGE OF PAUL IN AN ABANDONED ROWBOAT?
GO FOR IT, SISTER...

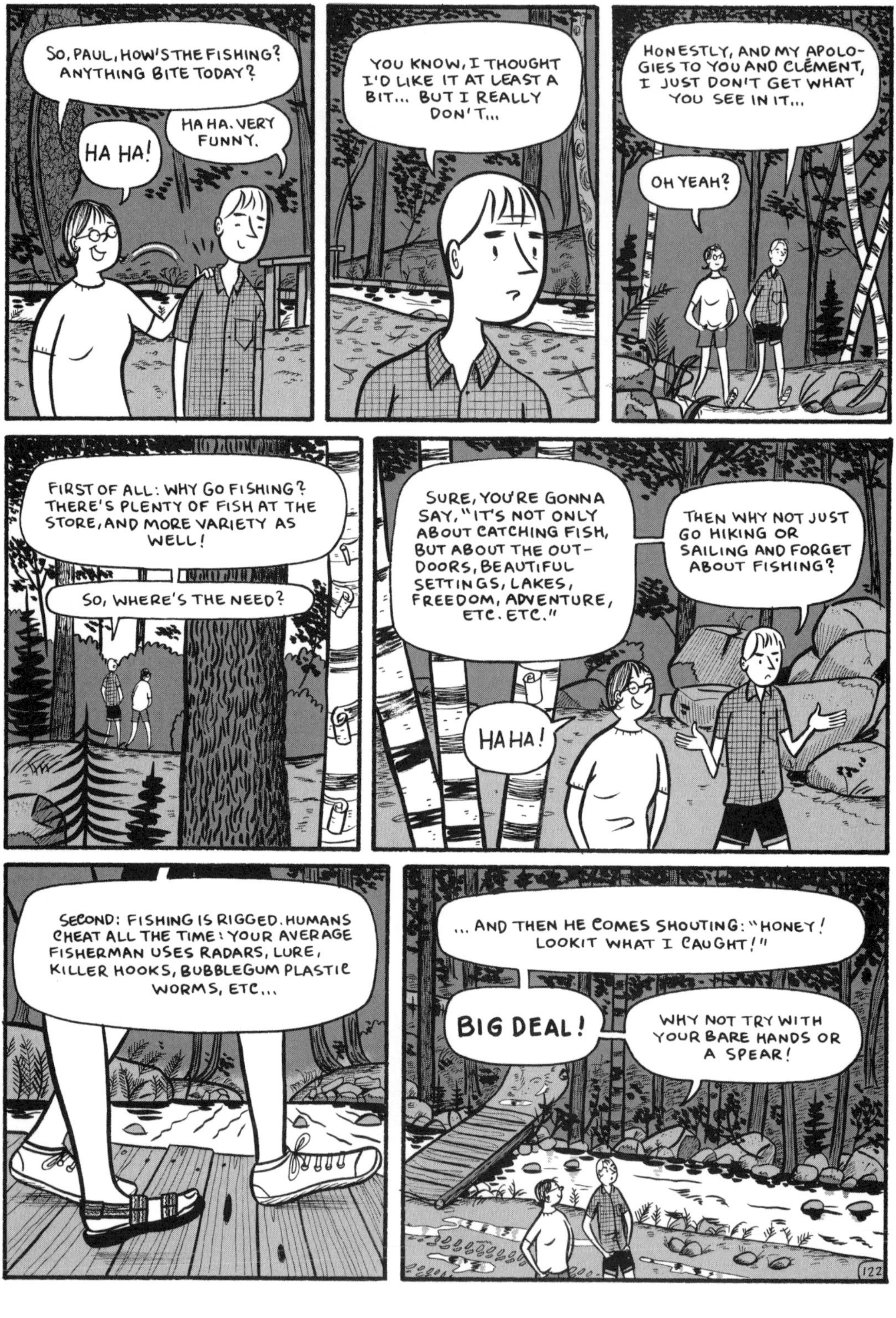
SO, PAUL, HOW'S THE FISHING? ANYTHING BITE TODAY?
HA HA!
HA HA. VERY FUNNY.
YOU KNOW, I THOUGHT I'D LIKE IT AT LEAST A BIT... BUT I REALLY DON'T...
HONESTLY, AND MY APOLOGIES TO YOU AND CLÉMENT, I JUST DON'T GET WHAT YOU SEE IN IT...
OH YEAH?
FIRST OF ALL: WHY GO FISHING? THERE'S PLENTY OF FISH AT THE STORE, AND MORE VARIETY AS WELL!
SO, WHERE'S THE NEED?
SURE, YOU'RE GONNA SAY, "IT'S NOT ONLY ABOUT CATCHING FISH, BUT ABOUT THE OUTDOORS, BEAUTIFUL SETTINGS, LAKES, FREEDOM, ADVENTURE, ETC. ETC."
THEN WHY NOT JUST GO HIKING OR SAILING AND FORGET ABOUT FISHING?
HA HA!
SECOND: FISHING IS RIGGED. HUMANS CHEAT ALL THE TIME: YOUR AVERAGE FISHERMAN USES RADARS, LURE, KILLER HOOKS, BUBBLEGUM PLASTIC WORMS, ETC...
... AND THEN HE COMES SHOUTING: "HONEY! LOOKIT WHAT I CAUGHT!"
BIG DEAL!
WHY NOT TRY WITH YOUR BARE HANDS OR A SPEAR!

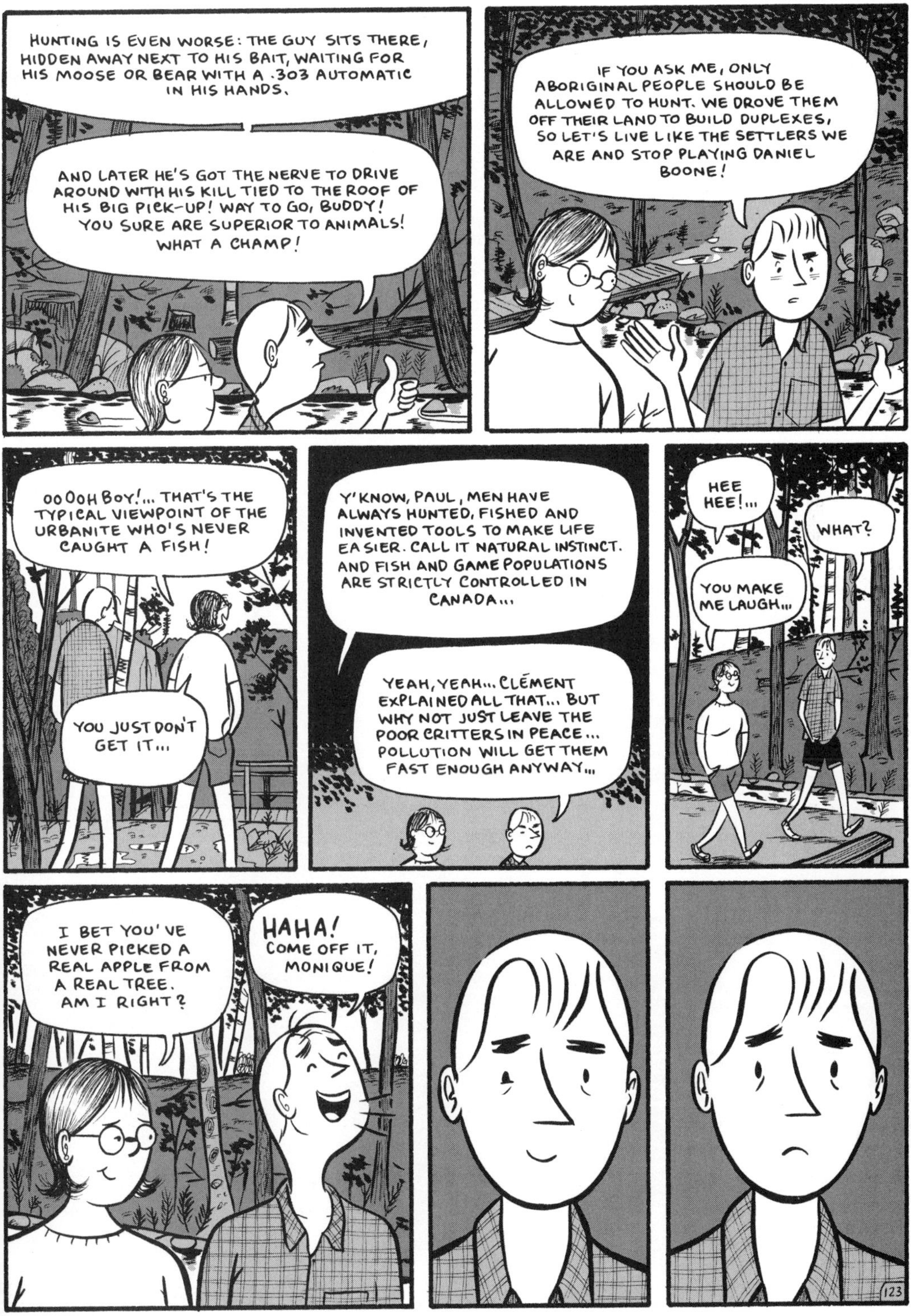
HUNTING IS EVEN WORSE: THE GUY SITS THERE, HIDDEN AWAY NEXT TO HIS BAIT, WAITING FOR HIS MOOSE OR BEAR WITH A .303 AUTOMATIC IN HIS HANDS.
AND LATER HE'S GOT THE NERVE TO DRIVE AROUND WITH HIS KILL TIED TO THE ROOF OF HIS BIG PICK-UP! WAY TO GO, BUDDY! YOU SURE ARE SUPERIOR TO ANIMALS! WHAT A CHAMP!
IF YOU ASK ME, ONLY ABORIGINAL PEOPLE SHOULD BE ALLOWED TO HUNT. WE DROVE THEM OFF THEIR LAND TO BUILD DUPLEXES, SO LET'S LIVE LIKE THE SETTLERS WE ARE AND STOP PLAYING DANIEL BOONE!
OOOOH BOY!... THAT'S THE TYPICAL VIEWPOINT OF THE URBANITE WHO'S NEVER CAUGHT A FISH!
YOU JUST DON'T GET IT...
Y'KNOW, PAUL, MEN HAVE ALWAYS HUNTED, FISHED AND INVENTED TOOLS TO MAKE LIFE EASIER. CALL IT NATURAL INSTINCT. AND FISH AND GAME POPULATIONS ARE STRICTLY CONTROLLED IN CANADA...
YEAH, YEAH... CLÉMENT EXPLAINED ALL THAT... BUT WHY NOT JUST LEAVE THE POOR CRITTERS IN PEACE... POLLUTION WILL GET THEM FAST ENOUGH ANYWAY...
HEE HEE!...
WHAT?
YOU MAKE ME LAUGH...
I BET YOU'VE NEVER PICKED A REAL APPLE FROM A REAL TREE. AM I RIGHT?
HAHA! COME OFF IT, MONIQUE!

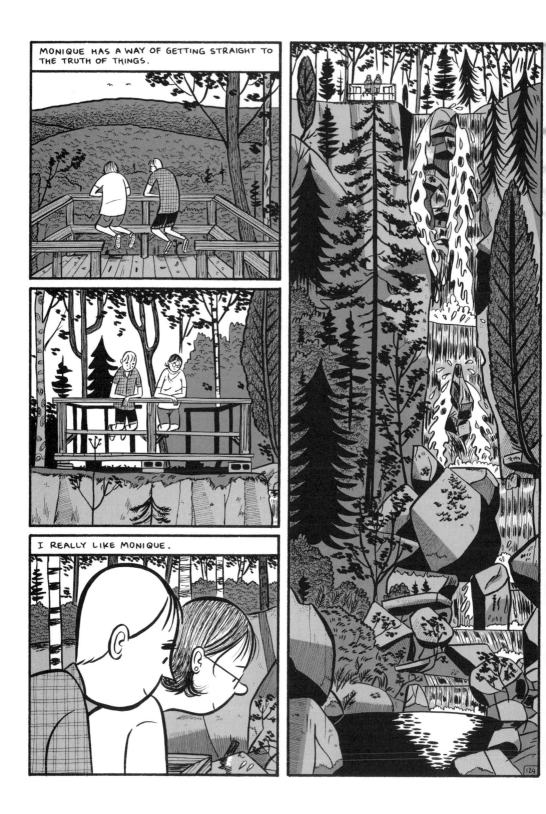

MONIQUE HAS A WAY OF GETTING STRAIGHT TO THE TRUTH OF THINGS.

I REALLY LIKE MONIQUE.

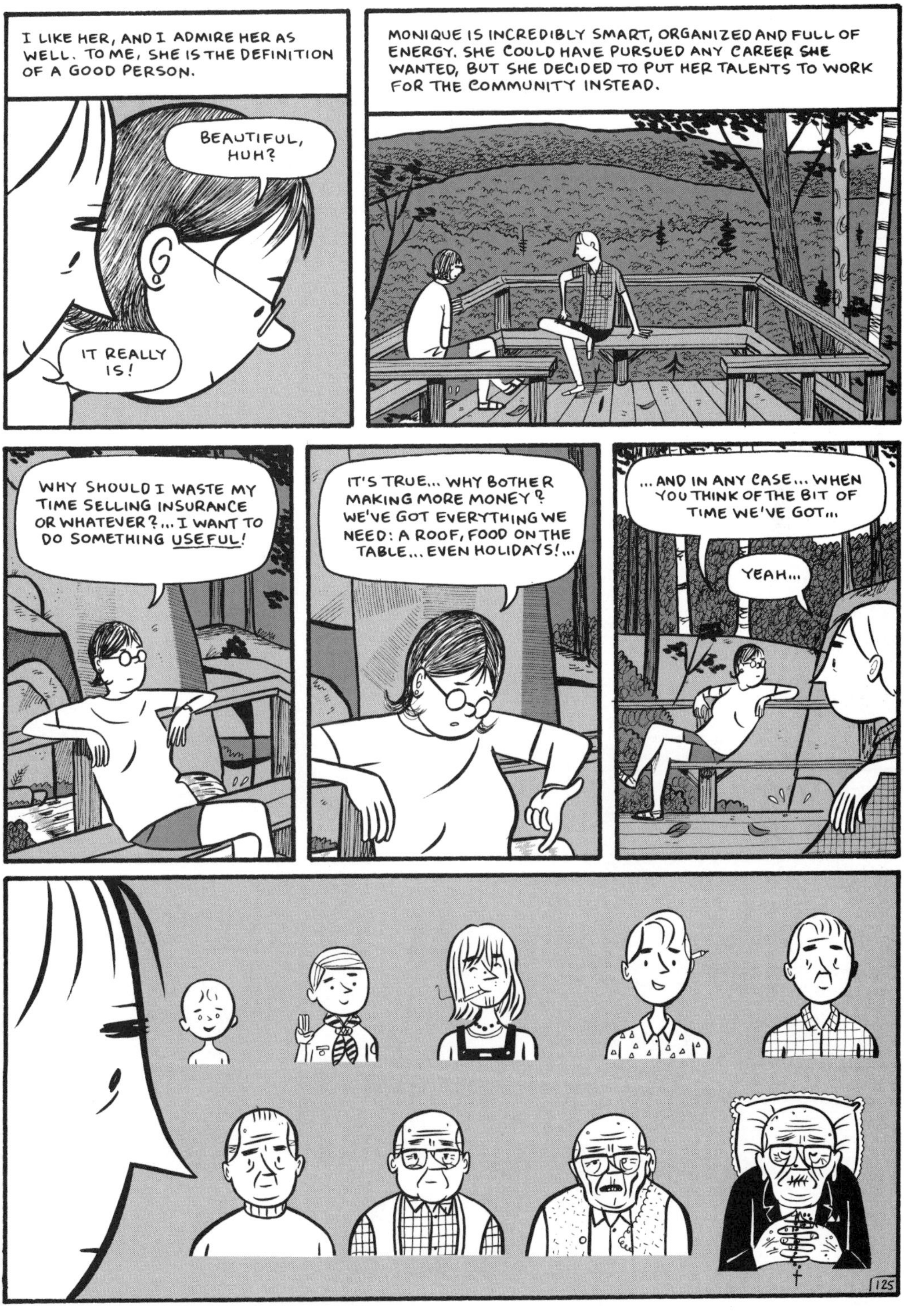
I LIKE HER, AND I ADMIRE HER AS WELL. TO ME, SHE IS THE DEFINITION OF A GOOD PERSON.
BEAUTIFUL, HUH?
IT REALLY IS!
MONIQUE IS INCREDIBLY SMART, ORGANIZED AND FULL OF ENERGY. SHE COULD HAVE PURSUED ANY CAREER SHE WANTED, BUT SHE DECIDED TO PUT HER TALENTS TO WORK FOR THE COMMUNITY INSTEAD.
WHY SHOULD I WASTE MY TIME SELLING INSURANCE OR WHATEVER?... I WANT TO DO SOMETHING USEFUL!
IT'S TRUE... WHY BOTHER MAKING MORE MONEY? WE'VE GOT EVERYTHING WE NEED: A ROOF, FOOD ON THE TABLE... EVEN HOLIDAYS!...
...AND IN ANY CASE... WHEN YOU THINK OF THE BIT OF TIME WE'VE GOT...
YEAH...

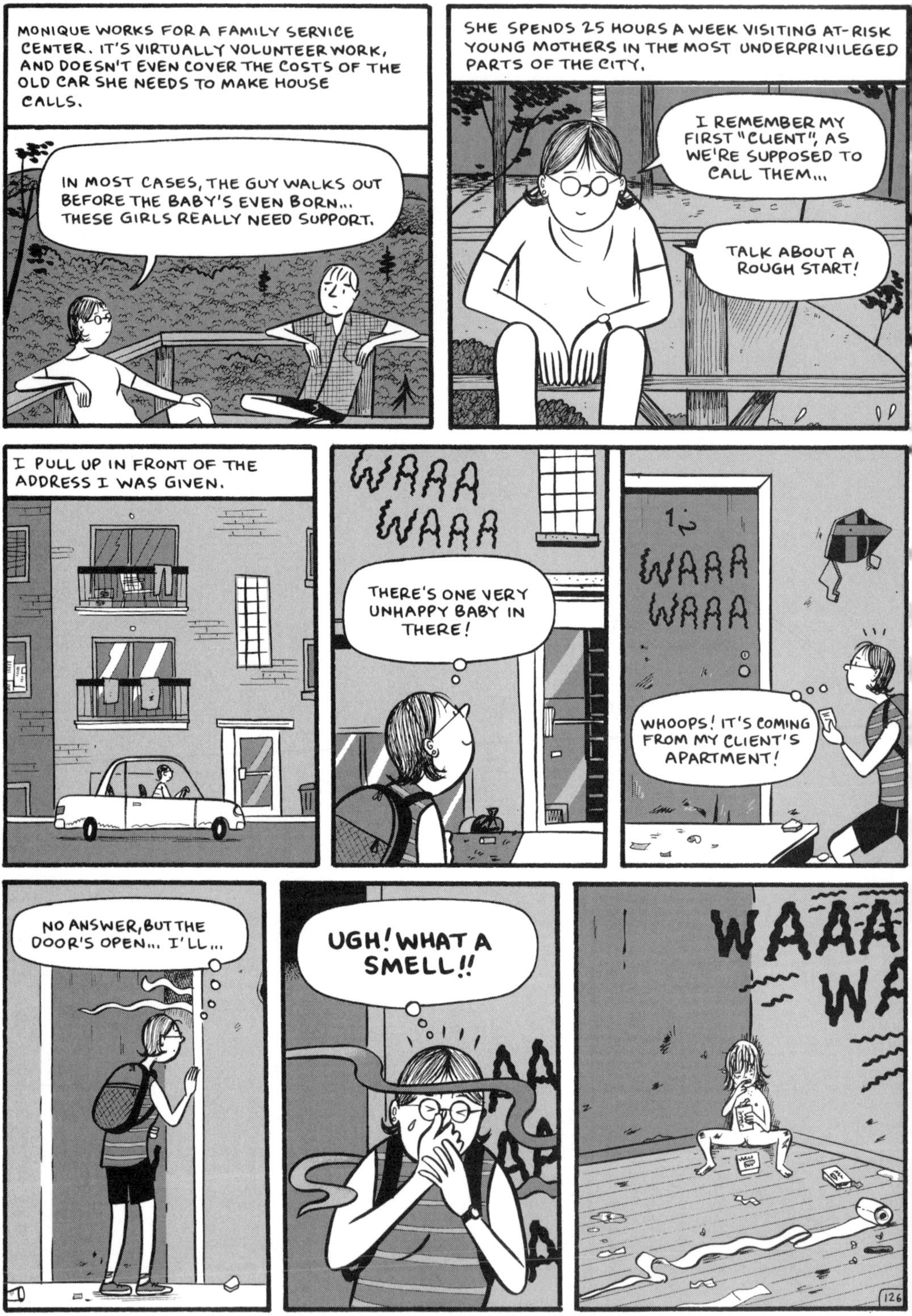
MONIQUE WORKS FOR A FAMILY SERVICE CENTER. IT'S VIRTUALLY VOLUNTEER WORK, AND DOESN'T EVEN COVER THE COSTS OF THE OLD CAR SHE NEEDS TO MAKE HOUSE CALLS.
IN MOST CASES, THE GUY WALKS OUT BEFORE THE BABY'S EVEN BORN... THESE GIRLS REALLY NEED SUPPORT.
SHE SPENDS 25 HOURS A WEEK VISITING AT-RISK YOUNG MOTHERS IN THE MOST UNDERPRIVILEGED PARTS OF THE CITY.
I REMEMBER MY FIRST "CLIENT", AS WE'RE SUPPOSED TO CALL THEM...
TALK ABOUT A ROUGH START!
I PULL UP IN FRONT OF THE ADDRESS I WAS GIVEN.
WAAA WAAA
THERE'S ONE VERY UNHAPPY BABY IN THERE!
WAAA WAAA
WHOOPS! IT'S COMING FROM MY CLIENT'S APARTMENT!
NO ANSWER, BUT THE DOOR'S OPEN... I'LL...
UGH! WHAT A SMELL!!
WAAA WA

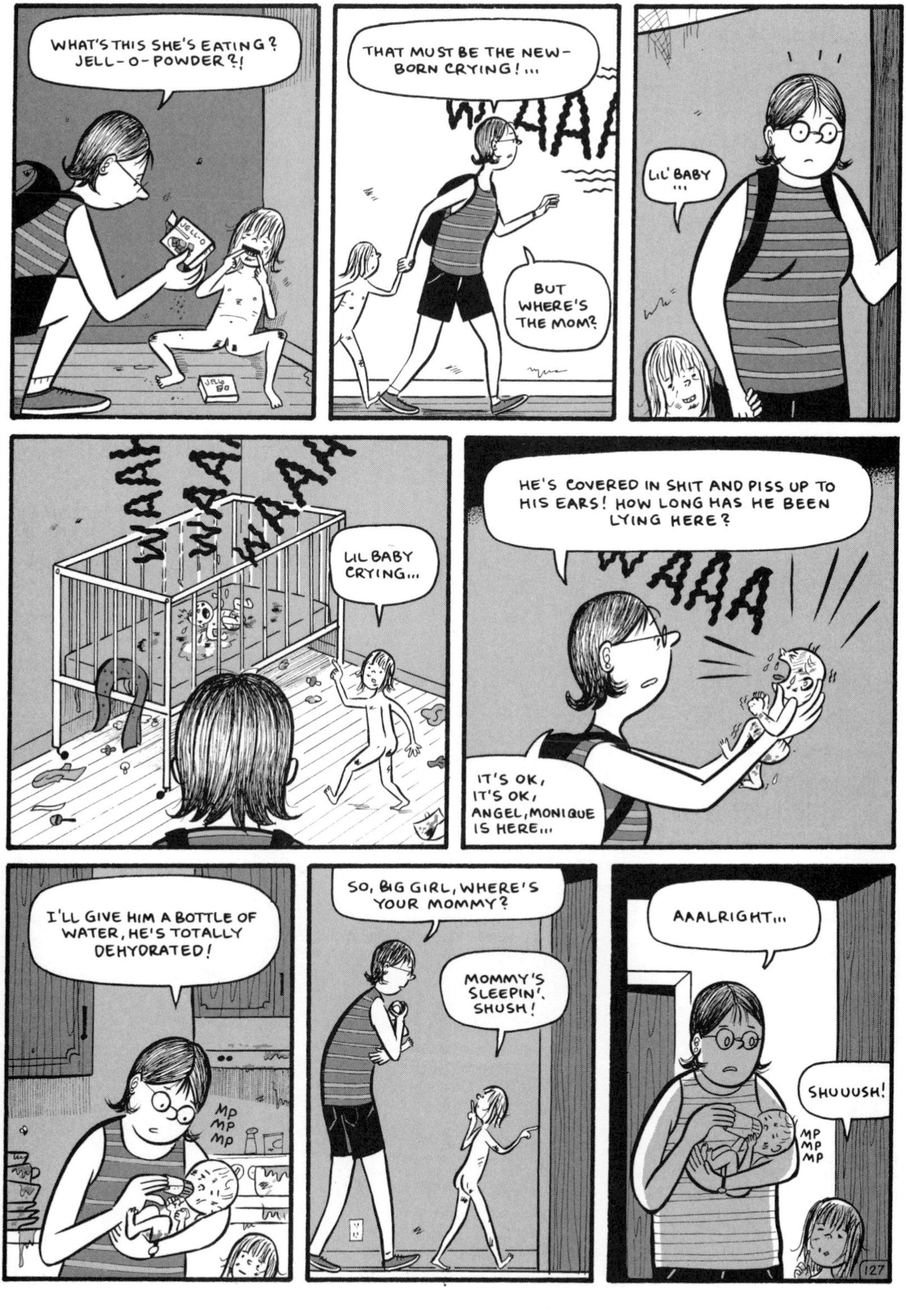
WHAT'S THIS SHE'S EATING? JELL-O-POWDER?!
JELL-O
THAT MUST BE THE NEW-BORN CRYING!...
WAAA
BUT WHERE'S THE MOM?
LIL' BABY ...
LIL BABY CRYING...
HE'S COVERED IN SHIT AND PISS UP TO HIS EARS! HOW LONG HAS HE BEEN LYING HERE?
WAAA
IT'S OK, IT'S OK, ANGEL, MONIQUE IS HERE...
I'LL GIVE HIM A BOTTLE OF WATER, HE'S TOTALLY DEHYDRATED!
MP MP MP
SO, BIG GIRL, WHERE'S YOUR MOMMY?
MOMMY'S SLEEPIN'. SHUSH!
AAALRIGHT...
SHUUUSH!
MP MP MP

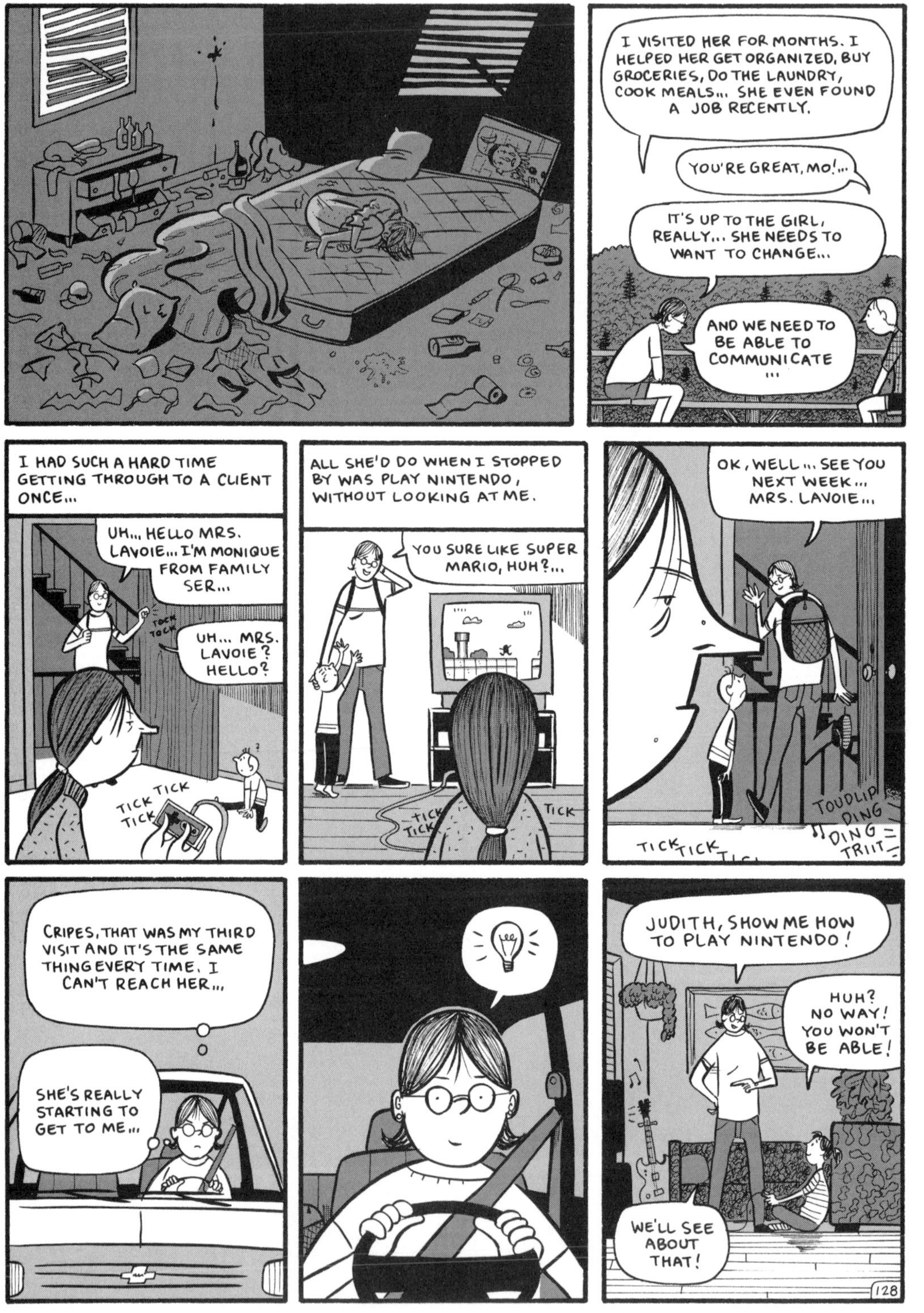
I VISITED HER FOR MONTHS. I HELPED HER GET ORGANIZED, BUY GROCERIES, DO THE LAUNDRY, COOK MEALS... SHE EVEN FOUND A JOB RECENTLY.
YOU'RE GREAT, MO!...
IT'S UP TO THE GIRL, REALLY... SHE NEEDS TO WANT TO CHANGE...
AND WE NEED TO BE ABLE TO COMMUNICATE ...
I HAD SUCH A HARD TIME GETTING THROUGH TO A CLIENT ONCE...
UH... HELLO MRS. LAVOIE... I'M MONIQUE FROM FAMILY SER...
TOCK TOCK
UH... MRS. LAVOIE? HELLO?
TICK TICK TICK
ALL SHE'D DO WHEN I STOPPED BY WAS PLAY NINTENDO, WITHOUT LOOKING AT ME.
YOU SURE LIKE SUPER MARIO, HUH?...
TICK TICK
TICK
OK, WELL... SEE YOU NEXT WEEK... MRS. LAVOIE...
TOUDLIP DING DING TRIIT
TICK TICK
CRIPES, THAT WAS MY THIRD VISIT AND IT'S THE SAME THING EVERY TIME. I CAN'T REACH HER...
SHE'S REALLY STARTING TO GET TO ME...
JUDITH, SHOW ME HOW TO PLAY NINTENDO!
HUH? NO WAY! YOU WON'T BE ABLE!
WE'LL SEE ABOUT THAT!

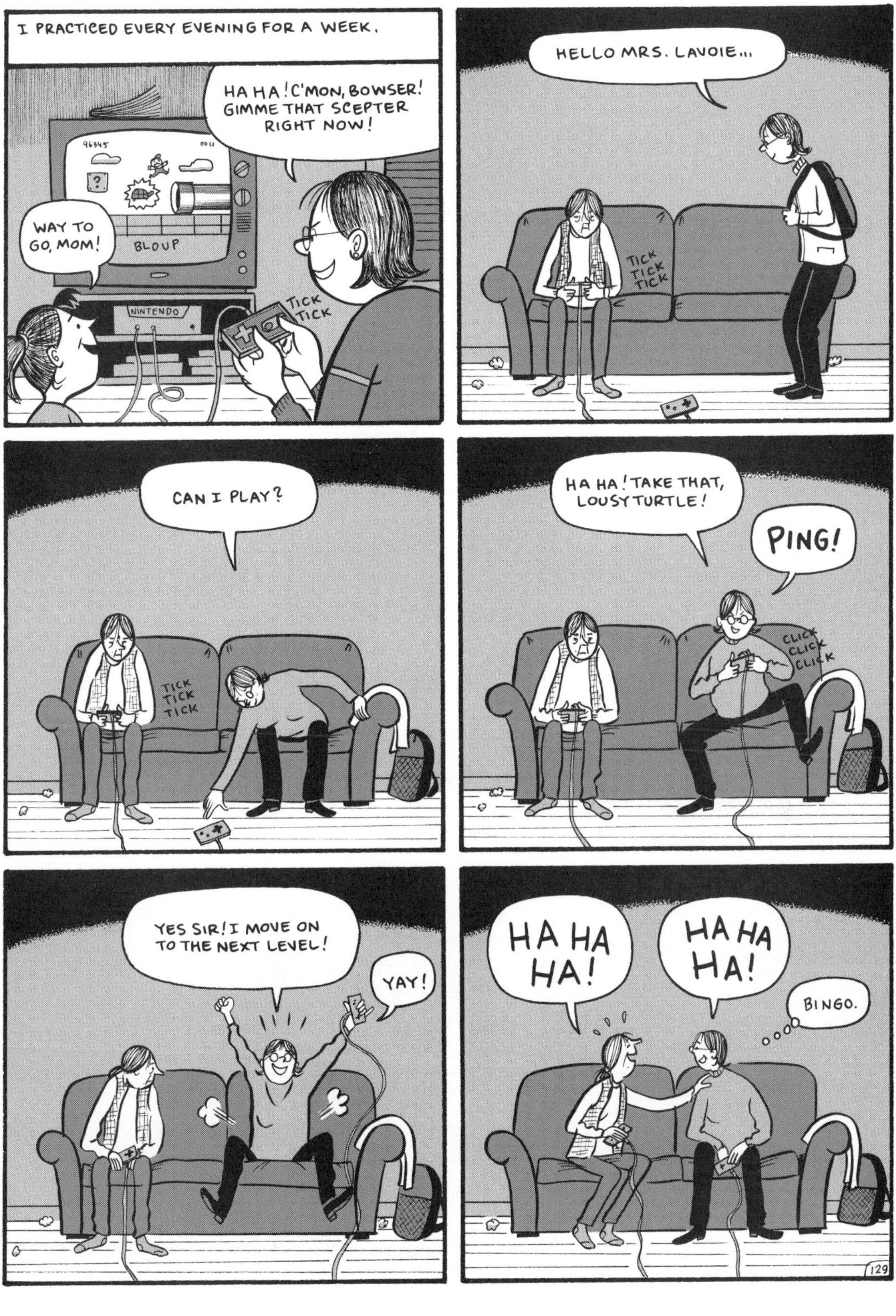
I PRACTICED EVERY EVENING FOR A WEEK.
HA HA! C'MON, BOWSER! GIMME THAT SCEPTER RIGHT NOW!
WAY TO GO, MOM!
BLOUP
NINTENDO
TICK TICK
HELLO MRS. LAVOIE...
TICK TICK TICK
CAN I PLAY?
TICK TICK TICK
HA HA! TAKE THAT, LOUSY TURTLE!
PING!
CLICK CLICK CLICK
YES SIR! I MOVE ON TO THE NEXT LEVEL!
YAY!
HA HA HA!
HA HA HA!
BINGO.

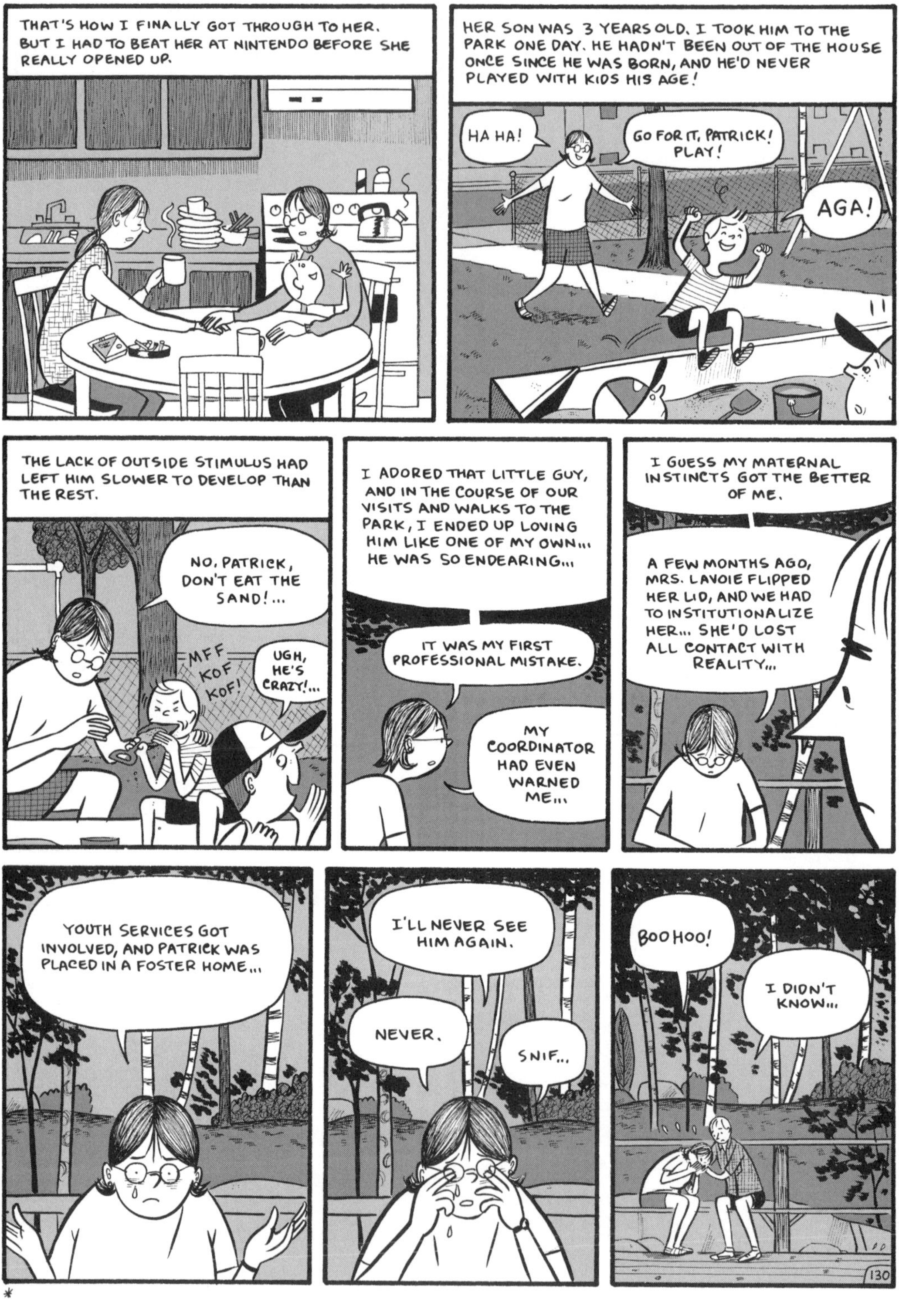
THAT'S HOW I FINALLY GOT THROUGH TO HER. BUT I HAD TO BEAT HER AT NINTENDO BEFORE SHE REALLY OPENED UP.
HER SON WAS 3 YEARS OLD. I TOOK HIM TO THE PARK ONE DAY. HE HADN'T BEEN OUT OF THE HOUSE ONCE SINCE HE WAS BORN, AND HE'D NEVER PLAYED WITH KIDS HIS AGE!
HA HA!
GO FOR IT, PATRICK! PLAY!
AGA!
THE LACK OF OUTSIDE STIMULUS HAD LEFT HIM SLOWER TO DEVELOP THAN THE REST.
NO, PATRICK, DON'T EAT THE SAND!...
MFF KOF KOF!
UGH, HE'S CRAZY!...
I ADORED THAT LITTLE GUY, AND IN THE COURSE OF OUR VISITS AND WALKS TO THE PARK, I ENDED UP LOVING HIM LIKE ONE OF MY OWN... HE WAS SO ENDEARING...
IT WAS MY FIRST PROFESSIONAL MISTAKE.
MY COORDINATOR HAD EVEN WARNED ME...
I GUESS MY MATERNAL INSTINCTS GOT THE BETTER OF ME.
A FEW MONTHS AGO, MRS. LAVOIE FLIPPED HER LID, AND WE HAD TO INSTITUTIONALIZE HER... SHE'D LOST ALL CONTACT WITH REALITY...
YOUTH SERVICES GOT INVOLVED, AND PATRICK WAS PLACED IN A FOSTER HOME...
I'LL NEVER SEE HIM AGAIN.
NEVER.
SNIF...
BOO HOO!
I DIDN'T KNOW...

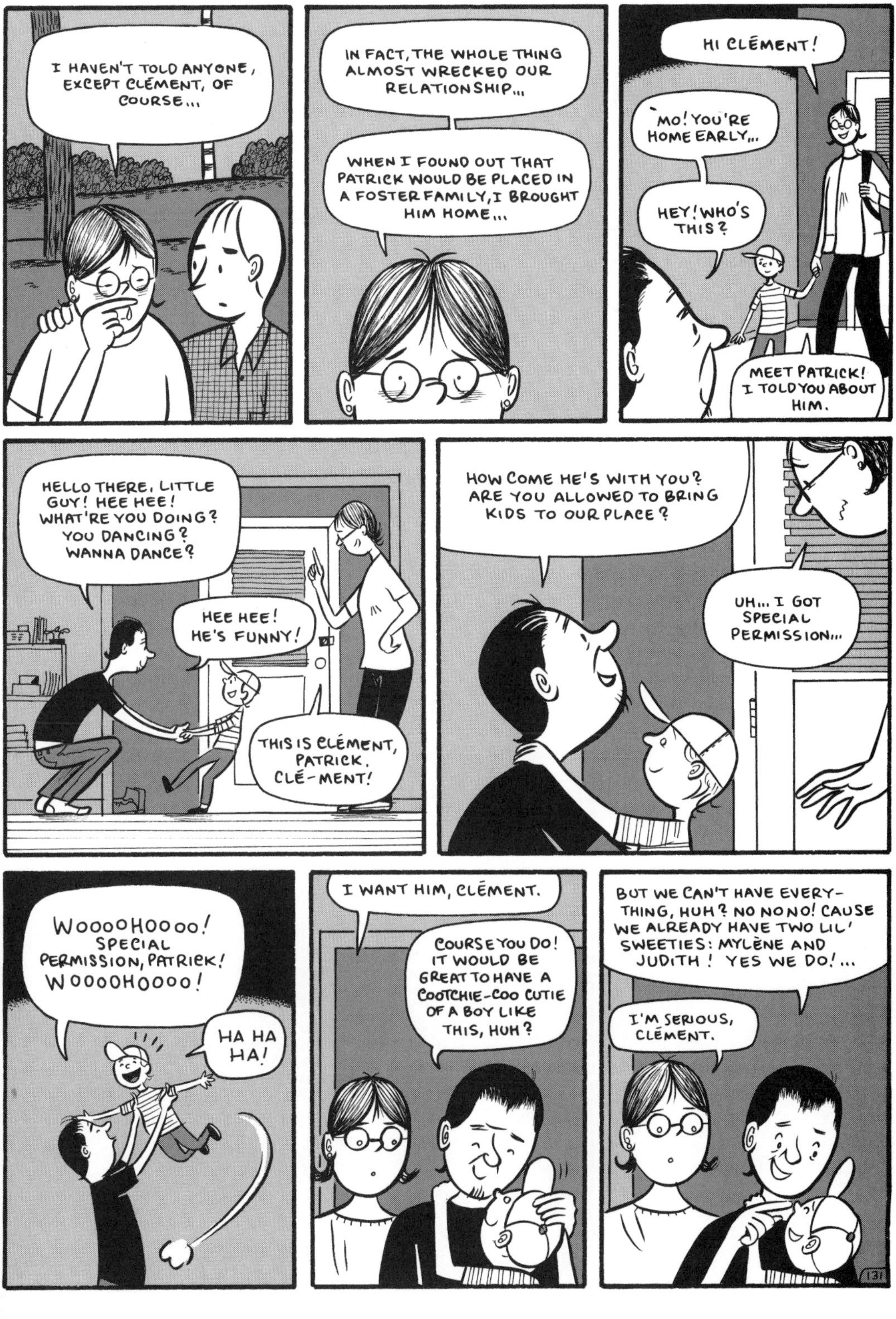

I HAVEN'T TOLD ANYONE, EXCEPT CLÉMENT, OF COURSE...
IN FACT, THE WHOLE THING ALMOST WRECKED OUR RELATIONSHIP...
WHEN I FOUND OUT THAT PATRICK WOULD BE PLACED IN A FOSTER FAMILY, I BROUGHT HIM HOME...
HI CLÉMENT!
MO! YOU'RE HOME EARLY...
HEY! WHO'S THIS?
MEET PATRICK! I TOLD YOU ABOUT HIM.
HELLO THERE, LITTLE GUY! HEE HEE! WHAT'RE YOU DOING? YOU DANCING? WANNA DANCE?
HEE HEE! HE'S FUNNY!
THIS IS CLÉMENT, PATRICK. CLÉ-MENT!
HOW COME HE'S WITH YOU? ARE YOU ALLOWED TO BRING KIDS TO OUR PLACE?
UH... I GOT SPECIAL PERMISSION...
WOOOOHOOOO! SPECIAL PERMISSION, PATRICK! WOOOOHOOOO!
HA HA HA!
I WANT HIM, CLÉMENT.
COURSE YOU DO! IT WOULD BE GREAT TO HAVE A COOTCHIE-COO CUTIE OF A BOY LIKE THIS, HUH?
BUT WE CAN'T HAVE EVERY-THING, HUH? NO NO NO! CAUSE WE ALREADY HAVE TWO LIL' SWEETIES: MYLÈNE AND JUDITH! YES WE DO!...
I'M SERIOUS, CLÉMENT.

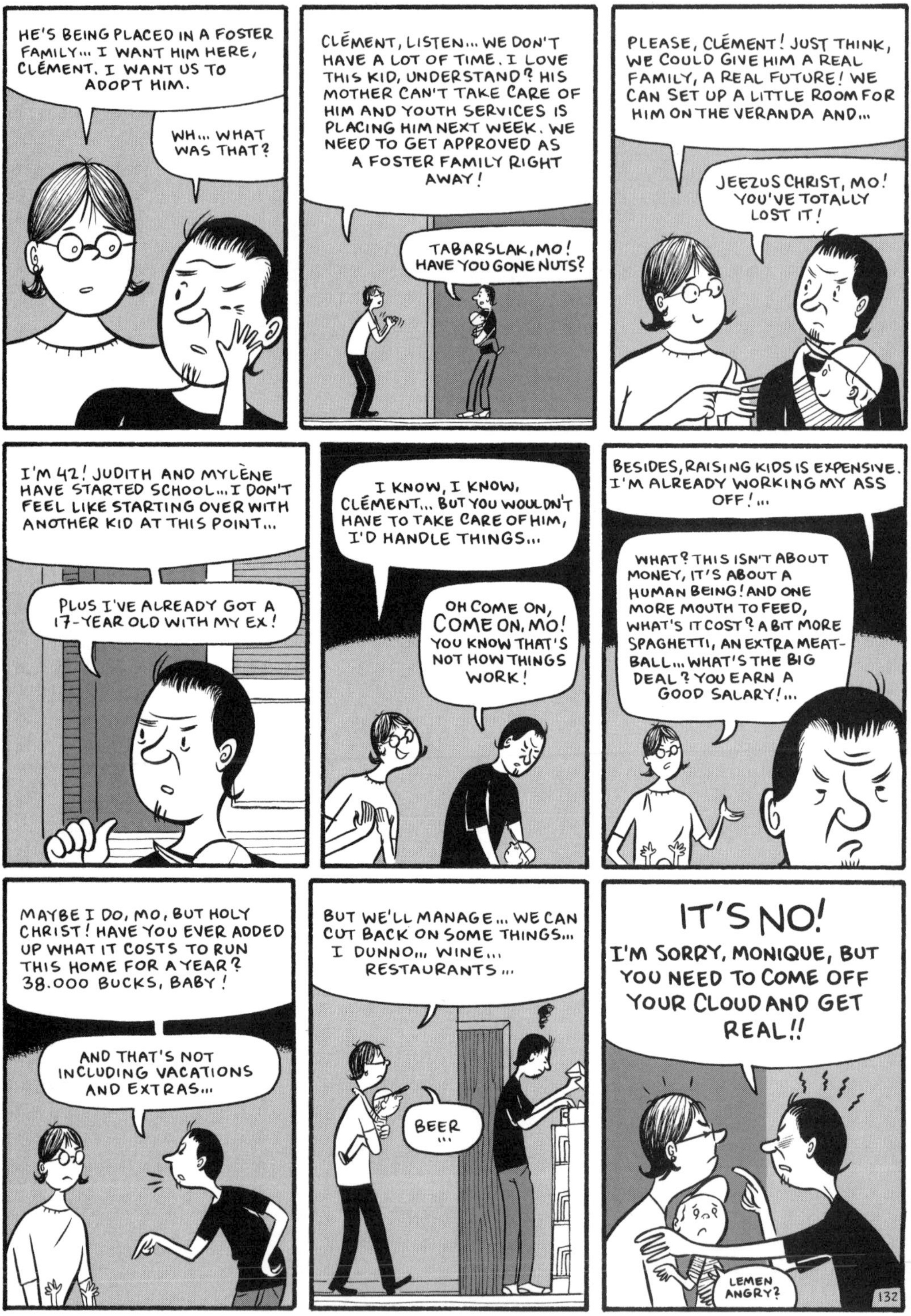
HE'S BEING PLACED IN A FOSTER FAMILY... I WANT HIM HERE, CLÉMENT. I WANT US TO ADOPT HIM.
WH... WHAT WAS THAT?
CLÉMENT, LISTEN... WE DON'T HAVE A LOT OF TIME. I LOVE THIS KID, UNDERSTAND? HIS MOTHER CAN'T TAKE CARE OF HIM AND YOUTH SERVICES IS PLACING HIM NEXT WEEK. WE NEED TO GET APPROVED AS A FOSTER FAMILY RIGHT AWAY!
TABARSLAK, MO! HAVE YOU GONE NUTS?
PLEASE, CLÉMENT! JUST THINK, WE COULD GIVE HIM A REAL FAMILY, A REAL FUTURE! WE CAN SET UP A LITTLE ROOM FOR HIM ON THE VERANDA AND...
JEEZUS CHRIST, MO! YOU'VE TOTALLY LOST IT!
I'M 42! JUDITH AND MYLÈNE HAVE STARTED SCHOOL... I DON'T FEEL LIKE STARTING OVER WITH ANOTHER KID AT THIS POINT...
PLUS I'VE ALREADY GOT A 17-YEAR OLD WITH MY EX!
I KNOW, I KNOW, CLÉMENT... BUT YOU WOULDN'T HAVE TO TAKE CARE OF HIM, I'D HANDLE THINGS...
OH COME ON, COME ON, MO! YOU KNOW THAT'S NOT HOW THINGS WORK!
BESIDES, RAISING KIDS IS EXPENSIVE. I'M ALREADY WORKING MY ASS OFF!...
WHAT? THIS ISN'T ABOUT MONEY, IT'S ABOUT A HUMAN BEING! AND ONE MORE MOUTH TO FEED, WHAT'S IT COST? A BIT MORE SPAGHETTI, AN EXTRA MEAT-BALL... WHAT'S THE BIG DEAL? YOU EARN A GOOD SALARY!...
MAYBE I DO, MO, BUT HOLY CHRIST! HAVE YOU EVER ADDED UP WHAT IT COSTS TO RUN THIS HOME FOR A YEAR? 38.000 BUCKS, BABY!
AND THAT'S NOT INCLUDING VACATIONS AND EXTRAS...
BUT WE'LL MANAGE... WE CAN CUT BACK ON SOME THINGS... I DUNNO... WINE... RESTAURANTS...
BEER...
IT'S NO!
I'M SORRY, MONIQUE, BUT YOU NEED TO COME OFF YOUR CLOUD AND GET REAL!!
LEMEN ANGRY?

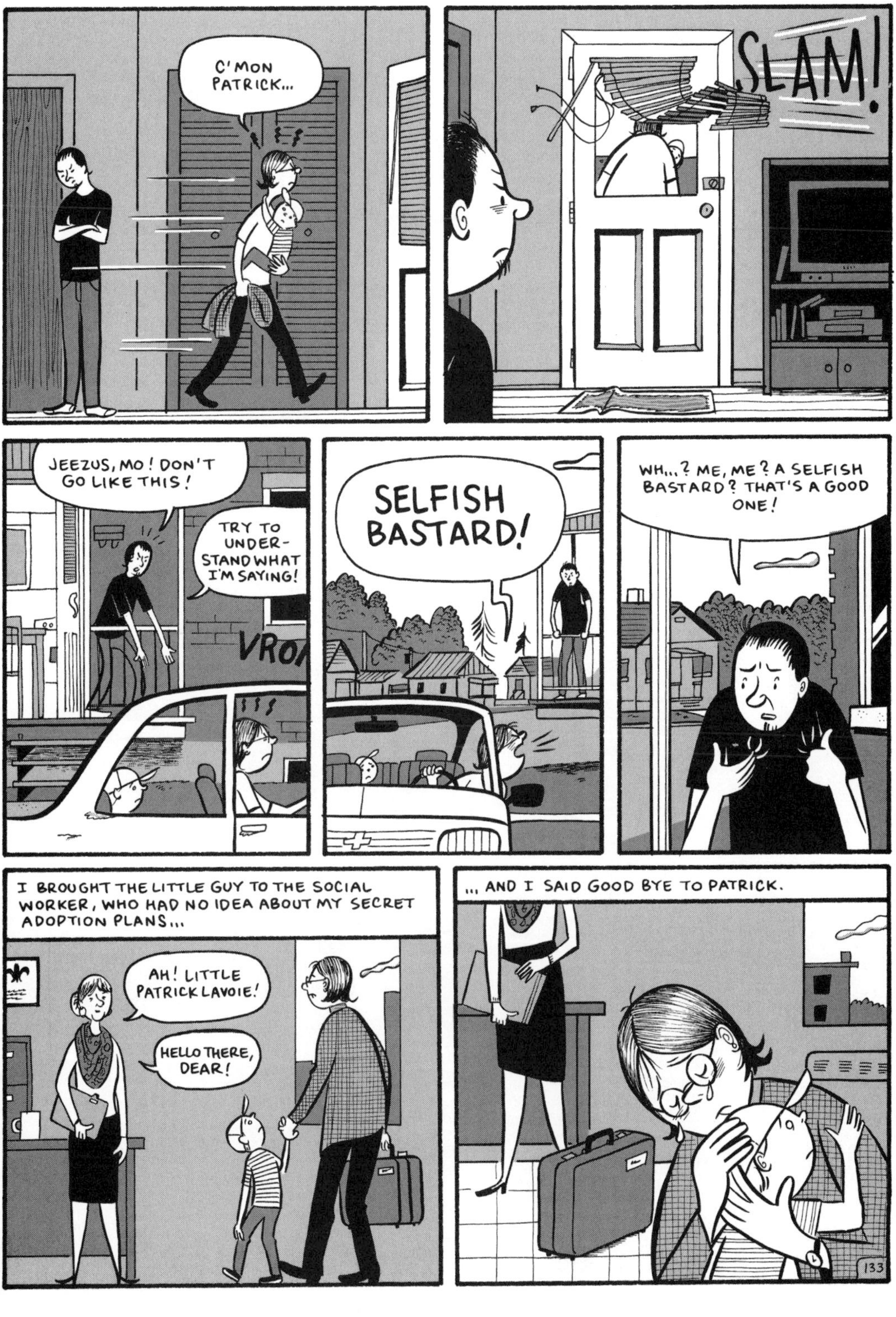
C'MON PATRICK...
SLAM!
JEEZUS, MO! DON'T GO LIKE THIS!
TRY TO UNDER-STAND WHAT I'M SAYING!
VRO
SELFISH BASTARD!
WH...? ME, ME? A SELFISH BASTARD? THAT'S A GOOD ONE!
I BROUGHT THE LITTLE GUY TO THE SOCIAL WORKER, WHO HAD NO IDEA ABOUT MY SECRET ADOPTION PLANS...
AH! LITTLE PATRICK LAVOIE!
HELLO THERE, DEAR!
... AND I SAID GOOD BYE TO PATRICK.

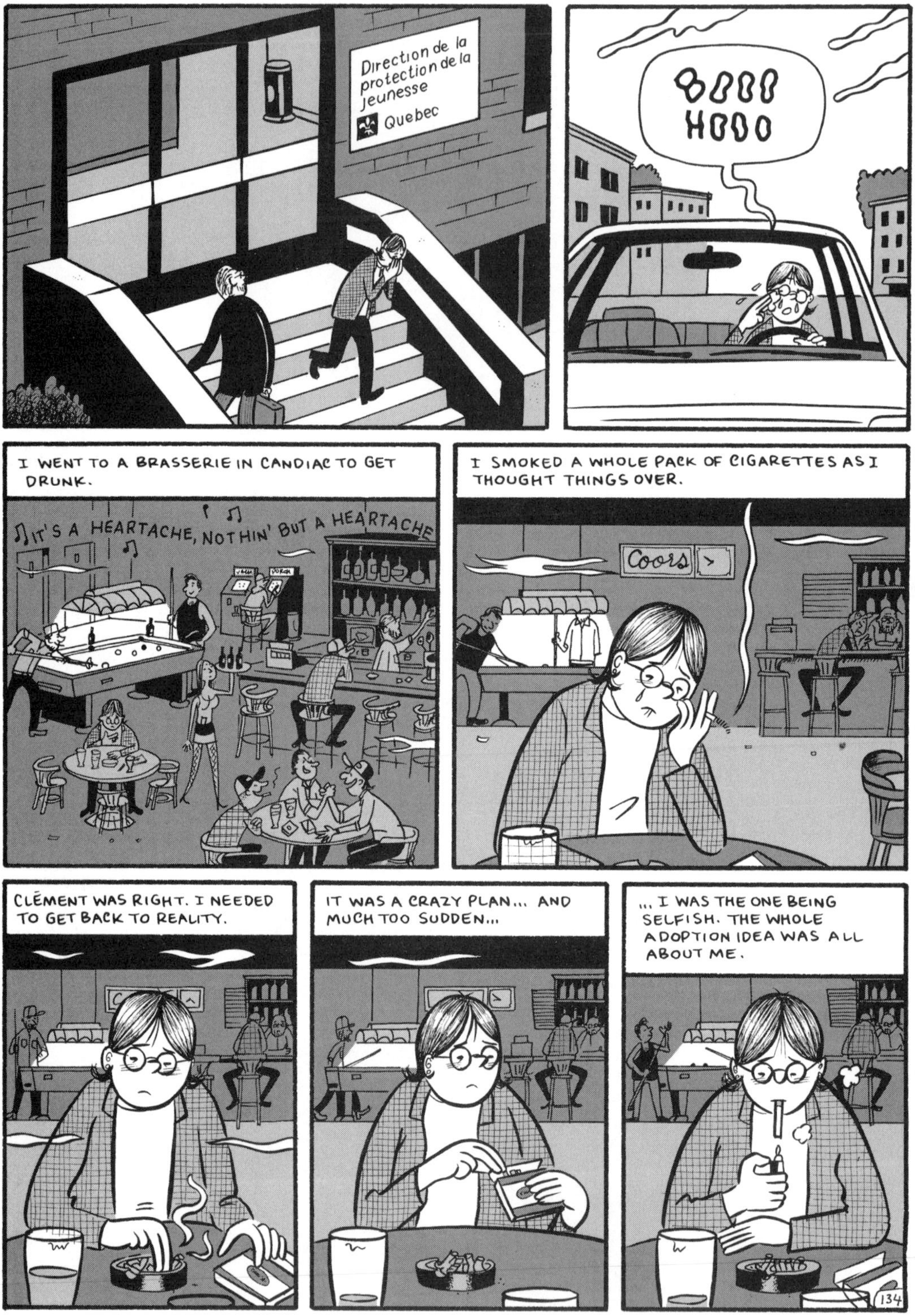

Direction de la protection de la jeunesse
Quebec
BOOO HOOO
I WENT TO A BRASSERIE IN CANDIAC TO GET DRUNK.
♫ IT'S A HEARTACHE, NOTHIN' BUT A HEARTACHE ♫
I SMOKED A WHOLE PACK OF CIGARETTES AS I THOUGHT THINGS OVER.
Coors
CLÉMENT WAS RIGHT. I NEEDED TO GET BACK TO REALITY.
IT WAS A CRAZY PLAN... AND MUCH TOO SUDDEN...
... I WAS THE ONE BEING SELFISH. THE WHOLE ADOPTION IDEA WAS ALL ABOUT ME.

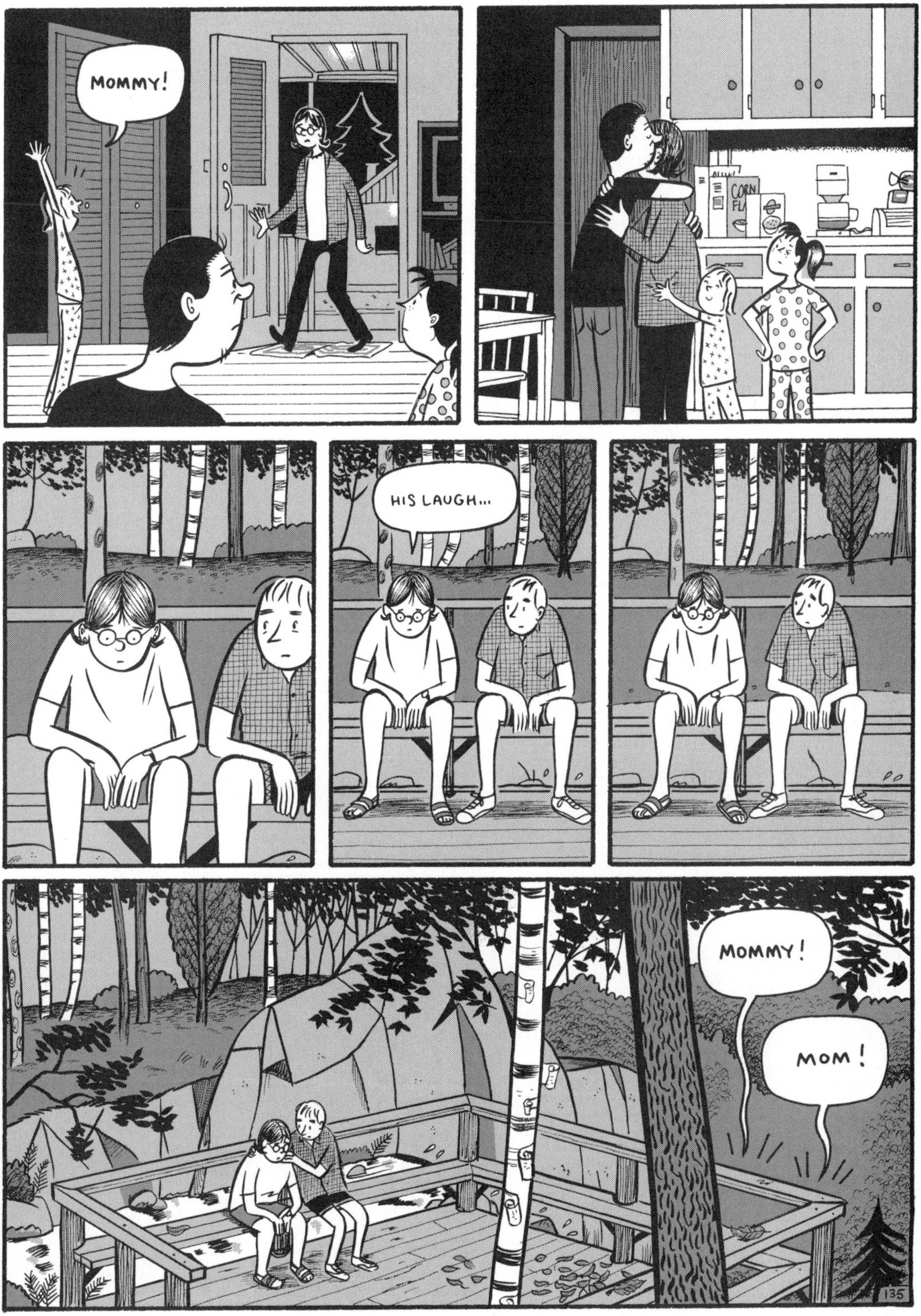
MOMMY!
HIS LAUGH...
MOMMY!
MOM!

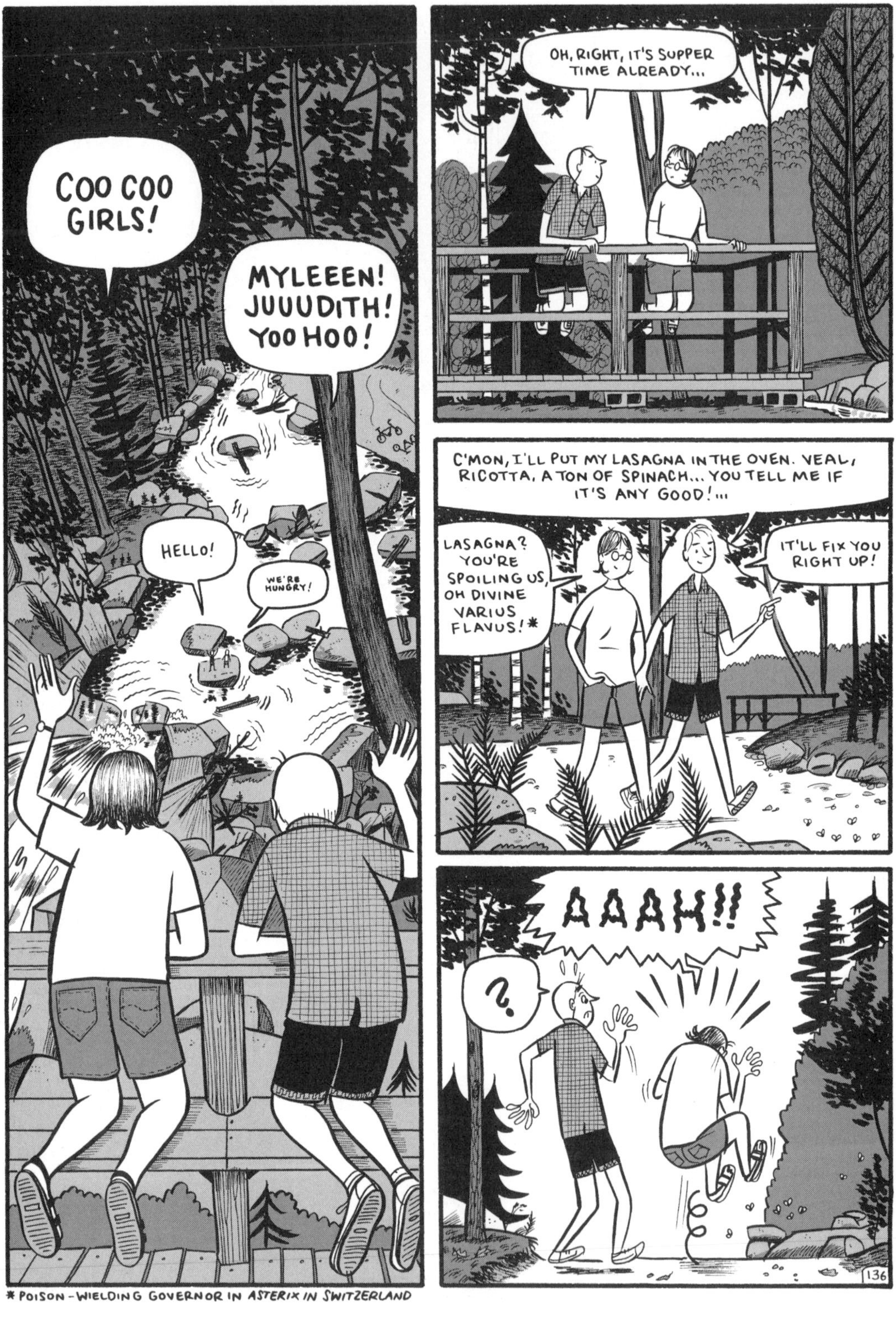
COO COO GIRLS!
MYLEEEN! JUUUDITH! YOO HOO!
HELLO!
WE'RE HUNGRY!
OH, RIGHT, IT'S SUPPER TIME ALREADY...
C'MON, I'LL PUT MY LASAGNA IN THE OVEN. VEAL, RICOTTA, A TON OF SPINACH... YOU TELL ME IF IT'S ANY GOOD!...
LASAGNA? YOU'RE SPOILING US, OH DIVINE VARIUS FLAVUS! *
IT'LL FIX YOU RIGHT UP!
AAAH!!
?

* POISON-WIELDING GOVERNOR IN *ASTERIX IN SWITZERLAND*

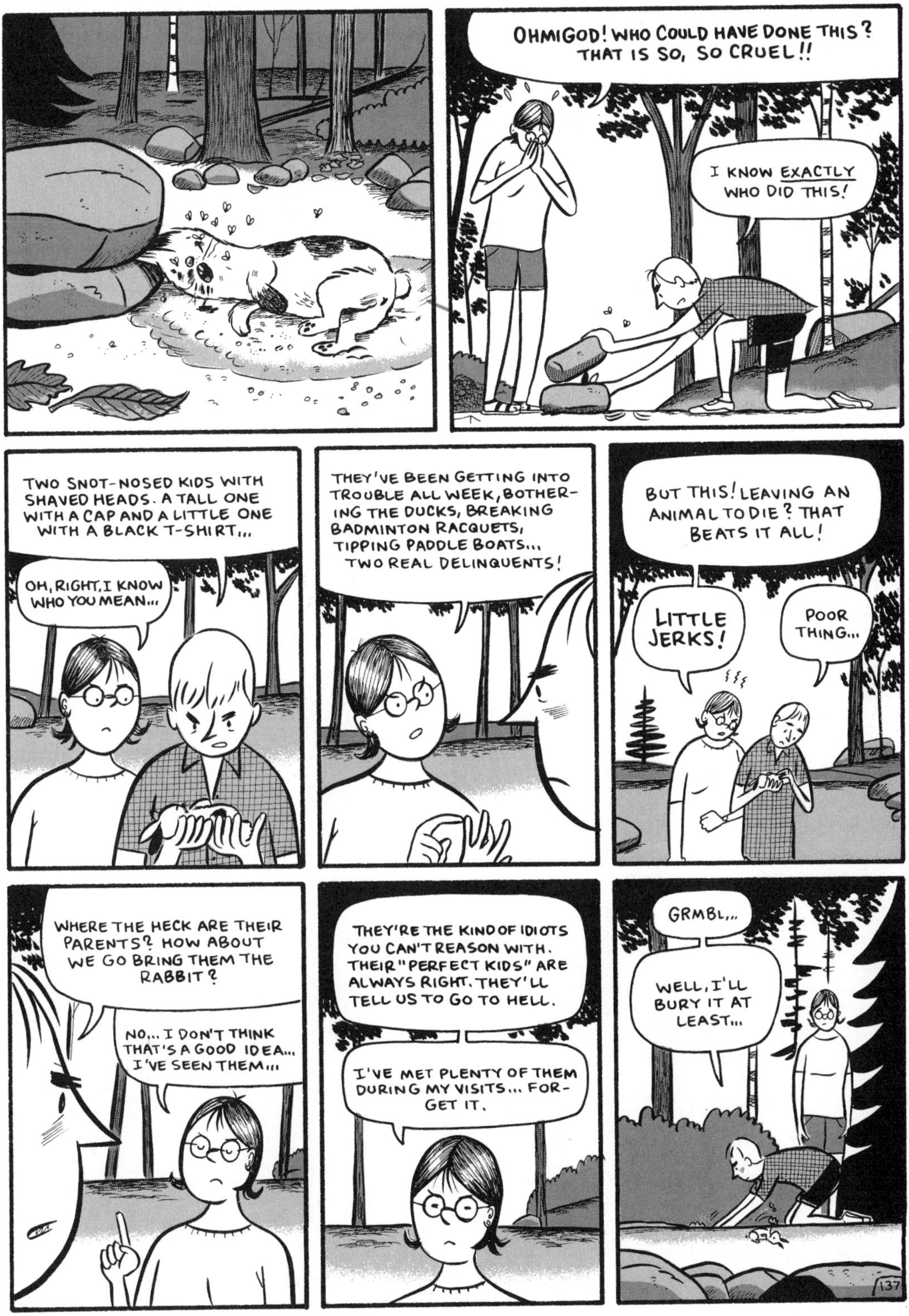
OHMIGOD! WHO COULD HAVE DONE THIS? THAT IS SO, SO CRUEL!!
I KNOW EXACTLY WHO DID THIS!
TWO SNOT-NOSED KIDS WITH SHAVED HEADS. A TALL ONE WITH A CAP AND A LITTLE ONE WITH A BLACK T-SHIRT...
OH, RIGHT, I KNOW WHO YOU MEAN...
THEY'VE BEEN GETTING INTO TROUBLE ALL WEEK, BOTHERING THE DUCKS, BREAKING BADMINTON RACQUETS, TIPPING PADDLE BOATS... TWO REAL DELINQUENTS!
BUT THIS! LEAVING AN ANIMAL TO DIE? THAT BEATS IT ALL!
LITTLE JERKS!
POOR THING...
WHERE THE HECK ARE THEIR PARENTS? HOW ABOUT WE GO BRING THEM THE RABBIT?
NO... I DON'T THINK THAT'S A GOOD IDEA... I'VE SEEN THEM...
THEY'RE THE KIND OF IDIOTS YOU CAN'T REASON WITH. THEIR "PERFECT KIDS" ARE ALWAYS RIGHT. THEY'LL TELL US TO GO TO HELL.
I'VE MET PLENTY OF THEM DURING MY VISITS... FORGET IT.
GRMBL...
WELL, I'LL BURY IT AT LEAST...

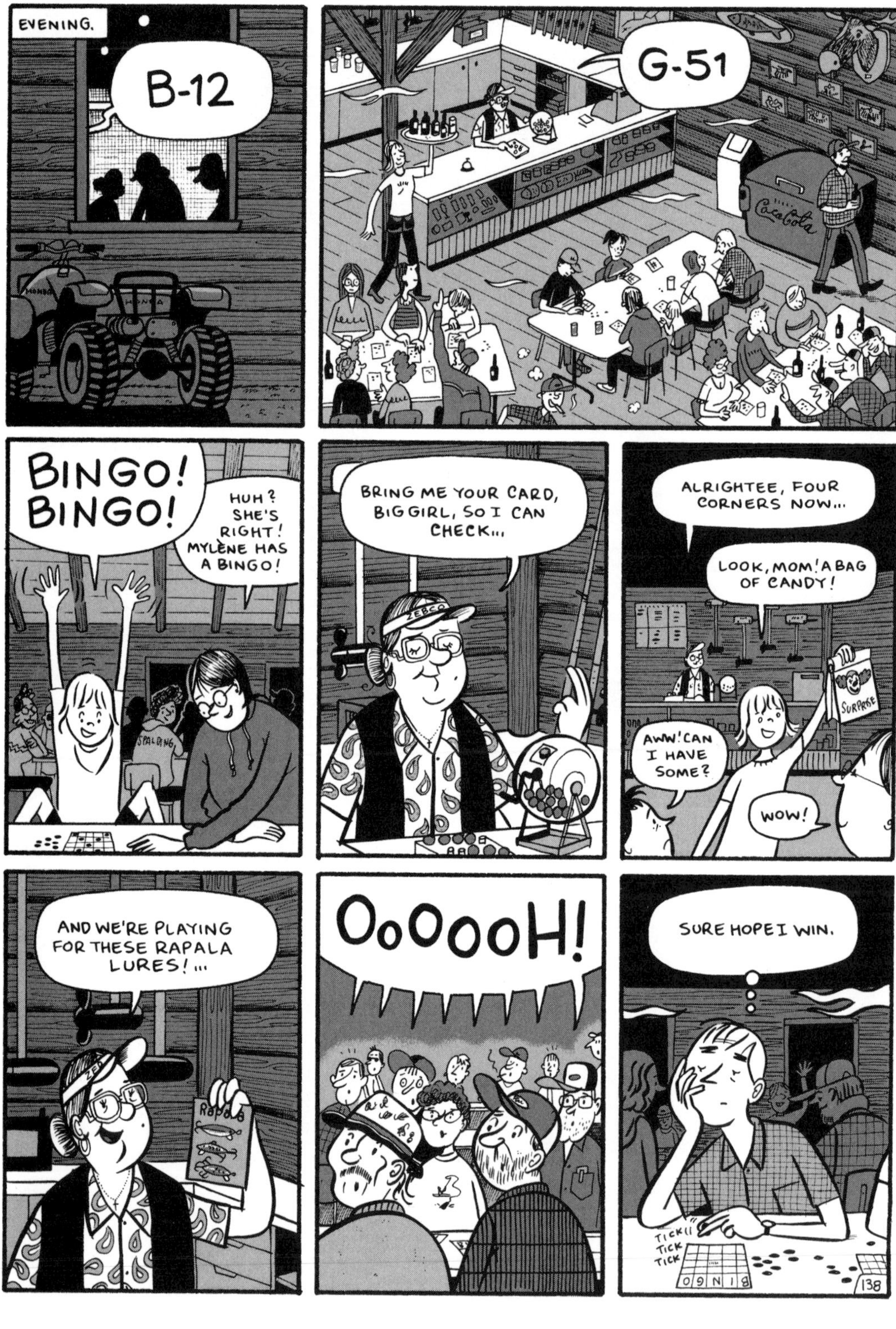
EVENING.
B-12
G-51
BINGO! BINGO!
HUH? SHE'S RIGHT! MYLÈNE HAS A BINGO!
BRING ME YOUR CARD, BIG GIRL, SO I CAN CHECK...
ALRIGHTEE, FOUR CORNERS NOW...
LOOK, MOM! A BAG OF CANDY!
AWW! CAN I HAVE SOME?
WOW!
AND WE'RE PLAYING FOR THESE RAPALA LURES!...
OoOOOH!
SURE HOPE I WIN.
TICK TICK TICK

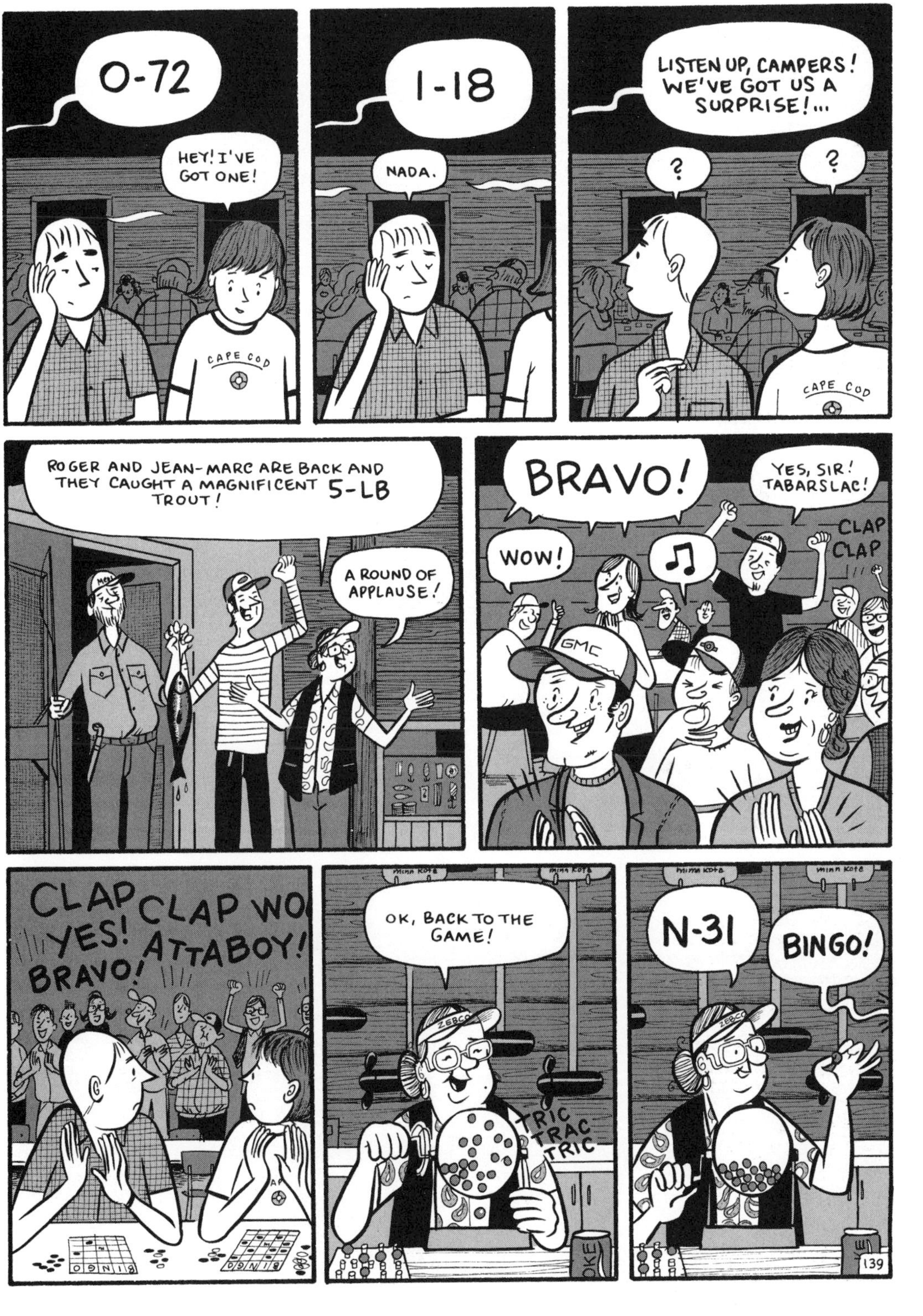
O-72
HEY! I'VE GOT ONE!
CAPE COD
1-18
NADA.
LISTEN UP, CAMPERS! WE'VE GOT US A SURPRISE!...
?
?
CAPE COD
ROGER AND JEAN-MARC ARE BACK AND THEY CAUGHT A MAGNIFICENT 5-LB TROUT!
A ROUND OF APPLAUSE!
BRAVO!
YES, SIR! TABARSLAC!
WOW!
CLAP CLAP
GMC
CLAP CLAP WO
YES!
ATTABOY!
BRAVO!
BINGO
BINGO
OK, BACK TO THE GAME!
ZEBCO
TRIC TRAC TRIC
N-31
BINGO!
ZEBCO

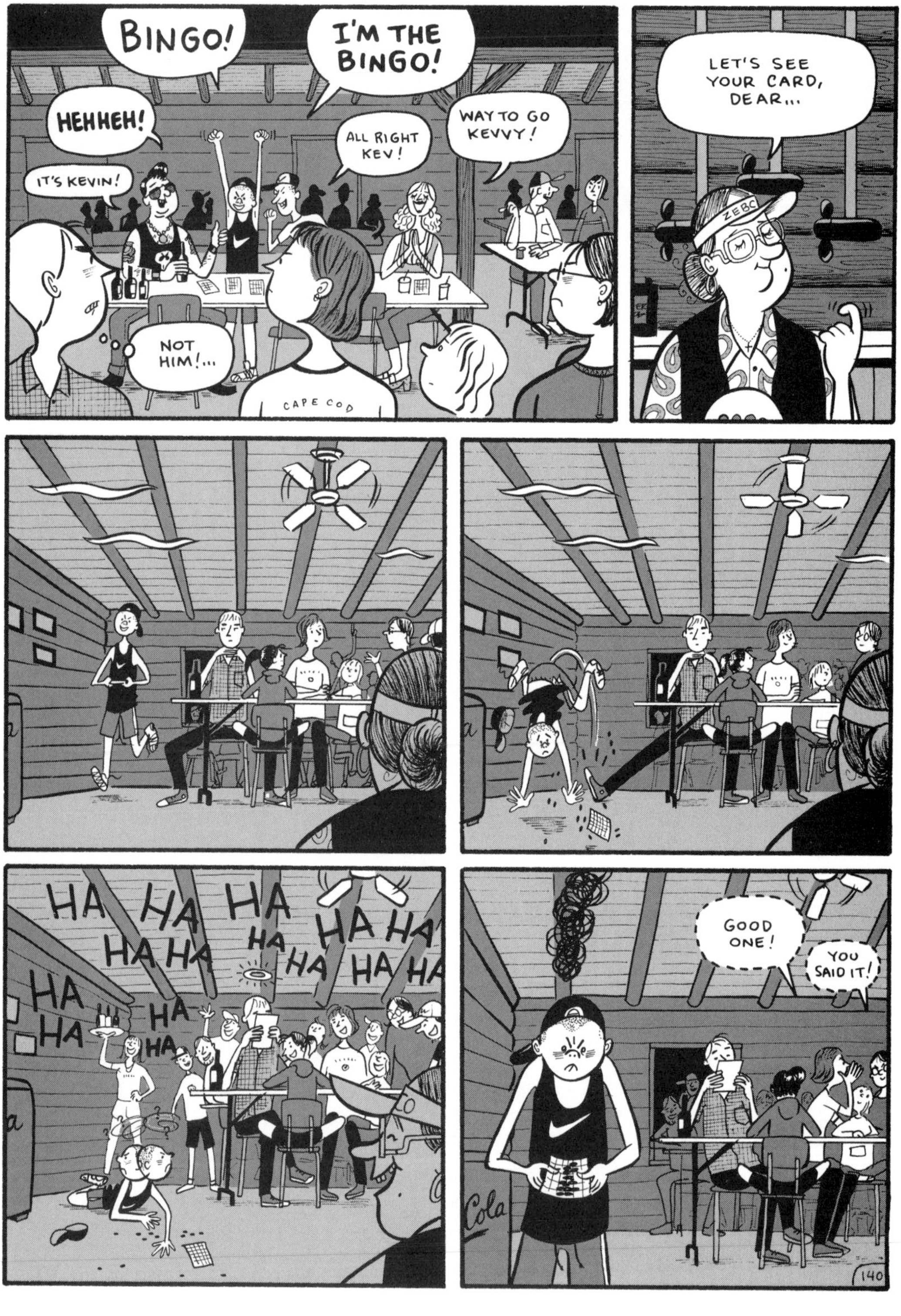
BINGO!
I'M THE BINGO!
HEHHEH!
ALL RIGHT KEV!
WAY TO GO KEVVY!
IT'S KEVIN!
NOT HIM!...
CAPE COD
LET'S SEE YOUR CARD, DEAR...
ZEBC
HA HA HA HA HA HA HA HA HA HA HA HA HA HA HA HA
GOOD ONE!
YOU SAID IT!
Cola

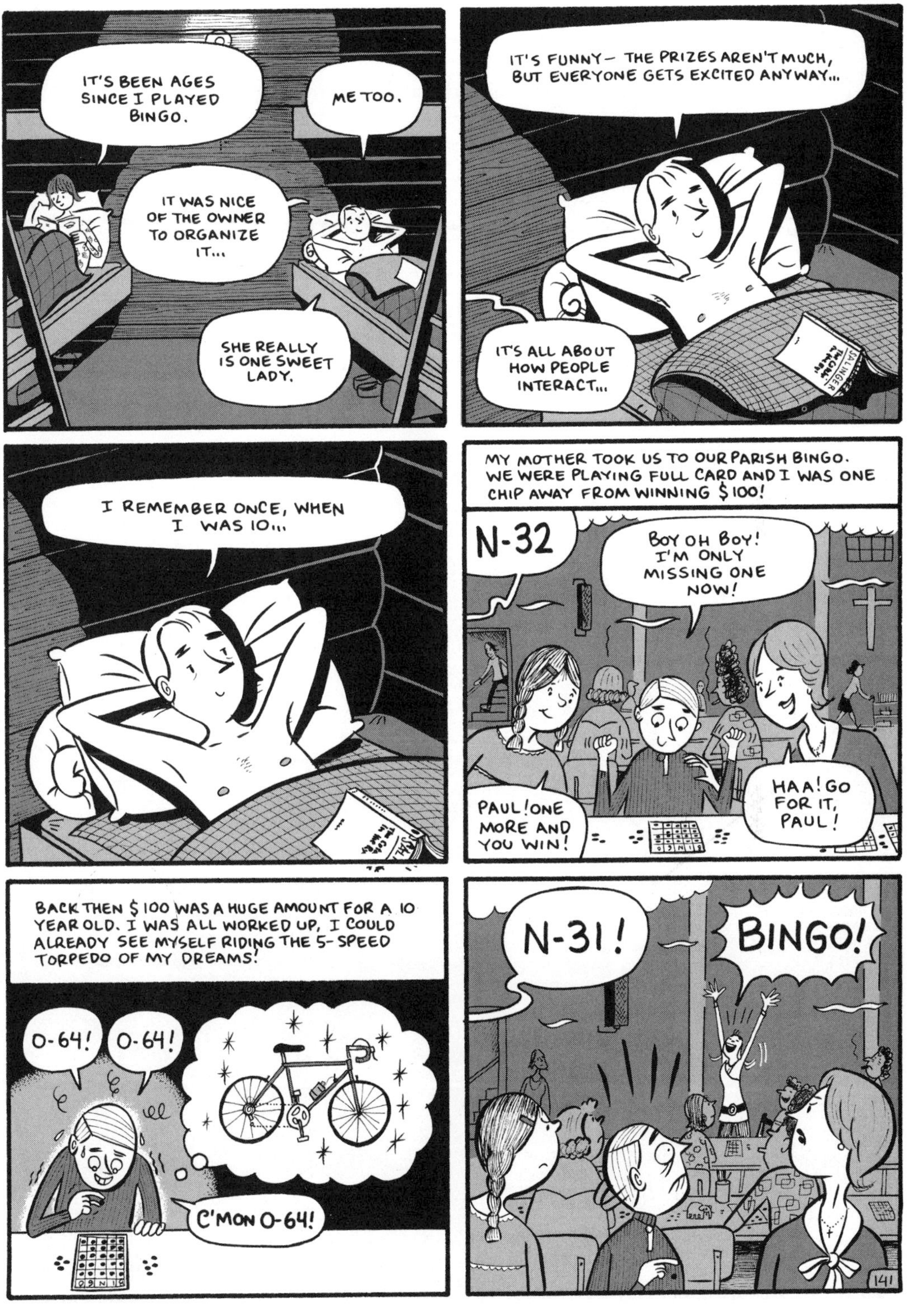
IT'S BEEN AGES SINCE I PLAYED BINGO.
ME TOO.
IT WAS NICE OF THE OWNER TO ORGANIZE IT...
SHE REALLY IS ONE SWEET LADY.
IT'S FUNNY— THE PRIZES AREN'T MUCH, BUT EVERYONE GETS EXCITED ANYWAY...
IT'S ALL ABOUT HOW PEOPLE INTERACT...
I REMEMBER ONCE, WHEN I WAS 10...
MY MOTHER TOOK US TO OUR PARISH BINGO. WE WERE PLAYING FULL CARD AND I WAS ONE CHIP AWAY FROM WINNING $100!
N-32
BOY OH BOY! I'M ONLY MISSING ONE NOW!
PAUL! ONE MORE AND YOU WIN!
HAA! GO FOR IT, PAUL!
BACK THEN $100 WAS A HUGE AMOUNT FOR A 10 YEAR OLD. I WAS ALL WORKED UP, I COULD ALREADY SEE MYSELF RIDING THE 5-SPEED TORPEDO OF MY DREAMS!
O-64!
O-64!
C'MON O-64!
N-31!
BINGO!

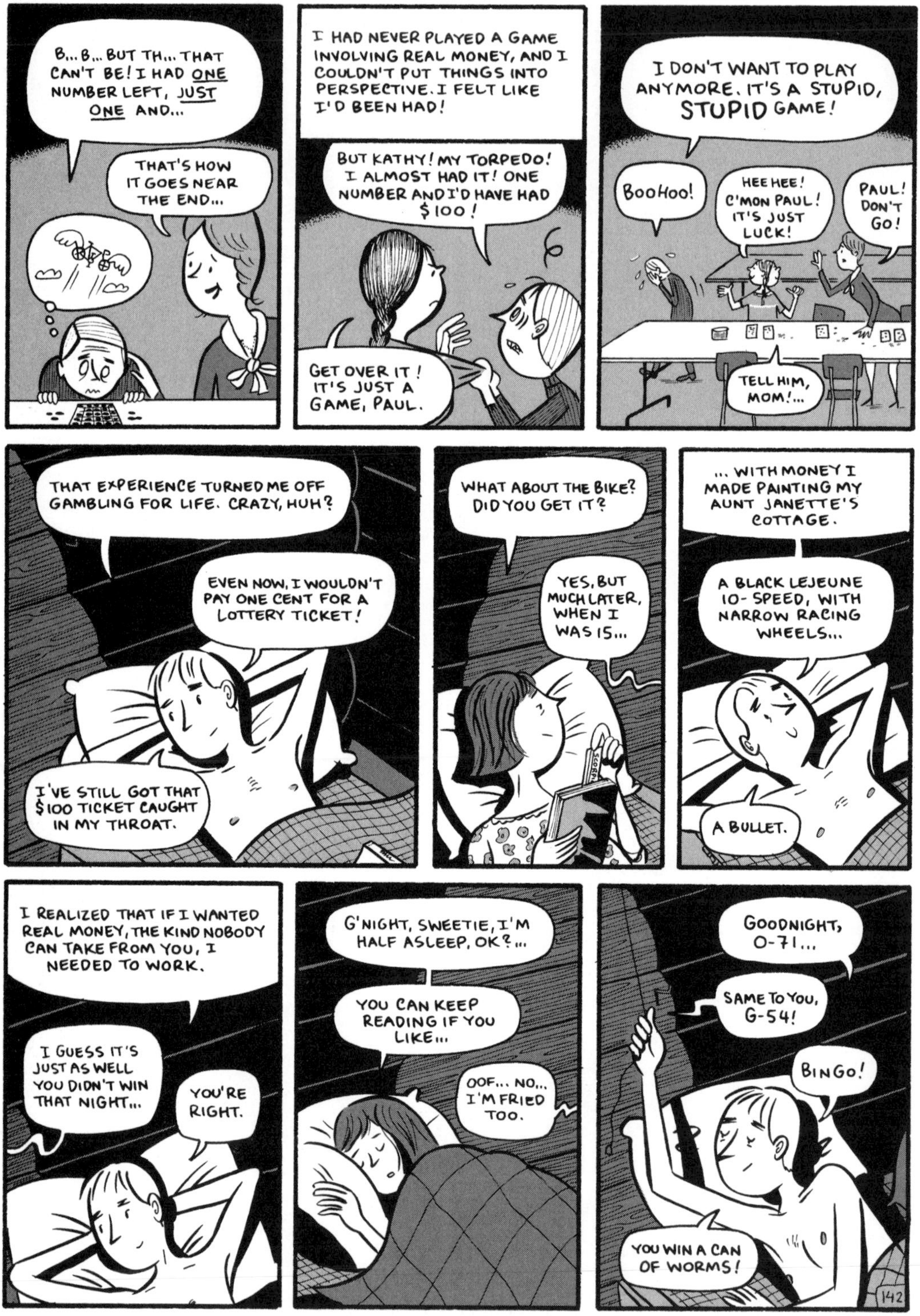
B... B... BUT TH... THAT CAN'T BE! I HAD ONE NUMBER LEFT, JUST ONE AND...
THAT'S HOW IT GOES NEAR THE END...
I HAD NEVER PLAYED A GAME INVOLVING REAL MONEY, AND I COULDN'T PUT THINGS INTO PERSPECTIVE. I FELT LIKE I'D BEEN HAD!
BUT KATHY! MY TORPEDO! I ALMOST HAD IT! ONE NUMBER AND I'D HAVE HAD $100!
GET OVER IT! IT'S JUST A GAME, PAUL.
I DON'T WANT TO PLAY ANYMORE. IT'S A STUPID, STUPID GAME!
BooHoo!
HEE HEE! C'MON PAUL! IT'S JUST LUCK!
PAUL! DON'T GO!
TELL HIM, MOM!...
THAT EXPERIENCE TURNED ME OFF GAMBLING FOR LIFE. CRAZY, HUH?
EVEN NOW, I WOULDN'T PAY ONE CENT FOR A LOTTERY TICKET!
I'VE STILL GOT THAT $100 TICKET CAUGHT IN MY THROAT.
WHAT ABOUT THE BIKE? DID YOU GET IT?
YES, BUT MUCH LATER, WHEN I WAS 15...
... WITH MONEY I MADE PAINTING MY AUNT JANETTE'S COTTAGE.
A BLACK LEJEUNE 10-SPEED, WITH NARROW RACING WHEELS...
A BULLET.
I REALIZED THAT IF I WANTED REAL MONEY, THE KIND NOBODY CAN TAKE FROM YOU, I NEEDED TO WORK.
I GUESS IT'S JUST AS WELL YOU DIDN'T WIN THAT NIGHT...
YOU'RE RIGHT.
G'NIGHT, SWEETIE, I'M HALF ASLEEP, OK?...
YOU CAN KEEP READING IF YOU LIKE...
OOF... NO... I'M FRIED TOO.
GOODNIGHT, O-71...
SAME TO YOU, G-54!
BinGo!
YOU WIN A CAN OF WORMS!

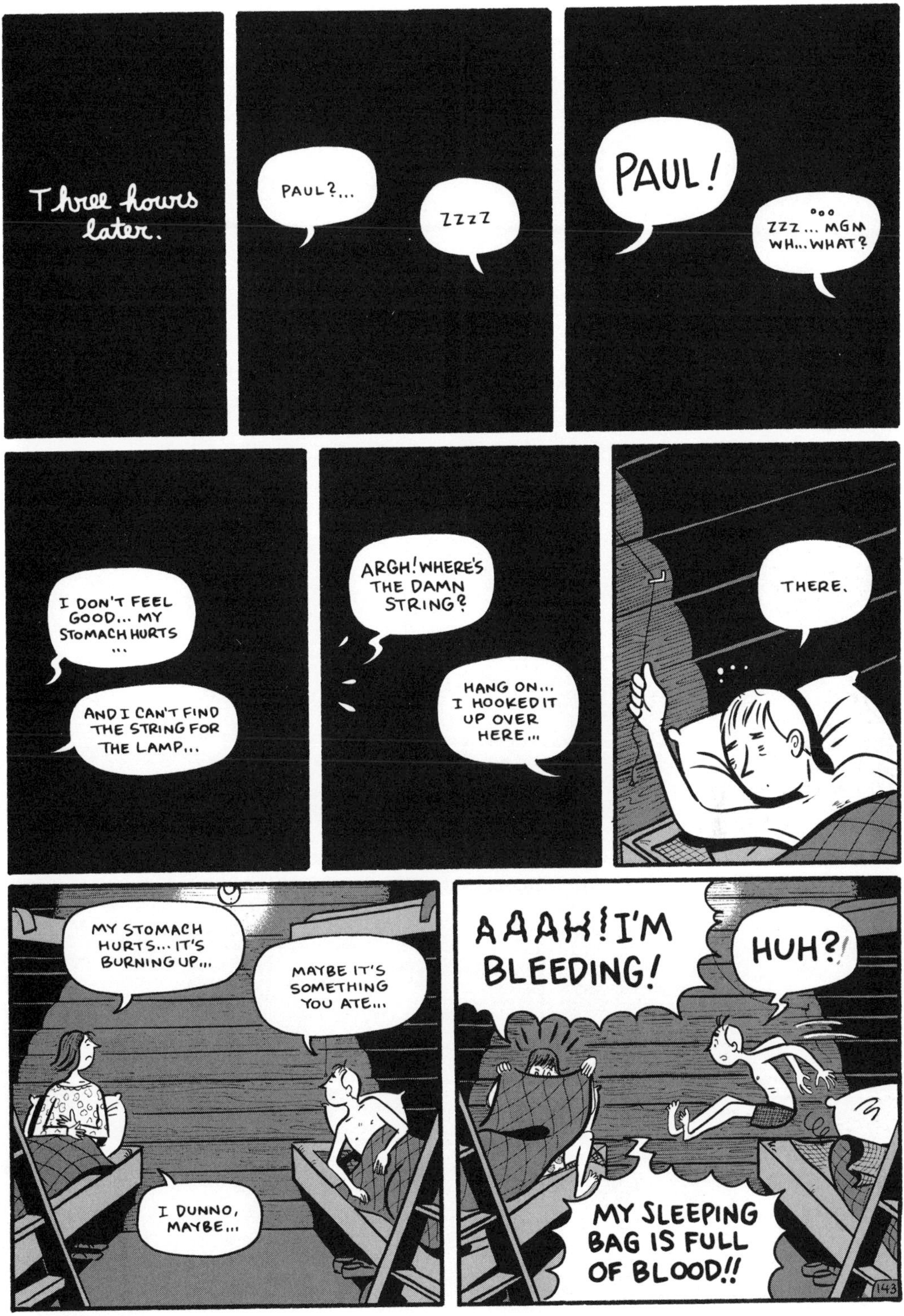
Three hours later.
PAUL?...
ZZZZ
PAUL!
ZZZ... MGM WH... WHAT?
I DON'T FEEL GOOD... MY STOMACH HURTS ...
AND I CAN'T FIND THE STRING FOR THE LAMP...
ARGH! WHERE'S THE DAMN STRING?
HANG ON... I HOOKED IT UP OVER HERE...
THERE.
MY STOMACH HURTS... IT'S BURNING UP...
MAYBE IT'S SOMETHING YOU ATE...
I DUNNO, MAYBE...
AAAH! I'M BLEEDING!
HUH?!
MY SLEEPING BAG IS FULL OF BLOOD!!
143

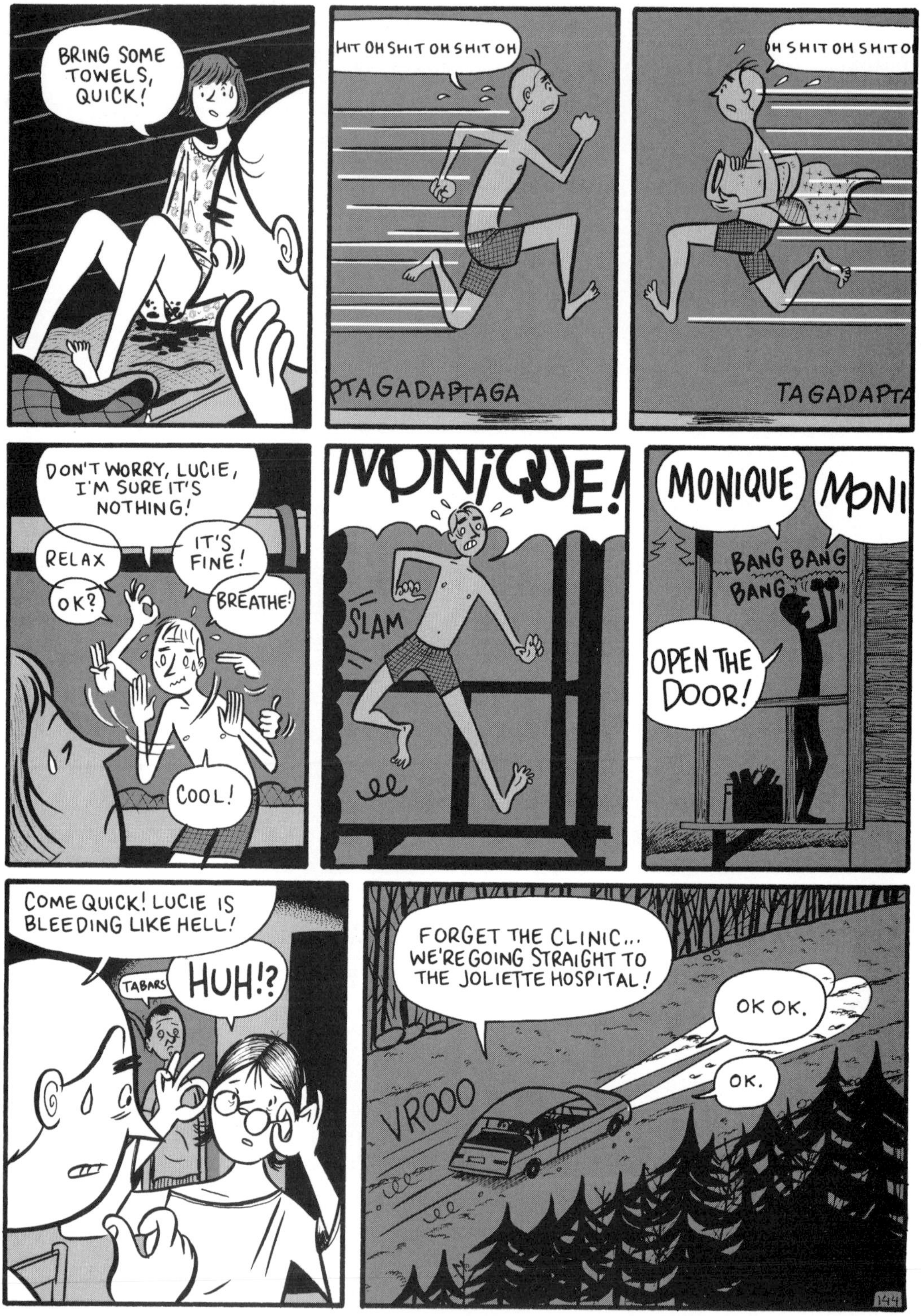
BRING SOME TOWELS, QUICK!
HIT OH SHIT OH SHIT OH
PTA GADAPTAGA
H SHIT OH SHIT O
TA GADAPTA
DON'T WORRY, LUCIE, I'M SURE IT'S NOTHING!
RELAX
IT'S FINE!
OK?
BREATHE!
COOL!
MONIQUE!
SLAM
MONIQUE
MONI
BANG BANG BANG
OPEN THE DOOR!
COME QUICK! LUCIE IS BLEEDING LIKE HELL!
TABARS
HUH!?
FORGET THE CLINIC... WE'RE GOING STRAIGHT TO THE JOLIETTE HOSPITAL!
OK OK.
OK.
VROOO
144

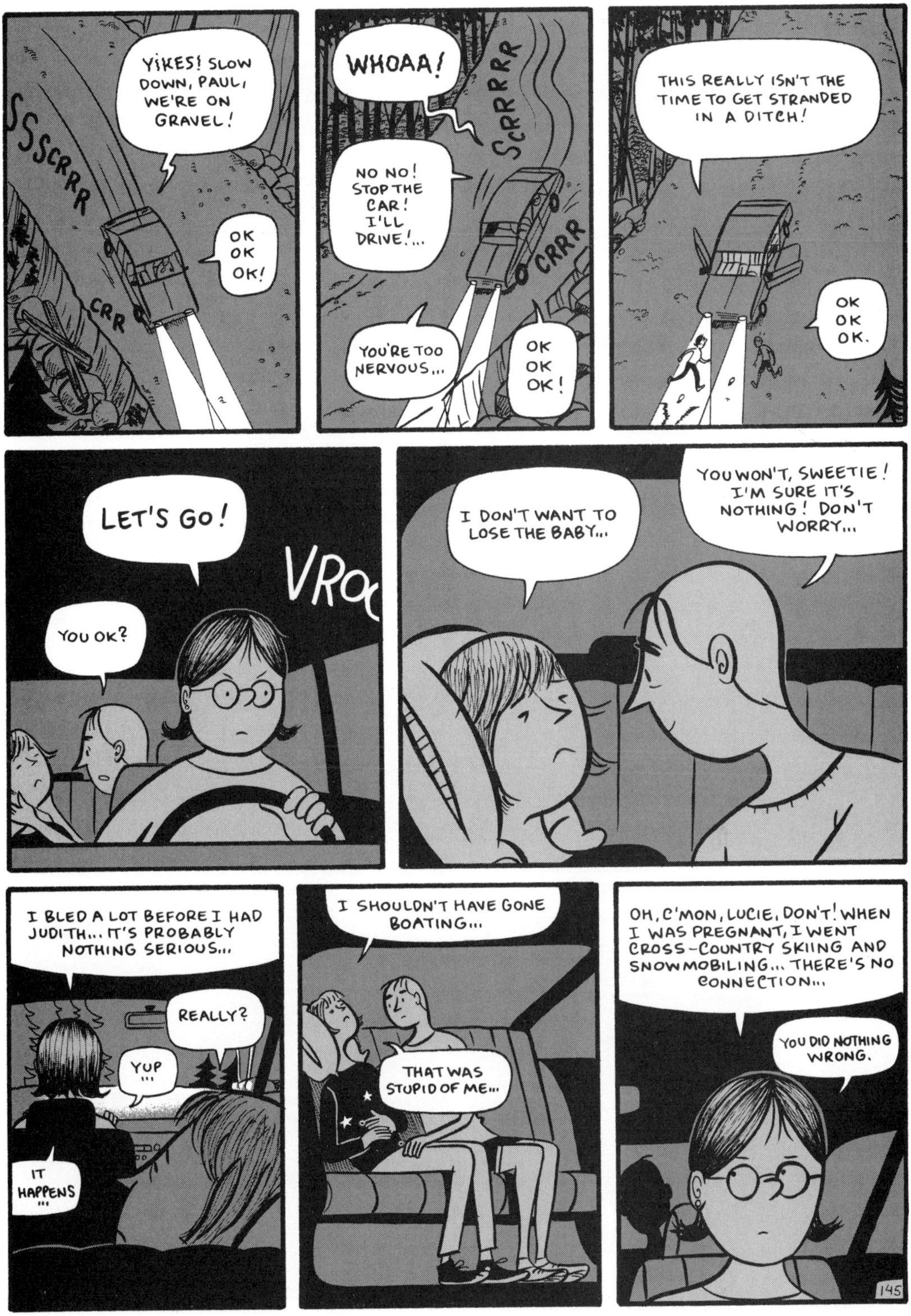

YIKES! SLOW DOWN, PAUL, WE'RE ON GRAVEL!
SSSCRRR
OK OK OK!
CRR
WHOAA!
SCRRRRR
NO NO! STOP THE CAR! I'LL DRIVE!...
CRRR
YOU'RE TOO NERVOUS...
OK OK OK!
THIS REALLY ISN'T THE TIME TO GET STRANDED IN A DITCH!
OK OK OK.
LET'S GO!
VROO
YOU OK?
I DON'T WANT TO LOSE THE BABY...
YOU WON'T, SWEETIE! I'M SURE IT'S NOTHING! DON'T WORRY...
I BLED A LOT BEFORE I HAD JUDITH... IT'S PROBABLY NOTHING SERIOUS...
REALLY?
YUP...
IT HAPPENS...
I SHOULDN'T HAVE GONE BOATING...
THAT WAS STUPID OF ME...
OH, C'MON, LUCIE, DON'T! WHEN I WAS PREGNANT, I WENT CROSS-COUNTRY SKIING AND SNOWMOBILING... THERE'S NO CONNECTION...
YOU DID NOTHING WRONG.

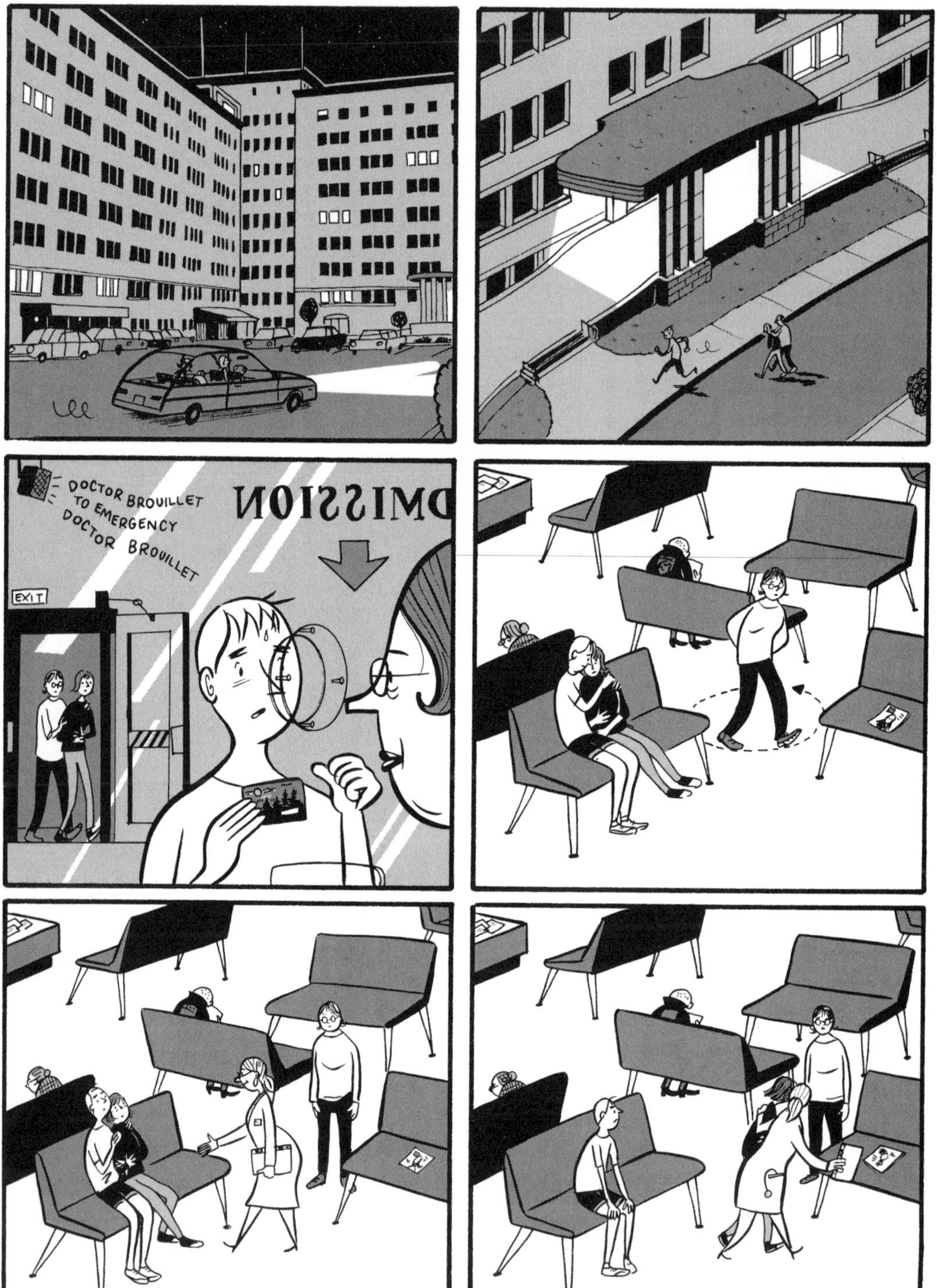
DOCTOR BROUILLET
TO EMERGENCY
DOCTOR BROUILLET
EXIT

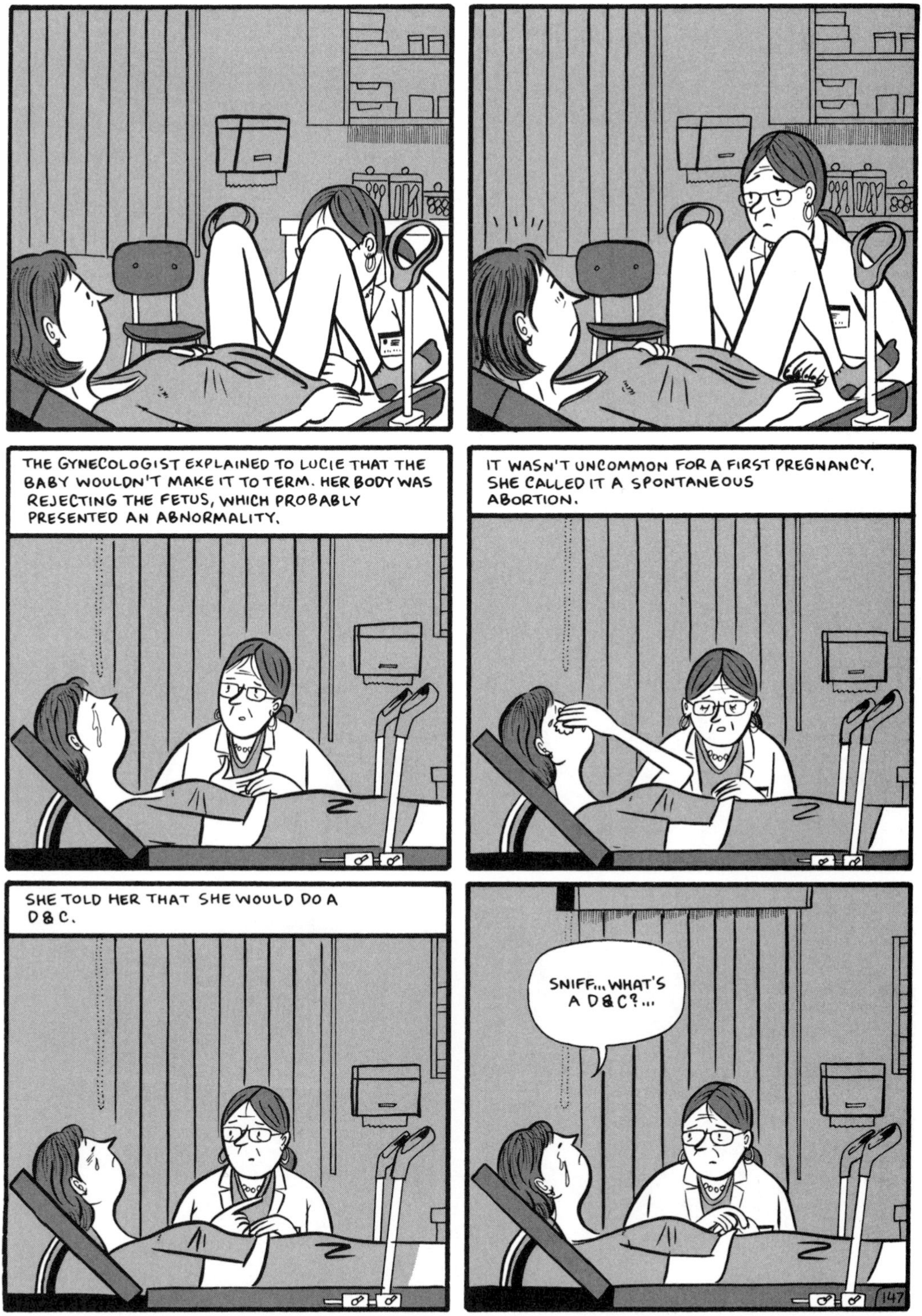
THE GYNECOLOGIST EXPLAINED TO LUCIE THAT THE BABY WOULDN'T MAKE IT TO TERM. HER BODY WAS REJECTING THE FETUS, WHICH PROBABLY PRESENTED AN ABNORMALITY.
IT WASN'T UNCOMMON FOR A FIRST PREGNANCY. SHE CALLED IT A SPONTANEOUS ABORTION.
SHE TOLD HER THAT SHE WOULD DO A D&C.
SNIFF... WHAT'S A D&C?...

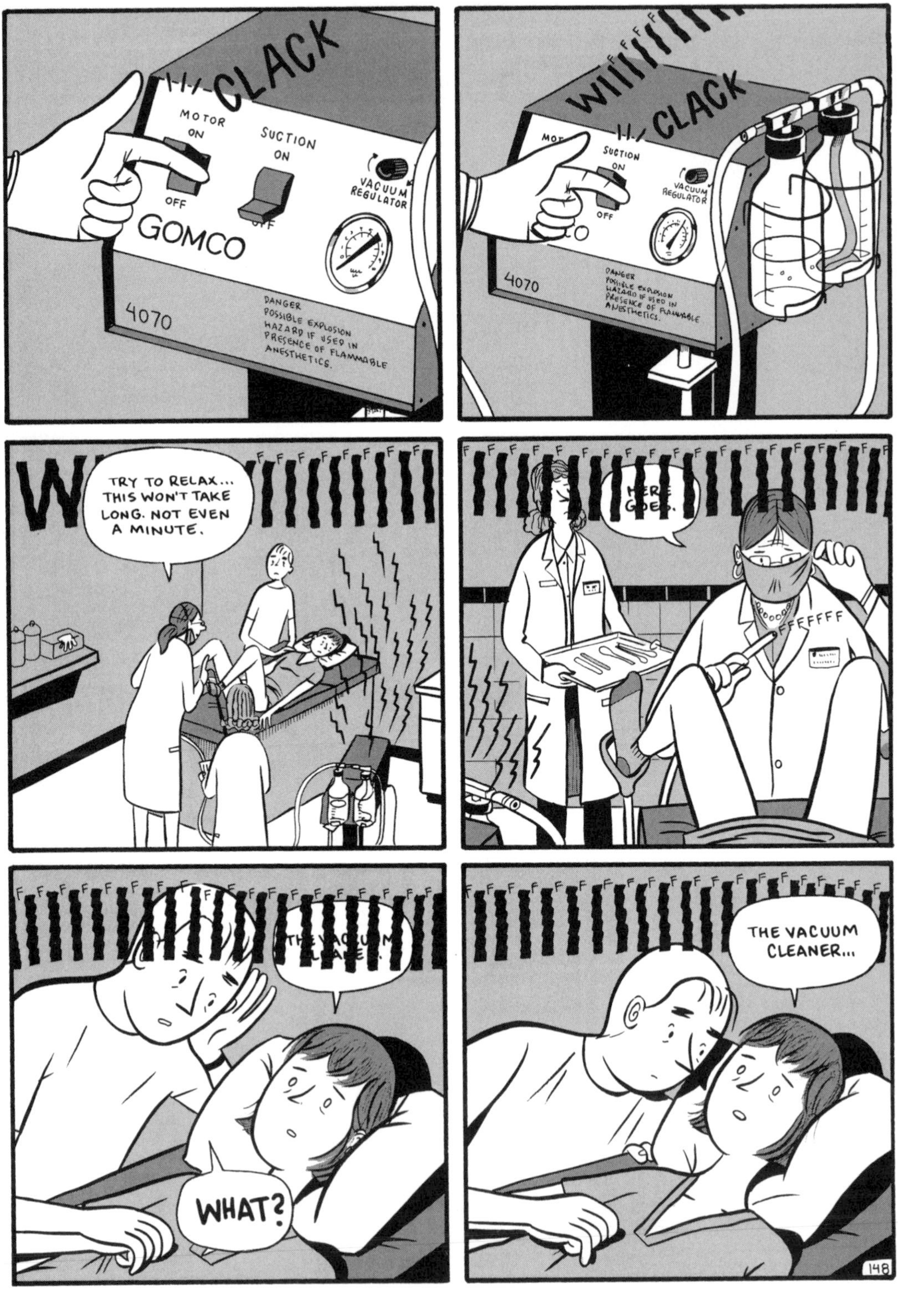
CLACK
MOTOR ON
OFF
SUCTION ON
VACUUM REGULATOR
GOMCO
4070
DANGER POSSIBLE EXPLOSION HAZARD IF USED IN PRESENCE OF FLAMMABLE ANESTHETICS.
CLACK
SUCTION ON
VACUUM REGULATOR
OFF
4070
DANGER POSSIBLE EXPLOSION HAZARD IF USED IN PRESENCE OF FLAMMABLE ANESTHETICS.
TRY TO RELAX... THIS WON'T TAKE LONG. NOT EVEN A MINUTE.
HERE GOES.
WHAT?
THE VACUUM CLEANER...

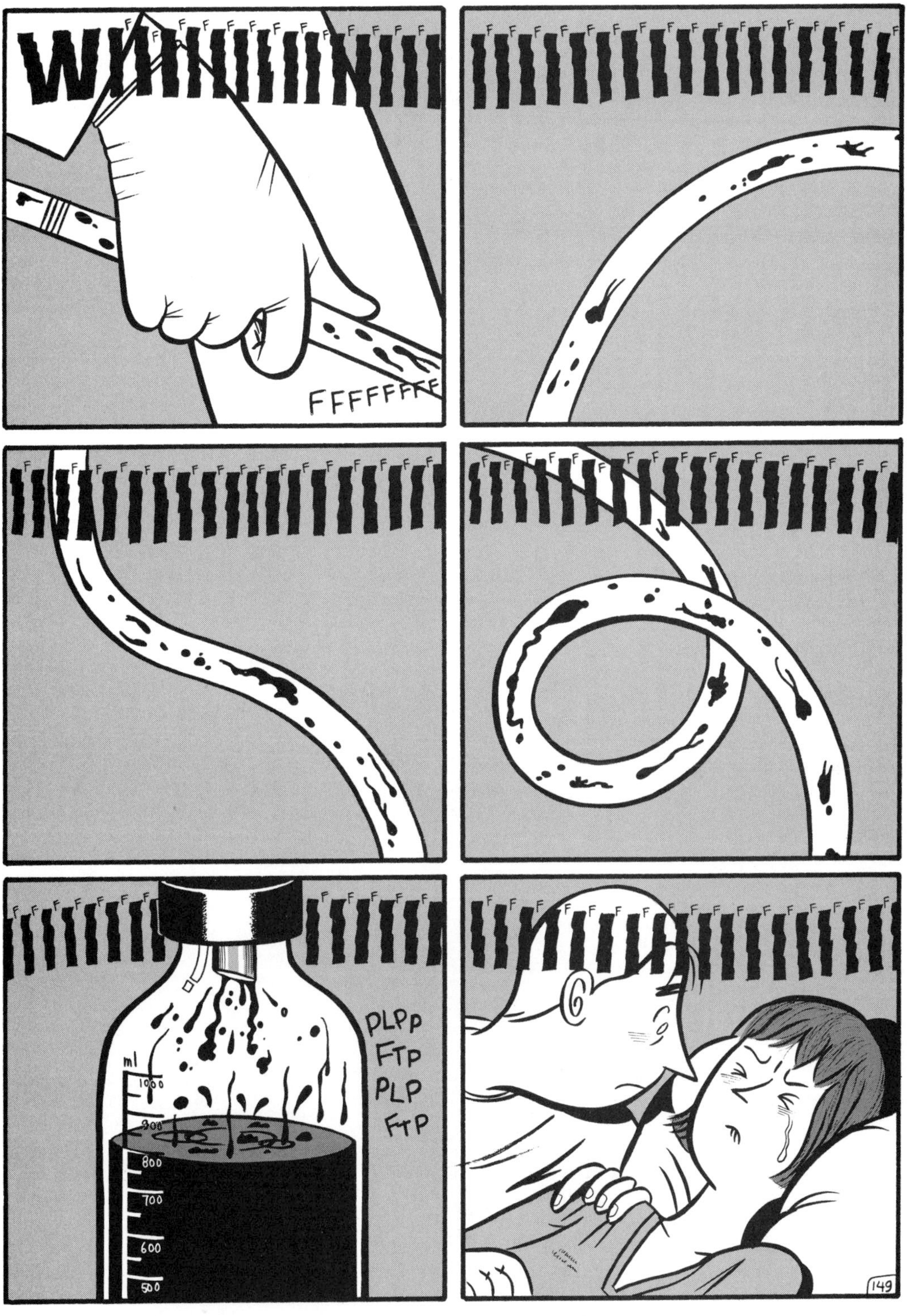
FFFFFFFF
PLPP
FTP
PLP
FTP

14 months later.

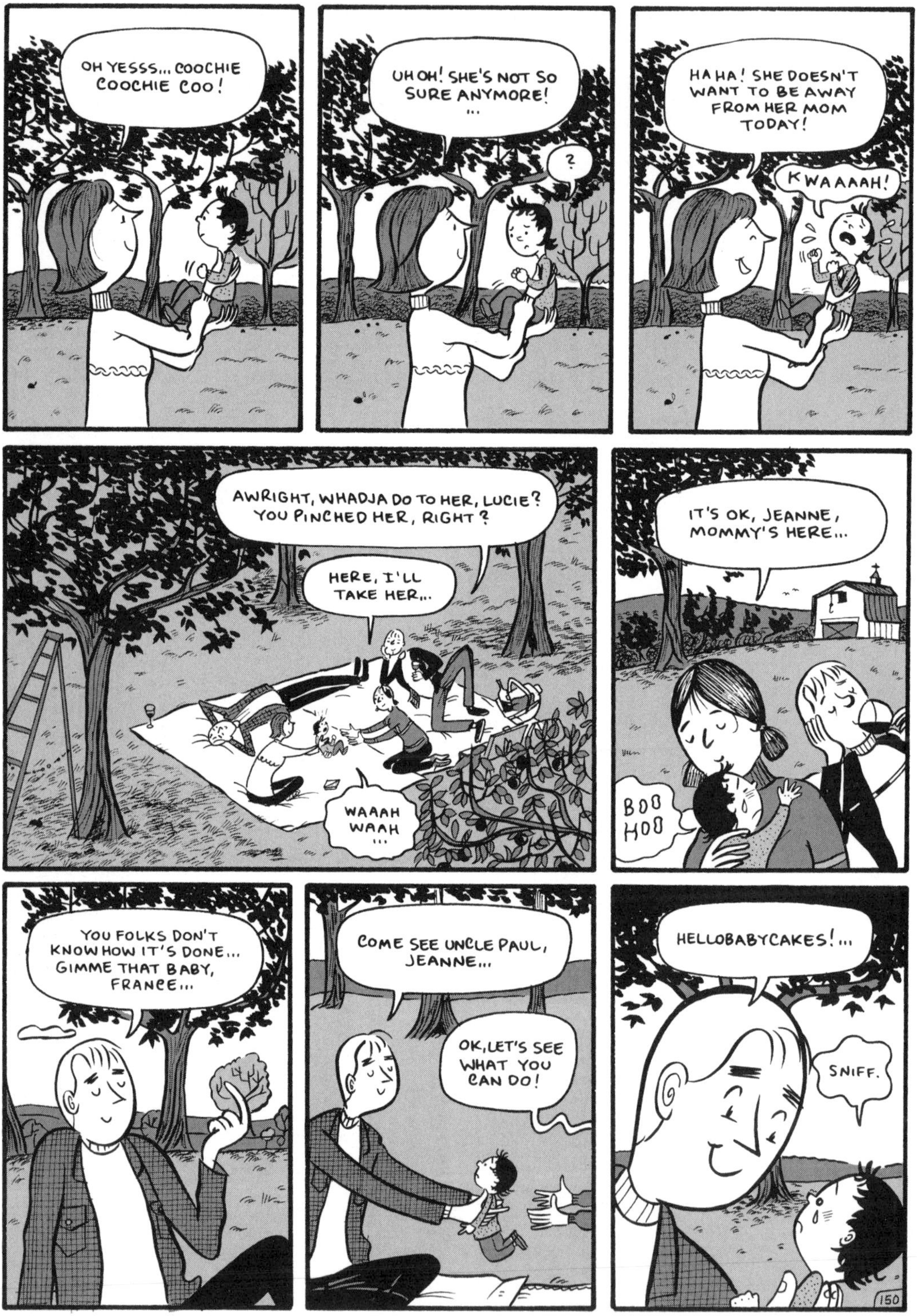
OH YESSS... COOCHIE COOCHIE COO!
UH OH! SHE'S NOT SO SURE ANYMORE! ...
?
HA HA! SHE DOESN'T WANT TO BE AWAY FROM HER MOM TODAY!
KWAAAAH!
AWRIGHT, WHADJA DO TO HER, LUCIE? YOU PINCHED HER, RIGHT?
HERE, I'LL TAKE HER...
WAAAH WAAH ...
IT'S OK, JEANNE, MOMMY'S HERE...
BOO HOO
YOU FOLKS DON'T KNOW HOW IT'S DONE... GIMME THAT BABY, FRANCE...
COME SEE UNCLE PAUL, JEANNE...
OK, LET'S SEE WHAT YOU CAN DO!
HELLOBABYCAKES!...
SNIFF.

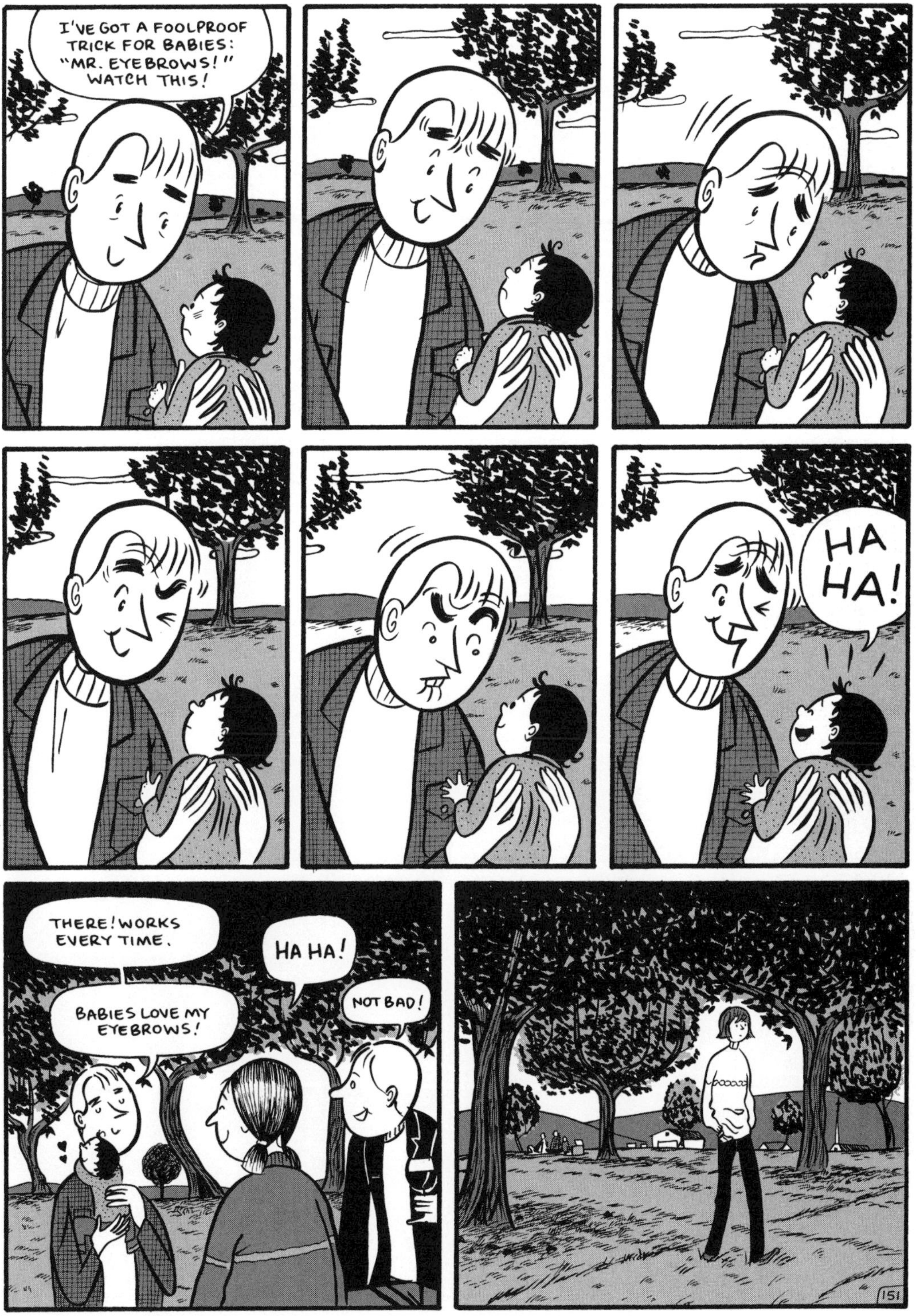

I'VE GOT A FOOLPROOF TRICK FOR BABIES: "MR. EYEBROWS!" WATCH THIS!
HA HA!
THERE! WORKS EVERY TIME.
BABIES LOVE MY EYEBROWS!
HA HA!
NOT BAD!

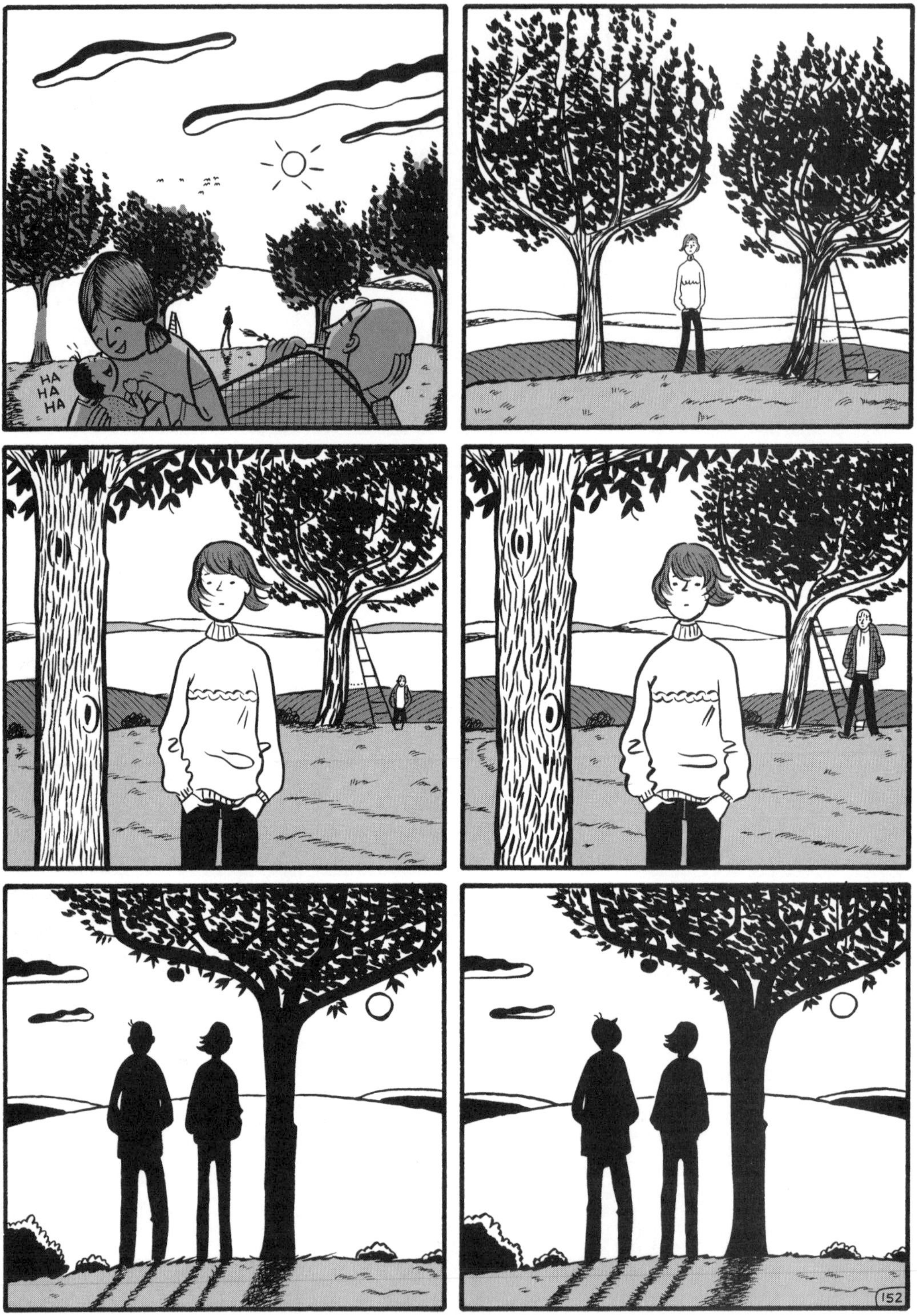
HA
HA
HA

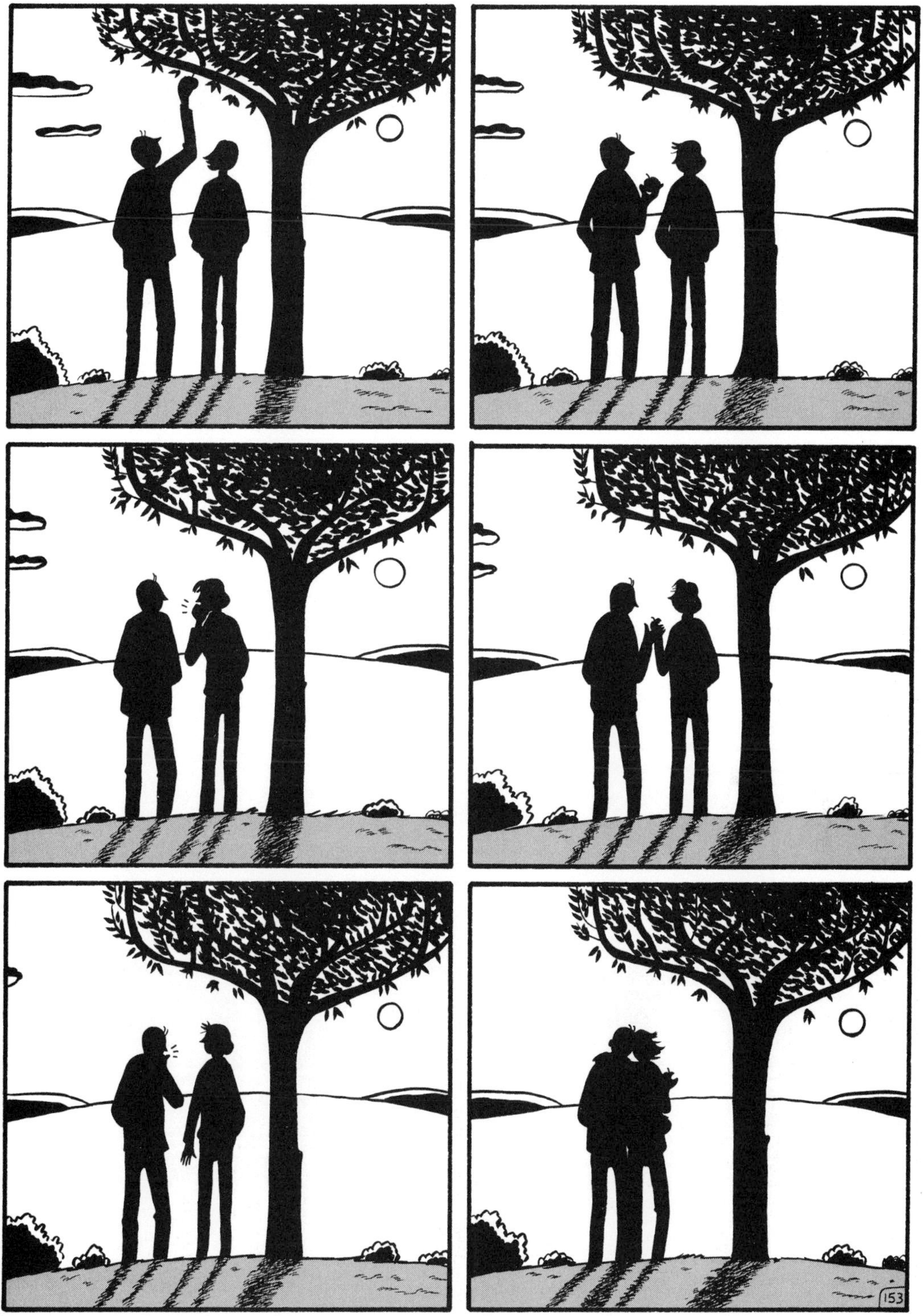

3 months later.

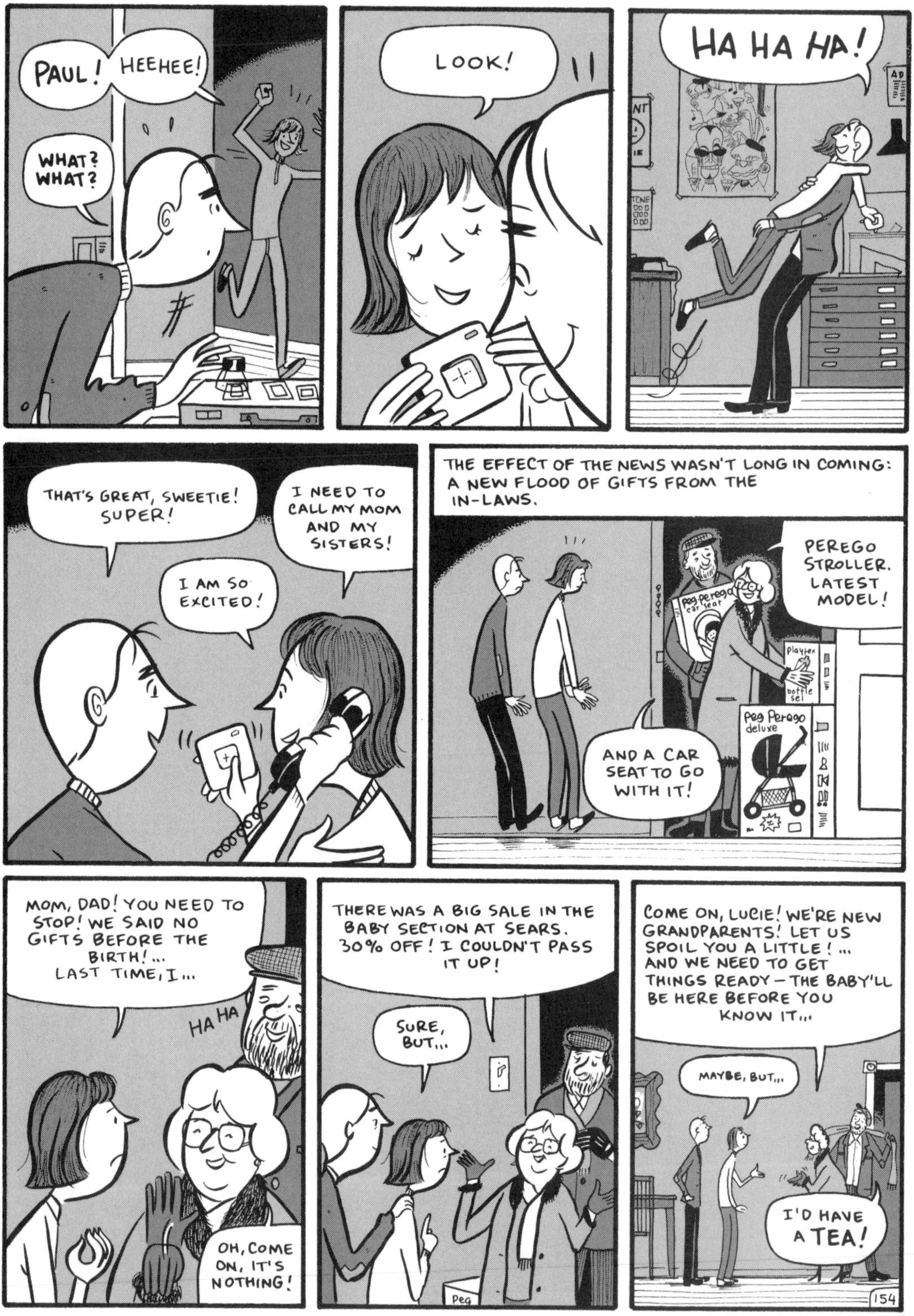
PAUL!
HEEHEE!
WHAT? WHAT?
LOOK!
HA HA HA!
THAT'S GREAT, SWEETIE! SUPER!
I NEED TO CALL MY MOM AND MY SISTERS!
I AM SO EXCITED!
THE EFFECT OF THE NEWS WASN'T LONG IN COMING: A NEW FLOOD OF GIFTS FROM THE IN-LAWS.
PEREGO STROLLER. LATEST MODEL!
AND A CAR SEAT TO GO WITH IT!
Peg-Perego car seat
playtex bottle set
Peg Perego deluxe
MOM, DAD! YOU NEED TO STOP! WE SAID NO GIFTS BEFORE THE BIRTH!... LAST TIME, I...
HA HA
OH, COME ON, IT'S NOTHING!
THERE WAS A BIG SALE IN THE BABY SECTION AT SEARS. 30% OFF! I COULDN'T PASS IT UP!
SURE, BUT...
Peg
COME ON, LUCIE! WE'RE NEW GRANDPARENTS! LET US SPOIL YOU A LITTLE! ... AND WE NEED TO GET THINGS READY — THE BABY'LL BE HERE BEFORE YOU KNOW IT...
MAYBE, BUT...
I'D HAVE A TEA!

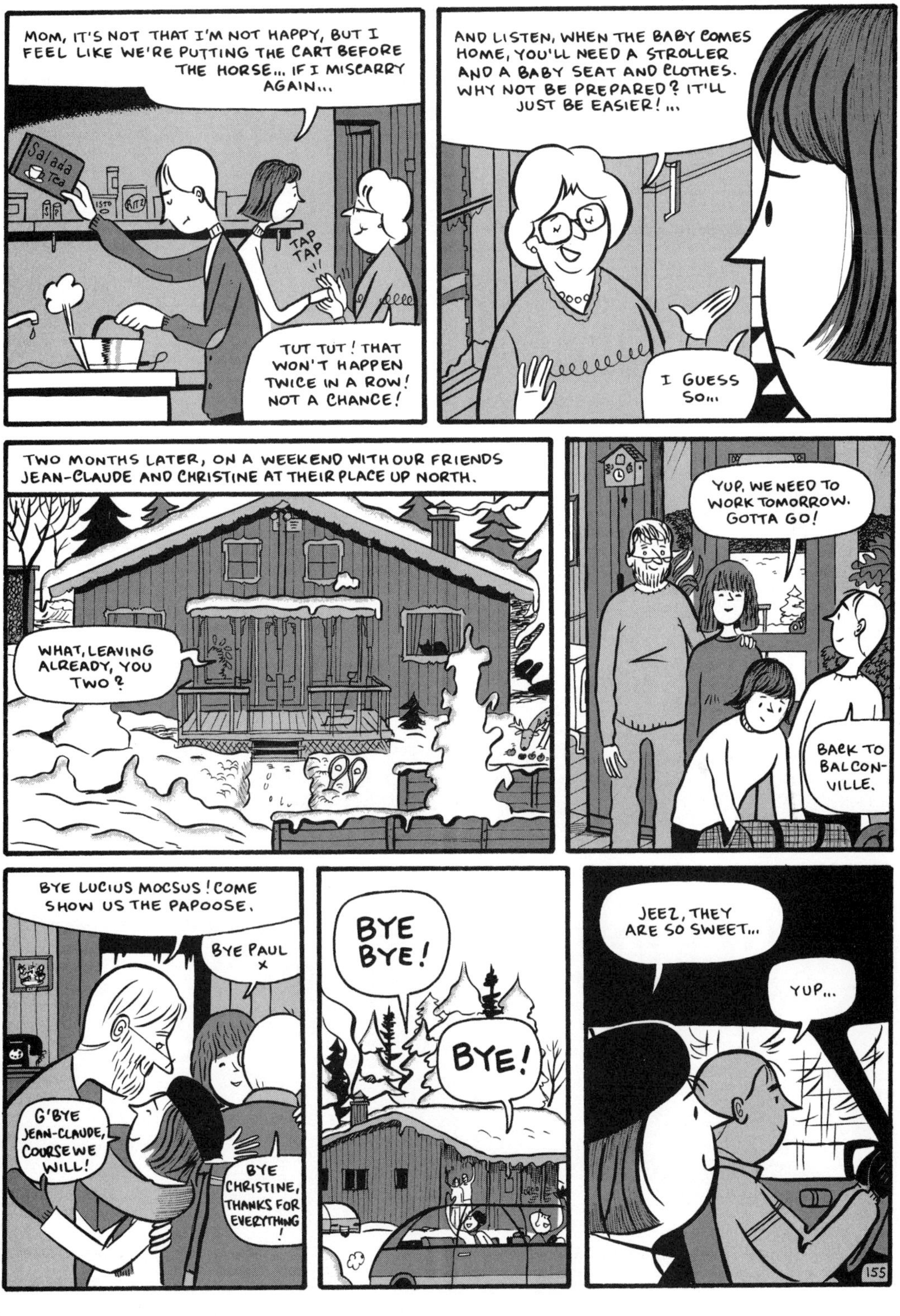
MOM, IT'S NOT THAT I'M NOT HAPPY, BUT I FEEL LIKE WE'RE PUTTING THE CART BEFORE THE HORSE... IF I MISCARRY AGAIN...
TAP TAP
TUT TUT! THAT WON'T HAPPEN TWICE IN A ROW! NOT A CHANCE!
AND LISTEN, WHEN THE BABY COMES HOME, YOU'LL NEED A STROLLER AND A BABY SEAT AND CLOTHES. WHY NOT BE PREPARED? IT'LL JUST BE EASIER!...
I GUESS SO...
TWO MONTHS LATER, ON A WEEKEND WITH OUR FRIENDS JEAN-CLAUDE AND CHRISTINE AT THEIR PLACE UP NORTH.
WHAT, LEAVING ALREADY, YOU TWO?
YUP, WE NEED TO WORK TOMORROW. GOTTA GO!
BACK TO BALCONVILLE.
BYE LUCIUS MOCSUS! COME SHOW US THE PAPOOSE.
BYE PAUL x
G'BYE JEAN-CLAUDE, COURSE WE WILL!
BYE CHRISTINE, THANKS FOR EVERYTHING!
BYE BYE!
BYE!
JEEZ, THEY ARE SO SWEET...
YUP...

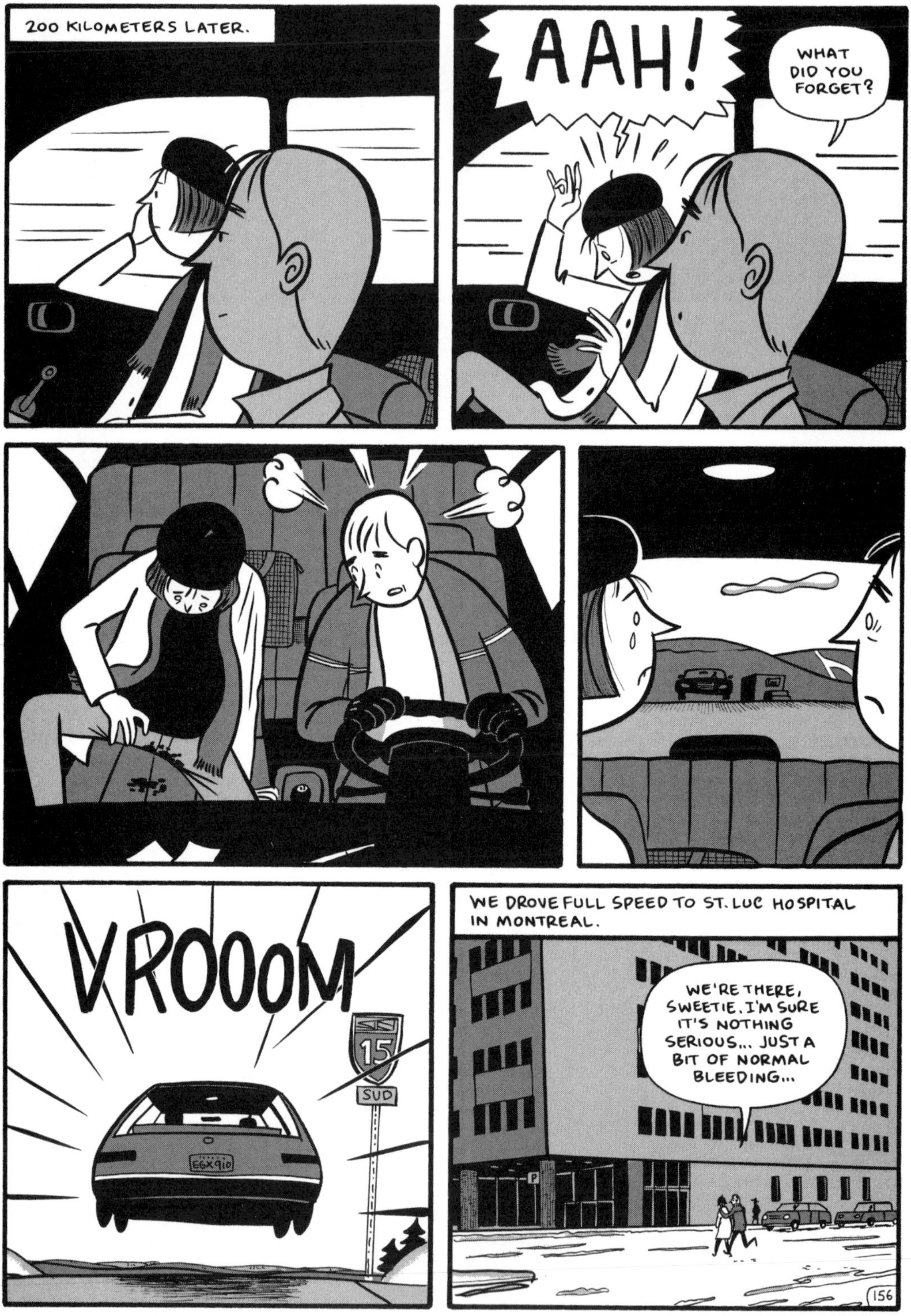

200 KILOMETERS LATER.
AAH!
WHAT DID YOU FORGET?
VROOOM
15
SUD
EGX 910
WE DROVE FULL SPEED TO ST. LUC HOSPITAL IN MONTREAL.
WE'RE THERE, SWEETIE. I'M SURE IT'S NOTHING SERIOUS... JUST A BIT OF NORMAL BLEEDING...
P

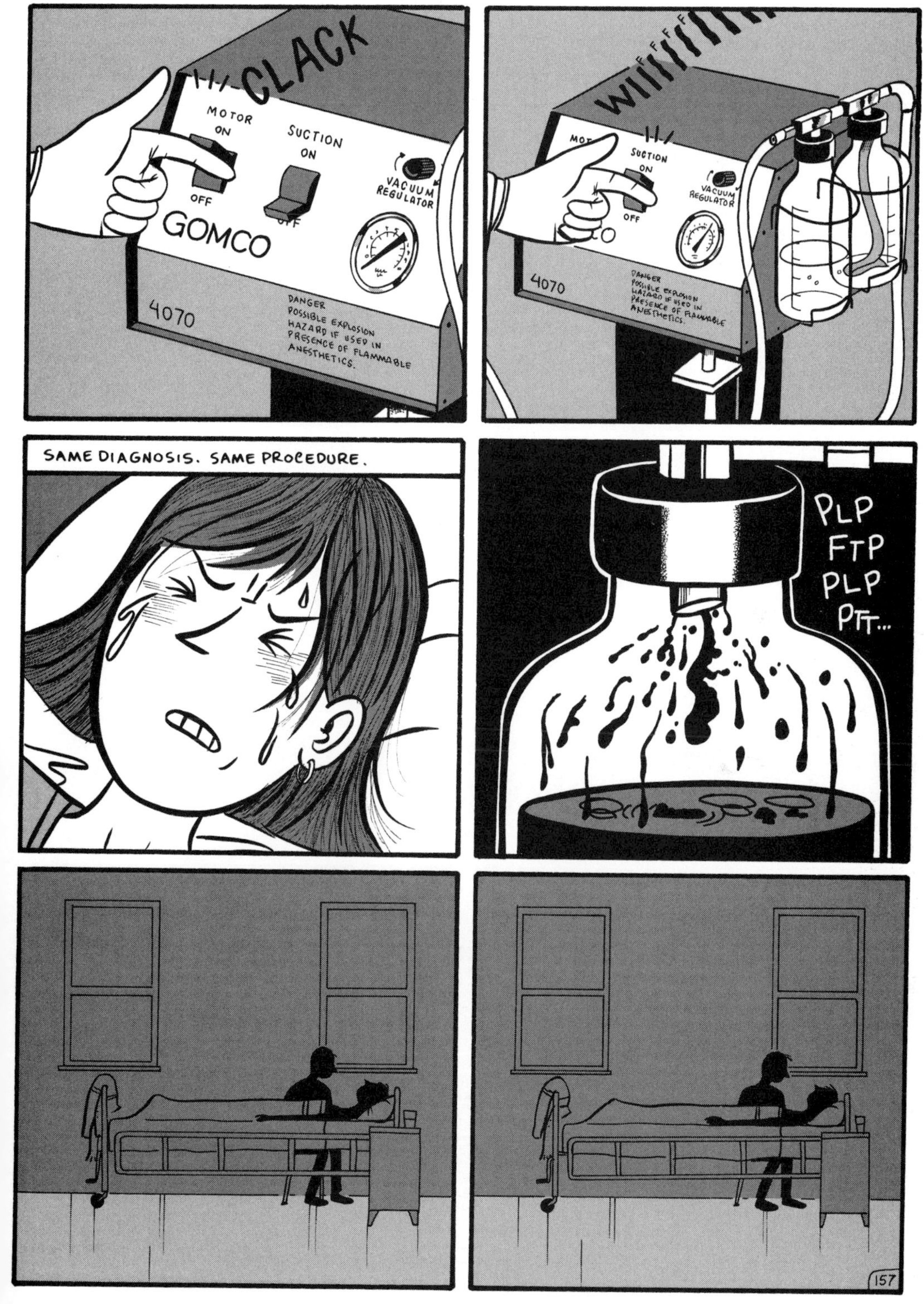
CLACK
MOTOR ON
OFF
SUCTION ON
OFF
VACUUM REGULATOR
GOMCO
4070
DANGER POSSIBLE EXPLOSION HAZARD IF USED IN PRESENCE OF FLAMMABLE ANESTHETICS.
SUCTION ON
OFF
VACUUM REGULATOR
4070
DANGER POSSIBLE EXPLOSION HAZARD IF USED IN PRESENCE OF FLAMMABLE ANESTHETICS.
SAME DIAGNOSIS. SAME PROCEDURE.
PLP
FTP
PLP
PFT...

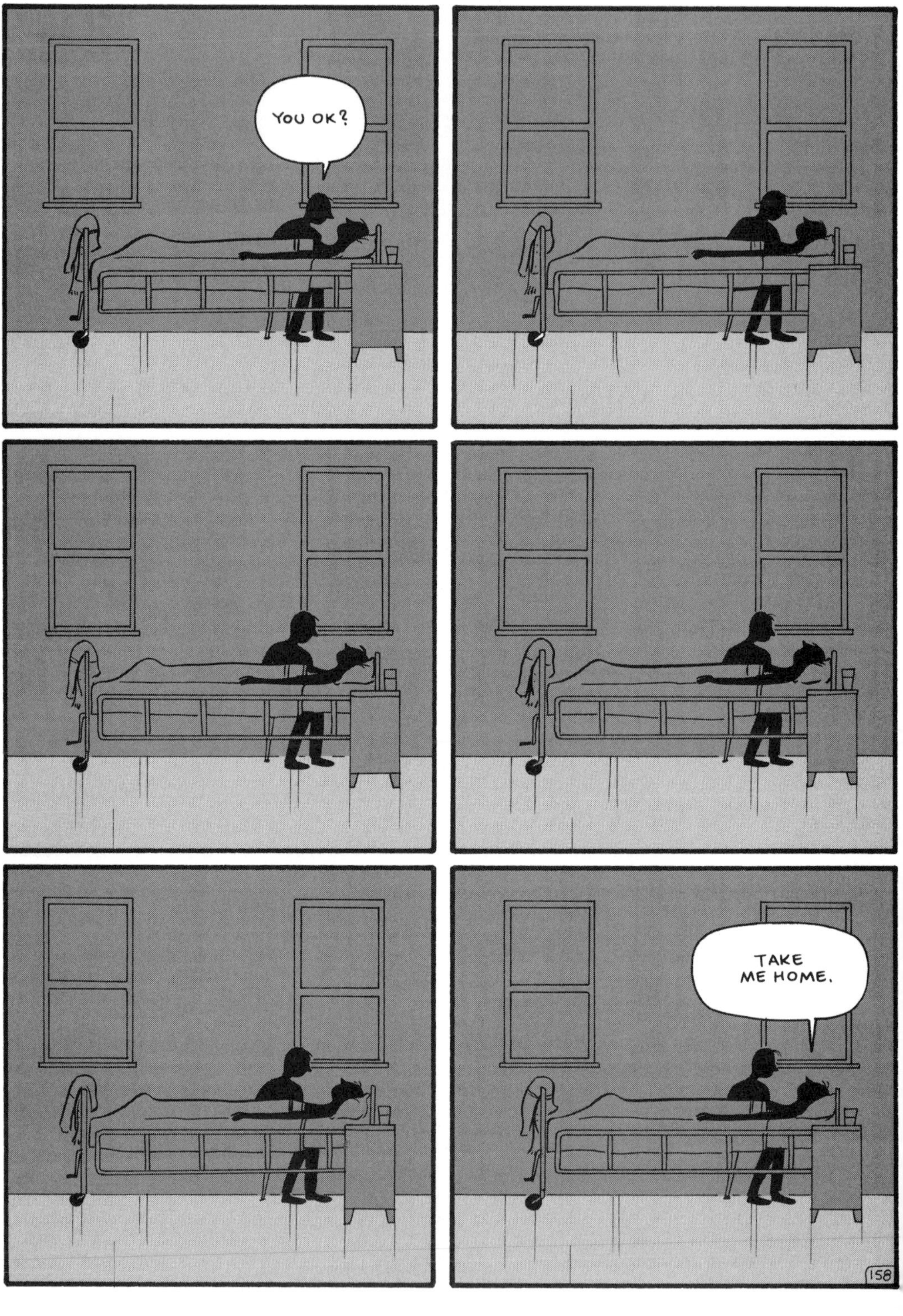
YOU OK?
TAKE ME HOME.
158

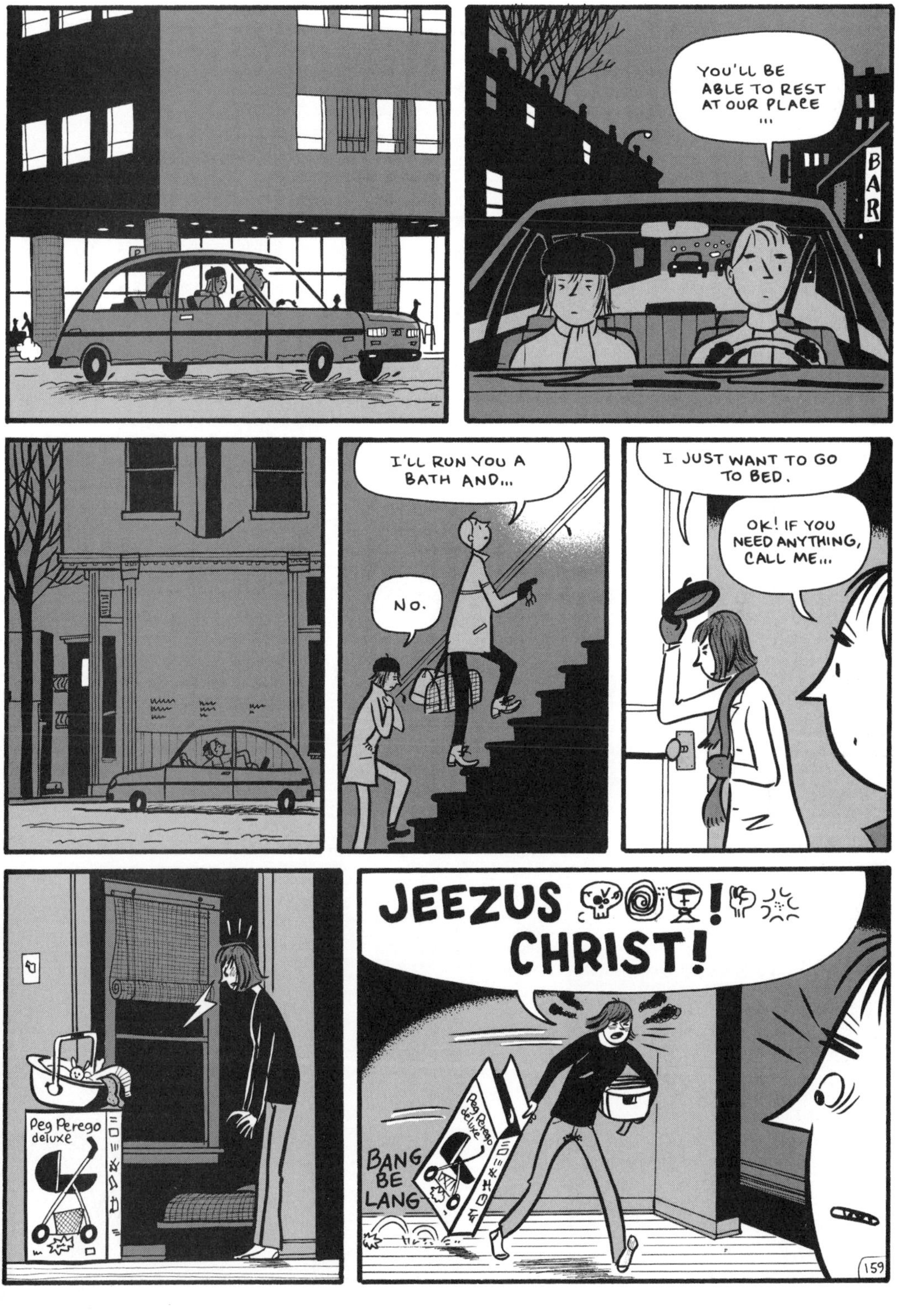

YOU'LL BE ABLE TO REST AT OUR PLACE ...
BAR
I'LL RUN YOU A BATH AND...
NO.
I JUST WANT TO GO TO BED.
OK! IF YOU NEED ANYTHING, CALL ME...
Peg Perego deluxe
JEEZUS CHRIST!
BANG BE LANG
Peg Perego deluxe

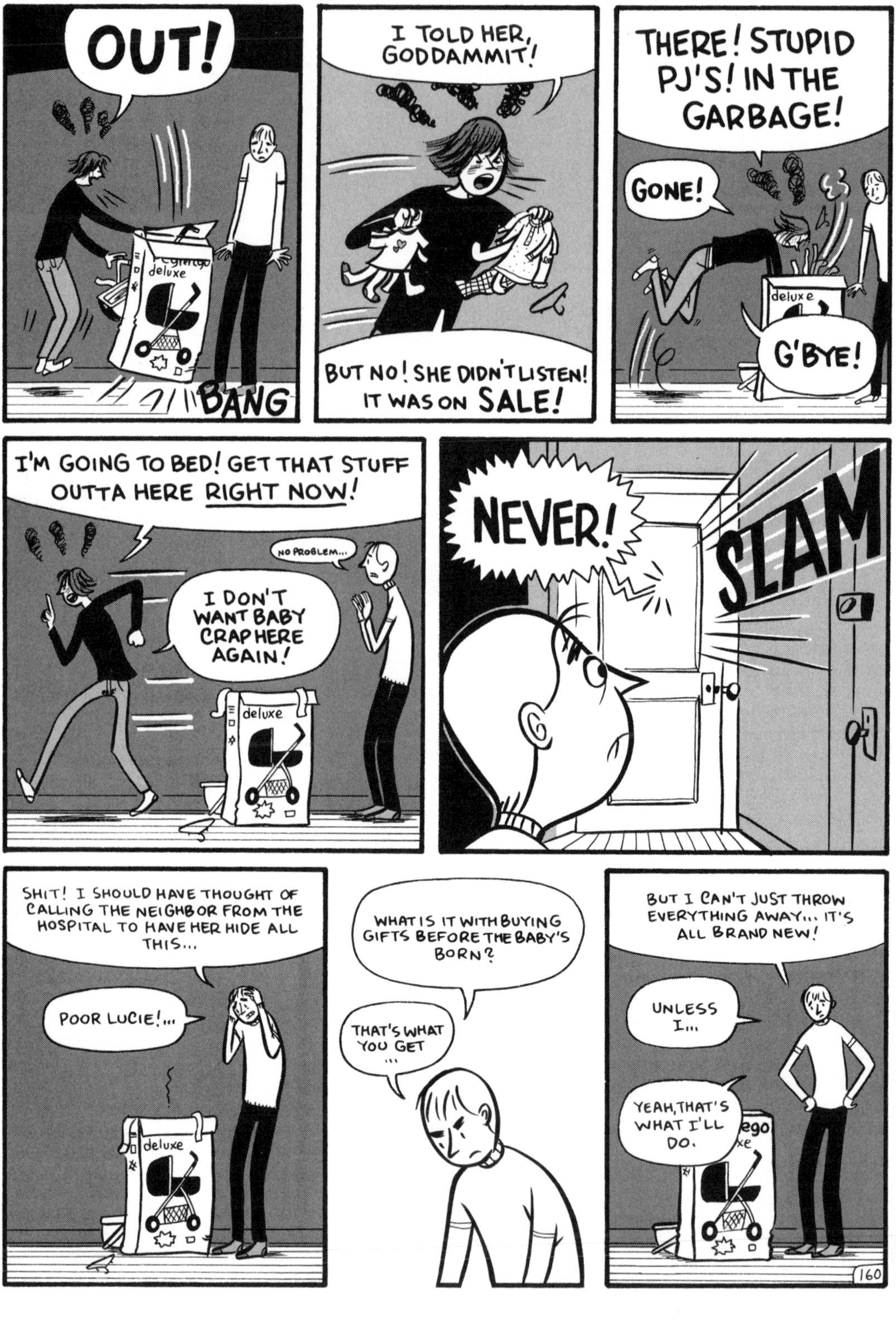
OUT!
BANG
I TOLD HER, GODDAMMIT!
BUT NO! SHE DIDN'T LISTEN! IT WAS ON SALE!
THERE! STUPID PJ'S! IN THE GARBAGE!
GONE!
G'BYE!
I'M GOING TO BED! GET THAT STUFF OUTTA HERE RIGHT NOW!
NO PROBLEM...
I DON'T WANT BABY CRAP HERE AGAIN!
NEVER!
SLAM
SHIT! I SHOULD HAVE THOUGHT OF CALLING THE NEIGHBOR FROM THE HOSPITAL TO HAVE HER HIDE ALL THIS...
POOR LUCIE!...
WHAT IS IT WITH BUYING GIFTS BEFORE THE BABY'S BORN?
THAT'S WHAT YOU GET ...
BUT I CAN'T JUST THROW EVERYTHING AWAY... IT'S ALL BRAND NEW!
UNLESS I...
YEAH, THAT'S WHAT I'LL DO.

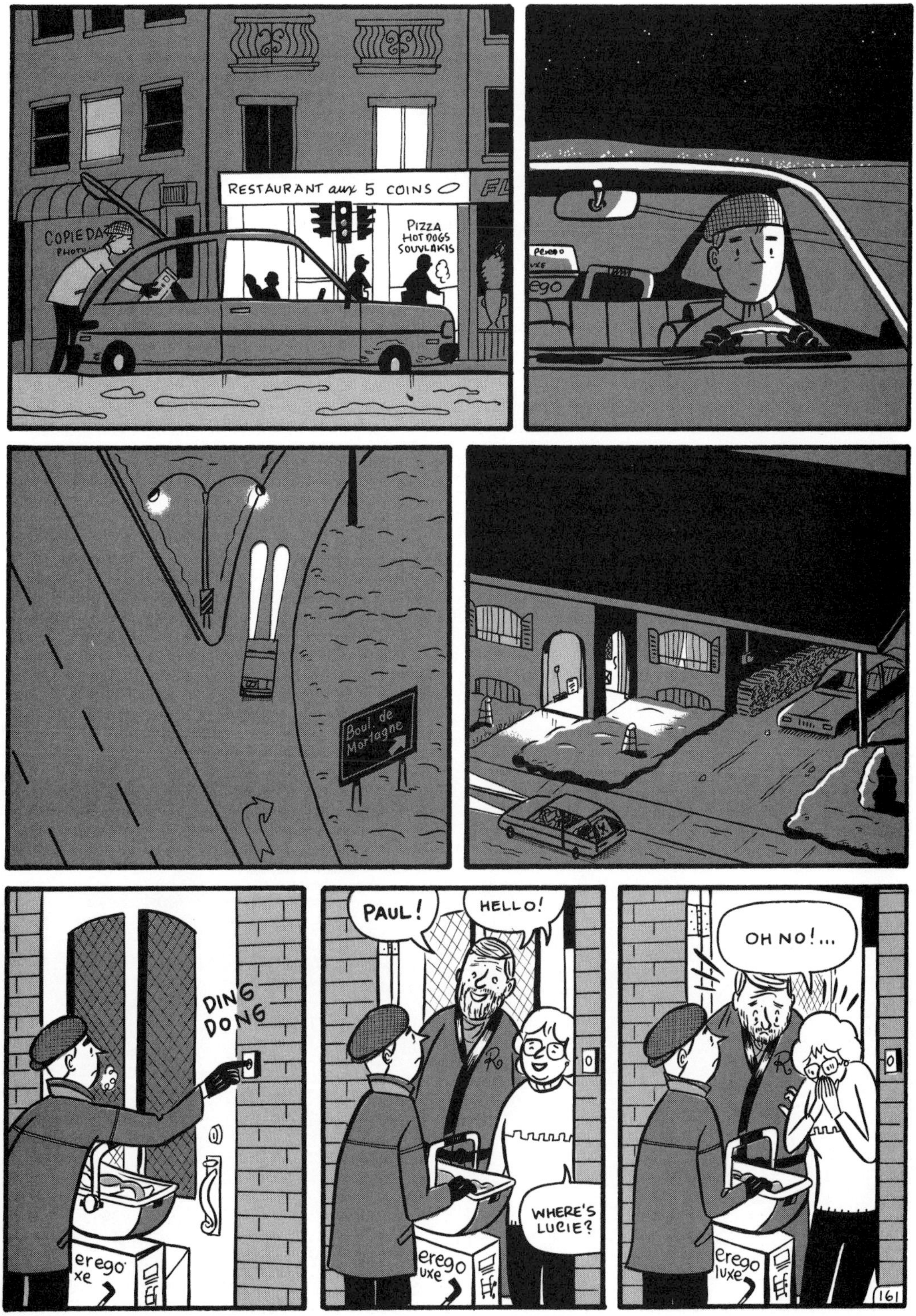
RESTAURANT aux 5 COINS
COPIEDA
PHOTO
PIZZA
HOT DOGS
SOUVLAKIS
Boul. de Mortagne
DING DONG
erego
xe
PAUL!
HELLO!
WHERE'S LUCIE?
erego
luxe
OH NO!...
erego
luxe

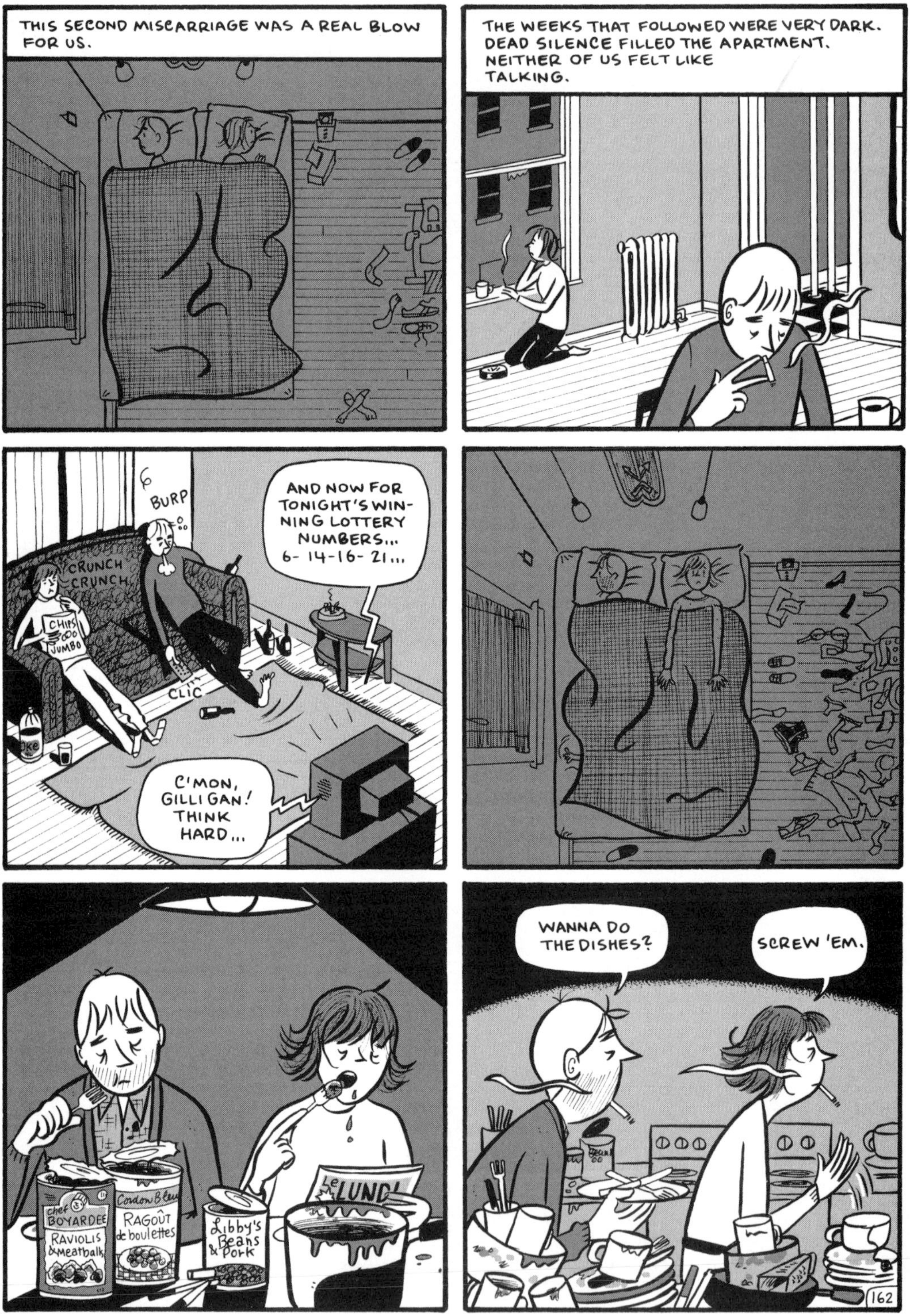
THIS SECOND MISCARRIAGE WAS A REAL BLOW FOR US.
THE WEEKS THAT FOLLOWED WERE VERY DARK. DEAD SILENCE FILLED THE APARTMENT. NEITHER OF US FELT LIKE TALKING.
BURP
CRUNCH CRUNCH
CHIPS JUMBO
AND NOW FOR TONIGHT'S WINNING LOTTERY NUMBERS... 6- 14-16- 21...
CLIC
C'MON, GILLIGAN! THINK HARD...
Chef BOYARDEE RAVIOLIS &Meatballs
Cordon Bleu RAGOÛT de boulettes
Libby's Beans & Pork
Le LUNDI
WANNA DO THE DISHES?
SCREW 'EM.

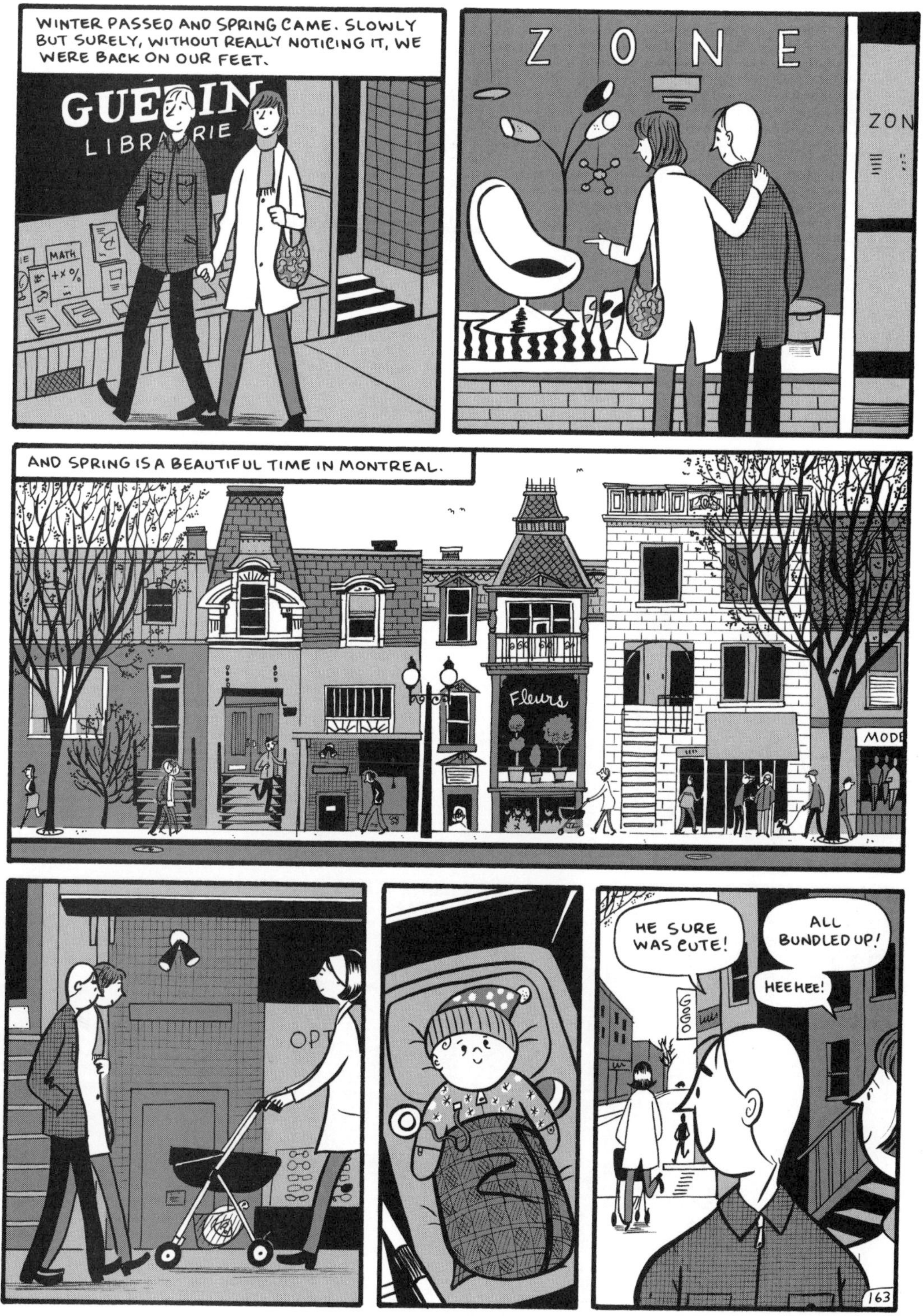
WINTER PASSED AND SPRING CAME. SLOWLY BUT SURELY, WITHOUT REALLY NOTICING IT, WE WERE BACK ON OUR FEET.
GUÉRIN
LIBRAIRIE
MATH
ZONE
ZON
AND SPRING IS A BEAUTIFUL TIME IN MONTREAL.
Fleurs
MODE
OPT
HE SURE WAS CUTE!
ALL BUNDLED UP!
HEE HEE!
GOGO

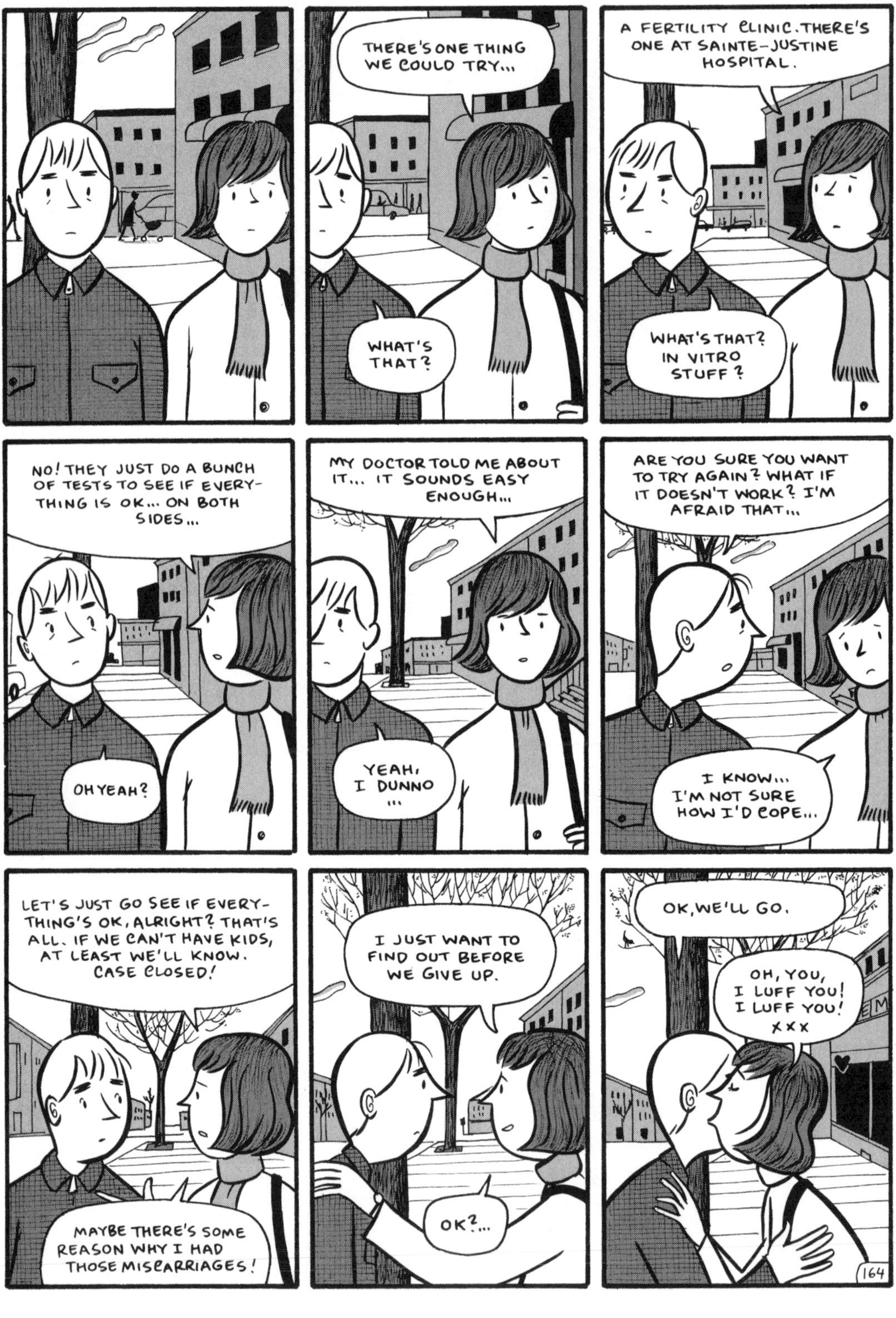
THERE'S ONE THING WE COULD TRY...
WHAT'S THAT?
A FERTILITY CLINIC. THERE'S ONE AT SAINTE-JUSTINE HOSPITAL.
WHAT'S THAT? IN VITRO STUFF?
NO! THEY JUST DO A BUNCH OF TESTS TO SEE IF EVERYTHING IS OK... ON BOTH SIDES...
OH YEAH?
MY DOCTOR TOLD ME ABOUT IT... IT SOUNDS EASY ENOUGH...
YEAH, I DUNNO ...
ARE YOU SURE YOU WANT TO TRY AGAIN? WHAT IF IT DOESN'T WORK? I'M AFRAID THAT...
I KNOW... I'M NOT SURE HOW I'D COPE...
LET'S JUST GO SEE IF EVERYTHING'S OK, ALRIGHT? THAT'S ALL. IF WE CAN'T HAVE KIDS, AT LEAST WE'LL KNOW. CASE CLOSED!
MAYBE THERE'S SOME REASON WHY I HAD THOSE MISCARRIAGES!
I JUST WANT TO FIND OUT BEFORE WE GIVE UP.
OK?...
OK, WE'LL GO.
OH, YOU, I LUFF YOU! I LUFF YOU! XXX

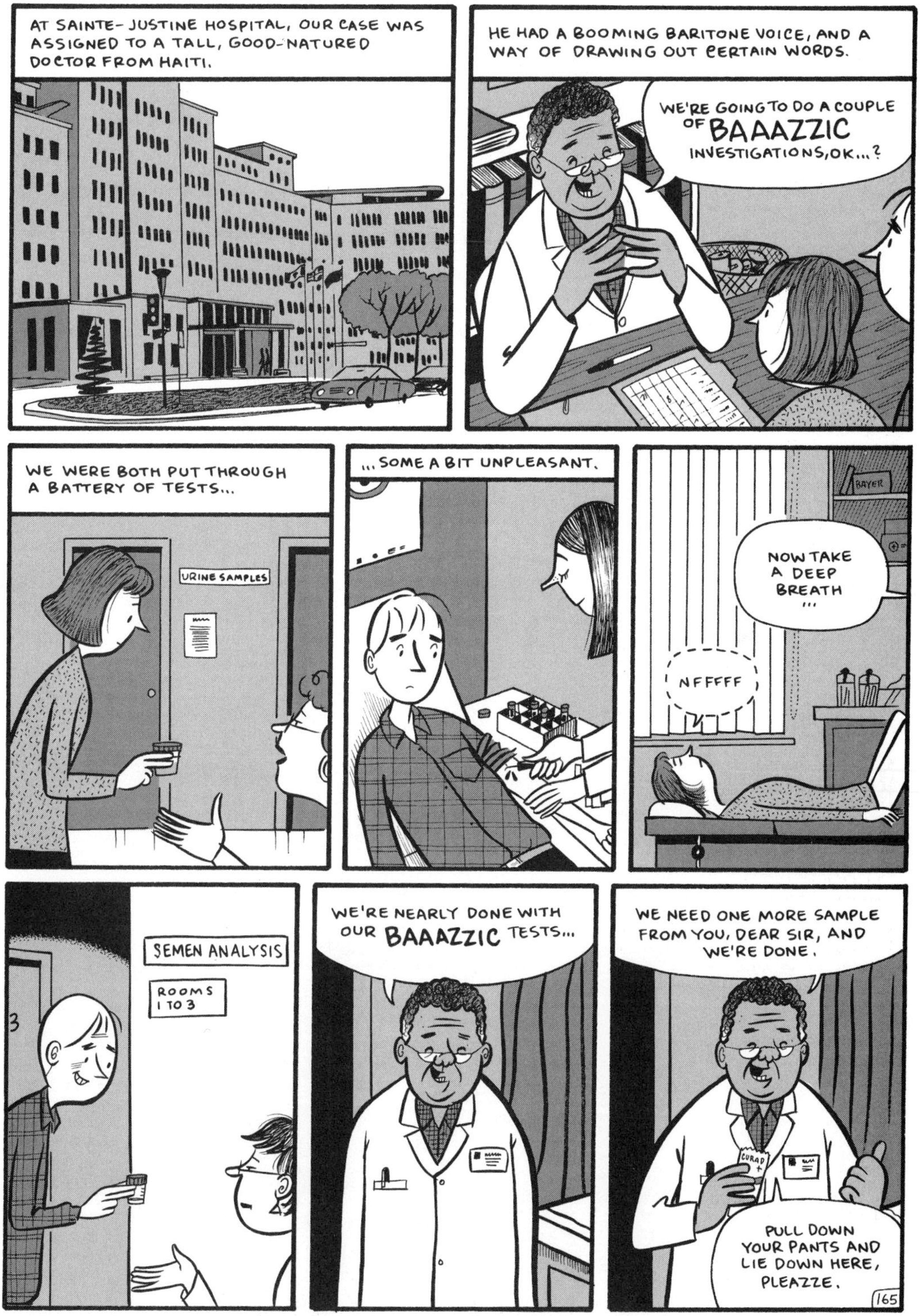
AT SAINTE-JUSTINE HOSPITAL, OUR CASE WAS ASSIGNED TO A TALL, GOOD-NATURED DOCTOR FROM HAITI.
HE HAD A BOOMING BARITONE VOICE, AND A WAY OF DRAWING OUT CERTAIN WORDS.
WE'RE GOING TO DO A COUPLE OF BAAAZZIC INVESTIGATIONS, OK...?
WE WERE BOTH PUT THROUGH A BATTERY OF TESTS...
URINE SAMPLES
...SOME A BIT UNPLEASANT.
BAYER
NOW TAKE A DEEP BREATH ...
NFFFFF
SEMEN ANALYSIS
ROOMS 1 TO 3
3
WE'RE NEARLY DONE WITH OUR BAAAZZIC TESTS...
WE NEED ONE MORE SAMPLE FROM YOU, DEAR SIR, AND WE'RE DONE.
CURAD
PULL DOWN YOUR PANTS AND LIE DOWN HERE, PLEAZZE.

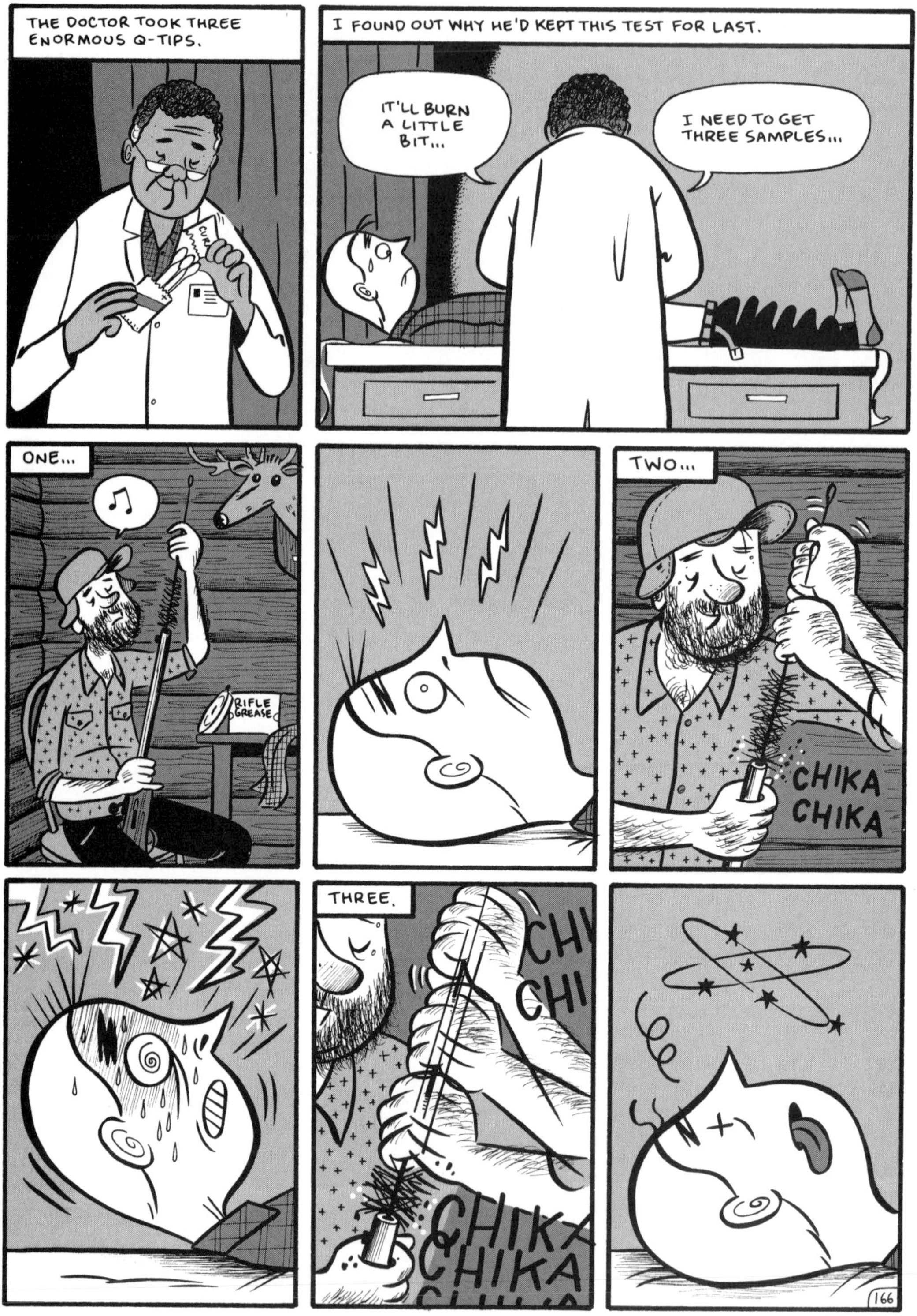

THE DOCTOR TOOK THREE ENORMOUS Q-TIPS.
CURI
I FOUND OUT WHY HE'D KEPT THIS TEST FOR LAST.
IT'LL BURN A LITTLE BIT...
I NEED TO GET THREE SAMPLES...
ONE...
RIFLE GREASE
TWO...
CHIKA CHIKA
THREE.
CHI CHI
CHIKA CHIKA

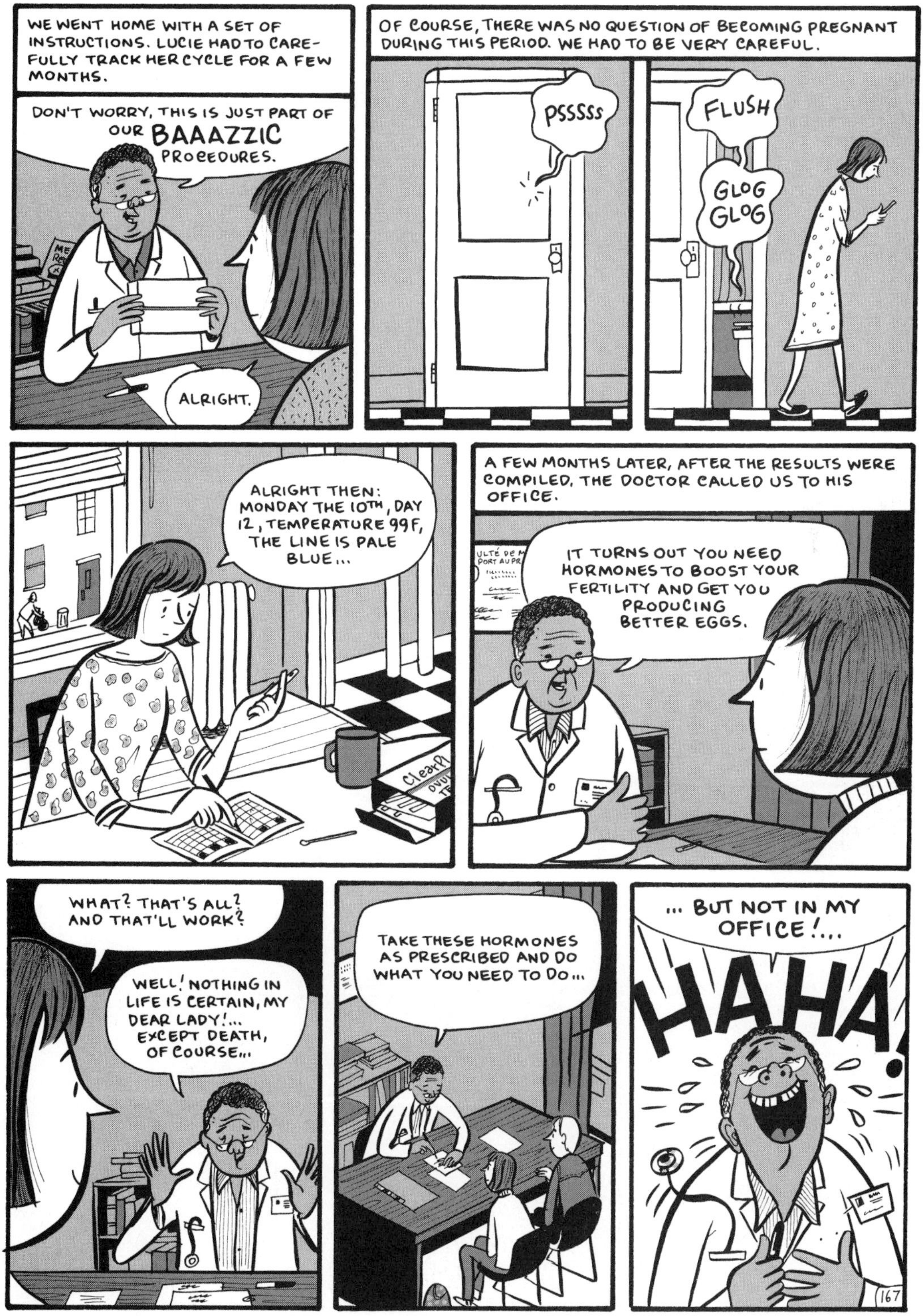
WE WENT HOME WITH A SET OF INSTRUCTIONS. LUCIE HAD TO CAREFULLY TRACK HER CYCLE FOR A FEW MONTHS.
DON'T WORRY, THIS IS JUST PART OF OUR BAAAZZIC PROCEDURES.
ALRIGHT.
OF COURSE, THERE WAS NO QUESTION OF BECOMING PREGNANT DURING THIS PERIOD. WE HAD TO BE VERY CAREFUL.
PSSSSS
FLUSH
GLOG GLOG
ALRIGHT THEN: MONDAY THE 10TH, DAY 12, TEMPERATURE 99F, THE LINE IS PALE BLUE...
A FEW MONTHS LATER, AFTER THE RESULTS WERE COMPILED, THE DOCTOR CALLED US TO HIS OFFICE.
IT TURNS OUT YOU NEED HORMONES TO BOOST YOUR FERTILITY AND GET YOU PRODUCING BETTER EGGS.
WHAT? THAT'S ALL? AND THAT'LL WORK?
WELL! NOTHING IN LIFE IS CERTAIN, MY DEAR LADY!... EXCEPT DEATH, OF COURSE...
TAKE THESE HORMONES AS PRESCRIBED AND DO WHAT YOU NEED TO DO...
... BUT NOT IN MY OFFICE!...
HAHA!

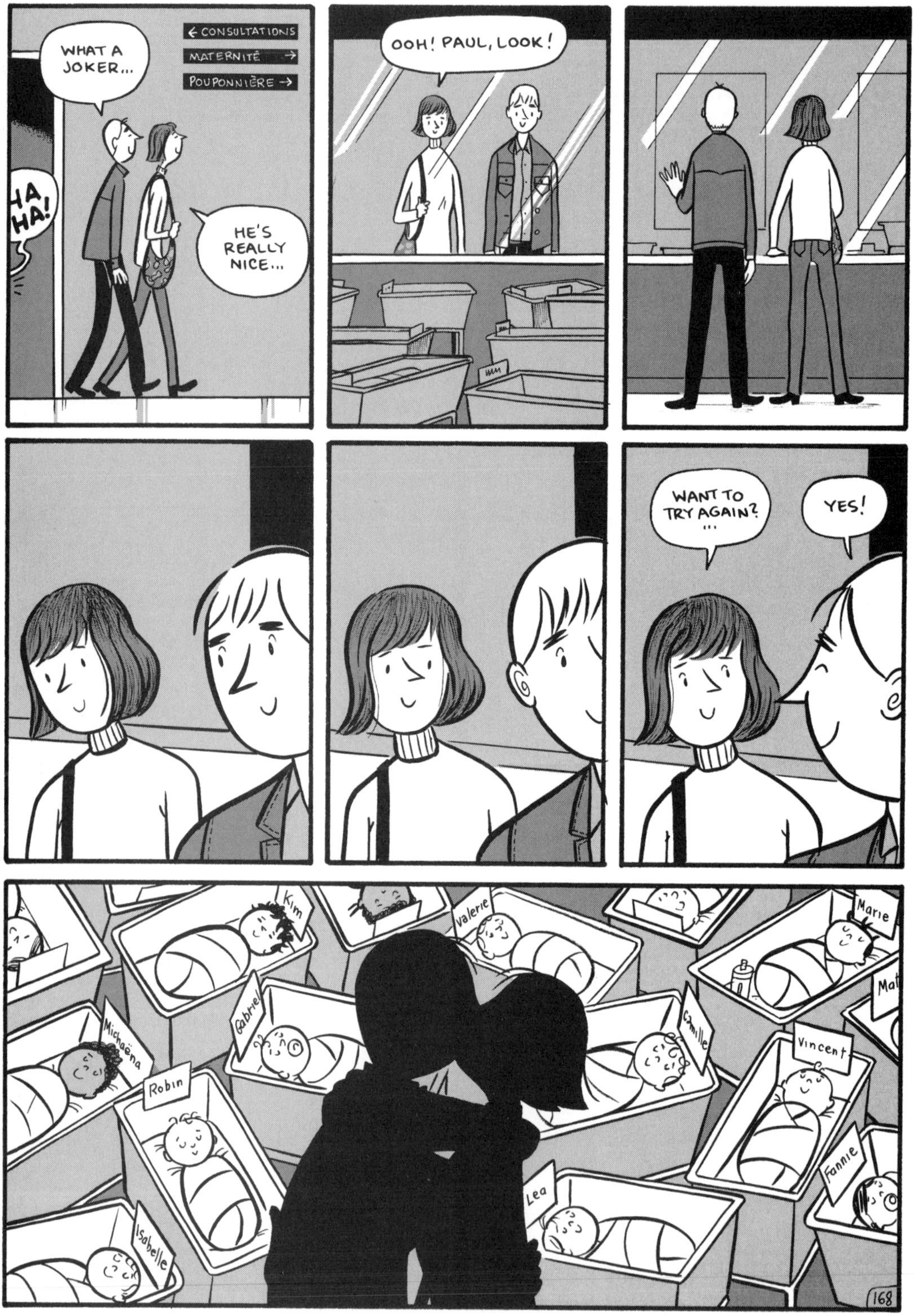
← CONSULTATIONS
MATERNITÉ →
POUPONNIÈRE →
WHAT A JOKER...
HA HA!
HE'S REALLY NICE...
OOH! PAUL, LOOK!
WANT TO TRY AGAIN? ...
YES!
Kim
Valerie
Marie
Gabriel
Camille
Michaëna
Robin
Vincent
Fannie
Lea
Isabelle

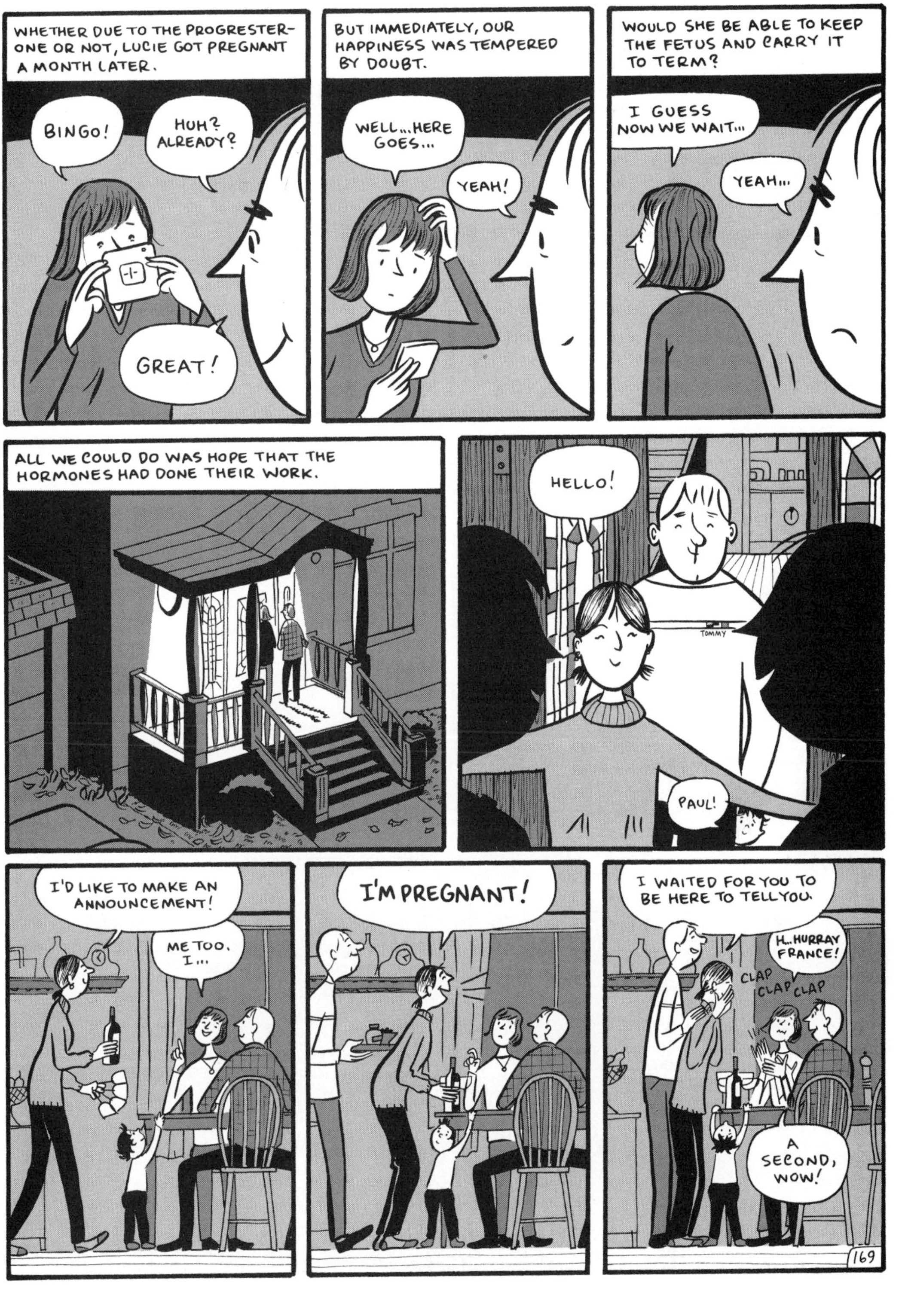
WHETHER DUE TO THE PROGRESTERONE OR NOT, LUCIE GOT PREGNANT A MONTH LATER.
BINGO!
HUH? ALREADY?
GREAT!
BUT IMMEDIATELY, OUR HAPPINESS WAS TEMPERED BY DOUBT.
WELL... HERE GOES...
YEAH!
WOULD SHE BE ABLE TO KEEP THE FETUS AND CARRY IT TO TERM?
I GUESS NOW WE WAIT...
YEAH...
ALL WE COULD DO WAS HOPE THAT THE HORMONES HAD DONE THEIR WORK.
HELLO!
TOMMY
PAUL!
I'D LIKE TO MAKE AN ANNOUNCEMENT!
ME TOO, I...
I'M PREGNANT!
I WAITED FOR YOU TO BE HERE TO TELL YOU.
H... HURRAY FRANCE!
CLAP CLAP CLAP
A SECOND, WOW!

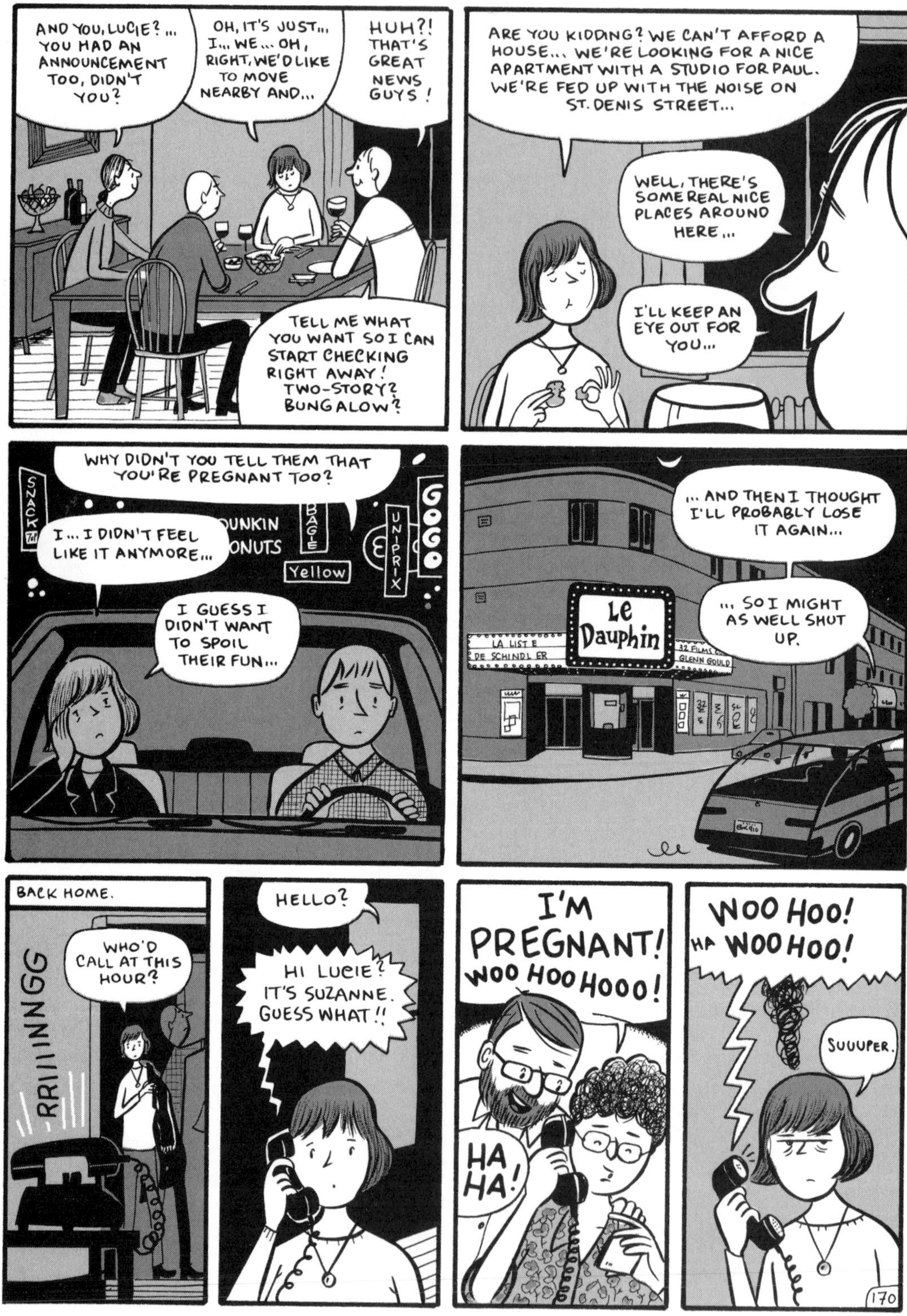
AND YOU, LUCIE? ... YOU HAD AN ANNOUNCEMENT TOO, DIDN'T YOU?
OH, IT'S JUST... I... WE... OH, RIGHT, WE'D LIKE TO MOVE NEARBY AND...
HUH?! THAT'S GREAT NEWS GUYS!
TELL ME WHAT YOU WANT SO I CAN START CHECKING RIGHT AWAY! TWO-STORY? BUNGALOW?
ARE YOU KIDDING? WE CAN'T AFFORD A HOUSE... WE'RE LOOKING FOR A NICE APARTMENT WITH A STUDIO FOR PAUL. WE'RE FED UP WITH THE NOISE ON ST. DENIS STREET...
WELL, THERE'S SOME REAL NICE PLACES AROUND HERE...
I'LL KEEP AN EYE OUT FOR YOU...
WHY DIDN'T YOU TELL THEM THAT YOU'RE PREGNANT TOO?
SNACK
DUNKIN DONUTS
BAGEL
UNIPRIX
GOGO
Yellow
I... I DIDN'T FEEL LIKE IT ANYMORE...
I GUESS I DIDN'T WANT TO SPOIL THEIR FUN...
... AND THEN I THOUGHT I'LL PROBABLY LOSE IT AGAIN...
... SO I MIGHT AS WELL SHUT UP.
Le Dauphin
LA LISTE DE SCHINDLER
32 FILMS GLENN GOULD
BACK HOME.
WHO'D CALL AT THIS HOUR?
RRIIIINNGG
HELLO?
HI LUCIE? IT'S SUZANNE. GUESS WHAT!!
I'M PREGNANT! WOO HOO HOOO!
HA HA!
WOO HOO! HA WOO HOO!
SUUUPER.

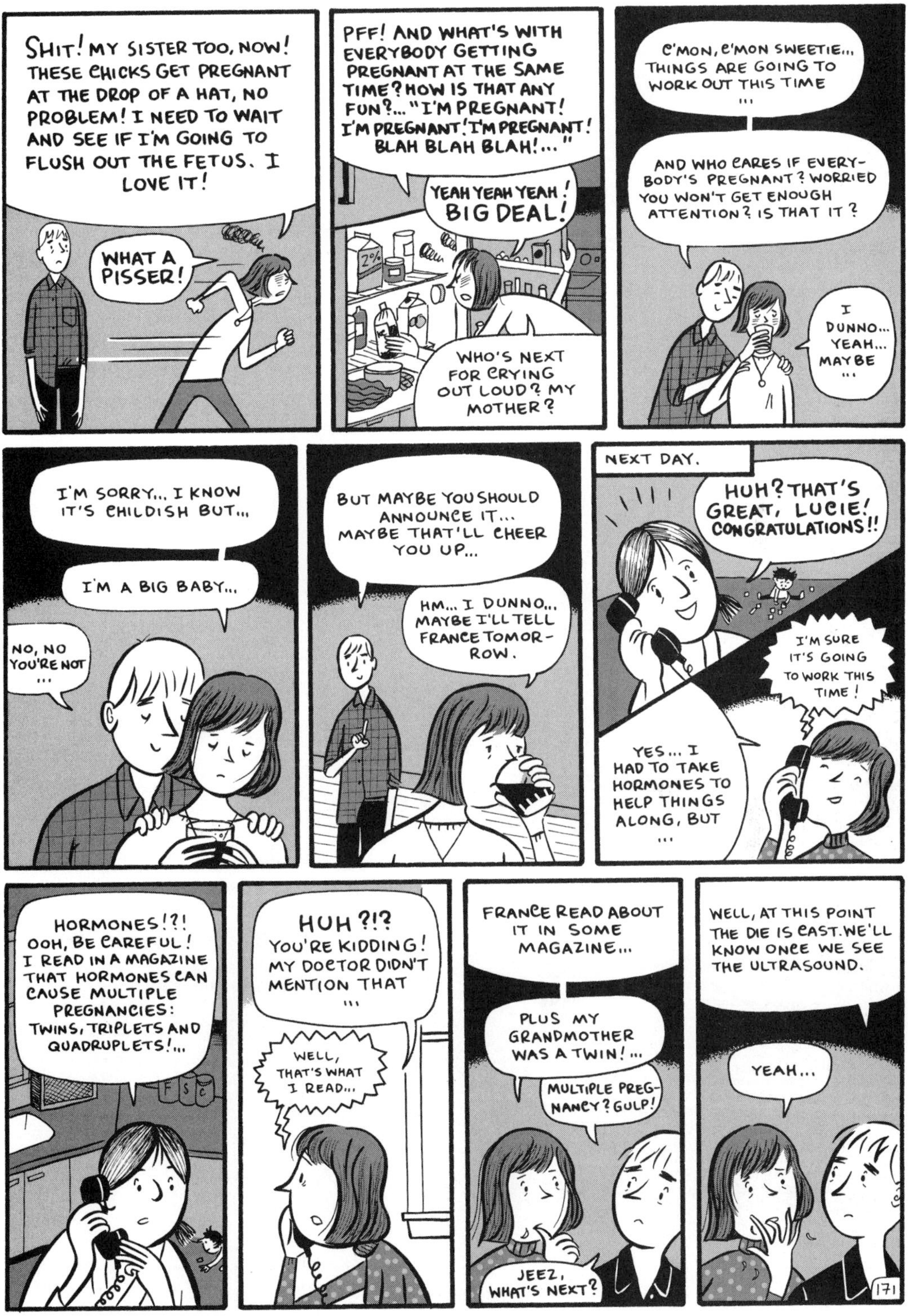
SHIT! MY SISTER TOO, NOW! THESE CHICKS GET PREGNANT AT THE DROP OF A HAT, NO PROBLEM! I NEED TO WAIT AND SEE IF I'M GOING TO FLUSH OUT THE FETUS. I LOVE IT!
WHAT A PISSER!
PFF! AND WHAT'S WITH EVERYBODY GETTING PREGNANT AT THE SAME TIME? HOW IS THAT ANY FUN?... "I'M PREGNANT! I'M PREGNANT! I'M PREGNANT! BLAH BLAH BLAH!..."
YEAH YEAH YEAH! BIG DEAL!
WHO'S NEXT FOR CRYING OUT LOUD? MY MOTHER?
C'MON, C'MON SWEETIE... THINGS ARE GOING TO WORK OUT THIS TIME ...
AND WHO CARES IF EVERYBODY'S PREGNANT? WORRIED YOU WON'T GET ENOUGH ATTENTION? IS THAT IT?
I DUNNO... YEAH... MAYBE ...
I'M SORRY... I KNOW IT'S CHILDISH BUT...
I'M A BIG BABY...
NO, NO YOU'RE NOT ...
BUT MAYBE YOU SHOULD ANNOUNCE IT... MAYBE THAT'LL CHEER YOU UP...
HM... I DUNNO... MAYBE I'LL TELL FRANCE TOMORROW.
NEXT DAY.
HUH? THAT'S GREAT, LUCIE! CONGRATULATIONS!!
I'M SURE IT'S GOING TO WORK THIS TIME!
YES... I HAD TO TAKE HORMONES TO HELP THINGS ALONG, BUT ...
HORMONES!?! OOH, BE CAREFUL! I READ IN A MAGAZINE THAT HORMONES CAN CAUSE MULTIPLE PREGNANCIES: TWINS, TRIPLETS AND QUADRUPLETS!...
HUH?!? YOU'RE KIDDING! MY DOCTOR DIDN'T MENTION THAT ...
WELL, THAT'S WHAT I READ...
FRANCE READ ABOUT IT IN SOME MAGAZINE...
PLUS MY GRANDMOTHER WAS A TWIN!...
MULTIPLE PREGNANCY? GULP!
JEEZ, WHAT'S NEXT?
WELL, AT THIS POINT THE DIE IS CAST. WE'LL KNOW ONCE WE SEE THE ULTRASOUND.
YEAH...

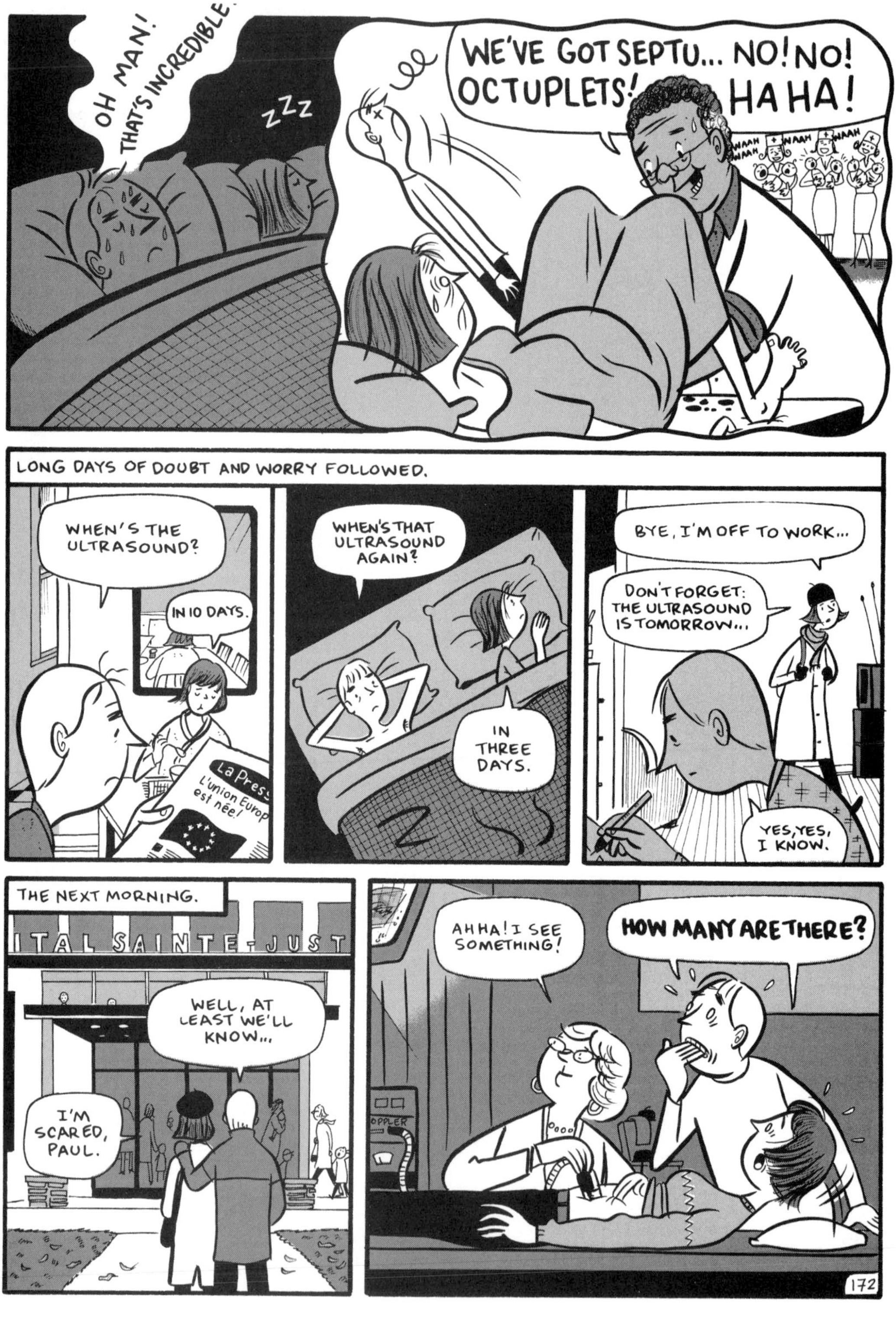
OH MAN! THAT'S INCREDIBLE.
ZZZ
WE'VE GOT SEPTU... NO! NO! OCTUPLETS! HAHA!
WAAH WAAH
WAAH
WAAH
LONG DAYS OF DOUBT AND WORRY FOLLOWED.
WHEN'S THE ULTRASOUND?
IN 10 DAYS.
La Press
L'union Europ est née!
WHEN'S THAT ULTRASOUND AGAIN?
IN THREE DAYS.
BYE, I'M OFF TO WORK...
DON'T FORGET: THE ULTRASOUND IS TOMORROW...
YES, YES, I KNOW.
THE NEXT MORNING.
ITAL SAINTE-JUST
WELL, AT LEAST WE'LL KNOW...
I'M SCARED, PAUL.
AH HA! I SEE SOMETHING!
HOW MANY ARE THERE?
OPPLER

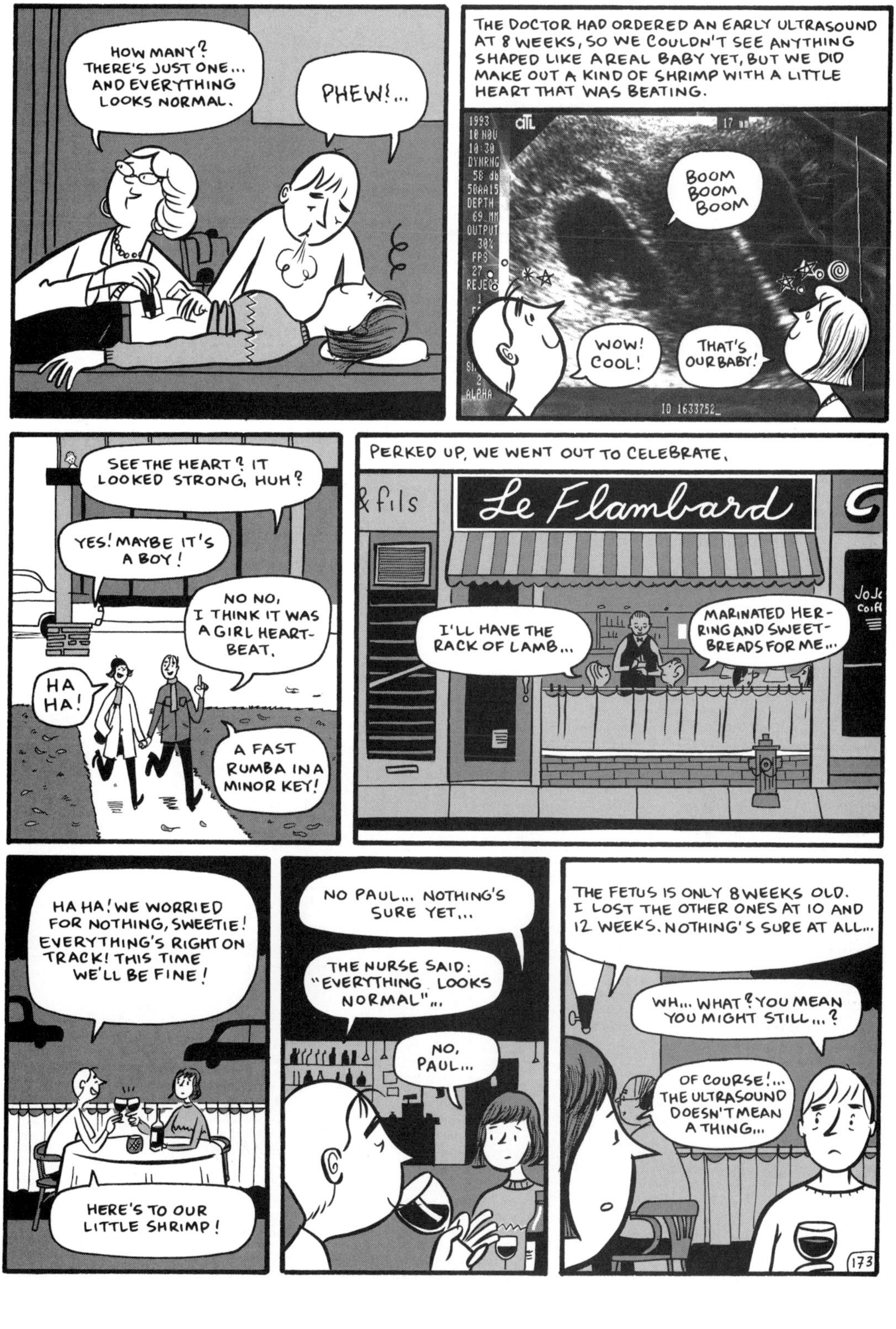

HOW MANY? THERE'S JUST ONE... AND EVERYTHING LOOKS NORMAL.
PHEW!...
THE DOCTOR HAD ORDERED AN EARLY ULTRASOUND AT 8 WEEKS, SO WE COULDN'T SEE ANYTHING SHAPED LIKE A REAL BABY YET, BUT WE DID MAKE OUT A KIND OF SHRIMP WITH A LITTLE HEART THAT WAS BEATING.
BOOM BOOM BOOM
WOW! COOL!
THAT'S OUR BABY!
SEE THE HEART? IT LOOKED STRONG, HUH?
YES! MAYBE IT'S A BOY!
NO NO, I THINK IT WAS A GIRL HEART-BEAT.
HA HA!
A FAST RUMBA IN A MINOR KEY!
PERKED UP, WE WENT OUT TO CELEBRATE.
Le Flambard
& fils
I'LL HAVE THE RACK OF LAMB...
MARINATED HER-RING AND SWEET-BREADS FOR ME...
HA HA! WE WORRIED FOR NOTHING, SWEETIE! EVERYTHING'S RIGHT ON TRACK! THIS TIME WE'LL BE FINE!
HERE'S TO OUR LITTLE SHRIMP!
NO PAUL... NOTHING'S SURE YET...
THE NURSE SAID: "EVERYTHING LOOKS NORMAL"...
NO, PAUL...
THE FETUS IS ONLY 8 WEEKS OLD. I LOST THE OTHER ONES AT 10 AND 12 WEEKS. NOTHING'S SURE AT ALL...
WH... WHAT? YOU MEAN YOU MIGHT STILL...?
OF COURSE!... THE ULTRASOUND DOESN'T MEAN A THING...

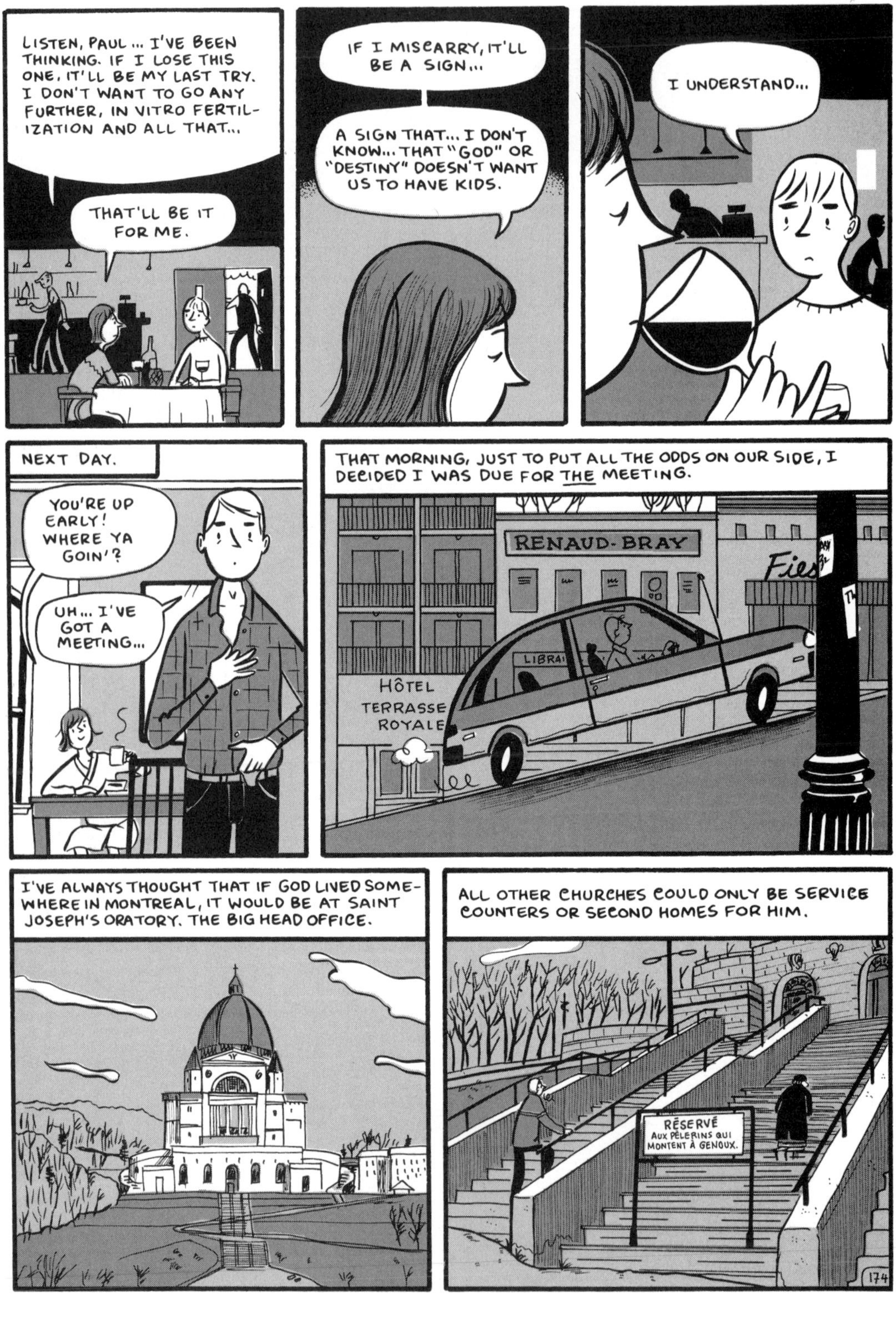
LISTEN, PAUL... I'VE BEEN THINKING. IF I LOSE THIS ONE, IT'LL BE MY LAST TRY. I DON'T WANT TO GO ANY FURTHER, IN VITRO FERTILIZATION AND ALL THAT...
THAT'LL BE IT FOR ME.
IF I MISCARRY, IT'LL BE A SIGN...
A SIGN THAT... I DON'T KNOW... THAT "GOD" OR "DESTINY" DOESN'T WANT US TO HAVE KIDS.
I UNDERSTAND...
NEXT DAY.
YOU'RE UP EARLY! WHERE YA GOIN'?
UH... I'VE GOT A MEETING...
THAT MORNING, JUST TO PUT ALL THE ODDS ON OUR SIDE, I DECIDED I WAS DUE FOR THE MEETING.
RENAUD-BRAY
HÔTEL TERRASSE ROYALE
I'VE ALWAYS THOUGHT THAT IF GOD LIVED SOMEWHERE IN MONTREAL, IT WOULD BE AT SAINT JOSEPH'S ORATORY. THE BIG HEAD OFFICE.
ALL OTHER CHURCHES COULD ONLY BE SERVICE COUNTERS OR SECOND HOMES FOR HIM.
RÉSERVÉ
AUX PÈLERINS QUI MONTENT À GENOUX.

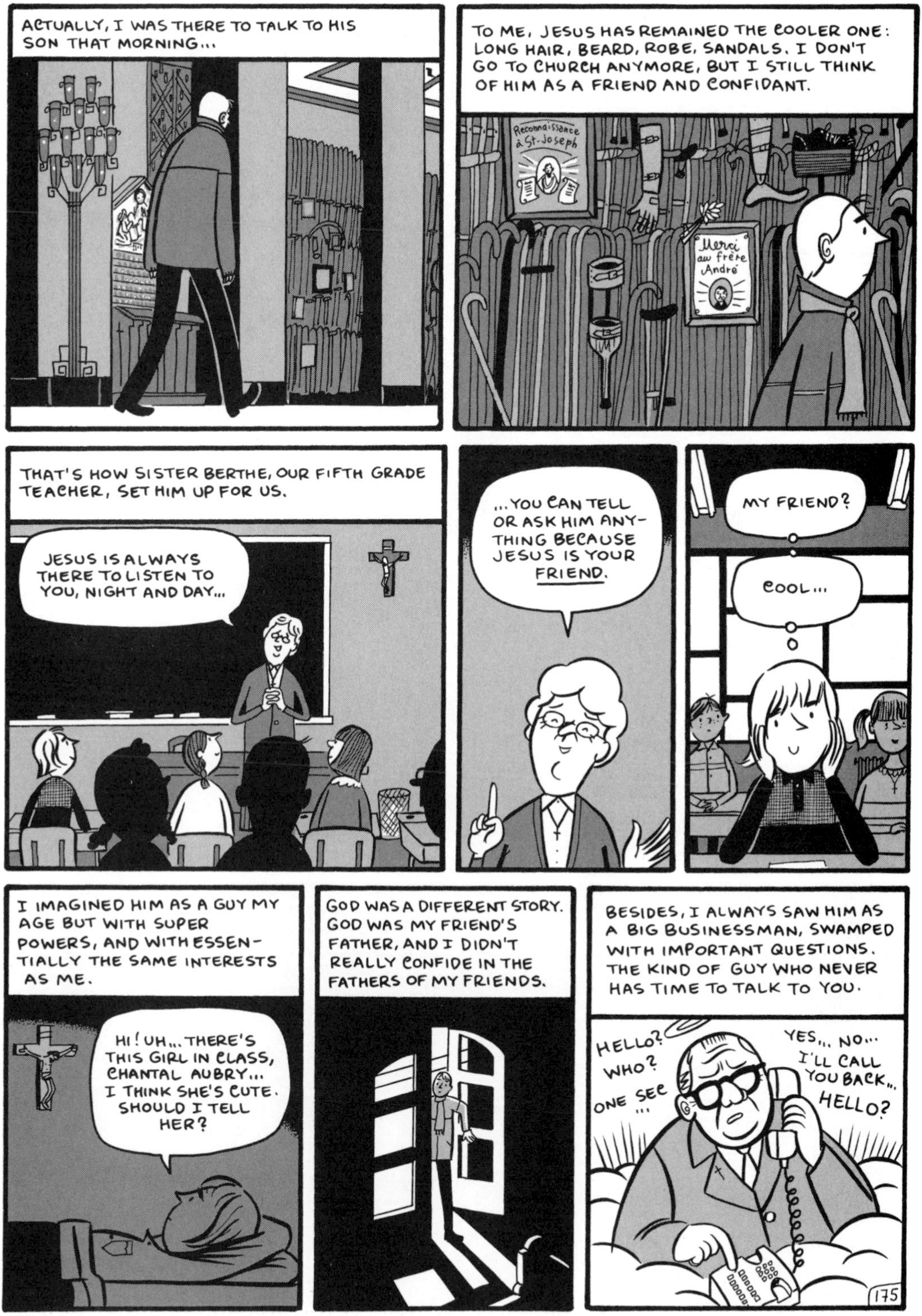
ACTUALLY, I WAS THERE TO TALK TO HIS SON THAT MORNING...
TO ME, JESUS HAS REMAINED THE COOLER ONE: LONG HAIR, BEARD, ROBE, SANDALS. I DON'T GO TO CHURCH ANYMORE, BUT I STILL THINK OF HIM AS A FRIEND AND CONFIDANT.
Reconnaissance à St-Joseph
Merci au frère André
THAT'S HOW SISTER BERTHE, OUR FIFTH GRADE TEACHER, SET HIM UP FOR US.
JESUS IS ALWAYS THERE TO LISTEN TO YOU, NIGHT AND DAY...
...YOU CAN TELL OR ASK HIM ANYTHING BECAUSE JESUS IS YOUR FRIEND.
MY FRIEND?
COOL...
I IMAGINED HIM AS A GUY MY AGE BUT WITH SUPER POWERS, AND WITH ESSENTIALLY THE SAME INTERESTS AS ME.
HI! UH... THERE'S THIS GIRL IN CLASS, CHANTAL AUBRY... I THINK SHE'S CUTE. SHOULD I TELL HER?
GOD WAS A DIFFERENT STORY. GOD WAS MY FRIEND'S FATHER, AND I DIDN'T REALLY CONFIDE IN THE FATHERS OF MY FRIENDS.
BESIDES, I ALWAYS SAW HIM AS A BIG BUSINESSMAN, SWAMPED WITH IMPORTANT QUESTIONS. THE KIND OF GUY WHO NEVER HAS TIME TO TALK TO YOU.
HELLO?
WHO?
ONE SEC...
YES... NO... I'LL CALL YOU BACK...
HELLO?

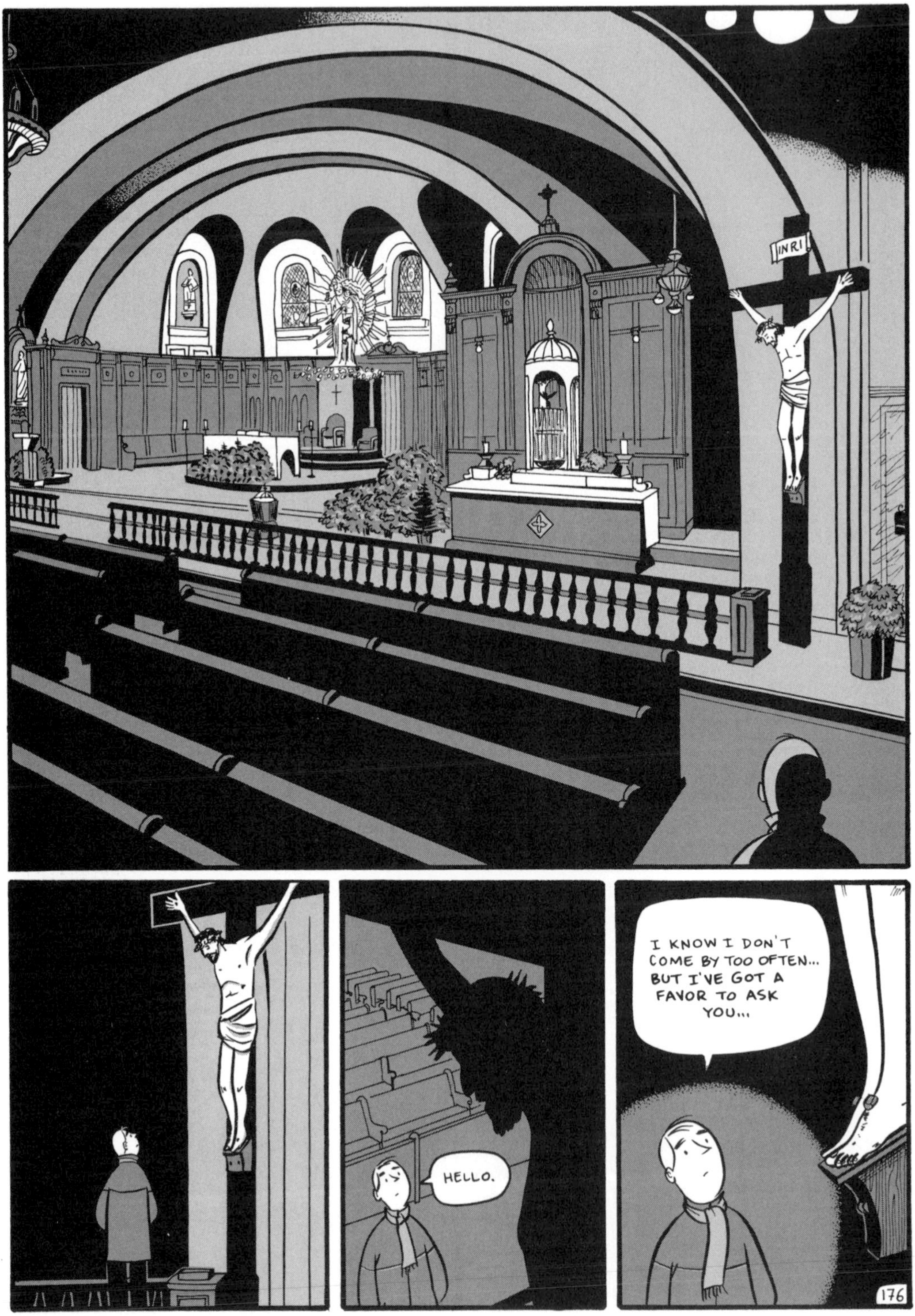
INRI
HELLO.
I KNOW I DON'T COME BY TOO OFTEN... BUT I'VE GOT A FAVOR TO ASK YOU...

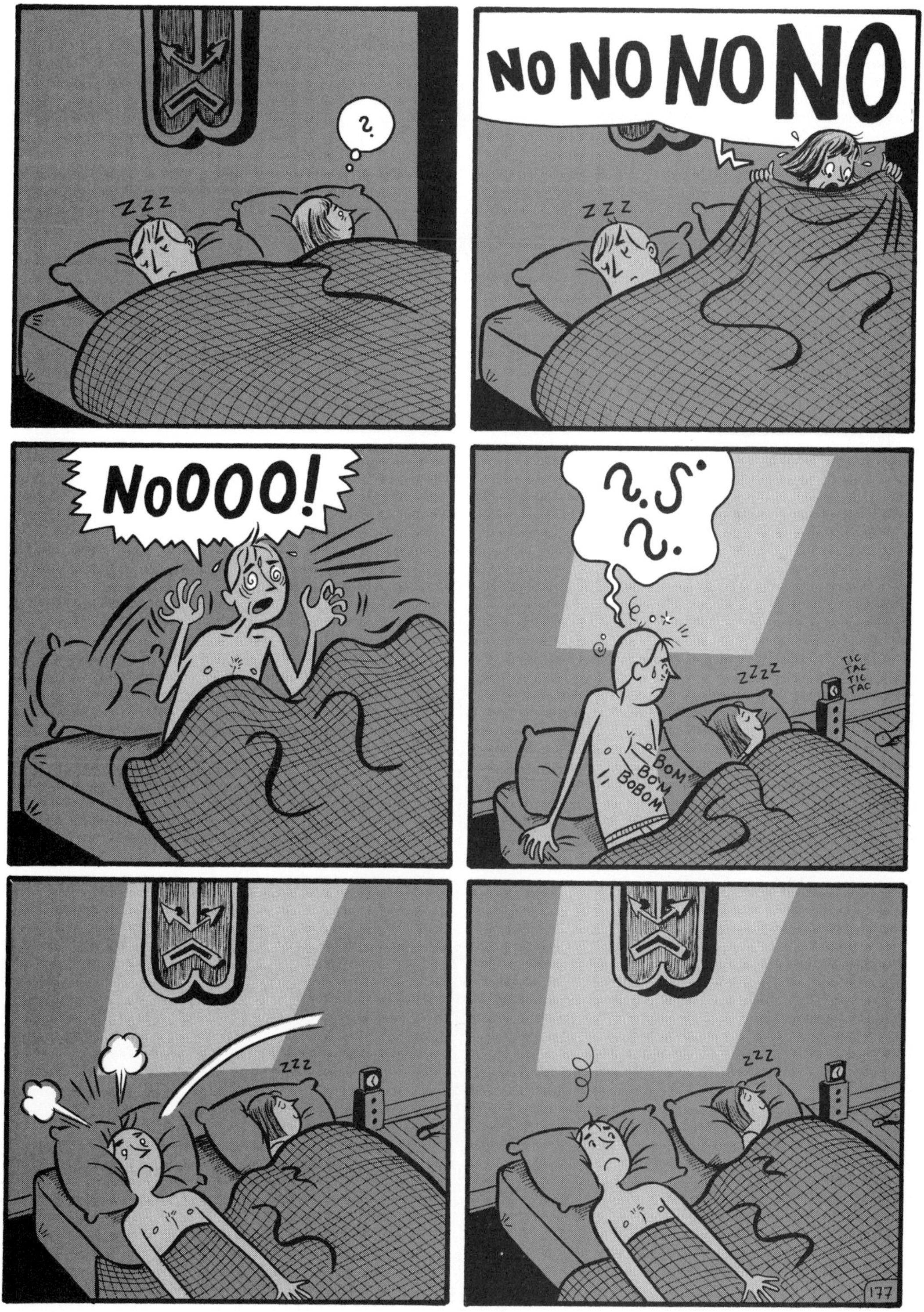

?
ZZZ
NO NO NO NO NO
ZZZ
NOOOO!
ZZZZ
TIC TAC TIC TAC
BOM BOM BOBOM
ZZZ
ZZZ

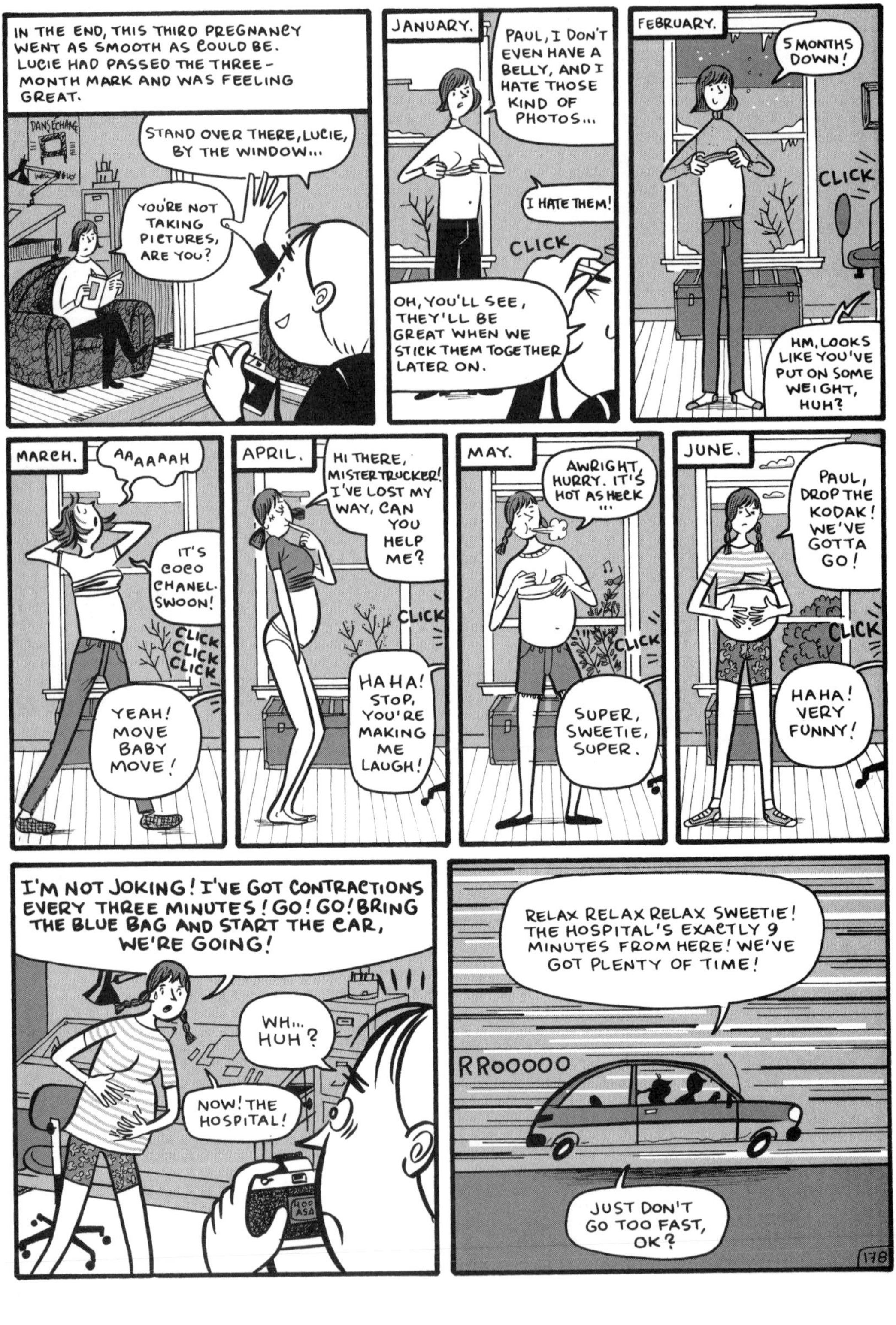

IN THE END, THIS THIRD PREGNANCY WENT AS SMOOTH AS COULD BE. LUCIE HAD PASSED THE THREE-MONTH MARK AND WAS FEELING GREAT.
STAND OVER THERE, LUCIE, BY THE WINDOW...
YOU'RE NOT TAKING PICTURES, ARE YOU?
JANUARY.
PAUL, I DON'T EVEN HAVE A BELLY, AND I HATE THOSE KIND OF PHOTOS...
I HATE THEM!
CLICK
OH, YOU'LL SEE, THEY'LL BE GREAT WHEN WE STICK THEM TOGETHER LATER ON.
FEBRUARY.
5 MONTHS DOWN!
CLICK
HM, LOOKS LIKE YOU'VE PUT ON SOME WEIGHT, HUH?
MARCH.
AAAAAAH
IT'S COCO CHANEL. SWOON!
CLICK CLICK CLICK
YEAH! MOVE BABY MOVE!
APRIL.
HI THERE, MISTER TRUCKER! I'VE LOST MY WAY, CAN YOU HELP ME?
CLICK
HAHA! STOP, YOU'RE MAKING ME LAUGH!
MAY.
AWRIGHT, HURRY. IT'S HOT AS HECK ...
CLICK
SUPER, SWEETIE, SUPER.
JUNE.
PAUL, DROP THE KODAK! WE'VE GOTTA GO!
CLICK
HAHA! VERY FUNNY!
I'M NOT JOKING! I'VE GOT CONTRACTIONS EVERY THREE MINUTES! GO! GO! BRING THE BLUE BAG AND START THE CAR, WE'RE GOING!
WH... HUH?
NOW! THE HOSPITAL!
400 ASA
RELAX RELAX RELAX SWEETIE! THE HOSPITAL'S EXACTLY 9 MINUTES FROM HERE! WE'VE GOT PLENTY OF TIME!
RROOOOO
JUST DON'T GO TOO FAST, OK?

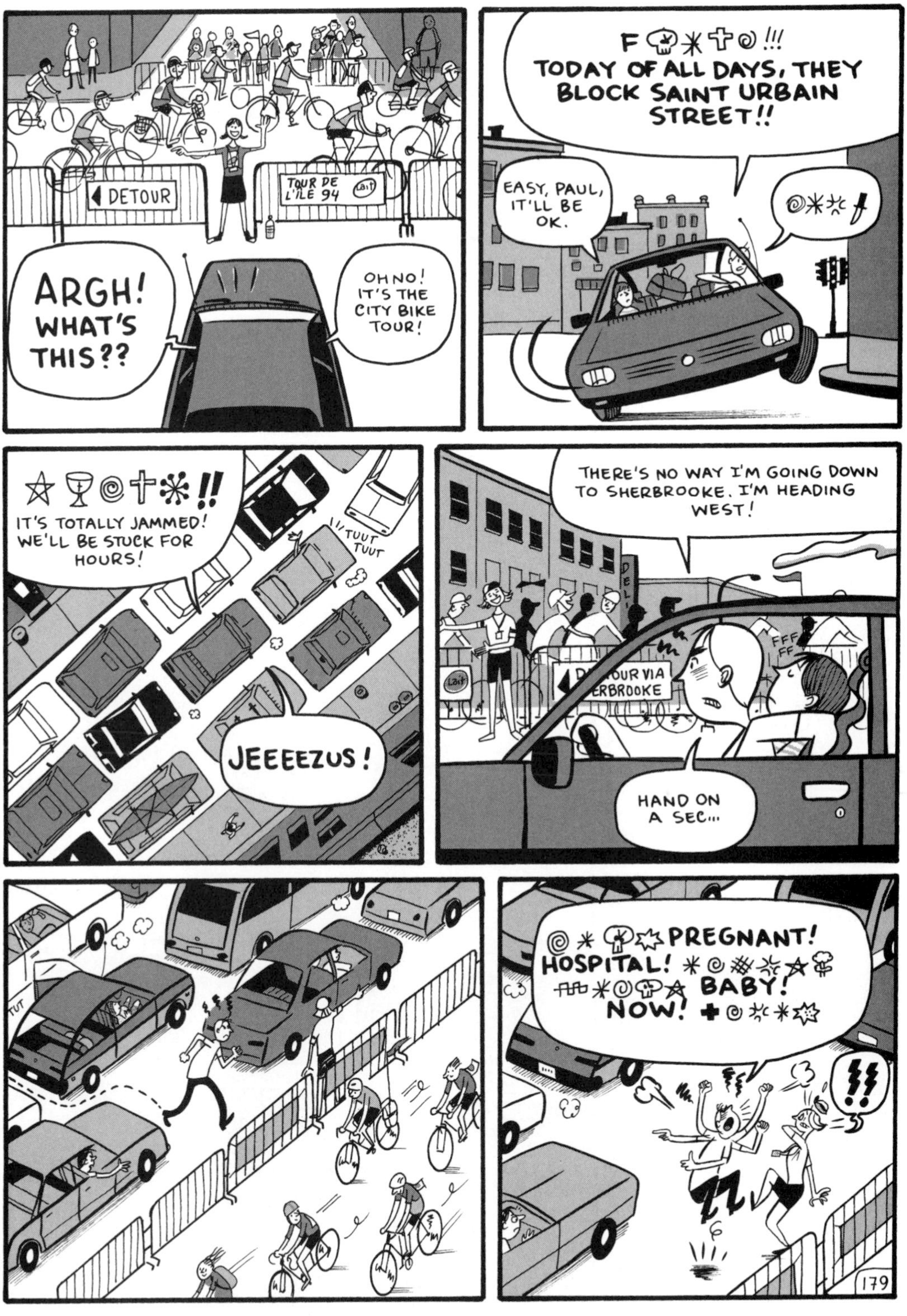
DETOUR
TOUR DE L'ILE 94
LAIT
ARGH! WHAT'S THIS??
OH NO! IT'S THE CITY BIKE TOUR!
TODAY OF ALL DAYS, THEY BLOCK SAINT URBAIN STREET!!
EASY, PAUL, IT'LL BE OK.
IT'S TOTALLY JAMMED! WE'LL BE STUCK FOR HOURS!
TUUT TUUT
JEEEEZUS!
THERE'S NO WAY I'M GOING DOWN TO SHERBROOKE. I'M HEADING WEST!
DELI
FFF FF
HAND ON A SEC...
TUT
PREGNANT! HOSPITAL! BABY! NOW!

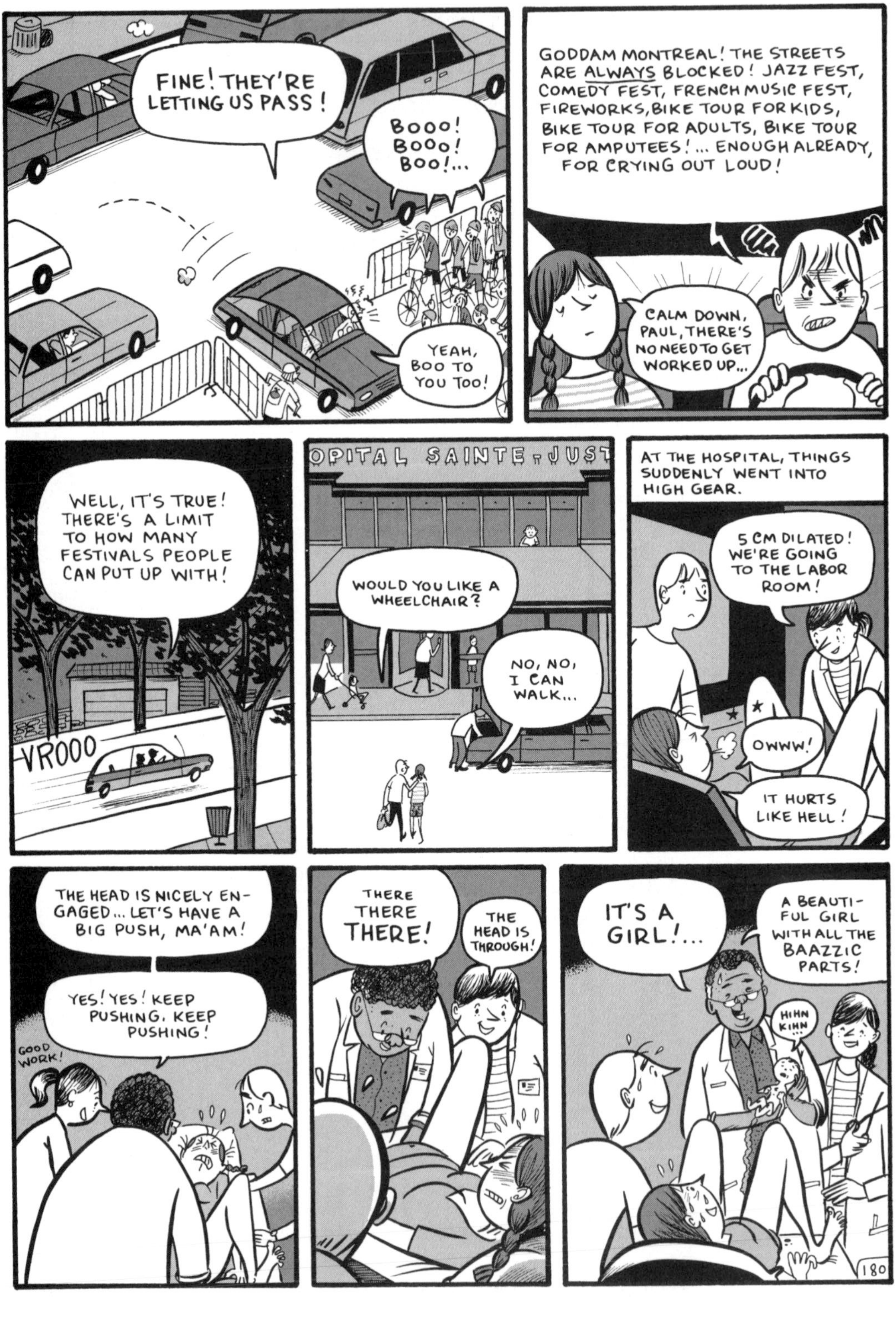
FINE! THEY'RE LETTING US PASS!
BOOO! BOOO! BOO!...
YEAH, BOO TO YOU TOO!
GODDAM MONTREAL! THE STREETS ARE ALWAYS BLOCKED! JAZZ FEST, COMEDY FEST, FRENCH MUSIC FEST, FIREWORKS, BIKE TOUR FOR KIDS, BIKE TOUR FOR ADULTS, BIKE TOUR FOR AMPUTEES! ... ENOUGH ALREADY, FOR CRYING OUT LOUD!
CALM DOWN, PAUL, THERE'S NO NEED TO GET WORKED UP...
WELL, IT'S TRUE! THERE'S A LIMIT TO HOW MANY FESTIVALS PEOPLE CAN PUT UP WITH!
VROOO
OPITAL SAINTE-JUST
WOULD YOU LIKE A WHEELCHAIR?
NO, NO, I CAN WALK...
AT THE HOSPITAL, THINGS SUDDENLY WENT INTO HIGH GEAR.
5 CM DILATED! WE'RE GOING TO THE LABOR ROOM!
OWWW!
IT HURTS LIKE HELL!
THE HEAD IS NICELY ENGAGED... LET'S HAVE A BIG PUSH, MA'AM!
YES! YES! KEEP PUSHING. KEEP PUSHING!
GOOD WORK!
THERE THERE THERE!
THE HEAD IS THROUGH!
IT'S A GIRL!...
A BEAUTIFUL GIRL WITH ALL THE BAAZZIC PARTS!
HIHN KIHN ...

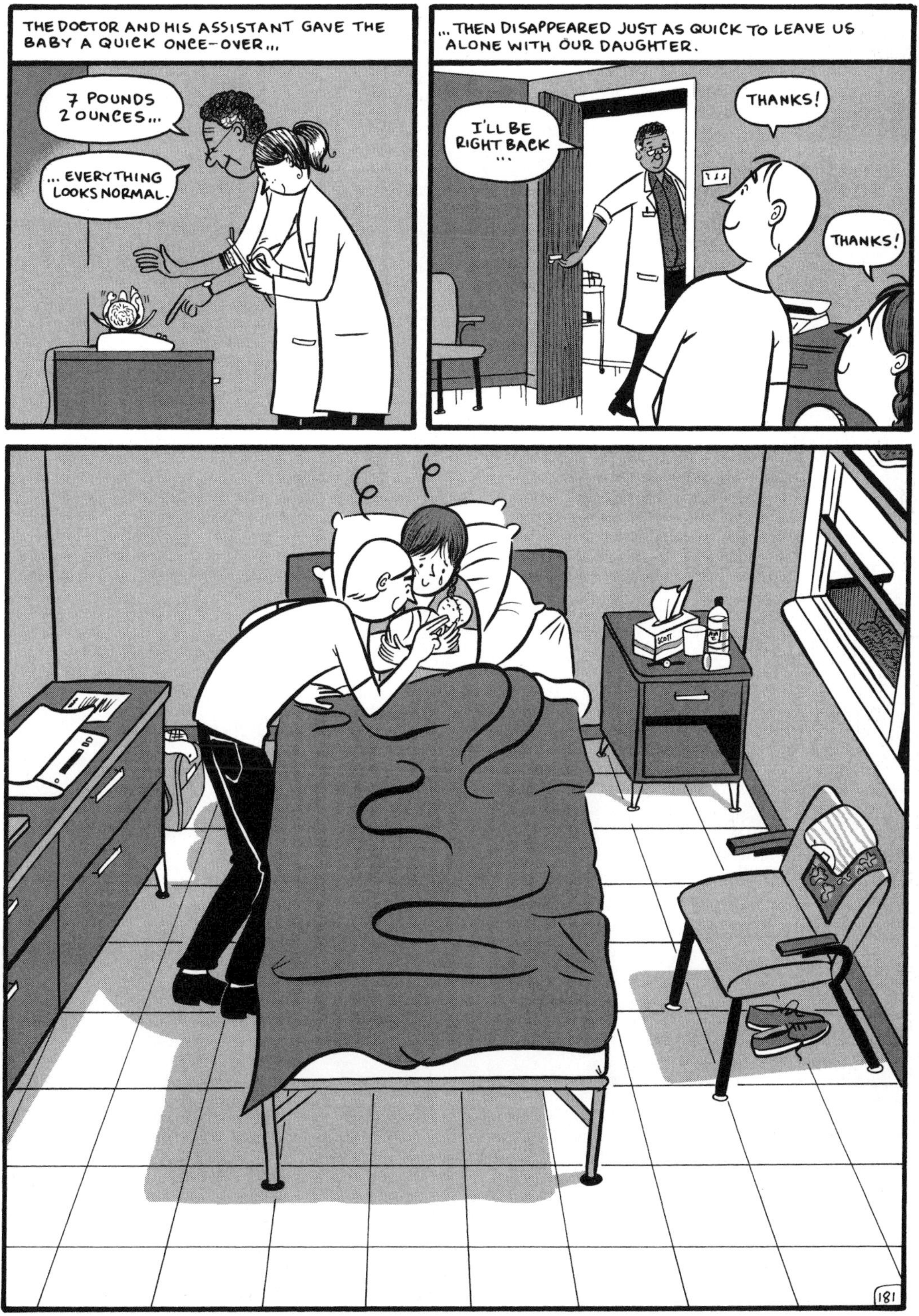
THE DOCTOR AND HIS ASSISTANT GAVE THE BABY A QUICK ONCE-OVER...
7 POUNDS 2 OUNCES...
... EVERYTHING LOOKS NORMAL.
...THEN DISAPPEARED JUST AS QUICK TO LEAVE US ALONE WITH OUR DAUGHTER.
I'LL BE RIGHT BACK ...
THANKS!
THANKS!
SCOTT

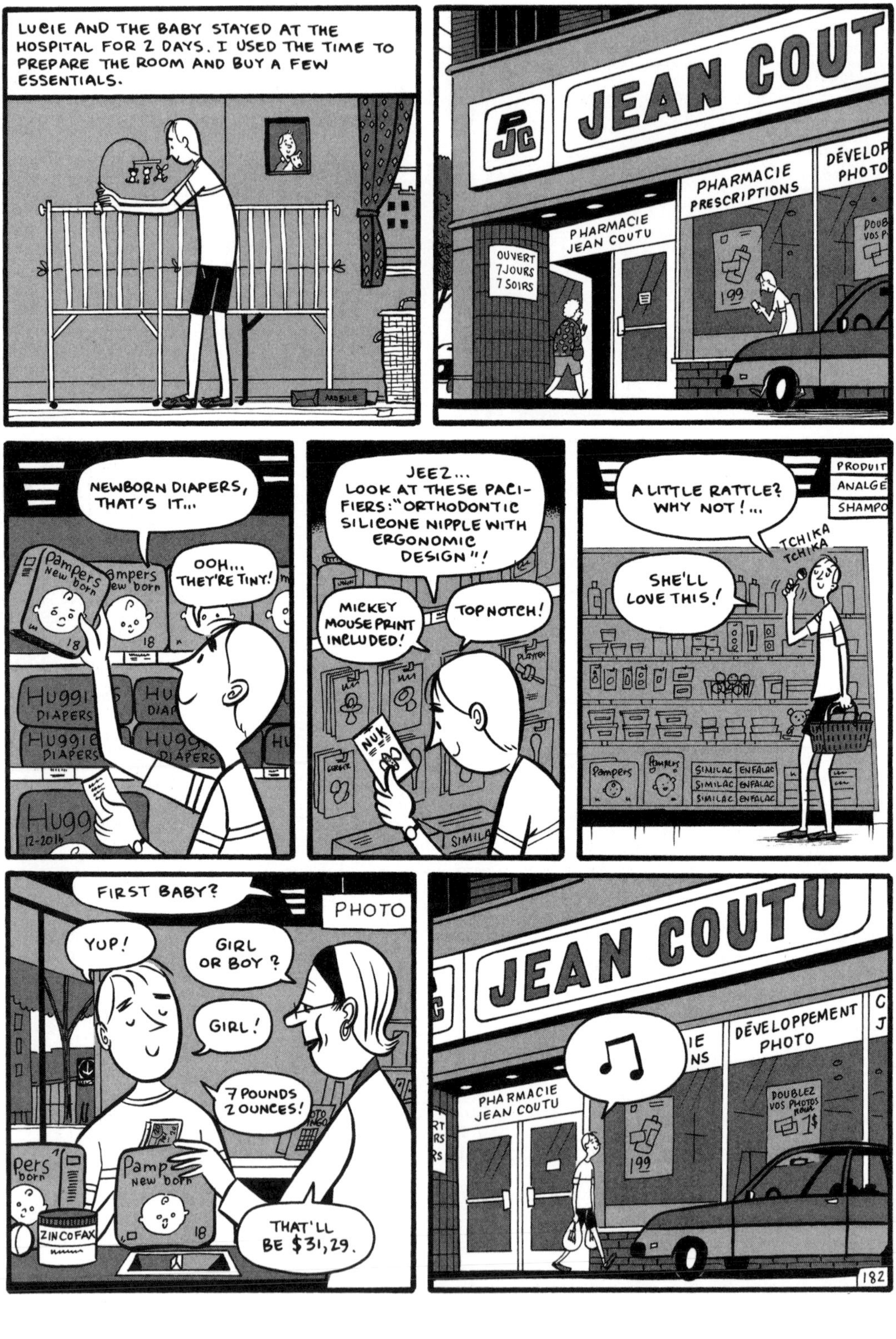
LUCIE AND THE BABY STAYED AT THE HOSPITAL FOR 2 DAYS. I USED THE TIME TO PREPARE THE ROOM AND BUY A FEW ESSENTIALS.
MOBILE
JEAN COUT
PJC
PHARMACIE PRESCRIPTIONS
DÉVELOP PHOTO
PHARMACIE JEAN COUTU
OUVERT 7 JOURS 7 SOIRS
199
NEWBORN DIAPERS, THAT'S IT...
OOH... THEY'RE TINY!
Pampers New born
18
Huggies DIAPERS
12-2016
JEEZ... LOOK AT THESE PACIFIERS: "ORTHODONTIC SILICONE NIPPLE WITH ERGONOMIC DESIGN"!
MICKEY MOUSE PRINT INCLUDED!
TOP NOTCH!
NUK
PLAYTEX
SIMILA
A LITTLE RATTLE? WHY NOT!...
TCHIKA TCHIKA
SHE'LL LOVE THIS!
PRODUIT
ANALGÉ
SHAMPO
SIMILAC ENFALAC
FIRST BABY?
PHOTO
YUP!
GIRL OR BOY?
GIRL!
7 POUNDS 2 OUNCES!
ZINCOFAX
THAT'LL BE $31,29.
JEAN COUTU
DÉVELOPPEMENT PHOTO
PHARMACIE JEAN COUTU
DOUBLEZ VOS PHOTOS POUR 1$
199

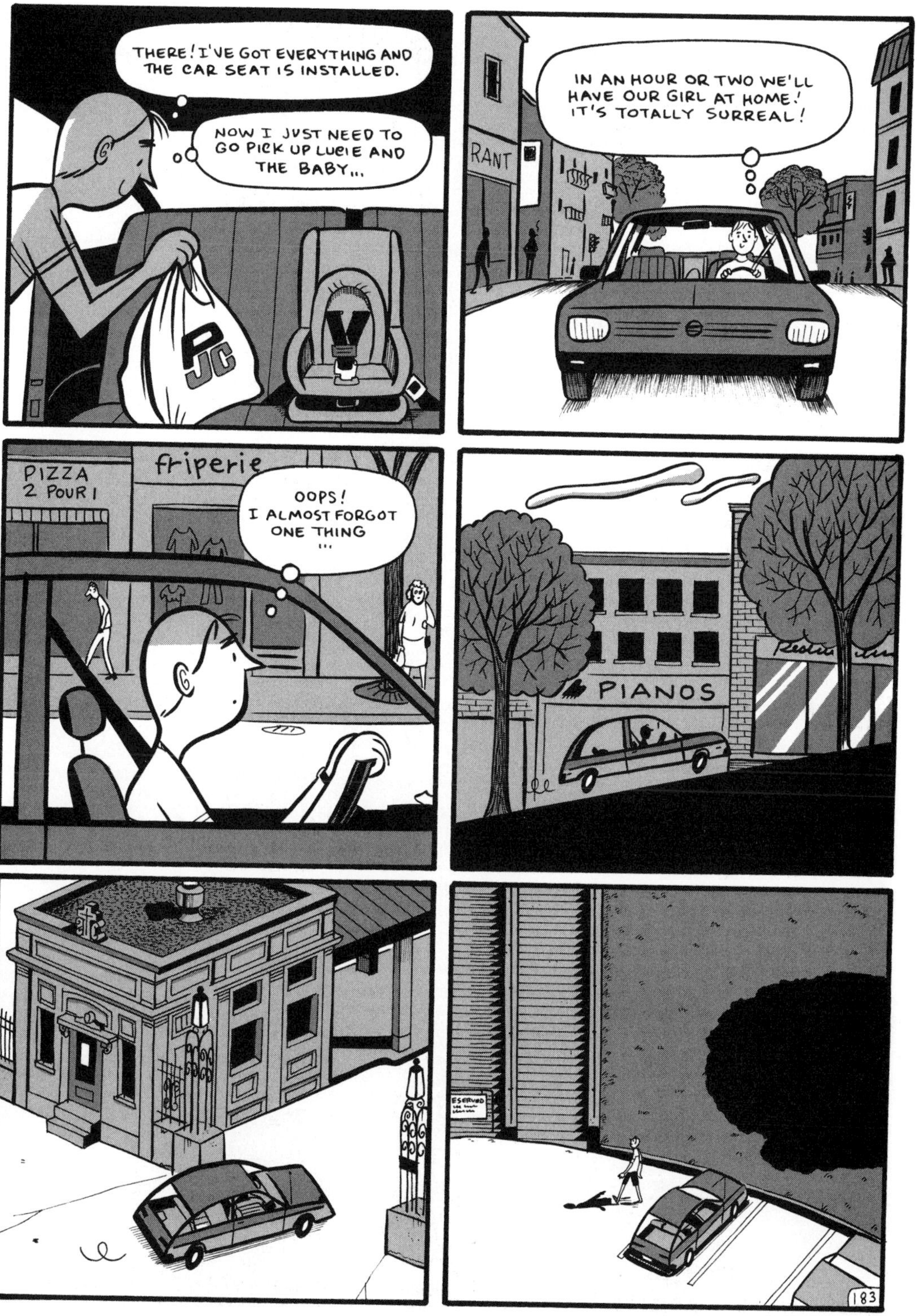
THERE! I'VE GOT EVERYTHING AND THE CAR SEAT IS INSTALLED.
NOW I JUST NEED TO GO PICK UP LUCIE AND THE BABY...
PJC
RANT
IN AN HOUR OR TWO WE'LL HAVE OUR GIRL AT HOME! IT'S TOTALLY SURREAL!
PIZZA 2 POUR 1
friperie
OOPS! I ALMOST FORGOT ONE THING ...
PIANOS

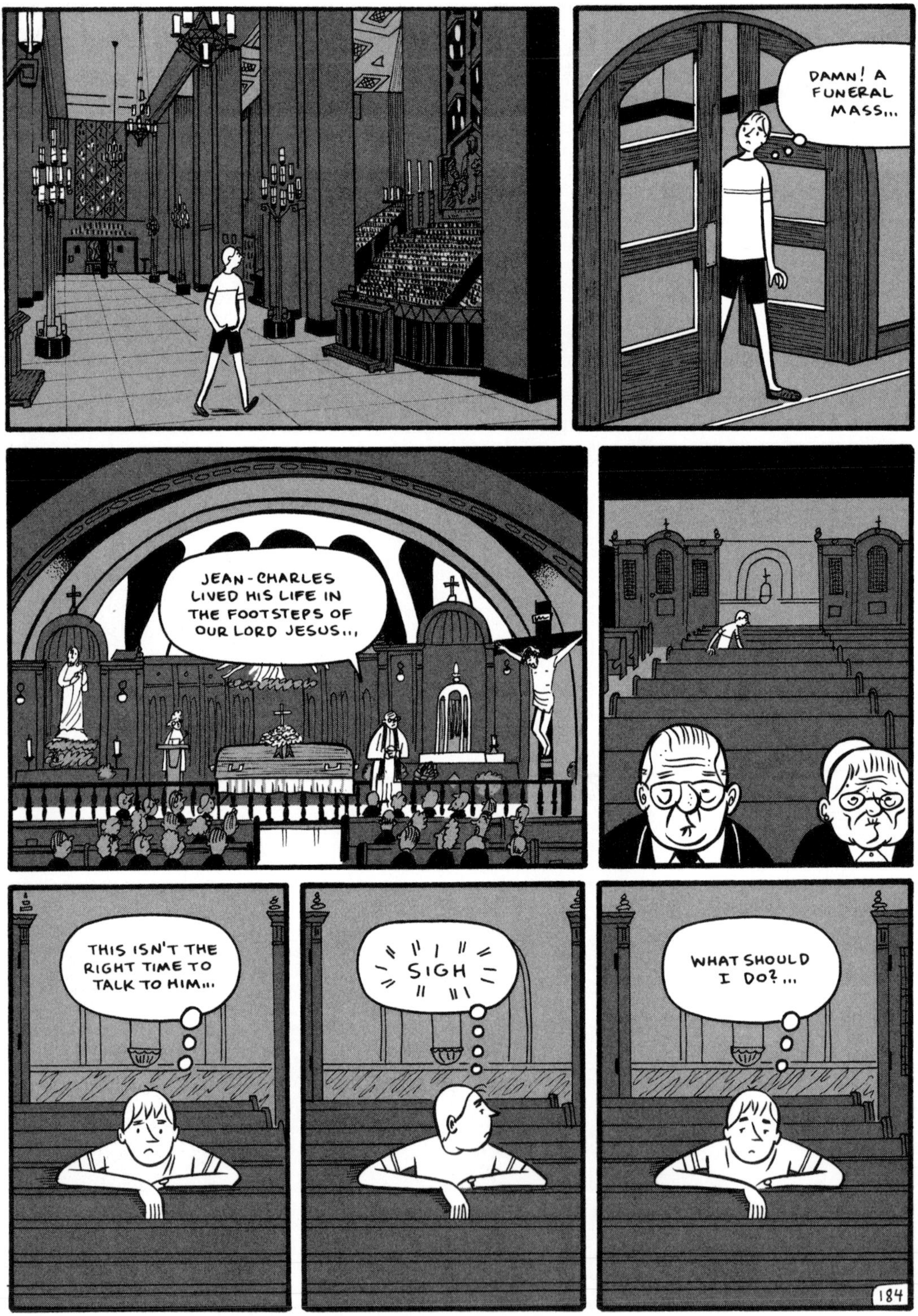
DAMN! A FUNERAL MASS...
JEAN-CHARLES LIVED HIS LIFE IN THE FOOTSTEPS OF OUR LORD JESUS...
THIS ISN'T THE RIGHT TIME TO TALK TO HIM...
SIGH
WHAT SHOULD I DO?...

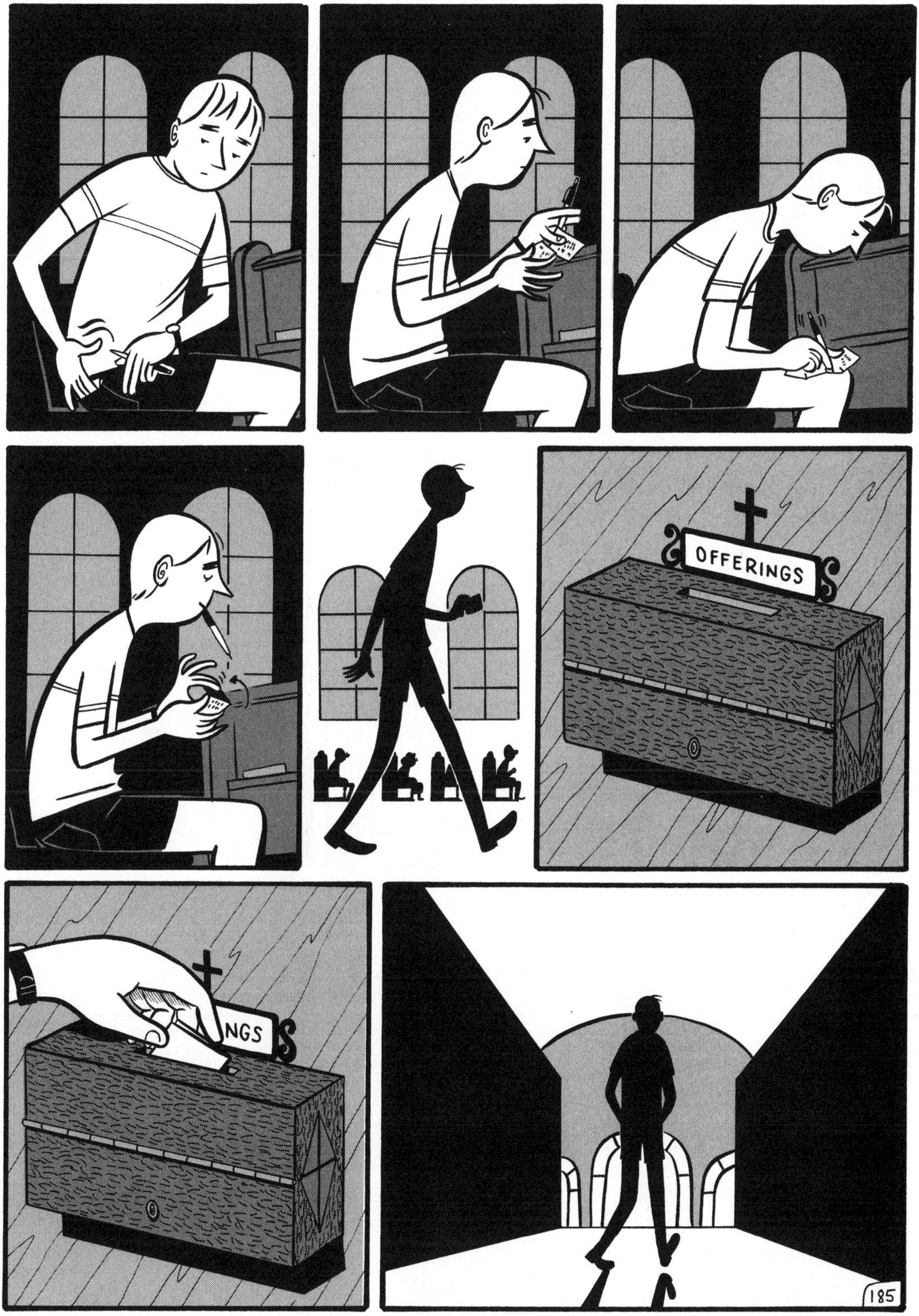
OFFERINGS
NGS

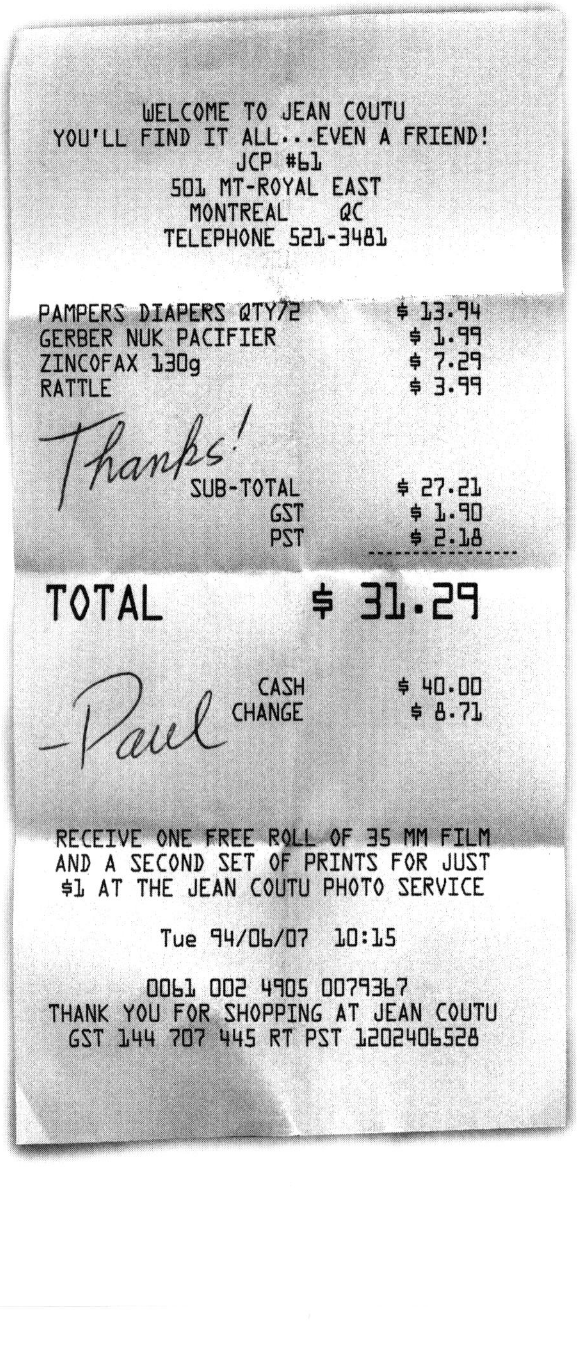
WELCOME TO JEAN COUTU
YOU'LL FIND IT ALL...EVEN A FRIEND!
JCP #61
501 MT-ROYAL EAST
MONTREAL QC
TELEPHONE 521-3481

PAMPERS DIAPERS QTY72	$ 13.94
GERBER NUK PACIFIER	$ 1.99
ZINCOFAX 130g	$ 7.29
RATTLE	$ 3.99

Thanks!

SUB-TOTAL	$ 27.21
GST	$ 1.90
PST	$ 2.18

TOTAL $ 31.29

CASH	$ 40.00
CHANGE	$ 8.71

-Paul

RECEIVE ONE FREE ROLL OF 35 MM FILM
AND A SECOND SET OF PRINTS FOR JUST
$1 AT THE JEAN COUTU PHOTO SERVICE

Tue 94/06/07 10:15

0061 002 4905 0079367
THANK YOU FOR SHOPPING AT JEAN COUTU
GST 144 707 445 RT PST 1202406528

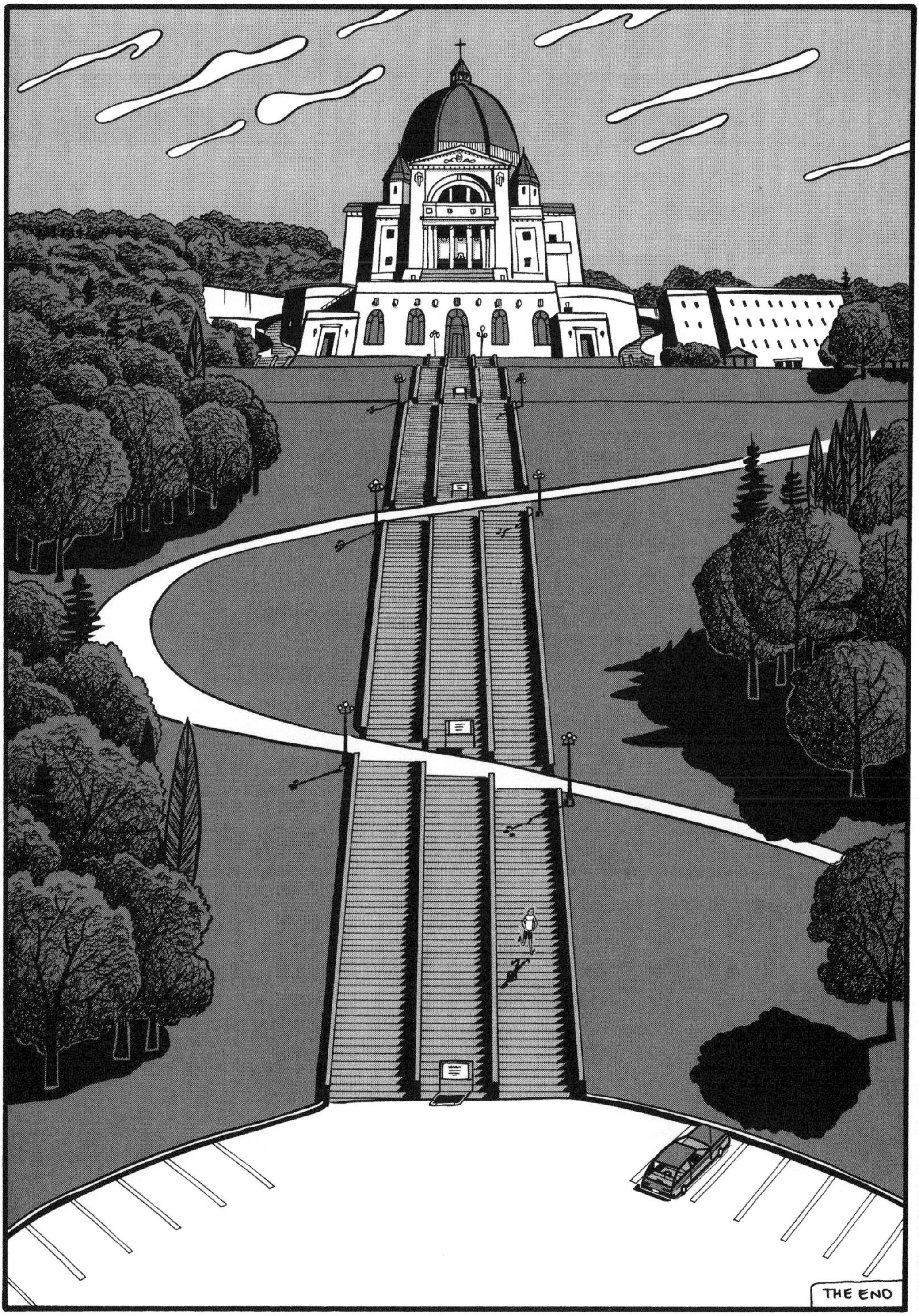
THE END

MICHEL RABAGLIATI JUNE 2006.

Songs

Lucky lucky (lyrics translated by Helge Dascher)
Richard Desjardins

That's Amore
Dean Martin

Jambalaya
Hank Williams

Hotel California
Eagles

It's a heartache
Bonnie Tyler

Sources

Ben Weider and E.Z. Massicotte,
Les hommes forts du Québec, de Jos Montferrand à Louis Cyr,
Éditions Trois-Pistoles, 1999.

Ben Weider
Louis Cyr, l'homme le plus fort du monde
Quebecor, 1993.

Acknowledgements

From Michel Rabagliati:
Thanks to Denis Aubin for sharing his knowledge about fishing and hunting.
Thanks to Michel Viau for his insights into the history of Quebec comics.
Thanks to Serge Brouillet for the documentation on uterine aspirators.

·

From Helge Dascher:
My thanks, as always, to Dag "The Moose" Dascher and Mark "Toothpick" Lang.
Special thanks also to Steve Louis.

By the same author

Paul In The Country
32 pages, 1999

(Harvey Award — Best New Talent 2001)
(Festival de la BD Francophone de Québec 2000 — Prix de l'espoir québécois)
(Bébélys Québec 2000 — Meilleur album québécois)

•

Paul Has A Summer Job
152 pages, 2003

(Bédélys Québec 2002 — Meilleur album québécois)
(Bédélys Média 2002)
(Festival de la BD francophone de Québec 2003 — Prix Réal-Fillion)

•

Paul Moves Out
120 pages, 2005

(Doug Wright Award — Best Book 2006)
(Festival de la BD francophone de Québec 2005 —
Grand Prix de la Ville de Québec)